Cornwall Coast
PATH

BUDE TO FALMOUTH
planning, places to stay, places to eat,
includes 100 large-scale walking maps

EDITH SCHOFIELD

THIRD EDITION RESEARCHED AND UPDATED BY

KEITH CARTER

TRAILBLAZER PUBLICATIONS

Acknowledgements

FROM KEITH In researching this third edition I wish to thank all the kind staff of the tourist information centres; the help they gave me was invaluable. I would also like to say how much I admire the men and women who drive the buses that ply Cornwall's narrow lanes, a job for which they get scant recognition and quite low wages.

Among the people who helped me in different ways are Mr and Mrs Davies of Nanterrow Farm, Gwithian, who came to my rescue when I was stranded and Alison and Martyn at The Lizard who saved me a long taxi ride.

My biggest debt is to my friend Jamie who joined me for two stages of the trail, a steady companion and good company along the way and my wife Annie who encouraged me in fair weather and foul. It is much better to have somebody with you on a walk to share the views, argue with over identifying the wildlife, and moan with over the tough uphill sections – James is a past master at all three.

We're grateful to all those readers who've written in with comments and suggestions, in particular Paul Bloomfield, Jim Manthorpe, Janice Booth, Hilary Bradt, Tony Howard and Di Taylor.

Thanks, too, to my editor Anna Jacomb-Hood, Nick Hill for updating the maps, Nicky Slade for proofreading, Jane Thomas for the index and Roderick Leslie for updating the fauna section.

FROM EDITH: Special thanks go to Nik for his support and encouragement to start the project, putting his own ambitions aside to come and keep me company on the track and for being there right through to the end.

Thank you also to those at Trailblazer who made it possible, Charlie Loram and Henry Stedman for all their hard work editing, Jane Thomas for the index, Nick Hill for the maps and Bryn Thomas for such an opportunity.

Updated information will shortly be available at:
💻 **www.trailblazer-guides.com**

Front cover: A perfect day near St George's Cove, just outside Padstow.
(Photo © Henry Stedman)

CONTENTS

INTRODUCTION

Synonymous with the sea and the sea's wild storms that created its dramatic coastline, Cornwall is a land of magic, myth and legend, of poetic writing and art. Its known history stretches back 5500 years and has witnessed Phoenician traders, pirates, smugglers and shipwrecks, the rise and fall of the tin-mining and fishing industries and a growing market in tourism which dates back to the days of Victorian villas built for long summer holidays.

Walking the coast path is one of the best ways to experience fully the sights and sounds that make Cornwall unique and special. As well as the sheer physical pleasure of walking, the sea breeze in your hair, the taste of the salt spray on your lips, you are treated to the most beautiful and spectacular views of this beguiling and sometimes hazardous coastline. The sky and the light change with the movement of even the smallest cloud over the sea that lies ultramarine and translucent on long hot summer days but becomes leaden and silver with mountainous white-crested waves in sudden storms. Watch for the seals that fool you by swimming under water for long periods, then bob up just when you'd thought they'd gone. You might see dolphins, too, or even a basking shark.

Walking allows you flexibility over the distances you want to cover, your speed depending on your level of fitness. You can be completely independent, carrying all the basics of life – food, shelter and clothes – on your back, or book B&Bs ahead and walk with the knowledge that your creature comforts – hot baths and comfortable beds – will be waiting for you at the end of the day.

As for rest stops, you'll be tempted time and time again. Explore quintessentially Cornish fishing villages or take a quick break on the Isles of Scilly. Try to identify some of Cornwall's profusion of wild flowers. Look into the little rock pools that are so full of life. Immerse yourself in contemporary art in St Ives. Investigate tin-mining history in a landscape so important that it has been declared a World Heritage Site. Try surfing or simply take a swim to cool off on a hot day.

For food, feast on Cornish pasties and crab sandwiches as you picnic on a clifftop or beach; in picturesque cottage tearooms gorge on scones piled high with strawberry jam and clotted cream. Above all eat fish fresh from the sea, superb shellfish, lobster, crab and scallops. As well as ubiquitous fish and chip shops and beach cafés there are several top-class seafood restaurants in Cornwall, some run by famous TV chefs: Rick Stein has been in Padstow for many years and Jamie Oliver opened a restaurant in Watergate Bay in 2006.

The Cornish coast is a holiday paradise that's easily accessible, where you'll enjoy some of the finest coastal walking Britain has to offer.

About this book

This guidebook is as practically useful, comprehensive and up to date as humanly possible. It is the **only** book you need; no phoning around for tourist brochures. You can find here everything for planning your trip including:
● All standards of places to stay from campsites and hostels to B&Bs, inns, guesthouses and hotels
● Walking companies if you want a self-guided or fully guided tour
● Varied itineraries for all types of walkers
● Answers to all your questions: when to go, degree of difficulty, what to pack and how much the whole walking holiday will cost

When you're all packed, there's comprehensive information to get you to and from the Cornwall Coast Path and 100 large-scale (1:20,000) walking maps to keep you on it. The route guide section has:

● Reviews of campsites, youth hostels, independent hostels, B&Bs, guesthouses, inns and hotels on and near the path
● Cafés, pubs, tea-shops, takeaways and restaurants as well as shops and supermarkets for buying supplies
● Rail, bus and taxi information for the villages and towns along the coast path
● Town plans including: Bude, Tintagel, Port Isaac, Rock, Padstow, Newquay, Perranporth, St Agnes, St Ives, St Just, Mousehole, Mullion, Mawnan Smith and Falmouth
● Historical, cultural and geographical background information

Minimum impact for maximum insight

Nature's peace will flow into you as the sunshine flows into trees. The winds will blow their freshness into you and storms their energy, while cares will drop off like autumn leaves.
John Muir (one of the world's earliest and most influential environmentalists, born in 1838)

It is no surprise that, since the time of John Muir, walkers and adventurers have been concerned about the natural environment; this book seeks to continue that tradition. There is a detailed, illustrated chapter on wildlife and conservation as well as a chapter devoted to minimum impact walking with ideas on how we can broaden that ethos.

By developing a deeper ecological awareness through a better understanding of nature and by supporting rural economies, local businesses, sensitive forms of transport and low-impact methods of farming and land-use we can all do our bit for a brighter future. There can be few activities as 'environmentally friendly' as walking.

Break clear away, once in awhile, and climb a mountain or spend a week in the woods. Wash your spirit clean.   **John Muir**

PART 1: PLANNING YOUR WALK

About the Cornwall Coast Path

HISTORY

The origins of the coast path lie in Cornwall's smuggling history. By the early 19th century smuggling had become so rife that in 1822 HM Coastguard was formed to patrol the entire British coastline. A coast-hugging footpath was created to enable the coastguards to see into every cove, inlet and creek and slowly but surely law and order prevailed and the smuggling decreased. By the beginning of the 20th century the foot patrols had been abandoned.

The South-West Coast Path

In 1948 a government report recommended the creation of a footpath around the entire south-west peninsula to improve public access to the coast which at that time was dire. It took until 1973 for the Cornwall Coast Path to be declared officially open and another five years for the rest of the South-West Coast Path to be completed. This is England's longest national trail, covering 613 miles (982 km) from Minehead in Somerset right round the bottom south-west corner of Britain to Poole Harbour in Dorset. If walking the Cornwall section whets your appetite there is plenty more to do!

HOW DIFFICULT IS THE COAST PATH?

No great level of experience is needed to walk the coast path as the walking is generally easy and you are never far from help. Villages and accommodation are reasonably close together so it is simple to adapt itineraries to suit all needs and levels of fitness.

The most challenging section of the coast path is the stretch from St Ives to Sennen Cove. The terrain is rugged and many of the places to stay and eat are located some way inland. As long as you plan ahead and are reasonably fit you should not experience any difficulties. Other points to bear in mind are basically common sense: don't wander too close to either the top or bottom of cliffs; take care when swimming; be aware of the tides; and listen to weather forecasts (for more information see pp58-9).

Route finding

For most of its length the coast path is well signposted. At confusing junctions the route is usually indicated by a finger-post sign with 'coast path' written on it. At other points, where there could be some confusion, there are wooden waymark posts with

Coast Path Waymarker

an acorn symbol and a yellow arrow to indicate which direction you should head. The waymarking is the responsibility of the local authorities along the trail who have a duty to maintain the path. Generally they do a good job but occasionally you will come across sections of the trail where waymarking is ambiguous, or even non-existent, but with the detailed trail maps and directions in this book and the fact that you always have the sea to one side it would be hard to get really lost.

GPS WAYPOINTS

If you have a handheld **GPS receiver** you will be able to take advantage of the waypoints marked on the maps, and listed on pp248-52 of this book.

Essentially a GPS will calculate your position on the earth using a number of satellites and this will be accurate to a few metres. That being so you might wonder what the point is of taking paper maps and a compass with you. The answer is that if the batteries go flat or the machine malfunctions you'll be left with only your sense of direction.

Having said this, it is **by no means necessary** that you use a GPS in con-junction with this guide and you should be able to get by with simply the sign-posts on the trail and the maps in this book. However, a GPS can be useful if for some reason you do get lost, or if you decide to explore off the trail and can't find your way back. It can also prove handy if you find yourself on the trail after dark when you can't see further than your torch beam.

If you do decide to use a GPS unit in conjunction with this book don't feel you need to be ticking off every waypoint as you reach it; you'll soon get bored and should get by without turning on your GPS for most of the trail. But if at any point you are **unsure of your position** your GPS can give a quick and reas-suring answer.

You can either manually key the nearest presumed waypoint from the list in this book into your unit as and when the need arises or, much less laboriously and with less margin for keystroke error, download the complete list (but not the descriptions) for free as a GPS-readable file from the Trailblazer website. You'll need the right cable and adequate memory in your unit (typically the ability to store 500 waypoints or more). This file, as well as instructions on how to inter-pret an OS grid reference, can be found on the Trailblazer website (⌨ www.trail blazer-guides.com).

HOW LONG DO YOU NEED?

If you're a fit walker who loves to spend all day on the trail you could manage Bude to Falmouth, or vice versa, a distance of around 203 miles (327km) depending on your exact route, in about 14 days. If you like your walking hol-iday to be a bit more relaxed with time to sit on the cliff tops, explore towns and villages as well as have a few rest days, three to three and a half weeks would be ample. Most walkers will fit somewhere between these two extremes, taking roughly two and a half weeks which still allows time for exploring and one or two rest days. There are some suggested itineraries on pp32-4.

For walkers with less time on their hands there are some superb day and weekend walks (see p35) along parts of the coast path.

Practical information for the walker

The practical information in this section will help you plan an excellent walk, covering every detail from what you need to do before you leave home to designing an itinerary to meet your particular preferences. More detailed information about the day-to-day walking and towns and villages along the trail can be found in **Part 4**.

ACCOMMODATION

There are plenty of places to stay all along the Cornwall Coast Path. It is always a good idea to book your accommodation ahead (see box p14). National holidays and any major festivals and events (see pp29-31) are likely to fill up the available accommodation quite quickly so make sure you are aware of what is taking place in the region.

Camping

Camping can be good fun; modern tents are easy to erect and light so carrying everything on your back need not be burdensome. Backpackers experience a sense of true independence by not having to rely on rules or timetables, instead being free to depend solely on themselves, arrive late, leave early, and generally behave like a free spirit. In today's modern age many of us forget how it feels to be truly independent and we can regain a sense of this self-reliance.

Most campsites are only open from Easter to October so camping in winter is not really practical. You will come across an enormous range of sites from a simple field on a farm with a toilet, shower and little else, to huge caravan and camping parks with washing machines, dryers, a small shop and a book of rules.

Prices range from £5 to about £9 per person and reach their peak in July and August when they increase to as much as £15-18. It's advisable to book ahead although there will almost always be room for a single tent. Unfortunately some sites will only take a minimum booking of one week during these months. Walkers camping alone can occasionally be at a disadvantage as prices are sometimes per pitch, which assumes two people sharing a tent.

The coast path is not really suited to **wild camping**. If you want to camp wild you should ask permission from whoever owns the land. Finding which farmhouse owns the field you want to camp in is no easy feat; you may find yourself trudging along miles of country lanes only to be told 'no'. Also, a lot of the coastline is owned by the National Trust who do not allow camping on their land. Having said that, there will always be independent-minded souls who put up their tent as the spirit moves them. By pitching late in the day and leaving before anyone else is up, it is unlikely that you will get noticed.

Hostels

There is a reasonable scattering of hostels along the coast path providing budget accommodation for between £9.95 and £21 per night (less for under 18s), usually in dormitories, although the demand for family accommodation in such places has led to many of them making private rooms available. Hostels come in two types: **youth hostels**, which are part of the Youth Hostel Association/ Hostelling International (YHA/HI; see box below), and **independent hostels**, also referred to as **backpacker hostels**, which as the name suggests are independently owned and are open to all. If you are planning to stay in hostels as often as possible you will have to make use of both types. In addition, in Penzance there is an excellent hostel run by the **YMCA** requiring no prior membership or affiliation of any kind.

Hostels are not just for young travellers, the young at heart will be more than welcome at most places. At YHA hostels, in particular, you'll often find more oldies than young 'uns, in fact oldies are positively encouraged, the YHA wooing the group referred to as the 'green greys', that is, conservation-minded older people who are an important market sector for them. If you find large groups of young people intimidating you can always check if the hostel has any double rooms. Older walkers might consider how they feel about sharing a dorm with a group of youngsters bearing in mind the Shakespearean dictum that 'crabbed youth and age cannot live together'. There is also the likelihood of the dorm being mixed, at least at independent hostels, and there are the pitfalls to be aware of.

One of the big advantages of staying in a hostel, aside from a cheap bed, is being able to cook your own food. Most hostels provide well-equipped kitchens and all they ask is that you clean up after yourself. The old rule of having to do a chore is a thing of the past, thankfully. There's also no need to carry a sleeping bag. Youth Hostels always provide linen and don't allow you to use a sleeping bag anyway and most independent hostels have linen available, although

---

❑ **Youth Hostel Association (YHA)**

You can join the YHA (☎ 01629-592700, 🖳 www.yha.org.uk) direct or at any hostel. You don't need to be a youth to stay in a YHA hostel nor do you need to be a member. The annual fee is £15.95 (£9.95 for under 26s) or £22.95 for family membership, valid for a year. One advantage of becoming a member is the YHA handbook issued annually and containing full details of all their properties. Another is that non members pay £3 a night more than members: the rates quoted in this guide and on the YHA's website are for YHA members.

If you are from another country other than Britain the equivalent organisation is **Hostelling International**: their website (🖳 www.hihostels.com) has lists of each country's contact details. HI cards are accepted at all YHA hostels in Britain.

sometimes you have to pay an extra £1-3 for its hire. Towels are hardly ever provided so it's worth remembering to pack one in your rucksack. In some cases camping is available at YHA hostels for £7 per person per night and campers can use the hostel's facilities.

Unfortunately, hostels aren't numerous enough or well-enough spaced to provide accommodation for every night of your walk so you will inevitably have to stay in B&Bs on several nights. The long stretch between Penzance and Falmouth is particularly barren with only two hostels (Lizard and Coverack).

Most YHA hostels (but not independent hostels) close between November and April; however, it is possible this will change so check the YHA website for up-to-date details.

Bed and breakfast (B&Bs)

B&Bs are a great British institution: for anyone unfamiliar with the concept you get a bedroom in someone's home along with a cooked breakfast the following morning; in many ways it is like being a guest of the family. However, the term B&B can equally apply to a night in someone's back bedroom in a suburban bungalow to one in a cliff-top farmhouse where every need is catered for, from a choice of herbal teas to free shampoos in the bathroom. It is an ideal way to walk in Cornwall as you can travel without too much clobber and relax in the evening in pleasant surroundings with the benefit of conversation with the proprietor and gain a fascinating insight into the local culture. Every night is a new experience.

What to expect For the long-distance walker tourist-board recommendations and star-rating systems may be a starting point although by no means all the places on or near the Coast Path are registered. Many walkers rely on the tourist information centres to book their next night's lodging for them. There are numerous guides listing Best Places to Stay and it can be difficult to choose especially in places like St Ives and Penzance which are practically wall-to-wall with guesthouses. Bear in mind they are not only accommodating walkers, in fact walkers are only one of the many types of people on holiday and B&Bs are not there simply for our benefit. At the end of a long day you will simply be glad of a hot bath or shower and clean bed to lay your head. If they have somewhere to hang your wet and muddy clothes so much the better. It is these criteria that have been used for places included in this guide – tea- and coffee-making facilities are more or less standard these days, even in the more out-of-the-way places round Land's End.

Bed and breakfast owners are often proud to boast that all rooms are **en suite** but this is sometimes merely a small shower and loo cubicle in the corner of the bedroom. Establishments without en suite rooms can be just as satisfactory as you may get sole use of a bathroom across the corridor and a hot bath is just what you need after a hard day on the trail. Sadly, baths are the exception, most B&Bs installing showers to tick the box marked 'en suite' when the Tourist Board come round to inspect. Rooms without private bathroom en suite are cheaper too. **Single** rooms are sometimes rather cramped 'box' rooms with barely enough room for the bed which can be restricting if you are travelling with quite a big pack. **Twin** rooms have two single beds, while a **double** is supposed to have one double bed, although just to confuse things, twins are sometimes called doubles because the beds can be moved together to make a 'double' bed. This can lead to awkward moments so it is best to specify if you prefer two single beds. Some establishments have **family** rooms, which sleep three or more, although to confuse matters even further, others call these **triple** rooms and may also have a family room sleeping four people or more.

Some B&Bs provide an **evening meal**, particularly if there is no pub or restaurant nearby. Others may offer you a lift to a local eatery, while some will expect you make your own arrangements. Check what the procedure is when you book.

All accommodation listed should be open year-round (unless stated otherwise). Remember, however, that B&B owners can, and do, change their minds at a moment's notice, deciding to redecorate when it's quiet, or closing the business when they want to go away on holiday. Smoking (see box p18-19) in enclosed public spaces is now banned so in effect every B&B is a non-smoking house. A tiny minority may set aside a room for smokers but few do.

Rates B&B prices are quoted either as per person per night or per room per night. Per person rates range from £24 for a simple room with a shared bathroom to over £40 for a very comfortable en suite room with all mod cons; the equivalent per room rates would be £48 and £80. In the large towns tariffs tend to drop in the low season, but in many small places they stay the same year-round. The rates quoted in the text reflect the seasonal variation.

In general B&B accommodation is cheaper if you are travelling as a pair. Since many places don't have a single room other rooms are sometimes let out on a single occupancy basis. However, for this there is often a supplement if the rate is per person or a discount on the room rate: in either case about £5-10: at peak times solo travellers may be expected to pay the full rate for two people.

Remember, many B&Bs do not take payment by credit or debit cards or even, if you turn up off the street, cheques, and you should have enough cash with you to pay your bill in the morning.

❏ **Booking accommodation in advance**

Booking ahead is a good idea for all types of accommodation as it guarantees you a bed for the night. If you are walking alone it also means somebody is expecting you. During the high season (July and August) you may need to book a few months ahead, whereas in the winter a few days, or even the night before, should suffice. If you are walking in the low season check the owner will provide an evening meal or that a local pub serves food. If you must cancel please telephone your hosts; it will save a lot of worry and allow them to provide a bed for somebody else.

If the idea of booking all your accommodation fills you with dread, you may want to consider using the services of one of the companies listed on pp21-3. For a fee they will happily do all the work for you, saving you a considerable amount of trouble, and most will also arrange for your baggage to be forwarded to the next night's accommodation in the price.

Inns and pubs

Putting up at an inn is a British tradition that goes back centuries and still appeals to many walkers. However, just because it's called an inn doesn't mean it will have old oak beams and a roaring log fire. Although there are some delightful traditional pubs, many places have been refurbished and have lost some of their character and charm. Inns tend to be more expensive than simple B&Bs with prices around £30 to £40 per person with breakfast included.

The biggest advantage of staying at an inn is convenience. Accommodation, meals and a bar are all provided under the same roof. If you've had a few too many pints of wonderful Cornish ale you don't have far to stagger at closing time. On the other hand if you want an early night you may find the noise from the bar keeps you awake.

Guesthouses

Guesthouses are often larger Victorian or Edwardian houses converted into en suite rooms, filling the gap between B&Bs and hotels. They are usually less personal and more expensive (£30-40 per person) but do offer more space and a lounge for guests. They are usually more geared to coping with holiday-makers and their owners are experienced in the hospitality trade, employing staff – if only young locals – to come in to do the bedrooms. They often take payment by credit and debit card and by cheque without quibble.

Hotels

Most hotels along the coast are classier and more expensive than B&Bs, inns or guesthouses and therefore put many walkers off. The other problem for the walker is having suitable smart clothes to wear in the evening, unless of course, you have the panache to carry off designer fleece and walking boots in the restaurant. Once in a while you may feel you deserve a treat and at the end of a long day that Jacuzzi could be well worth paying extra for!

In general, hotels do not pay walkers any particular attention. They are simply one more guest who, if anything, requires rather more than the average guest when they arrive with pack, heavy boots and sometimes wet gear. Facilities for drying clothes will be minimal – one walker of my acquaintance was given a hair-dryer when asking if there was anywhere he could dry his soaking wet clothes.

Self-catering holiday cottages

It is possible to walk a considerable amount of the coast path from a fixed base using the excellent public transport to get to and from the trail each day; see box p31 for more information and ideas.

Renting a self-catering cottage makes a lot of sense for a group of walkers as it will work out a lot cheaper than staying in B&Bs and you won't have the headache of booking accommodation for lots of people. Holiday cottages are normally let on a weekly basis but short breaks are often possible. Cottages haven't been listed in this book; search on the internet or contact the tourist information centre in the area you want to stay for further details (see p40).

Alternatively, contact the Landmark Trust (information ☎ 01628-825920, booking ☎ 01628-825925, 🖳 www.landmarktrust.org.uk) or the National Trust (☎ 0844-800 2070, 🖳 www.nationaltrustcottages.co.uk), both of which have several properties in Cornwall.

FOOD AND DRINK

Breakfast, lunch and evening meals

The traditional B&B **breakfast** is the celebrated 'full English' breakfast, or in Cornwall, the 'full Cornish': this consists of a choice of cereals and/or fruit juice followed by a plate of eggs, bacon, sausages, mushrooms, beans, fried bread and tomatoes, with toast and marmalade or jams to end and all washed down with tea or coffee. This is good for a day's walking, but after a week not so good for your cholesterol level. Sometimes B&B owners offer a continental breakfast option or will charge you less if all you want is a bowl of muesli or some toast. Alternatively, and also if you want an early start, it is worth asking if they would substitute the breakfast for a packed lunch. Most B&Bs will fill your flask with tea or coffee for the day, often without charge.

For **lunch** there are several options. The cheapest and easiest is to buy a picnic lunch or pasty (see box opposite) at one of the many shops or bakeries you'll pass. Many B&Bs and hostels are happy to make a packed lunch for you for between £4 and £5. Otherwise you could eat out but you need to plan ahead to make sure the pub or restaurant is open and that you'll reach it in time for lunch. In recent times it has become quite the norm for walkers to travel light, taking only water and possibly a fruit bar or piece of fruit, confining their eating to the evening meal. Another alternative is to have a light lunch and then indulge in a **cream tea** (see box opposite).

During the summer you will also come across seasonal snack shacks by popular beaches and car parks serving light snacks such as filled sandwiches or baguettes, cakes, ice creams and soft drinks; the only trouble is not knowing exactly when they will be open.

For your **evening meal** the local pub is often the best place to head if your B&B does not provide a meal, or if you have not pre-booked one. Most pubs have a relatively standard bar menu that falls under the category of 'pub grub' featuring such regulars as scampi and chips, steak and ale pie and steaks supplemented by one or two 'specials' such as fresh fish probably from a local source, and many establishments also have an attached à la carte restaurant with more elaborate meals.

Most menus include at least two vegetarian options although this may only be a pasta dish smothered in melted cheese. All the towns along the coast have Indian and Chinese takeaways/restaurants as well as fish and chip shops. If you want to splash out on fine-dining there are lots of nice restaurants along the coast path and local seafood is invariably on the menu. If they can't serve freshly caught fish in Cornwall they are just not trying.

❑ Traditional Cornish food

● **The Cornish pasty** Visitors to Cornwall, whether walkers or not, cannot go home without having tried the ubiquitous pasty at least once. For some, once is enough whilst for others it becomes a lifetime's favourite. The pasty, for those who thought it was just a glorified meat pie, is shaped like a letter 'D', crimped on the curved side, with a filling of beef with swede or turnip, potato and onion with a light peppery seasoning. The pastry is slow-cooked to a golden colour and is glazed with milk or egg.

Originally Cornish tin miners were sent off to work by their wives with their lunch in the form of a pasty containing a savoury filling at one end and fruit at the other, two for the price of one so to speak. Today they are mainly savoury. Pasties are eaten widely and available everywhere providing a meal on the run. Such is the iconic status of the pasty that the Cornish Pasty Makers Association has applied for Protected Geographical Indication Status so that in future pasties can be recognised as unique to Cornwall. Perhaps they will have their own *appellation contrôllée*! Try one – you might get hooked.

● **Cornish cream tea** This is another walkers' favourite and you'll never be far from places offering this afternoon treat of scones, jam and clotted cream accompanied by a pot of tea; surely the cheapest decadent food available. Choose carefully and check that the scones are made on the premises or you may be disappointed. Prices start at around £4.50 per person.

● **Fish** The fishing industry has been one of the biggest influences on the culinary traditions of Cornwall, and local favourites such as **stargazy pie**, sometimes referred to as 'starry gazey' pie, made with fish heads sticking out of the crust looking towards the sky, are on some menus. Fish pie is widely served, usually a good option washed down with a pint of the local ale. Even if you're on a tight budget the ubiquitous **fish and chips** can be satisfying if cooked with fresh fish. At the other end of the scale there are plenty of restaurants around the coast offering mouth-watering dishes concocted from **locally caught fish**. Species found in Cornwall's inshore waters include Dover sole, plaice, turbot, brill, gurnard, pollock, lemon sole, ray, cod, whiting, red mullet, John Dory, mackerel, sea bass and many more. There's also shellfish: lobsters, crabs, scallops, langoustines, clams and mussels, which are often fished for from the smaller coastal villages.

For further information about Cornish food and farmers' markets in Cornwall visit: 🖥 www.foodfromcornwall.co.uk.

Self-catering

The coast-path walker doesn't need to carry much food. Almost every village you pass through has a small shop or convenience store with plenty of food for snacks and picnic lunches and often cut sandwiches and pasties and a limited choice for cooking in the evening. Larger stores are well-stocked with a range of groceries including lightweight campers' food such as instant mashed potato and pasta and sauce mixes and they'll usually have a selection of wine and beer too. **Fuel** for camp stoves requires a little more planning. Gas canisters are the easiest to come by with most general stores and campsite shops stocking them.

Methylated spirit and Coleman fuel is sold in many outdoor shops and hardware stores and can occasionally be found in other shops too. Fuel canisters for stoves are now universally available.

Drinking water

I wouldn't recommend filling your water bottle or pouch from any stream or river on the coast path. Most streams run through farmland before reaching the coast. It may also have run off roads, housing or agricultural fields picking up heavy metals, pesticides and other chemical contaminants that we humans use liberally. Tap water is safe to drink unless a sign specifies otherwise. Carry a two or three-litre bottle or pouch and fill it up wherever you stay the night. During the day you could refill it in public toilets although not all meet reasonable standards of cleanliness and the taps are often awkward. Shops and bars are

---

❏ Information for foreign visitors

● **Currency** The British pound (£) comes in notes of £100, £50, £20, £10 and £5, and coins of £2 and £1. The pound is divided into 100 pence (usually referred to as 'p', pronounced 'pee') which comes in silver coins of 50p, 20p, 10p and 5p, and copper coins of 2p and 1p.

● **Rates of exchange** Up-to-date rates of exchange can be found at ⌨ www.xe.com/ucc.

● **Business hours** Most **post offices** are open from Monday to Friday 9am-5.30pm and Saturday 9am-12.30pm except in the smaller places where they will close one afternoon a week, often Wednesday. **Banks** are generally open Monday to Friday 9am-3.30pm and **shops** Monday to Saturday 9am-5.30pm though some close at lunchtime on Saturday. **Supermarkets** and **food shops** often open longer hours, the national chain stores often opening for 12 hours a day or even longer and on Sunday as well. It is rare now for food shops to have an early closing day, as in the past, or to close for an hour for lunch.

Pubs are usually open from 11am-11pm Monday to Saturday, and noon-3pm and 7-10.30pm on Sundays. Even if a pub is open all day food is only likely to be available between noon-2pm and 6.30-9pm except in the busiest season when many do serve food all day. Since the licensing laws enable each pub to choose its opening hours, most are open the hours mentioned above.

● **National (bank) holidays** On any national public holiday Cornwall can be flooded with people. Businesses generally close on these days, accommodation prices often increase and you may find it difficult to book somewhere for just one night. The following are holidays in England: New Year's Day (1 January); Good Friday and Easter Monday (March/April); May Bank Holiday (first Monday in May); Whit Weekend or Spring Bank Holiday (last Monday in May); Summer Bank Holiday (last Monday of August); Christmas Day and Boxing Day (25-26 December).

● **School holidays** School holiday periods in England are generally as follows: a one-week break late October, two weeks around Christmas and the New Year, a week mid-February, two weeks around Easter, and from late July to early September.

● **Smoking** A ban on smoking in public places came into force in England in July 2007. The ban relates not only to pubs and restaurants, but also to B&Bs, hostels and hotels. These latter have the right to designate one or more bedrooms where the occupants can smoke, but the ban affects all enclosed areas open to the public – even if they are in a private home such as a B&B. Many pubs have a smoker's corner but it

becoming increasingly reluctant to fill water bottles for you, some even posting a notice to the effect that they don't do it. A 3-litre 'platypus' style bag should be sufficient for all but the hottest days.

Real ales and cider

The process of brewing beer is believed to have been in Britain since the Neolithic period and is an art local brewers have been perfecting ever since. Real ale is beer that has been brewed using traditional methods. **Real ales** are not filtered or pasteurised, a process which removes and kills all the yeast cells, but instead undergo a secondary fermentation at the pub which enhances the natural flavours and brings out the individual characteristics of the beer. It's served at cellar temperature with no artificial fizz added unlike keg beer which is pasteurised and has the fizz added by injecting nitrogen dioxide.

can only be outdoors at the back or at the picnic tables in the garden area. Should you be foolhardy enough to light up in a no-smoking area, which includes pretty well any indoor public place, you could be fined £50, but it's the owners of the premises who carry the can if they fail to stop you, with a potential fine of £2500.

● **EHICs and travel insurance** The European Health Insurance Card (EHIC) entitles EU nationals (on production of the EHIC card) to necessary medical treatment under the UK's National Health Service while on a temporary visit here. However, this is not a substitute for proper medical cover on your travel insurance for unforeseen bills and for getting you home should that be necessary. Also consider cover for loss and theft of personal belongings, especially if you are camping or staying in hostels, as there will be times when you'll have to leave your luggage unattended.

● **Weights and measures** In 2007 the European Commission announced they would no longer attempt to ban the pint or the mile: so in Britain milk can be sold in pints, as can beer in pubs, though most other liquid including petrol (gasoline) and diesel is sold in litres. Road distances will also continue to be given in miles rather than kilometres. Most food is sold in metric weights (g and kg) but the imperial weights of pounds (lb) and ounces (oz) are frequently displayed too. The population remains split between those who still use inches, feet and yards and those who are happy with millimetres, centimetres and metres; you'll often be told that 'it's only a hundred yards or so' to somewhere, rather than a hundred metres or so. The weather – a frequent topic of conversation – is also an issue: while most forecasts predict temperatures in °C, many people continue to think in terms of °F.

● **Time** During the winter, the whole of Britain is on Greenwich Mean Time (GMT). The clocks move forward one hour on the last Sunday in March, remaining on British Summer Time (BST) until the last Sunday in October.

● **Telephone** From outside Britain the international country access code for Britain is ☎ 44 followed by the area code minus the first 0, and then the number you require. Within Britain, to call a number with the same code as the phone you are calling from, the code can be omitted: dial the number only. It is cheaper to ring at weekends, and after 6pm and before 8am on weekdays. If you're using a mobile phone that is registered overseas, consider buying a local SIM card to keep costs down.

● **Emergency services** For police, ambulance, fire or coastguard dial ☎ 999 or the EU standard number (☎ 112).

There are plenty of pubs along the coast path serving an excellent range of real ales from around the country. The strength of beer is denoted by the initials ABV which means alcohol by volume followed by a percentage starting with the lowest at about 3.8%. Distinctive Cornish beers watching out for include Betty Stoggs Bitter (4%), a strong hoppy beer, and Cornish Knocker Ale (4.5%) with its beautiful golden colour, both of which are brewed by Skinner's who have won a number of awards. Sharp's Brewery also produces some fine ales, in particular Doom Bar Bitter (4%) named after the Doom Bar (see box p110) near Padstow, Eden Bitter (4.3%) and IPA (4.8%) which can be the undoing of the unsuspecting drinker. St Austell Brewery was first established in 1851 and their most popular brews are Tribute (4%), voted by CAMRA as Supreme Champion of Cornwall, and Tinners Ale (3.7%), a light, chestnut, malty beer. Truro Brewery has a range of bitters with names inspired by buccaneers including Pirate's Gold (4%), Cornish Buccaneer (4.3%) and Cornish Mutiny (4.8%), a darkish, hoppy beer with a slightly biscuity flavour. The most common of these ales are St Austell's Tribute and Sharp's Doom Bar, both widely available.

Scrumpy (rough cider) is another Cornish favourite and well worth trying if you come across it on draught. You will immediately notice the difference from keg cider as it will be cloudy, with 'bits' floating in it and no fizz. You may also notice the difference afterwards; scrumpy is notorious for inducing wild nights out with subsequent periods of memory loss, sweating, dizziness, prolonged headaches, shaking, nausea and hot flushes. Another pint, anyone?

MONEY

Most campsites, hostels, B&Bs and small shops will require you to pay with **cash**, or by cheque from a British bank account, as they won't have credit/debit card facilities. You don't need to carry large amounts of money with you as all towns have banks with cash machines (ATMs) which are also found in convenience stores and supermarkets. Some ATMs charge (£1.50-1.85) for withdrawals though there are clear signs warning you of this before you actually withdraw the money. Alternatively, many supermarkets will advance cash

---

❏ Cornish words and place names

Along the coast path you will come across many place names which are easily translated once you've become familiar with a few Cornish words. To get you started here are some of the most common words used in place names.

Boel/Voel – cliff	*Kellys* – lost, hidden or grove	*Ros* – heath or moor
Bos/Bud – dwelling		*Tol* – holed
Carrack – rock	*Men/Maen* – stone	*Towan* – sandhill
Chy – house	*Mor* – sea	*Tre* – hamlet or homestead
Cornovii – cliff castles	*Penn/Pen/Pedn* – headland	
Dinas – hill fort		*Treath* – beach
Dhu/Du – black	*Pol* – pool	*Wheal* – mine
Enys – island	*Porth* – harbour or cove	*Zawn* – cleft

against a card (cashback) often asking if you require cash when you go through the checkout with your purchases.

Use the table of town and village facilities (see pp24-7) to plan how much money you'll need to withdraw at any one time. **Travellers' cheques** can be cashed only at banks, foreign exchange bureaus and a few of the larger hotels. See also p39.

Using the Post Office for banking

Some UK banks have an agreement with the Post Office allowing customers to withdraw cash from branches using their debit card and pin number, or cheque-book and debit card. As many towns and villages have post offices, this is an extremely useful facility.

OTHER SERVICES

Almost all villages have at least a **general store**, a **post office** and **public telephone**. Where they exist special mention has also been made in Part 4 of other services that may be of use to walkers such as **banks**, **cash machines**, **laundrettes**, **outdoor equipment shops**, **internet access**, **pharmacies**, **medical centres** and **tourist information centres**.

WALKING COMPANIES

For walkers wanting to make their holiday as easy and trouble free as possible there are several specialist companies offering a range of services from accommodation booking to fully guided group tours.

Baggage carriers

The thought of carrying a large pack puts many people off walking long-distance trails. Let's Go Walking (see p22) offer a baggage-transfer service. Alternatively some of the **taxi** firms listed in this guide can provide a similar service within a local area if you want a break from carrying your bags for a day or so. Also, don't rule out the possibility of your B&B/guesthouse owner taking your bags ahead for you; plenty of them are glad to do since it supplements their income and adds to the service they offer. Depending on the distance they may make no charge at all, or charge £10 to £15; this may be less than a taxi so is worth enquiring about.

Self-guided holidays

The following companies provide customised packages for walkers which usually include detailed advice and notes on itineraries and routes, maps, accommodation booking, daily baggage transfer and transport arrangements at the start and end of your walk. If you don't want the whole all-in package some of the companies may be able to arrange just **accommodation booking** or **baggage carrying**.

● **Celtic Trails** (☎ 0800-970 7585, 🖳 www.celtic-trails.com) Organise walking holidays round the whole footpath. Time options are from four days to a week or more. Plus tailor-made tours.

● **Compass Holidays** (☎ 01242-250642, 🖥 www.compass-holidays.com) Organise seven/eight-day walks around the Lizard Peninsula (Helston to Mullion).

● **Contours Walking Holidays** (☎ 01768-480451, 🖥 www.contours.co.uk) Holidays include Padstow to St Ives, St Ives to Penzance and Penzance to Falmouth in various combinations of three to ten days' walking plus tailor-made tours.

● **Explore Britain** (☎ 01740-650900, 🖥 www.xplorebritain.com) Operate a variety of holidays including one based at Land's End, five to six days St Ives to Land's End, three days Bude to Tintagel, fourteen days Padstow to Frenchman's Creek, six days Newquay to Land's End.

● **Footpath Holidays** (☎ 01985-840049, 🖥 www.footpath-holidays.com) Operates a range of walking holidays: inn-to-inn holidays, single centre from Boscastle for North Cornwall, and Penzance for far west Cornwall. They also offer short breaks or one-week holidays plus tailor-made tours. Baggage transfer is included as part of inn-to-inn holidays.

● **HF Holidays** (☎ 0845-470 8558, 🖥   www.hfholidays.co.uk/trails) Offer six-day holidays based in St Ives and walking from there to north or south Cornwall.

● **Let's Go Walking** (☎ 01837-880075, 🖥 www.letsgowalking.com) Offer holidays which cover the whole of the coast path with length of stay to suit.

● **Lightfoot Walking Holidays** (☎ 01736-850715, 🖥 www.lightfootwalking holidays.co.uk) Specialises in Cornwall walking holidays. Custom-made trips for any length (three nights to four weeks or more) along all parts of the coastal path.

● **Sherpa Expeditions** (☎ 020-8577 2717, 🖥 www.sherpa-walking-holidays .co.uk) Offer an eight-day walking holiday from Mevagissey to Marazion including the Lizard and Roseland peninsulas.

● **Westcountry Walking Holidays** (☎ 0845-094 3848, 🖥 www.westcountry-walking-holidays.com) Offer custom-made trips for any number of days to suit anywhere along the coast path.

Group/guided walking tours

Fully guided tours are ideal for individuals wanting to travel in the company of others and for groups of friends wanting to be guided. The packages usually include meals, accommodation, transport arrangements, minibus back-up, baggage transfer, as well as a qualified guide and are often for sections of the trail such as Padstow to St Ives, a popular route for a week's walking. The companies differ widely in terms of the size of the groups they take, the standards of accommodation, the age range of clients, the distances walked and the professionalism of the guides, so it's worth checking out several before making a booking.

● **Adventureline** (☎ 01209-820847, 🖥 www.adventureline.co.uk) Has a base in St Agnes and offers a variety of walks along different stretches of the coast path in most areas of Cornwall, from seven days plus.

● **Celtic Trails** (see p21) Offers a one-week guided walking holiday based in two centres, one on the Atlantic coast and one on the English Channel coast.
● **Footpath Holidays** (see opposite) Fully guided tours (short breaks or one week) are offered from their base in Penzance.
● **HF Holidays** (see opposite) Two itineraries (six days) based in St Ives.
● **Ramblers Countrywide Holidays** (☎ 01707-386800, 🖳 www.ramblers countrywide.co.uk) Offers a six-day holiday based in Penzance with four day-walks covering the coast path between Penzance and St Ives.

WALKING WITH DOGS

Providing your dog is fit enough there is no legal reason why it can't come and enjoy your holiday with you. As long as you act responsibly to help prevent conflict with other walkers, farmers and landowners this happy situation will continue.

Remember that it is a legal requirement to **keep dogs under close control** on Rights of Way. It is particularly important to **keep your dog on a lead** when crossing farmland with livestock in it. You need to be especially vigilant around lambing time and from March to July when ground-nesting birds are busy lay-ing and hatching their eggs. Incidents of dogs worrying sheep do nothing to endear dog-walkers to farmers and a farmer can legally shoot a dog that is apparently worrying livestock. Also take care around crops. Dogs that run through and flatten fields of wheat, barley and hay are affecting a farmer's livelihood.

You may encounter some problems when walking with a dog, particularly where the coast path crosses a beach (with no alternative route) on which there's a dog ban (usually between Easter and October). In such a situation Right of Way legislation over-rides the dog ban but you should cross the beach directly and keep your dog on a short lead. The current legislation is not common knowledge and you may find people will challenge you, telling you that you are not allowed on the beach with your dog. Beaches with dog restrictions are marked on the trail maps.

Carry a 'pooper scooper' or bags to remove waste if your dog fouls on the path, or in heavily used areas such as parks, playgrounds and beaches. You should also remove dog waste when crossing sensitive areas such as heathland and dunes. These are nutrient-poor sites and over time failure to remove faeces enriches the soil, acting as an unwanted fertiliser which leads to invasion by plant species not usually associated with these environments.

Remember if booking accommodation to mention you have a dog with you. Many places will not accept dogs apart from guide dogs.

PLANNING YOUR WALK

VILLAGE AND

Place name (Places in brackets are a short walk off the coast path)	Distance from previous place approx miles/km	Cash Machine	Post Office	Tourist Information Centre/Point (TIC/TIP)/Visitor Centre (VC)
Bude & Upton		✔	✔	TIC
Widemouth Bay	3/5		✔	
Crackington Haven	7/11			
Boscastle	7/11	✔	✔	VC
Bossiney	4/6			
Tintagel	1/2	✔	✔	TIC
Trebarwith Strand	2/3			
Port Gaverne	6/10			
Port Isaac	1/2		✔	
Polzeath	9/14	✔	✔	
Padstow	3/5	✔	✔	TIC
Trevone	5/8			
Harlyn Bay	1.5/2			
Mother Ivey's Bay	1.5/2			
Constantine Bay	2/3			
Treyarnon	0.5/1			
Porthcothan	2/3			
Mawgan Porth	4.5/7	✔		
Watergate Bay	2/3			
Porth	2/3			
Newquay	4/6	✔	✔	
Crantock	2/3-6/10	✔	✔	
Holywell	3.5/6			
Perranporth	4.5/7	✔	✔	TIP
(St Agnes)	3.5/6 to Trevaunance Cove	✔	✔	TIC
Porthtowan	4.5/7		✔	
Portreath	3/5	✔	✔	
Gwithian	8/13			
Hayle	4/6	✔	✔	TIC
St Ives	5/8	✔	✔	TIC
(Zennor)	6/10 to Zennor Head			
(Gurnard's Head/Treen)	1/2 to Lean Point			
(Pendeen/Trewellard)	6/10 to Pendeen Watch	✔	✔	
(Botallack)	2/3 to Zawn a Bal			
(St Just)	2/3 to Cape Cornwall	✔	✔	TIC
Sennen Cove/Mayon	5/8		✔	
Land's End	1/2			VC
Porthcurno	5/8		✔	
Treen	0.5/1			
Lamorna	4.5/7			
Mousehole	2/3		✔	
Newlyn	2.5/4	✔	✔	
Penzance	1.5/2	✔	✔	TIC

(cont'd on p26)

TOWN FACILITIES

Eating Place ✔ = one ✔✔ = a few ✔✔✔ = four + (✔) = seasonal	Food Store	Campsite	Hostels YHA or H (Ind Hostel) (H)=seasonal	B&B-style accommodation ✔ = one ✔✔ = two ✔✔✔ = three +	Place name (Places in brackets are a short walk off the coast path)
✔✔	✔	✔	H	✔✔✔	**Bude & Upton**
(✔✔)		✔		✔✔	**Widemouth Bay**
✔(✔✔)				✔	**Crackington Haven**
✔✔	✔		(YHA)	✔✔✔	**Boscastle**
		✔		✔✔	**Bossiney**
✔✔	✔	✔	(YHA)	✔✔✔	**Tintagel**
✔✔				✔	**Trebarwith Strand**
✔				✔✔	**Port Gaverne**
✔(✔✔)	✔			✔✔✔	**Port Isaac**
✔✔	✔	✔		✔	**Polzeath**
✔✔✔	✔	✔		✔✔✔	**Padstow**
				✔✔	**Trevone**
(✔)				✔	**Harlyn Bay**
		✔		✔	**Mother Ivey's Bay**
(✔)	✔			✔	**Constantine Bay**
(✔)		✔	YHA		**Treyarnon**
	✔				**Porthcothan**
(✔✔)	✔	✔		✔✔	**Mawgan Porth**
✔✔✔		✔			**Watergate Bay**
✔✔		✔		✔✔✔	**Porth**
✔✔✔	✔	✔	H	✔✔✔	**Newquay**
✔✔	✔	✔		✔✔✔	**Crantock**
✔(✔)		✔			**Holywell**
✔✔✔	✔	✔	(YHA)	✔✔✔	**Perranporth**
✔✔	✔	✔		✔✔✔	**(St Agnes)**
✔(✔)	✔	✔		✔✔	**Porthtowan**
✔✔	✔		YHA	✔✔	**Portreath**
✔(✔)		✔		✔✔	**Gwithian**
✔✔✔	✔			✔✔✔	**Hayle**
✔✔✔	✔	✔	H	✔✔✔	**St Ives**
✔		✔	H	✔✔✔	**(Zennor)**
✔				✔✔✔	**(Gurnard's Head/Treen)**
✔✔	✔	✔		✔✔✔	**(Pendeen/Trewellard)**
✔		✔		✔	**(Botallack)**
✔✔	✔	✔ (Kelynack)	(YHA)	✔✔✔	**(St Just)**
✔✔✔	✔	✔	H	✔✔	**Sennen Cove/Mayon**
✔		✔		✔	**Land's End**
(✔)	✔			✔✔	**Porthcurno**
✔		✔		✔	**Treen**
✔✔				✔✔	**Lamorna**
✔✔✔	✔ snacks only			✔✔✔	**Mousehole**
✔✔✔	✔			✔✔✔	**Newlyn**
✔✔✔	✔	✔	YHA/H	✔✔✔	**Penzance**

(cont'd on p27)

VILLAGE AND

(cont'd from p24) Place name (Places in brackets are a short walk off the coast path)	Distance from previous place approx miles/km	Cash Machine	Post Office	Tourist Information Centre/Point (TIC/TIP)/Visitor Centre (VC)
Marazion	3/5	✔	✔	
Praa Sands	6/10		✔	
Porthleven	4/6		✔	
(Mullion Cove/Mullion)	6/10 to Mullion Cove	✔	✔	
(Lizard)	6/10 to Lizard Point	✔	✔	
Cadgwith	4/6			
Coverack	7/11		✔	
Porthallow	4/6			
Helford	6/10		✔	
Gweek	5/8		✔	
Helford Passage	5.5/9 via Gweek; 0/0 by ferry			
(Mawnan Smith)	1/2 to Durgan		✔	
Falmouth	9/14	✔	✔	TIC
TOTAL DISTANCE	203 miles/327km			

Budgeting

By **camping** and cooking your own meals you can get by on about £12 to £15 per day outside the holiday season but much more during it. If you envisage having the odd meal out and like to finish the day with a glass or two of wine or a pint at the pub £20 would be more realistic. Remember that the time of year you're walking will have a significant impact on your budget; during the height of the season campground charges can sometimes escalate dramatically.

As noted on p13, it isn't possible to stay in **hostels** every night. However, for the nights you do stay in one expect to pay £9-21. If you cook your own meals you will need about £25 to £30 per day. If you eat the meals provided in some YHA hostels expect to pay £4.50 for breakfast; £4/5.10 for a child/adult packed lunch and £6.50/9 for an child/adult evening meal.

On the nights when you have to stay in a B&B there won't be the facilities to cook for yourself, so you will have to eat out. For these days budget in the vicinity of £30 if you can make do with a takeaway for dinner, or £35 if you intend having a more substantial meal out.

If you stay in standard **B&Bs** you can keep your daily budget within £40-60 by requesting a picnic lunch from the proprietor or making your own and not being too indulgent in the pub each night. If you plan to stay in more expensive B&Bs, inns, guesthouses or hotels budget for at least £60-70 per day inclusive

(cont'd from p25)

TOWN FACILITIES

Eating Place ✔= one ✔✔= a few ✔✔✔= four + (✔✔) = seasonal	Food Store	Campsite	Hostels YHA or H (Ind Hostel) (H)=seasonal	B&B-style accommodation ✔= one ✔✔= two ✔✔✔= three +	Place name (Places in brackets are a short walk off the coast path)
✔✔✔	✔	✔		✔✔✔	**Marazion**
✔(✔)	✔	✔		✔✔	**Praa Sands**
✔✔✔	✔			✔✔✔	**Porthleven**
✔✔✔	✔	✔ (Tenerife Farm)		✔✔✔	**(Mullion Cove/Mullion)**
✔✔✔	✔	✔	(YHA)	✔✔✔	**(Lizard)**
✔		✔(Kennack Sands)		✔	**Cadgwith**
✔(✔)	✔	✔	(YHA)	✔✔	**Coverack**
					Porthallow
✔	✔	✔ (Gear Farm)			**Helford**
✔✔	✔				**Gweek**
					Helford Passage
✔	✔			✔✔✔	**(Mawnan Smith)**
✔✔✔	✔	✔	H	✔✔✔	**Falmouth**

of lunch and evening meal. (See also p14-15). Don't forget to set some money aside for the inevitable **extras**: postcards, stamps, washing and drying clothes, entrance fees for various attractions, cream teas, beer, buses and taxis, any changes of plan.

When to go

The decision of when to go may be out of your hands. However, if you are in a position to choose which time of the year to come, make your plans carefully. Do you prefer the vibrant colours of springtime wildflowers, or the rich tones of autumnal foliage and heather? Do you want weather warm enough for swimming? Do you like the buzz of big crowds, or do you prefer to walk in solitude? The following information should help you decide when is best for you.

SEASONS

Spring and early summer

April, **May** and **June** are possibly the best months to go walking in Cornwall. The weather is warm enough without being too hot, the days are getting longer, the holiday crowds have yet to arrive and this is usually the driest time of the year. Perhaps the most beautiful advantage is the abundance of wild flowers

PLANNING YOUR WALK

which reach their height in May. Cornwall starts to get busier in June as by now the sun is making an average appearance of seven hours a day.

Summer

July and **August** are the hottest months and also the busiest. This is the time of the school summer holidays when families and holidaymakers flock in their thousands to Cornwall. Demand for accommodation is high and many B&B owners and some campsites will only take bookings of at least two nights if not a full week. Surprisingly most of the coast path itself is not that busy, but you'll encounter the crowds at beaches, car parks and in towns, especially if the sun is out. The weather is generally good in July, although during particularly settled periods it can be too hot for walking. August can be wetter and overcast: August 2008 was the wettest on record.

Autumn

September is often a wonderful month for walking. The days are still long, the temperature has not dropped noticeably and the summer crowds have long disappeared. The first signs of winter will be felt in **October** but there's nothing really to deter the walker. In fact there's still much to entice you, such as the colours of the heathland, which come into their own in autumn; a magnificent blaze of brilliant purples and pinks, splashed with the yellow flowers of gorse.

Winter

November can bring crisp clear days which are ideal for walking, although you'll definitely feel the chill when you stop on the cliff tops for a break. Winter temperatures rarely fall below freezing but the incidence of gales and storms definitely increases. You need to be fairly hardy to walk in **December** and **January** and you may have to alter your plans because of the weather. By **February** the daffodils and primroses are already appearing but even into **March** it can still be decidedly chilly if the sun is not out.

While winter is definitely the low season with many places closed, this can be more of an advantage than a disadvantage. Very few people walk at this time of year, giving you long stretches of the trail to yourself. When you do stumble across other walkers they are as happy as you to stop and chat. Finding B&B accommodation is easier as you will rarely have to book more than a night ahead (though it is still worth checking in advance as some B&Bs close out of season), but if you are camping, or on a small budget, you will find places to stay much more limited. Few campsites bother to stay open all year and many hostels will be closed.

WEATHER

The Cornish climate is considerably milder than in the rest of Britain because of its southerly location and the influence of the Gulf Stream.

Winter **temperatures** rarely fall below freezing and the mean maximum in summer is around 19°C. Sea temperatures range from about 9°C in February to about 17°C in August.

Rainfall is highest in the winter due to the regular procession of weather fronts moving east across the Atlantic. In the summer these fronts are weaker, less frequent and take a more northerly track.

Mean **wind speeds** are force 3-4 in summer and 4-5 in winter. Gales can be expected around ten days per month between December and February and less than one day per month from May to August.

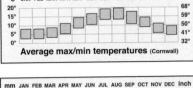

Average max/min temperatures (Cornwall)

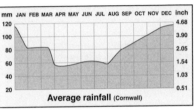

Average rainfall (Cornwall)

DAYLIGHT HOURS

If you are walking in autumn, winter or early spring you must take into account how far you can walk in the available light. It may not be possible to cover as many miles as you would in the summer.

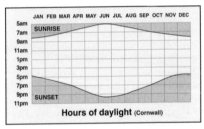

Hours of daylight (Cornwall)

The sunrise and sunset times in the table (see opposite) are based on information for the town of Penzance on the 15th of each month. This gives a rough picture for the rest of Cornwall. Please also bear in mind that you will get a further 30-45 minutes of usable light before sunrise and after sunset depending on the weather.

FESTIVALS AND EVENTS

Passing through a town or village in the middle of a festival or major event can provide a great atmosphere and give you an opportunity to join in the fun. However, if you unknowingly walk into a town heaving with people you may find it more of a headache when searching for accommodation.

The events and festivities listed take place every year, though the dates may vary slightly. Contact the tourist information board (see p40), the relevant tourist information centres, or visit the actual websites (see pp30-1) if you want more details. In addition to festivals you are likely to come across bands or groups of singers performing in pubs or in the open air in the main season. Be prepared to join in the Floral Dance if you are lucky enough to be in a village on the right evening.

March to May

● **St Piran's Day (5 March)** Festivities and processions throughout Cornwall (see box p136).

● **Giant Bolster Festival (May Day Bank Holiday), St Agnes** Re-enactment of the legend of the Giant Bolster culminating in a torchlight procession of giant puppets to the cliff top where the wicked giant was tricked into killing himself whilst proving his love for Agnes (see pp141-4).

● **'Obby 'Oss Day (May Day Bank Holiday), Padstow** Festivities and procession as the hobby horse (see box p109) dances through the town.

June to August

● **Golowan (mid to late June), Penzance** Celebration of the midsummer Feast of St John and of west Cornwall's ancient Celtic traditions. During the ten days of festivities there is film, theatre, dance, traditional and contemporary music and a colourful, lively street procession (see 🖥 www.golowan.com and pp196-201).

● **Lafrowda Festival (mid-July), St Just** A week-long culture and music festival with all kinds of music from Irish to Cornish to jazz. It culminates in Lafrowda Day when there are bands performing all day long in the square and at the Plen an Gwarry amphitheatre by the clock tower (see 🖥 www.lafrowda-festival.co.uk for details and also pp177-8).

● **St Ives Biathlon (June/July)** An annual event that involves running along the coast path from St Ives to Carbis Bay then swimming back (see pp158-63).

● **Padstow Carnival Week (end July)** Various events throughout the town and a carnival parade at the end of the week (see pp108-112).

● **Hayle Heritage Festival (late July to early August)** Events include a summer art show, horticultural show, Old Cornwall Society exhibition, traditional music and dancing, and Cornish wrestling (see pp153-5).

● **Camel Sailing Week (early August)** Major regatta on the Camel Estuary.

● **Survival (August), Porthmeor Beach, St Ives** The main event in the UK surf-lifesaving calendar (see pp158-63).

● **Falmouth Classics and Regatta Week (first two weeks in August)** The highlight of Falmouth's sailing season catering for every class of boat including traditional classic yachts (🖥 www.falmouthweek.co.uk). It begins with the parade of the Falmouth Classics, a procession of wooden boats followed by races in Carrick Roads and ending with a firework display (see pp242-7).

● **Bude Jazz Festival (last week of August), Bude** Eight days of jazz in 20 venues around the town (🖥 www.budejazzfestival.co.uk, see p73).

● **Newlyn Fish Festival (August bank holiday weekend)** The harbour is crammed with boats and the market filled with stalls, displays, cookery demonstrations and entertainment (see 🖥 www.newlynfishfestival.org.uk and pp193-5).

September to December

● **St Ives September Festival of Music and Art (mid-September)** From classical music to jazz and folk, comedy, theatre and poetry. Also hosts performances by international artists, painting, pottery and craft exhibitions and talks on literature and art (see 🖥 www.stivesseptemberfestival.co.uk and pp158-63).

● **Falmouth Oyster Festival and Fresh Seafood Week (mid to late October)**
Celebrates one of the only remaining oyster fisheries still dredging under sail
and oar. A must for lovers of the exquisite bivalve with trips to the oyster fisheries, an oyster-shucking competition, oyster tasting and sales on Custom
House Quay and live music (see 🖳 www.falmouthoysterfestival.co.uk and
pp242-7). A lively and fascinating event.
● **Lowender Peran Celtic Festival (mid to late October), Perranporth**
Celtic dance and parade (🖳 www.lowenderperan.co.uk. see pp138-40).
● **Tom Bawcock's Eve (23 December), Mousehole** In memory of a fisherman
who put out to sea in a storm so that the starving population would not have a
hungry Christmas. The event is celebrated with a carol concert, a torchlit procession and the consumption of an enormous stargazy pie (see box p17). The
story is retold in a popular children's classic *The Mousehole Cat* by Antonia
Barber. Mousehole (see pp191-3) is also illuminated with Christmas lights from
mid December to early January.

Itineraries

All walkers are individuals. Some like to cover large distances as quickly as
possible, others are happy to stroll along, stopping whenever the fancy takes
them. You may want to walk the coast path all in one go, tackle it over a series
of weekends or use the trail for linear day walks; the choice is yours.

To accommodate these differences this guidebook has not been divided
into rigid daily stages which often leads to a fixed mindset of how you should
walk. Instead, it's been designed to make it easy for you to plan your own perfect itinerary.

The **planning map** (see opposite the inside back cover) and **table of town
and village facilities** (see pp24-7) summarise the essential information and
make it straightforward to make a plan of your own. Alternatively, to make it
even easier, have a look at the **suggested itineraries** (pp32-4) and simply
choose your preferred type of accommodation and speed of walking. There are
also suggestions (see box p35) for those who want to experience the best of the

❏ **Walking from a fixed base**
An option to consider when making your plans is to stay at one place and use public
transport to get to and from different stretches of the coast path – rather than moving
on every day. This style of walking would particularly suit those on a short break, or
groups who wanted to rent a self-catering cottage (see pp15-16).

When choosing a place to base yourself you need somewhere with good public
transport (see pp45-50), a variety of coast-path walks nearby and preferably somewhere with a bit of atmosphere so that you can enjoy yourself when you are not walking. Consider Padstow (pp108-12), Newquay (pp126-30), St Just (p177-8), Mousehole
(pp191-3), Newlyn (pp193-5), Penzance (pp196-201), and Marazion (pp202-4).

trail over a day or a weekend, or who want to plan a series of day walks from a fixed base (see box p31).

The **public transport maps** on pp46-7 and **service table** (pp48-50) may also be useful at this stage. Having made a rough plan, turn to **Part 4** where you will find: summaries of the route; full descriptions of accommodation, places to eat and other services in each village and town; as well as detailed trail maps.

WHICH DIRECTION?

Although the route in this book has been described from Bude to Falmouth, it doesn't make much difference whether you decide to walk the coast path in a

PLANNING YOUR WALK

CAMPING (EASTER TO OCTOBER ONLY)					
Relaxed pace		**Medium pace**		**Fast pace**	
Place	Approx Distance	Place	Approx Distance	Place	Approx Distance
Night	miles/km		miles/km		miles/km
0 Bude		Bude		Bude	
1 Widem'th Bay	3/5	Widem'th Bay	3/5	Widem'th Bay	3/5
2 Bossiney	18/28	Bossiney	18/28	Bossiney	18/28
3 Polzeath	19/31	Polzeath	19/31	Polzeath	19/31
4 Padstow	3/5	Padstow	3/5	Padstow	3/5
5 Mother Ivey's	8/13	Treyarnon	10/16	Treyarnon	10/16
6 Mawgan P'th	9/14	Mawgan P'th	7/11	Newquay	13/21
7 Newquay	6/10	Crantock	8/13-12/19*	St Agnes	13.5/22-17.5/28*
8 Holywell	5.5/9-9.5/15*	St Agnes	11.5/19	Gwithian	15.5/25
9 St Agnes	8/13	Gwithian	15.5/25	St Ives	9/14
10 Porthtowan	4.5/7	St Ives	9/14	Pendeen	13/21
11 Gwithian	11/18	Zennor	6/10	Treen	15.5/25
12 St Ives	9/14	Botallack	9/14	Marazion	13.5/22
13 Zennor	6/10	Treen	13.5/22	Praa Sands	6/10
14 Pendeen	7/11	Penzance	10.5/17	Lizard	16/26
15 Sennen Cove	9/14	Praa Sands	9/14	Coverack	11/18
16 Treen	6.5/10	Tenerife Farm (Nr Mullion)	11/18	Gear Farm (Nr Helford)	13/21
17 Penzance	10.5/17	Kennack Sands (Nr Cadgwith)	11/18	Falmouth	13/21**
18 Praa Sands	9/14	Coverack	5/8		
19 Tenerife Farm (Nr Mullion)	11/18	Gear Farm (Nr Helford)	13/21		
20 Lizard	5/8	Falmouth	13/21**		
21 Coverack	11/18				
22 Gear Farm (Nr Helford)	13/21				
23 Falmouth	13/21**				

* Depends on route across The Gannel (see pp131-2)
** Using ferry from Helford to Helford Passage (see p230)

clockwise or anti-clockwise direction. There is virtually the same amount of ascent and descent either way and the prevailing south-westerly wind will be in your face for one half of the walk and behind you for the other whichever way you go.

If you're walking solely on the north coast, or solely on the south, it may be worth walking west to east so that the wind is predominantly behind you.

SUGGESTED ITINERARIES

The itineraries that follow are suggestions only; feel free to adapt them to your needs. They have been divided into different accommodation types and each

	Medium pace			**Fast pace**		
Place	**Hostel**	**Approx Distance**	**Place**	**Hostel**	**Approx Distance**	
Night		miles/km			miles/km	
0 Bude	H		Bude	H		
1 Crack'ton Haven		10/16	Crack'ton Haven		10/16	
2 Boscastle§	YHA	7/11	Boscastle§	YHA	7/11	
3 Port Isaac		14/23	Port Isaac		14/23	
4 Padstow		12/19	Padstow		12/19	
5 Treyarnon	YHA	10/16	Treyarnon	YHA	10/16	
6 Newquay	H	13/21	Newquay	H	13/21	
7 Perranporth	YHA	10/16-14/23*	Perranporth	YHA	10/16-14/23*	
8 Portreath	YHA	11/18	Portreath	YHA	11/18	
9 Hayle		12/19	St Ives	H	17/27	
10 St Ives	H	5/8	Zennor	H	6/10	
11 Zennor	H	6/10	Sennen Cove		16/26	
12 St Just	YHA	12/19	Penzance	YHA & H	17/27	
13 Sennen Cove		4/6	Porthleven		13/21	
14 Porthcurno		6/9	Lizard	YHA	12/19	
15 Penzance	YHA & H	11/18	Coverack	YHA	11/18	
16 Porthleven		13/21	Falmouth	H	20/32**	
17 Lizard	YHA	12/19				
18 Coverack	YHA	11/18				
19 Mawnan Smith		11/18**				
20 Falmouth	H	9/14				

§ Tintagel Youth Hostel is also a possibility but staying there would make the following day (Tintagel to Port Isaac) pretty short
* Depends on route across The Gannel (see pp131-2)
** Using ferry from Helford to Helford Passage (see p230)

YHA = YHA hostel available; H=independent hostel available; where there is no hostel it will be necessary to camp or stay in a B&B

STAYING IN B&Bs

Night	Relaxed pace Place	Approx Distance miles/km	Medium pace Place	Approx Distance miles/km	Fast pace Place	Approx Distance miles/km
0	Bude		Bude		Bude	
1	C'ton Haven	10/16	C'ton Haven	10/16	Boscastle	17/27
2	Boscastle	7/11	Boscastle	7/11	Port Isaac	14/23
3	Tintagel	5/8	Port Isaac	14/23	Padstow	12/19
3	Port Isaac	14/23	Padstow	12/19	Porthcothan	12.5/20
4	Padstow	12/19	Constantine Bay	9.5/15	Crantock	12.5/20-16.5/27*
5	Mother Ivey's	8/13	Newquay	13.5/22	St Agnes	11.5/19
6	Mawgan Porth	9/14	Perranporth	10/16-14/23*	Gwithian	15.5/25
7	Crantock	8/13-12/19*	Porthtowan	8/13	St Ives	9/14
8	Perranporth	8/13	Gwithian	11/18	Pendeen	13/21
9	Porthtowan	8/13	St Ives	9/14	Porthcurno	15/24
10	Portreath	3/5	Zennor	6/10	Marazion	14/23
11	Gwithian	8/13	St Just	11/18	Mullion	16/26
12	St Ives	9/14	Porthcurno	11/18	Coverack	17/27
13	Zennor	6/10	Penzance	11/18	Falmouth	20/32**
14	Pendeen	7/11	Porthleven	13/21		
15	Sennen Cove	9/14	Lizard	12/19		
16	Porthcurno	6/10	Coverack	11/18		
17	Mousehole	7/11	Mawnan Smith	11/18**		
18	Marazion	7/11	Falmouth	9/14		
19	Porthleven	10/16				
20	Mullion	6/10				
21	Lizard	6/10				
22	Coverack	11/18				
23	Helford	10/16				
24	Falmouth	10/16**				

* Depends which route across The Gannel (see pp131-2)
** Using ferry from Helford to Helford Passage (see p230)

table has different itineraries to encompass different walking paces. **Don't forget to add your travelling time before and after the walk**.

Note that most campsites are open from Easter to October only; also there are not enough hostels along the coast path to allow you to stay in one every night and not all are open throughout the year; see also p25 and p27.

❏ DAY AND WEEKEND WALKS

There's nothing quite like walking along a long-distance footpath for several days or even weeks but some people just don't have the time. The following highlights offer outstanding walking and scenery coupled with good public transport (see pp46-50) at the start and finish.

Day walks

● **Crackington Haven to Boscastle**, 7 miles/11km (see pp82-7) An exhilarating day's walk along the top of beautiful green cliffs; some of the highest in Cornwall. Begin at the tiny hamlet of Crackington Haven and finish in the enchanting village of Boscastle with its pretty pubs and stone houses.

● **Tintagel to Port Isaac**, 9 miles/15km (see pp94-101) This is one of the toughest sections on the whole coast path but despite the unforgiving ups and downs it is also one of the most enjoyable. Beginning at historic Tintagel with its castle and Arthurian legend, the path continues past historic mine workings and past the beautiful beaches of Trebarwith and Tregardock before a roller-coaster cliff-top path leads eventually to the pretty white-washed buildings of Port Isaac.

● **Crantock to Perranporth**, 8 miles/13km (see pp134-40) An excellent day's walk starting from the picturesque village of Crantock and finishing along the expansive sands of Perran Beach. Take a picnic to have at secluded Porth Joke, or stop for lunch in Holywell at the thatched-roofed Treguth Inn.

● **St Ives to Zennor**, 6 miles/10km (see pp162-8) This walk offers a combination of wild Atlantic coastline, exquisite light and a feeling of remoteness that can't be found anywhere else on the coast path. It's also one of the toughest parts of the whole trail with many rocky, uneven, boggy sections and some relentless ascents and descents. However, there is a good bus service so you can walk one way and take the bus back.

● **Porthcurno to Mousehole**, 7 miles/11km (see pp186-93) A charming walk with lots of coves and headlands to explore.

● **Mullion Cove to the Lizard**, 7 miles/11km (see pp218-23) A cliff-top walk from a classic Cornish fishing village to the southernmost point in mainland Britain, taking in long stretches of windswept heath and beautiful Kynance Cove. This route can be very exposed in bad weather.

Weekend walks

● **Crackington Haven to Port Isaac**, 21 miles/34km (see pp82-101) This challenging walk combines the first two day walks as detailed above, with the addition of the easy cliff-top section between Boscastle and Tintagel which takes in some wonderful coves, inlets and the lovely beach at Bossiney Haven.

● **Padstow to Mawgan Porth**, 17 miles/27km (see pp113-22) The highlights of this section include Pepper and Round Holes, Trevose Head lighthouse, Park Head, Bedruthan Steps and a long section of coastline as wonderfully indented and eroded as the crooked man's crooked smile.

● **St Ives to Land's End**, 23 miles/37km (see pp162-83) Pass through tough granite villages, head out onto Cape Cornwall and enjoy the rugged atmosphere of this walk.

● **Sennen Cove to Mousehole**, 13 miles/21km (see pp182-93) Start and finish in tiny fishing villages, walk to Land's End, the furthest point west in England, and enjoy picnic lunches in beautiful coves crying out to be explored.

● **Praa Sands to the Lizard**, 17 miles/27km (see pp207-18) Pack your camera for the scenic highlights of Mullion and Kynance coves and enjoy striding out across the windswept heath and turf of the Lizard Peninsula.

What to take

What and how much to take are very personal choices that take experience to get right. For those who are new to long-distance walking the suggestions below will help you reach a balance of comfort, safety and minimal weight.

KEEP IT LIGHT

When packing your rucksack it cannot be emphasised enough that the less weight you are carrying the more you will enjoy your walk. If you pack a lot of unnecessary items you will undoubtedly find yourself gradually discarding them as you go. If you are in doubt about taking something, be ruthless and leave it at home.

RUCKSACK

If you are staying in B&Bs or hostels you will need a medium-sized pack of about 40-60 litres' capacity; just big enough to hold a change of clothes, a waterproof jacket, a few toiletries, a water bottle/pouch and a packed lunch. Hostellers may require a few extras such as a towel, food for cooking and possibly a sleeping bag. Those camping are going to need a rucksack big enough to carry a tent, sleeping bag, towel, cooking equipment and food. A pack of about 60-80 litres should be ample.

If you are walking with an organised tour or using a baggage-carrying service (see pp21-2) you will be able to pack the bulk of your gear into a suitcase or holdall. While walking you only need a lightweight daypack for a spare jumper, waterproof jacket, water bottle/pouch and lunch but don't forget the camera, map and guide book, walking pole, binoculars and first-aid kit for the fully-equipped walker.

It's advisable to pack everything inside a large plastic bag; there is nothing worse than discovering that all your clothes and sleeping bag have got wet. Most outdoor shops stock large bags made from tough plastic, or you can use two rubbish bags instead.

FOOTWEAR

A comfortable, sturdy pair of leather or fabric **boots** are ideal for walking the coast path. If you don't already own a pair and the cost of purchasing them is prohibitive you could get by with a lightweight pair of trainers or trail shoes between late spring and early autumn. However, they don't give as much support and on rough ground it can be easy to sprain or twist your ankle. Certainly, if you're carrying a heavy rucksack, trail shoes will not be good enough although you do see people wearing them on the trail.

If you are walking in the winter you'll be much more comfortable if your boots are waterproof; wet feet equals cold feet. To waterproof leather boots cover them in a layer of wax and take the wax with you so you can redo them a couple of times during your walk.

Gaiters are not really necessary but if you have a pair you may find them useful when it's wet and muddy, or to keep the sand out when walking across dunes and beaches.

CLOTHING

Even if you are just on a day walk you should always have suitable clothing to keep you warm and dry however nice the weather is when you set out. Most walkers pick their clothes according to the versatile layering system, which consists of an outer layer or 'shell' to protect you from the wind and rain, a mid-layer or two to keep you warm, and a base layer to transport sweat away from your skin.

The most important item is a **waterproof/windproof jacket**. Even in summer it can rain for a week and if the sun isn't out the sea breeze can make it feel distinctly chilly. The most comfortable jackets are those made from breathable fabrics that let moisture (your sweat) out, but don't let moisture (the rain) in.

A polyester **fleece**, or **woollen jumper**, makes a good middle layer as they remain warm even when wet. The advantage of fleece is that it is lightweight and dries relatively quickly. In winter you may want to carry an extra jumper to put on when you stop as you can get cold very quickly.

In summer cotton T-shirts are fine for a **base layer**, but at other times of the year you will be more comfortable wearing a thin thermal layer. Those made from synthetic material such as polypropylene are now condemned because they retain smells and there are several new, technical fabrics available, of which one of the best is Merino wool which is lightweight, high-wicking, quick-drying and washable. Cotton absorbs sweat, trapping it next to the skin which will chill you rapidly when you stop exercising. Modern synthetic fabrics on the other hand, 'wick' sweat away from the body and dry rapidly.

Shorts are great to walk in during the summer, although you'll probably want to bring a pair of **long trousers** for cooler days. Also, some sections of the path can become overgrown with stinging nettles and you may appreciate having your legs covered. Don't wear jeans; if they get wet they become incredibly heavy and stick uncomfortably to your skin and take forever to dry.

It is worthwhile investing in good **socks**. There are many on the market that are designed with walkers in mind – check out the Thousand-Mile sock range. You will notice the difference particularly when they don't become hard and stiff after the first day of walking. How many pairs you take is a personal preference but I prefer to change my socks daily, hence five pairs would be about right.

Underwear goes without saying and how many pairs to take is a personal preference. Women may find a **sports bra** more comfortable because pack straps can cause bra straps to dig into your shoulders.

A **hat** is always a good idea: during the summer a **sun hat** helps to keep you cool and prevent sunburn, in the winter a hat can help to keep you warm. In the cooler months I would also recommend a pair of **gloves**. Don't forget your **swimming gear** and a **towel**; the white-sand beaches and crystal-clear aquamarine seas are extremely inviting.

You will also need a **change of clothing** for the evening. If you're staying in B&Bs and eating out you may feel more comfortable with something tidy. A spare pair of shoes such as lightweight sandals or trainers is also worth carrying, even if they do add a bit of weight. There's nothing worse than having to put wet, dirty (not to mention smelly) boots back on after you've showered and changed. If you're camping, early spring and late autumn nights can be decidedly chilly, so pack something warm.

TOILETRIES

Only take the minimum. Essentials are **soap, shampoo, toothbrush, toothpaste**, any **medication** and, for women, **sanitary towels** and **tampons**. **Loo paper** is generally provided in public toilets, but bring a roll just in case and carry a small lightweight **trowel** for burying excrement if you get caught out far from a toilet (see p53-4 for the code of the outdoor loo). **Sunscreen** and something to put on cracked lips is also a good idea. Deodorants, hair brushes, razors and so forth are up to you. If you are hostelling or camping you will also need a **towel**.

FIRST-AID KIT

Medical facilities in Britain are good so you only need to take a first-aid kit to deal with basic injuries. In a waterproof bag or container you should have: **scissors** for cutting tape and cutting away clothing; **aspirin** or **paracetamol** for treating mild to moderate pain; one or two **stretch bandages** for holding dressings or splints in place and for sprained ankles or sore knees; if you think your knees will give you trouble **elastic supports** are invaluable; a **triangular bandage** for broken/sprained arms; a small selection of **sterile dressings** for wounds; **porous adhesive tape** to hold them in place; **plasters/Band Aids** for minor cuts; a sturdier, preferably waterproof **adhesive tape** for blister prevention; **Compeed, Second Skin** or **Moleskin** for treating blisters; **safety pins**; **antiseptic cream** or **liquid**; **tweezers**; and treatment such as **Imodium** for acute diarrhoea – you never know when it might come in handy.

GENERAL ITEMS

Other **essential** items you should carry are: a **torch** (flashlight) in case you end up walking in the dark; a **whistle** to attract attention if you get lost or find yourself in trouble (see box p59); a **water bottle or pouch** (two litres is the best size); a **watch**; a current **tide chart** (available for about £1 from newsagents or TICs in coastal areas); and a **plastic bag** for carrying any rubbish you accumulate.

You should also carry some emergency **food** with you such as chocolate, dried fruit and biscuits.

Walking poles are now widely used and can help in taking some of the weight off your feet. Using them requires some practice but once you get used to them they become a quite normal part of the walker's equipment.

Useful items to carry are: a **pen-knife**; a **camera**; a **notebook** to record your impressions in a different way; **sunglasses** to protect your eyes from the glare off water and beaches on sunny days; **binoculars**; something to **read**; and a **vacuum flask** for hot drinks (worth the investment if you're on a budget as buying all those cups of tea or coffee can get expensive). A **map-case** can be a useful extra for protecting your map and guide book in the rain, which can very quickly reduce both to pulp.

CAMPING GEAR

Campers will need a decent **tent** able to withstand wind and rain; a **sleeping mat**; a two- or three-season **sleeping bag** (you can always wear clothes inside your sleeping bag if you are cold); a **camping stove** and **fuel**; **cooking equipment** (a pot with a pot-grabber and a frying pan that can double as a lid is enough for two people); a **bowl**, **mug**, **cutlery** (don't forget a can-opener), **pen-knife** and a **scrubber** for washing up.

MONEY AND DOCUMENTS

It is most convenient to carry your money as **cash**. A **debit/credit card** (with a PIN) is the easiest way to withdraw money either from banks or cash machines and can be used to pay in larger shops, restaurants and hotels. A **cheque book** is very useful for walkers with accounts in British banks as a cheque will often be accepted where a card is not.

Always keep your money and documents in a safe place and in a waterproof container. In particular, those camping or staying in hostels should take care not to leave them lying around; it's much safer to carry them on you.

MAPS

The hand-drawn maps in this book cover the trail at a scale of 1:20,000; plenty of detail and information to keep you on the right track. If you wish to explore inland, Ordnance Survey (☎ 0845-605 0505, 💻 www.ordnancesurvey.gov.uk) produce five excellent maps covering west Cornwall in their Explorer series; the ones with the orange cover. The numbers you'll require are: 111 Bude, Boscastle and Tintagel; 106 Newquay and Padstow; 104 Redruth and St Agnes; 102 Land's End, Penzance and St Ives; and 103 The Lizard, Falmouth and Helston. These maps are also good for those with a particular interest in Cornwall's ancient sites as all sites, however minor, are shown.

Harvey Maps (☎ 01786-841202, 💻 www.harveymaps.co.uk) produce a superb series of maps of the entire South West Coast Path: Map 2 covers Bude

PLANNING YOUR WALK

❏ SOURCES OF FURTHER INFORMATION

Trail information

● **South-West Coast Path Association** (SWCPA; ☎ 01752-896237, 🖳 www.swcp .org.uk) The SWCPA promotes the interests of users of the South-West Coast Path by, amongst other things, lobbying the numerous bodies responsible for the path in order to ensure it is maintained to a high standard. There are several places where the Association is actively seeking for the path to be re-routed so that it can genuinely be called a coast path. They publish an annual guide to the entire *South West Coast Path* (£8 to non-members) and are happy to provide advice and information to assist your coast-path walk. Membership costs £11 per year (£12.50 joint and £16 for non-UK).

Tourist information

● **Tourist information centres (TICs)** TICs are based in towns throughout Britain and provide all manner of locally specific information for visitors and an accommodation-booking service (for which there is usually a charge). Visitor centres generally provide information about their particular attraction, though they sometimes have general leaflets for other places of interest in the area but the staff will probably not be able to help with accommodation or similar queries.

There are TICs along the coast path in Bude (see p73), Boscastle (see p85), Tintagel (see p92), Padstow (see p109), Hayle (see p242), St Ives (see p158), St Just (see p177), Penzance (see p196) and Falmouth (see p242).

● **Tourist information points** Many village shops, libraries or post offices have an area set aside with a noticeboard and folders displaying local tourist information. There are also seasonal TIPs in Perranporth (see p138), St Agnes (see p142) and Lands End (see p182).

● **Tourist boards** For general information about the whole of Cornwall contact Cornwall Tourist Board (☎ 01872-322900, 🖳 www.visitcornwall.com), Pydar House, Pydar St, Truro TR1 1EA.

Organisations for walkers

● **Backpackers' Club** (🖳 www.backpackersclub.co.uk) A club for people who are involved or interested in lightweight camping through walking, cycling, skiing, canoeing, etc. They produce a quarterly magazine, provide members with a comprehensive advisory and information service on all aspects of backpacking, organise weekend trips and also publish a farm-pitch directory. Membership is £12 per year.

● **Long Distance Walkers' Association** (🖳 www.ldwa.org.uk) An association of people with the common interest of long-distance walking. Membership includes a journal three times per year giving details of challenge events and local group walks as well as articles on the subject. Information on over 500 Long Distance Paths is presented in the LDWA's Long Distance Walkers' Handbook. Membership is currently £13 per year, £19.50 for a family.

● **Ramblers' Association** (☎ 020-7339 8500, 🖳 www.ramblers.org.uk) Looks after the interests of walkers throughout Britain. They publish a large amount of useful information including their annual handbook *Walk Britain* (£5.99 to non-members); a full directory of services for walkers. Membership costs £27 per year for an individual and £36 for joint membership.

● **Walking World** (🖳 www.walkingworld.com) Online organisation. Membership fee of £17.45 allows access to hundreds of walks throughout the UK including many in Cornwall with a Find a walk feature. Type in the location and all the walks in that area are shown.

to Portreath; Map 3 covers Portreath to Lizard Point and Map 4 covers from Lizard Point to Plymouth.

Both OS and Harvey maps can also be obtained online from Mapkiosk (☎ 01785-241010, 🖳 www.mapkiosk.com).

Enthusiastic map buyers can reduce the often-considerable expense of purchasing them: the **Ramblers' Association** (see box opposite) has the complete range of OS Explorer and Landranger maps and members can borrow up to 10 for a period of four weeks at £1 per weatherproof map and 50p per paper map plus postage; members of the **Backpackers' Club** (see box opposite) can purchase maps at a significant discount through the club.

USEFUL BOOKS

Flora and fauna

The following books are likely to be of interest to the enthusiast but may be too heavy to carry around.

● *Wildflowers of Britain and Europe* by W Lippert and D Podlech (Collins, £9.99) is a good compact book for beginners. It is organised by flower colour making it easy to flip immediately to the right section.

● *The Wild Flower Key* by Francis Rose and Clare O'Reilly (Frederick Warne, £19.99) is an excellent book for more serious botanists. It is very comprehensive and allows identification of plants whether in flower or not.

● *Birds of Cornwall* by Trevor and Endymion Beer (Tor Mark Press, £2.99) is an extremely lightweight book. Its low price makes it an excellent buy and it's usually stocked in TICs and local bookshops.

● *Birds of Britain and Europe* by J Nicolai, D Singer and K Wothe (Collins, £9.99) is a compact book. It features photographs and is organised by habitat making it easy to flip straight to the right section.

● The RSPB's *Pocket Guide to British Birds* by Simon Harrap and David Nurney (£4.99) identifies birds by their plumage and song.

● *Where to watch birds – Devon & Cornwall* by David Norman & Vic Tucker (A&C Black 2009, 5th ed, £16.99)

● *Collins Bird Guide* by Mullarney, Svensson, Zetterström & Grant (Harper Collins 1999, Sbk £16.99, Hbk £24.99)

● *Seashore Life of Britain and Europe* by Bob Gibbons, Denys Ovenden and Melanie Perkins (Michelin Green Guides, £2.50) is a conveniently sized guide to 150 species of seaweeds, molluscs, crustaceans and insects likely to be found along Britain's coastline.

● *Sea Shore of Britain and Europe* by Peter Hayward, Tony Nelson-Smith and Chris Shields (Collins, £16.99) is a more detailed guide to the seashore ecology.

● The Field Studies Council (🖳 www.field-studies-council.org) publishes a series of *Identification Guides* (fold-out charts) which are also practical.

Others

Good **non-fiction** reads include: *A History of Cornwall* by Ian Soulsby (Phillimore and Co., 1986); *King Arthur: The Dream of a Golden Age* by Geoffrey Ashe (Thames and Hudson, 1990); *The Lost Gardens of Heligan* by Tim Smit (Victor Gollancz, 1997) and *Poldark's Cornwall* by Winston Graham (Webb and Bower, 1983).

If you are interested in the ancient sites of Cornwall, *Ancient Cornwall* by Paul White (Tor Mark Press, £2.99) is a slim volume that makes good night-time reading. It has a useful map of the sites.

The National Trust (NT) publish a series of leaflets titled the *Coast of Cornwall* with history, information and maps about their coastal properties in each area. They cost £1 each (plus a charge for post and packing) and are available from NT shops in Cornwall or by post from the NT Regional Office (☎ 01208-265952; Lanhydrock House Shop, Bodmin, Cornwall PL30 5AD).

Recommended **fiction** includes: *To the Lighthouse* by Virginia Woolf (first published 1932); *Rebecca* (1938), *Jamaica Inn* (1936) and *Frenchman's Creek* (1941) by Daphne du Maurier; the *Poldark* novels by Winston Graham (12 volumes between 1945 and 2002); *The Minack Chronicles* by Derek Tangye (over 20 books describing the author's attempts to set up a flower farm in Cornwall though not all are relevant to Cornwall); *The Lamorna Wink* by Martha Grimes (Headline Books, 1999); *Zennor in Darkness* by Helen Dunmore (Viking Books, 1993); *The Mousehole Cat* by Antonia Barber (1990).

Getting to and from the Cornwall Coast Path

All the major towns along the coast path are reasonably well served by rail and/or coach services from the rest of Britain. Travelling by train or coach is the most convenient way to get to the trail as you do not need to worry about where to leave your car, how safe it will be while you're walking, or how to get back to it at the end of your holiday.

Choosing to travel by public transport is choosing to help the environment; a creative step in minimising your impact on the countryside. It can also be an enjoyable experience in itself. How many of us have fond memories of relaxing to the click-click of the train wheels while sleepily watching the scenery pass by?

NATIONAL TRANSPORT

By rail

The main Cornwall line (operated by First Great Western, ☎ 0845-7000 125, 🖳 www.firstgreatwestern.co.uk) runs from London Paddington through Exeter and Plymouth to finish at **Penzance**, with branch lines connecting major towns on the coast path. There are several services every day as well as a night train

❑ GETTING TO BRITAIN

By air
The best international gateway to Britain for the Cornwall Coast Path is London with its five airports: Heathrow (the main airport), Gatwick, Stansted, Luton and London City. However, some charter and budget airlines such as Flybe (🖳 www.flybe.com) and Monarch (🖳 www.flymonarch.com) have flights to Newquay, Exeter and Bristol airports.

From Europe by train
Eurostar (🖳 www.eurostar.com) operates a high-speed passenger service via the Channel Tunnel between Paris, Brussels and Lille and London. The Eurostar terminal in London is at St Pancras International station with connections to the London Underground and to all other main railway stations in London. Trains to Cornwall leave from Paddington station; see opposite and below for details.

There are also various rail services from the Continent to Britain; for more information contact Rail Europe (🖳 www.raileurope.com).

From Europe by coach
Eurolines (🖳 www.eurolines.com) have a wide network of long-distance bus services connecting over 500 destinations in 25 European countries to London (Victoria Coach Station). Visit the Eurolines website for details of services from your country.

From Europe by car
P&O (🖳 www.poferries.com) runs frequent passenger **ferries** between Calais and Dover, Rotterdam and Zeebrugge and Hull, and Bilbao and Portsmouth. Hoverspeed (🖳 www.hoverspeed.com) offers a slightly faster journey between Calais and Dover. Brittany Ferries (🖳 www.brittanyferries.com) has services from Santander and Roscoff to Plymouth as well as from Cherbourg, St Malo and Caen to Poole and Portsmouth. There are also several other ferries plying routes between mainland Europe and ports on Britain's eastern coast. Look at 🖳 www.ferry savers.com or 🖳 www.directferries.com for a full list of companies and services.

Eurotunnel (🖳 www.eurotunnel.com) operates a **shuttle train service** for vehicles via the Channel Tunnel between Calais and Folkestone taking one hour between the motorway in France and the motorway in Britain.

(the Night Riviera, Sun-Fri). Cross Country (☎ 0844-811 0124, 🖳 www.cross countrytrains.co.uk) operates services from Scotland, the North-East and the Midlands to Penzance.

To get to **Bude** it's best to take a train to Exeter St David's and then get one of the connecting buses (see p49). However, the last train from London may arrive too late for the last bus to Bude so check in advance. Barnstaple, 35 miles to the north of Bude, and Okehampton, 30 miles to the east, are other possibilities though services only call at the latter in the summer months. In the summer First Great Western runs connecting buses regularly and daily from Okehampton to Bude. In contrast, from Barnstaple there are just one or two buses a day to Bude.

For **Padstow** get off the train at Bodmin Parkway station and catch the connecting Western Greyhound bus service No 555 (see box p48) to Padstow, for

Newquay you have to change at Par, for **Falmouth** you need to change at Truro, for **St Ives** change at St Erth.

National rail enquiries (☎ 08457-484950, 24hrs, 💻 www.nationalrail.co .uk) is the only number you need to find out all timetable and fare information. Information is also available in the Cornwall public transport timetable booklets (see opposite). Rail tickets are generally cheaper if you book them well in advance and also if you buy through tickets. Most discounted tickets carry some restrictions so check what they are before you purchase them. Tickets can be bought through the relevant companies, at any rail station, or online at 💻 www .thetrainline.com and 💻 www.qjump.co.uk.

If you think you may want to book a **taxi** when you arrive visit 💻 www.tr aintaxi.co.uk or phone ☎ 01733-237037 for details of taxi companies operating at rail stations throughout England. Alternatively, My Local Taxi (💻 www .mylocaltaxi.co.uk) provides a similar service.

It is often possible to buy a train ticket that includes bus travel at your destination: for further information visit the **Plusbus** website (💻 www.plusbus.info).

By coach

National Express (☎ 0871-781 8181, lines open 8am-10pm daily; 💻 www .nationalexpress.com) is the principal coach (long-distance bus) operator in Britain. Travel by coach is usually cheaper than by rail but does take longer.

❏ **Coach services**

Note: the services listed below operate daily but not all stops are included.

NX315 Eastbourne to Helston along the south coast via Brighton, Worthing, Southampton, Bournemouth, Exeter, Plymouth, Truro & **Falmouth**, daily 1/day

NX330 Nottingham to **Penzance** via Leicester, Birmingham, Worcester, Bristol, Plymouth, Bodmin, Wadebridge, St Columb Major & Minor, **Newquay**, **Hayle**, **Lelant**, **Carbis Bay**, **St Ives**, St Erth & Crowlas, daily 1/day

NX336 Edinburgh to **Penzance** via Glasgow, Carlisle, Lancaster, Manchester, Birmingham, Bristol, Exeter, Plymouth, Truro, **Hayle**, **Lelant**, **Carbis Bay**, **St Ives**, St Erth & Crowlas, daily 1/day

NX404 London to **Penzance** via Heathrow Airport, Chippenham, Bath, Bristol, Exeter, Paignton, Plymouth, Truro, **Hayle**, St Erth & Crowlas, daily 1/day

NX406 London to **Newquay** via Heathrow, Bridgwater, Taunton, Exeter, Plymouth & Bodmin, daily 1/day

NX500 London to **Penzance** via Heathrow, Taunton, Plymouth, Truro, **Hayle**, **Lelant**, **Carbis Bay**, **St Ives**, St Erth & Crowlas, daily 1-2/day

NX502 London to Westward Ho! via Heathrow, Bridgwater, Taunton, Tiverton, Barnstaple and Bideford, daily 3-4/day

NX504 London to **Penzance** via Heathrow, Plymouth, Bodmin, Wadebridge, St Columb Major and Minor, Newquay, Redruth, Pool, Camborne, **Hayle**, **Lelant**, **Carbis Bay**, **St Ives**, St Erth & Crowlas, daily 1/day

NX504 London to **Penzance** via Heathrow, Plymouth, Lisekard, St Austell, Truro, Penryn, **Falmouth**, Helston & **Porthleven**, Fri-Mon 1/day

To get the cheapest fares you need to book seven days ahead. You can purchase tickets from coach and bus station ticket offices, National Express agents, directly from the driver (though not always, so do check with locals in advance), by telephone, or online. You need to allow four working days for posted tickets.

At the time of writing there were no direct National Express services to **Bude** for the start of the walk, so it is best to take one of their services to Exeter, where you can connect with First's service to Bude. Alternatively take a coach to **Barnstaple** and get one of Stagecoach's services from there to Bude. There are several coach services to other towns on the coast path and also services from **Falmouth** to London and other destinations.

By car

The easiest way to drive into Cornwall is to join the M5 to Exeter and then take either the A30 or A38 depending on your final destination. A good road atlas is essential for navigating Cornwall's country lanes. You can get detailed driving directions from the AA website (🖳 www.theaa.com/route-planner/index.jsp) by clicking on the route planner.

Parking your car can be a problem. The safest place to leave it is in a garage that offers long-term parking or a long-stay car park, though these have no security and you can only purchase weekly tickets, necessitating a trip back to your car if you are going to be away longer. To avoid this hassle you may want to consider using public transport instead.

By air

Please bear in mind that air travel is by far the least environmentally sound option (see 🖳 www.chooseclimate.org for the true costs of flying). However, if you prefer to fly, visit Newquay Airport's website (🖳 www.newquaycornwall airport.com) for details of the airlines flying there.

LOCAL TRANSPORT

Bus services

Cornwall has a comprehensive public transport network linking almost all the coastal villages with at least one bus per day in the summer, sometimes fewer in winter. This is great news for the walker as it opens up the possibility of linear day and weekend walks, or a series of walks from a fixed base (see p31 for more ideas) without having to organise two cars. Just sit back and enjoy the ride along some of Britain's most scenic bus routes.

Timetables There's one overall timetable and five separate timetables covering Cornwall but you need only the blue, pink and purple timetables to cover all the bus services along the coast path.

In Cornwall you can pick the timetables up for free from bus stations, train stations, and tourist information centres, or contact the Passenger Transport Unit (☎ 01872-322003, 🖳 www.cornwallpublictransport.info), Cornwall Council, New County Hall, Treyew Rd, Truro TR1 3AY; there is usually a charge for posting them to you. The service numbers of the most useful buses are given in the tables on pp48-50 so you can flip straight to the page you need in the actual timetable.

Bus companies and customer helplines If the contact details in the box on pp48-50 prove unsatisfactory, you can contact **traveline** (☎ 0871-200 2233, 7am-9pm; 💻 www.traveline.org.uk) which has public transport information for the whole of the UK.

Tickets If you are going to be using the bus frequently over several days Explorer tickets are good value. They are valid for one, three or seven days and allow you unlimited travel within the county on the relevant company's services. Contact the bus operators for further details.

At the time of writing anyone over 60 could obtain a free NOW card which allows them to travel for nothing on local buses after 9.30am. This invaluable

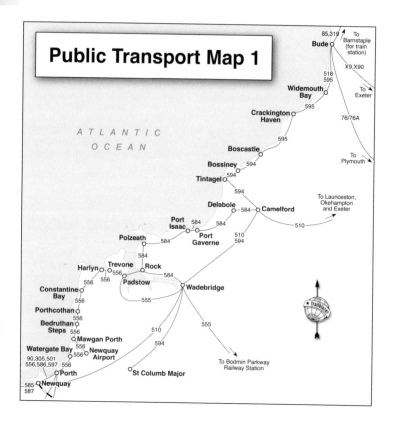

government-sponsored scheme has been enthusiastically welcomed by pensioners, less so by the bus companies although it helps to fill their seats, which can't be bad.

Public transport at a glance The maps below and tables on pp48-50 are designed to make it easy for you to plan your day using public transport. Use the **public transport maps** to see which towns each service covers then turn to the **tables** to check the frequency of that service. Take time to read the tables carefully; some services only run one day a week, or not on Saturdays or Sundays. The definition of a summer service depends on the company and the route; in some cases it is from Easter to October but in others May/July to September so check before you plan to use a summer service.

Note that **bus services do change** from year to year. Use this information as a rough guide and confirm details with the bus operators before travelling.

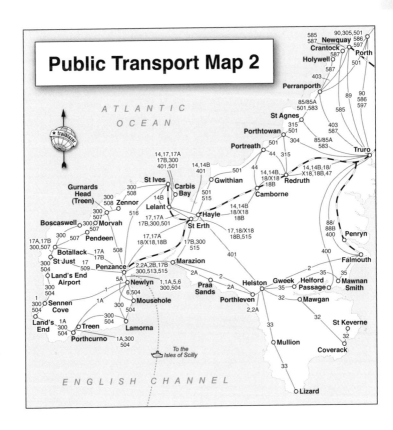

❏ Public transport services

Buses

Western Greyhound (WG; ☎ 01637-871871, 🖥 www.westerngreyhound.com)

501   Newquay–St Ives via Porth, Perran Sands (Holiday Camp), Perranporth, St Agnes, Porthtowan, Portreath, Gwithian, Hayle, Lelant & Carbis Bay, Sun-Fri 1/day, plus 2/day mid May to late Sep, plus 1/day Perranporth to St Ives; does not operate on Sat

504   Penzance–St Just via Newlyn Bridge, Newlyn, Mousehole, Lamorna Wink, Merry Maidens, Treen, Porthcurno, Minack Theatre, Lands End, Sennen First & Last, Sennen Cove, Lands End Airport & Kelynack, Mon-Sat 2/day plus Penzance–Lamorna Wink 1-2/day

507   St Just–Gurnard's Head via Botallack, Pendeen & Morvah, Mon-Sat 3-5/day

508   Penzance–St Ives via Gurnard's Head (Hotel) & Zennor, Mon-Sat 4/day plus 1/day Penzance to Zennor

509   St Just–Penzance, Mon-Sat 4-5/day

510   Exeter–Newquay via Okehampton, Launceston, Camelford & Wadebridge, Mon-Sat 3/day, Sun 1/day

513   Penzance–Marazion, Mon-Sat 3/day

515   Penzance–Gwithian via Marazion, St Erth & Hayle, Mon-Sat 3/day; (services from Gwithian–Penzance may require a change of bus)

516   St Ives–Penzance, Mon-Sat 10/day

518   Bude circular route via Marhamchurch & Widemouth Bay, Mon-Sat 6-9/day, Sun 4/day

555   Bodmin Parkway–Padstow via Wadebridge, Mon-Sat 1/hr, Sun 6/day

556   Padstow–Newquay via Windmill (for Trevone Bay), Harlyn Bay, Constantine Bay, Porthcothan, Mawgan Rd for Mawgan Porth, St Mawgan, Newquay Airport, Watergate Bay & Porth, Mon-Sat 1/hr, Sun 5/day plus Sun 6/day Newquay Airport to Newquay; route goes via Bedruthan Steps (Hotel) and Trenance 4-5/day

583   Truro–Perranporth via St Agnes, Sat only 5/day

584   Camelford–Wadebridge via Delabole, Port Gaverne, Port Isaac, Trewetha, St Endellion, Port Quin (crossroads), Polzeath, Trebetherick & Rock, Mon-Sat 5-6/day, Sun 4/day

585   Truro–Newquay via Crantock, Mon-Sat 1/hr

586   Truro–Newquay via Porth, Mon-Sat 1/hr

587   Truro–Newquay via Perranporth, Holywell Bay & Crantock, Mon-Sat 1/hr, Sun 1/hr

       Truro–Perranporth, Mon-Sat 1/hr

588   Newquay–Pentire Head circular route, Mon-Sat 1/hr

594   St Columb Major–Boscastle via Wadebridge, Camelford, Bossiney & Tintagel, Mon-Sat 5/day plus Camelford to Boscastle route 3/day, Sun Camelford to Boscastle only 4/day

595   Bude–Boscastle via Widemouth Bay & Crackington Haven, Mon-Sat 4-6/day, Sun 4/day

597   Truro–Newquay via Porth, Mon-Sat 2/hr, Sun 1/hr

Hookways Jennings (☎ 01288-352359, 🖳 www.hookways.com)
X90   Exeter–Bude, Mon-Sat 2/day

Stagecoach (🖳 www.stagecoachbus.com/devon)
85   Barnstaple–Bude, Mon-Sat 1/day
319   Barnstaple–Bude, Sun 2/day (May-Sep)

First Devon and Cornwall (☎ 0845-600 1420, 🖳 www.firstgroup.com/ukbus/southwest/devon/home/index.php)
X9   Exeter–Bude, Mon-Sat 5/day (plus Fri/Sat only dep Exeter 20.30 arr Bude
        22.29), Sun 2/day (note: the late and Sunday services may change in
        summer 2009 so check in advance)
1   Penzance–Lands End via Newlyn Bridge, Lamorna Turn, Sennen Cove,
        Sennen First & Last, Mon-Sat 4/day, Sun 3/day
1A   Penzance–Lands End via Newlyn Bridge, Lamorna Turn, Treen &
        Porthcurno, Mon-Sat 5/day, Sun 2/day
2   Penzance–Falmouth via Marazion, Perran (Crossroads), Porthleven &
        Helston, Mon-Sat 7/day; route goes via Praa Sands 2/day
2A   Penzance–Helston via Marazion, Perran (Crossroads), Praa Sands &
        Porthleven, Mon-Sat 9-10/day, Sun 5/day
2B   Penzance–Perranuthnoe via Marazion & Perran (Crossroads), Mon-Sat
        8-10/day
5   Penzance–Newlyn, daily 1/hr
5A   Penzance–Mousehole, Mon-Sat 3/day, evenings only
6   Penzance–Mousehole via Newlyn Bridge & Newlyn, Mon-Sat 2/hr, Sun 1/hr
14   Truro–St Ives via Redruth, Camborne, Hayle, Lelant & Carbis Bay,
        Mon-Sat 1/hr
14B   Truro–St Ives via Redruth, Camborne, Hayle, Lelant & Crowlas, Sun 4/day
17   St Ives–St Just via Carbis Bay, Lelant, St Erth, Crowlas & Penzance, Mon-
        Sat 1/hr
17A   St Ives–St Just via Carbis Bay, Lelant, St Erth, Crowlas, Penzance &
        Botallack, Mon-Sat 1/hr
17B   St Ives–St Just via Carbis Bay, Lelant, St Erth, Crowlas, Marazion, Penzance
        & Botallack, Mon-Sat 3/day evening only & change in Penzance
        St Ives–St Just via Carbis Bay, Lelant, St Erth, Crowlas, Marazion, Penzance
        & Botallack, Sun 5/day, plus St Ives-Penzance only, Sun 10/day
        Note: the timetable for the 17/17A & 17B is likely to change in July 2009
18/X18 Truro–Penzance via Redruth, Camborne, Hayle, St Erth & Crowlas,
        Mon-Sat 1/hr
18B   Truro–Penzance via Redruth, Camborne, Hayle, St Erth & Crowlas, Sun
        6/day
32   Helston–St Keverne via Mawgan & Coverack, Mon-Sat 6-8/day, Sun
        (2/day) services call at Gweek & Coverack

(cont'd on p50)

❑ **Public transport services**

Buses *(cont'd from p49)*

33   Lizard Green–Helston via Ruan Minor, Mullion & Poldhu Cove, Mon-Sat 12-15/day (note that some services start at Ruan Minor bus shelter and then go to Lizard Green), Sun 5/day

35   Falmouth–Helston via Mawnan Smith & Gweek, Mon-Sat 6/day (2/day call at Helford Passage) plus Falmouth–Helford Passage 4/day, Sun 2-3/day all call at Helford Passage

44   Redruth–Camborne via Portreath Beach & Illogan Churchtown, Mon-Sat 9-11/day

47   Truro–Redruth, Mon-Sat 11/day

76/76A   Plymouth–Bude, Mon-Sat 6/day

85/85A   Truro–St Agnes, Mon-Sat 1/hr plus 1-2/day to Perranporth, Sun Truro-Perranporth via St Agnes, 6/day

88/88B   Truro–Falmouth, Mon-Sat 4/hr, Sun 1/hr

89   Truro–Newquay via Trenance Gardens, Mon-Sat 6/day

90   Truro–Newquay via Porth, Mon-Sat 6/day

300   Penzance circular route via Marazion, Crowglas, St Erth, Lelant, Carbis Bay, St Ives, Zennor, Gurnard's Head, Morvah, Boscaswell, Geevor, Botallack, St Just, Lands End Airport, Sennen Cove, Sennen (First & Last), Lands End, Porthcurno, Treen, Lamorna Turn, Newlyn Bridge, daily mid May to end Aug 4/day; Sep 3/day and then the bus calls at Kelynack and does not call at Porthcurno, Treen, or Lamorna Turn

305   Porth–Newquay, mid May to end Sep daily 2/hr

314   Camborne–St Ives via Hayle, Lelant & Carbis Bay, May-Sep Mon-Fri 6-9/day

400   (The Falmouth Explorer) Truro–Maenporth Beach via Falmouth Moor, Falmouth Maritime Museum, Gyllyngvase Beach, Swanpool Beach & Pennance Mill, Mon-Fri 3/day plus 1/day Falmouth–Maenporth Beach, Truro–Falmouth Mon-Fri 5/day and Truro–Helford Passage 1/day

Williams Travel (☎ 01209-717152, 🖳 www.williams-travel.co.uk)

401   St Ives–Helston via Carbis Bay, Lelant & Hayle, mid May to late Sep Sun-Fri 3-4/day, not Sat

Summercourt Travel (🖳 www.summercourttravel.com)

403   Newquay–Truro via Perranporth & St Agnes, Mon-Fri 9-10/day

Hopley's Coaches (☎ 01872-553786, 🖳 www.hopleyscoaches.com)

304   Truro–Porthtowan, Mon-Fri, 9/day, Sat 6/day

315   Redruth–St Agnes via Porthtowan, Mon-Sat 6/day

Trains

First Great Western (☎ 0845-7000 125, 🖳 www.firstgreatwestern.co.uk)

● St Erth–St Ives via Lelant Saltings, Lelant & Carbis Bay, Mon-Sat 2/hour in summer, Sun hourly, pm only in winter

● Newquay–Par, Mon-Sat, 4-6/day, Sun 6/day in summer

● Truro–Falmouth Docks, Mon-Sat hourly, Sun 10/day.

PART 2: MINIMUM IMPACT AND OUTDOOR SAFETY

Minimum impact walking

By visiting Cornwall you are having a positive impact, not just on your own well-being, but on local communities as well. Your presence brings money and jobs into the local economy and also pride in and awareness of Cornwall's environment and culture. Cornwall receives four million visitors annually (with the coast path attracting at least a quarter of those) who bring an estimated £15 million into the regional economy.

However, the environment should not just be considered in terms of its value as a tourist asset. Its long-term survival and enjoyment by future generations will only be possible if both visitors and local communities protect it now. The following points are made to help you reduce your impact on the environment, encourage conservation and promote sustainable tourism in the area.

ECONOMIC IMPACT

If every person, tourist and business in Cornwall switched one per cent of their current spending to local products and services this would put an extra £1 million directly into the local economy every week. **Soil Association** *Local Food Routes*

The keyword here is 'local'. By supporting local services and businesses and the production and sale of local produce you are also supporting the local environment. Money generated by tourists in local economies provides extra incentives for local initiatives such as better-quality maintenance of an area, improved conservation and better local amenities, all of which can be achieved using local resources, labour and materials.

Buy local
Look and ask for local produce to buy and eat. By supporting local farmers and producers you are helping those people who are best placed to conserve and protect the land to do so. You are also reducing the pollution and congestion caused by the transportation of food, so-called 'food miles'. Websites such as 🖥 www.farmersmarkets.net and 🖥 www.foodfromcornwall.co.uk list the farmers' markets and farm shops in Cornwall.

Support local businesses
It's a fact of life that money spent at local level – perhaps in a market, or at the greengrocer, or in an independent pub – has a far greater impact for good on that community than the equivalent spent in a branch of a national chain store or restaurant. While no-one would advocate that walkers should boycott the larger supermarkets, which after all do provide local employment, it's worth

remembering that businesses in rural communities rely heavily on visitors for their very existence. If we want to keep these shops and post offices, we need to use them. The more money that circulates locally and is spent on local labour and materials, the greater the impact on the local economy and the more power the community has to effect the change it wants to see.

ENVIRONMENTAL IMPACT

By choosing a walking holiday you are already minimising your impact on the environment. Your interaction with the countryside and its inhabitants, whether they be plant, animal or human, can bring benefits to all. It is time we all started thinking beyond simply closing the gate and not leaving litter. With increasing numbers of people heading into the outdoors we all have to learn to look after and conserve the very environment we've come to enjoy.

Use public transport whenever possible
More use of public transport encourages the provision of better services which benefits visitors, local people and the global environment. During peak periods traffic congestion in Cornwall is a major headache and you're doing yourself (and everybody else in the vehicle with you) a big favour by avoiding it. There's detailed information in this book on public transport services; turn to pp48-50 to make good use of it.

Never leave litter
Litter is a worldwide problem that is unsightly, pollutes the environment and kills wildlife. **Please** carry a rubbish bag with you so you can dispose of rubbish in a bin at the next town rather than dropping it. You can even help by picking up a few pieces of litter that other people leave behind.

● **The lasting impact of litter** You may think a small piece of rubbish has little effect but consider the following: silver foil lasts 18 months; textiles hang around for 15 years; a plastic bag lasts for 10 to 12 years; an aluminium drinks can will last for 85 years on the ground, or 75 years in the sea; and iron takes more than two centuries to break down. An estimated one million seabirds and 100,000 marine mammals and sea turtles die every year from entanglement in, or ingestion of, plastics.

● **Is it OK if it's biodegradable?** Not really. Remember, a bit of orange peel lasts six months before decomposing. Apple cores, banana skins and the like are not only unsightly but they encourage flies, ants and wasps and can ruin a picnic spot for others.

Consider walking out of season
By walking the coast path at less busy times of the year you help to reduce overuse of the path at peak periods. Many fragile habitats, such as dunes, are unable to withstand the heavy use and consequent trampling. You also help to generate year-round income for local services and may find your holiday a more relaxing experience; there'll be less stress involved in finding accommodation and fewer people on the trail.

Erosion

Erosion is a natural process on any coastline, but it's accelerated by thousands of pairs of feet. Do your best to **stay on the main trail** and use managed footpaths wherever possible. If you are walking during the winter, or a particularly wet period, be aware that braiding (the creation of more than one path) usually occurs when the path is muddy. Come prepared with good walking boots that don't mind a little dirt.

Respect all wildlife

Remember that all wildlife you come across on the coast path has just as much right to be there as you. Tempting as it may be to pick wild flowers you should leave all flora alone so the next people who pass can enjoy the sight as well. You never know if you may be inadvertently picking a rare flower, destroying its chances of future survival.

If you come across young animals or birds leave them alone. Every year hundreds of well-meaning but misguided people hand in supposedly abandoned young to the RSPCA, when in fact the only thing keeping the mother away was them.

The code of the outdoor loo

As more and more people discover the joys of walking in the natural environment issues such as how to go to the loo outdoors rapidly gain importance. How many of us have shaken our heads at the sight of toilet paper strewn beside the path, or even worse, someone's dump left in full view? Human excrement is not only offensive to our senses but, more importantly, can infect water sources.

Where to go The coast path is a high-use area and many habitats will not benefit from your fertilisation. As far as 'number twos' are concerned try whenever possible to **use public toilets**. There is no shortage of public toilets along the coast path and they are all marked on the trail maps. However, there are those times when the only time is now. If you have to go outdoors help the environment to deal with your deposit in the best possible way by following a few simple guidelines:

● **Choose your site carefully** It should be at least 30 metres away from running water and out of reach of the high tide and not on any site of historical or archaeological interest. Carry a small trowel or use a sturdy stick to **dig a small hole** about 15cm (6") deep to bury your faeces in. Faeces decompose quicker when in contact with the top layer of soil or leaf mould; by using a stick to stir loose soil into your deposit you will speed decomposition up even more. Do not squash it under rocks as this slows down the decomposition process. If you have to use rocks as a cover make sure they are not in contact with your faeces.

● **Pack out toilet paper and tampons** Toilet paper takes a long time to decompose whether buried or not. It is easily dug up by animals and will then blow into water sources or onto the trail. The best method for dealing with used toilet paper is to **pack it out**. Put it in a paper bag placed inside a plastic bag and then dispose of it at the next toilet. **Tampons** and **sanitary towels** also need to be packed out in a similar way. They take years to decompose and may be dug up and scattered about by animals.

ACCESS

Access to the countryside has always been a hot topic in Britain. In the 1940s soldiers coming back from the Second World War were horrified and disgruntled to find that landowners were denying them the right to walk across the moors; ironically the very country that they had been fighting to protect. Since then it has been an ongoing battle and it is a battle that has finally been won as new legislation came into force in 2005 granting public access to thousands of acres of Britain's wildest land.

All those who enjoy access to the countryside must respect the land, its wildlife, the interests of those who live and work there and other users; we all share a common interest in the countryside. Knowing your rights and responsibilities gives you the information you need to act with minimal impact.

Rights of way

As a designated **National Trail** the coast path is a **public right of way**. A public right of way is either a footpath, a bridleway or a byway. The Cornwall coast path is a footpath for almost all its length which means that anyone has the legal right to use it on foot only.

Rights of way are theoretically established because the owner has dedicated them to public use. However, very few paths are formally dedicated in this way. If members of the public have been using a path without interference for 20 years or more the law assumes the owner has intended to dedicate it as a right of way. If a path has been unused for 20 years it does not cease to exist; the guiding principle is 'once a highway, always a highway'.

On a public right of way you have the right to 'pass and repass along the way' which includes stopping to rest or admire the view, or to consume refreshments. You can also take with you a 'natural accompaniment' (!) which includes a dog, but it must be kept under close control (see p23).

Farmers and land managers must ensure that paths are not blocked by crops or other vegetation, or otherwise obstructed, that the route is identifiable and the surface is restored soon after cultivation. If crops are growing over the path you have every right to walk through them, following the line of the right of way as closely as possible. If you find a path blocked or impassable you should report it to the appropriate **highway authority**. Highway authorities are responsible for maintaining footpaths. In Cornwall the highway authority is the **Cornwall Council** (see box p61). The council is also the surveying authority with responsibility for maintaining the official definitive map of public rights of way.

Wider access

The access situation to land around the coast path is a little more complicated. Trying to unravel and understand the seemingly thousands of different laws and acts is never easy in any legal system. Parliamentary Acts give a right to walk over certain areas of land such as some, but by no means all, common land and some specific places such as Dartmoor and the New Forest. However, in other places, such as Bodmin Moor and many British beaches, right of access is not written in law. It is merely tolerated by the landowner and could be terminated at any time.

Some landowners, such as the Forestry Commission, water companies and the National Trust, are obliged by law to allow some degree of access to their land. Land covered by schemes such as the Environmental Stewardship Scheme, formerly the Countryside Stewardship Scheme, gives landowners a financial incentive to manage their land for conservation and to provide limited public access. There are also a few truly altruistic landowners who have allowed access over their land and these include organisations such as the RSPB, the Woodland Trust, and some local authorities. Overall, however, access to most of Britain's countryside is forbidden to Britain's people, in marked contrast to the general rights of access that prevail in other European countries.

Right to roam

For many years groups such as the **Ramblers Association** (see box p40) and the **British Mountaineering Council** (💻 www.thebmc.co.uk) campaigned for new and wider access legislation. This finally bore fruit in the form of the Countryside and Rights of Way Act of November 2000, colloquially known as the CRoW Act, which granted access for 'recreation on foot' to mountain, moor, heath, down and registered common land in England and Wales. In essence it allows walkers the freedom to roam responsibly away from footpaths, without being accused of trespass, on about four million acres of open, uncultivated land.

On 28 August 2005 the South-West became the sixth region in England/Wales to be opened up under this act; however, restrictions may still be in place from time to time – check the situation on 💻 www.openaccess.gov.uk.

The Countryside Agency (now part of Natural England) has mapped the new agreed areas of open access. These areas are clearly marked on all the latest Ordnance Survey Explorer (1:25,000) maps. In the future it is hoped that the legislation can be extended to include other types of land such as cliff, foreshore, woodland, riverside and canal side.

The Countryside Code

The countryside is a fragile place which every visitor should respect. The Countryside Code seems like common sense but sadly some people still seem to have no understanding of how to treat the countryside they walk in. Everyone visiting the countryside has a responsibility to minimise the impact of their visit so that

> ❏ **The Countryside Code**
> ● Be safe – plan ahead and follow any signs
> ● Leave gates and property as you find them
> ● Protect plants and animals, and take your litter home
> ● Keep dogs under close control
> ● Consider other people

other people can enjoy the same peaceful landscapes. It does not take much effort; it really is common sense.

Below is an expanded version of the new Countryside Code, launched under the logo 'Respect, Protect and Enjoy':

● **Be safe** Walking on the Coast path is pretty much hazard free but you're responsible for your own safety so follow the simple guidelines outlined on p58-9.

● **Leave all gates as you found them** Normally a farmer leaves gates closed to keep livestock in but may sometimes leave them open to allow livestock access to food or water. Leave them as you find them and if there is a sign, follow the instructions.

● **Leave livestock, crops and machinery alone** Help farmers by not interfering with their means of livelihood.

● **Take your litter home** 'Pack it in, pack it out'. Litter is not only ugly but can be harmful to wildlife. Small mammals often become trapped in discarded cans and bottles. Many walkers think that orange peel and banana skins do not count as litter. Even biodegradable foodstuffs attract common scavenging species such as crows and gulls to the detriment of less dominant species. See p52.

● **Keep your dog under control** Across farmland dogs should be kept on a lead. During lambing time they should not be taken with you at all; see also p23.

● **Enjoy the countryside and respect its life and work** Access to the countryside depends on being sensitive to the needs and wishes of those who live and work there. Being courteous and friendly to those you meet will ensure a healthy future for all based on partnership and co-operation.

● **Keep to paths across farmland** Stick to the official path across arable or pasture land. Minimise erosion by not cutting corners or widening the path.

● **Use gates and stiles to cross fences, hedges and walls** The path is well supplied with stiles where it crosses field boundaries. If you have to climb over a gate because you can't open it always do so at the hinged end. Traditional Cornish hedges (see p65) are often ancient and easily damaged.

● **Help keep all water clean** Leaving litter and going to the toilet near a water source can pollute people's water supplies. See pp53-4 for more advice.

● **Take special care on country roads** Drivers often go dangerously fast on narrow winding lanes. To be safe, walk facing the oncoming traffic and carry a torch or wear highly visible clothing when it's getting dark. If you travel by car drive with care and reduced speed on country roads. Park your car with consideration for others' needs; never block a gateway.

● **Protect wildlife, plants and trees** Care for and respect all wildlife you come across along the path. Don't pick plants, break trees or scare wild animals. If you come across young birds that appear to have been abandoned leave them alone.

● **Guard against all risk of fire** Accidental fire is a great fear for farmers and foresters. Never make a camp fire: the deep burn damages turf and destroys flora and fauna. Take cigarette butts with you to dispose of safely.

● **Make no unnecessary noise** Stay in small groups and act unobtrusively. Avoid noisy and disruptive behaviour which might annoy residents and other visitors and frighten farm animals and wildlife.

Health and safety

HEALTH

You will enjoy your walk more if you have a reasonable level of fitness. Carrying a pack for five to seven hours a day is demanding and any preparation you have done beforehand will pay off.

Water
You need to drink lots of water (see p18-19) while you're walking; 3-5 litres per day depending on the weather. If you start to feel tired, lethargic or get a headache it may be that you are not drinking enough. Thirst is not a good indicator of when to drink; stop and have a drink every hour or two. A good indication of whether you are drinking enough is the colour of your urine, the lighter the better. If you are not needing to urinate much and your urine is dark yellow you need to increase your fluid intake.

Hypothermia
Hypothermia, or exposure, occurs when the body can't generate enough heat to maintain its core temperature. It's usually as a result of being wet, cold, unprotected from the wind, tired and hungry. It is easily avoided by wearing suitable clothing (see pp37-8), carrying and eating enough food and drink, being aware of the weather conditions and checking the morale of your companions. Early signs to watch for are feeling cold and tired with involuntary shivering. Find some shelter as soon as possible and warm the person up with a hot drink and some chocolate or other high-energy food. If possible give them another warm layer of clothing and allow them to rest until feeling better.

If allowed to worsen, strange behaviour, slurring of speech and poor co-ordination will become apparent and the victim can quickly progress into unconsciousness, followed by coma and death. Quickly get the victim out of wind and rain, improvising a shelter if necessary. Rapid restoration of bodily warmth is essential and best achieved by bare-skin contact: someone should get into the same sleeping bag as the patient, both having stripped to their underwear, any spare clothing under or over them to build up heat. Send urgently for help.

Hyperthermia
Heat exhaustion is often caused by water depletion and is a serious condition that could eventually lead to death. Symptoms include thirst, fatigue, giddiness, a rapid pulse, raised body temperature, low urine output and later on, delirium and coma. The only remedy is to re-establish water balance. If the victim is suffering severe muscle cramps it may be due to salt depletion.

Heatstroke is caused by failure of the body's temperature-regulating system and is extremely serious. It is associated with a very high body temperature and an absence of sweating. Early symptoms can be similar to those of hypothermia, such as aggressive behaviour, lack of co-ordination and so on. Later the victim goes into a coma or convulsions and death will follow if effective treatment is not given. To treat heatstroke sponge the victim down or cover with wet towels and vigorously fan them. Get help immediately.

Sunburn

Even on overcast days the sun still has the power to burn. Sunburn can be avoided by regularly applying sunscreen. Don't forget your lips and those areas affected by reflected light off the ground; under your nose, ears and chin. You may find that you quickly sweat sunscreen off, so consider wearing a sun hat. If you have particularly fair skin wear a light, long-sleeved top and trousers.

Footcare

Caring for your feet is vital; you're not going to get far if they are out of action. Wash and dry them properly at the end of the day, change your socks every few days and if it is warm enough take your boots and socks off when you stop for lunch to allow your feet to dry out in the sun.

Blisters can make or break a walk and the best treatment for them really is prevention. All methods of prevention work on the idea of reducing friction between the skin and the boot. You need to take action as soon as you feel a rub developing, don't make the mistake of waiting just a little longer. There are many different ideas around, but one of the most effective is to strap the affected area with tape; waterproof tape that has a smooth shiny surface works best. You may need to do this for a quite a few days until the skin toughens up.

If you've left it too late and you already have a blister one of the best ways to treat it is to cover it with Compeed or Second Skin (see p38 for first-aid kit). Another way is to build a layer of 'Moleskin' around the blister. Keep a careful eye on blisters to make sure they don't become infected.

OUTDOOR SAFETY

Weather forecasts

It is a good idea to listen to weather forecasts and in particular pay attention to wind and gale warnings. Winds on any coastline can get very strong and if the wind is high it is advisable not to walk. Walking in high winds is difficult particularly if you are carrying a pack which can act as a sail. If you are walking on a steep incline or above high cliffs it is dangerous. Even if the wind direction is inland it can literally blow you right over (unpleasant if there are gorse bushes around!), or if it suddenly stops or eddies (a common phenomenon when strong winds hit cliffs) it can cause you to lose your balance and stagger in the direction in which you have been leaning, ie towards the cliffs!

Another hazard on the coast is sea mist or fog which can dramatically decrease visibility. If a coastal fog blows over take extreme care where the path runs close to cliff edges.

Detailed weather forecasts for Cornwall and Devon are available through Weathercall (☎ 09068-500404, 🖥 www.weathercall.co.uk), but be aware that the phone number is a premium-rate number (60p/min) and information from their website is on a subscription basis. Alternatively, 🖥 www.destination-corn wall.co.uk, 🖥 www.bbc.co.uk/weather and 🖥 www.met-office.gov.uk have up-to-date forecasts; 🖥 www.metcheck.com is also a useful source of information.

Swimming

If you are not an experienced swimmer or familiar with the sea, plan ahead and swim at beaches where there is a lifeguard service; these beaches have all been marked on the trail maps. On such beaches you should swim between the red and yellow flags as this is the patrolled area. Don't swim between black and white chequered flags as these areas are only for surfboards. If there is a red flag flying this indicates that it is dangerous to enter the water. If you are not sure about anything ask one of the lifeguards; after all they are there to help you.

If you are going to swim at unsupervised beaches never do so alone and always take care. Some beaches are prone to strong rips. Never swim off headlands or near river mouths as there may be strong currents running. Always be aware of changing weather conditions and tidal movement. Cornwall has a huge tidal range and it can be very easy to get cut off by the tide.

If you see someone in difficulty do not attempt a rescue until you have contacted the coastguard (see box below). Once you know help is on the way try to assist the person by throwing something to help them stay afloat. Many beaches have rescue equipment located in red boxes; these are marked on the trail maps.

Walking alone

If you are walking alone you must appreciate and be prepared for the increased risk. It is always a good idea to leave word with somebody about where you are going; you can always ring ahead to book accommodation and let them know you are walking alone and what time you expect to arrive. Don't forget to contact whoever you have left word with to let them know you've arrived safely. Carrying a mobile phone can be useful though you cannot rely on getting good reception.

MINIMUM IMPACT & OUTDOOR SAFETY

❏ **Dealing with an accident**
- Use basic first aid to treat any injuries to the best of your ability.
- Try to attract the attention of anybody else who may be in the area. The **emergency signal** is six blasts on a whistle, or six flashes with a torch.
- If possible leave someone with the casualty while others go for help. If there is nobody else, you have a dilemma. If you decide to get help leave all spare clothing and food with the casualty.
- Telephone ☎ **999** and ask for the coastguard. They are responsible for dealing with any emergency that occurs on the coast or at sea. Make sure you know exactly where you are before you call.
- Report the exact position of the casualty and their condition.

PART 3: THE ENVIRONMENT AND NATURE

The Cornish coastline provides a diverse range of habitats – ocean, beaches, sand dunes, steep cliffs, cliff-top grasslands and heathland – resulting in a rich variety of wildlife. For the walker interested in the natural environment it is a feast for the senses.

It would take a book several times the size of this one to list the thousands of species which you could come across on your walk. What follows is a brief description of the more common species you may encounter as well as some of the more special plants and animals which are found in Cornwall. If you want to know more refer to the field guides listed on p41.

Conservation issues are also explored on the premise that to really learn about a landscape you need to know more than the names of all the plants and animals in it. It is just as important to understand the interactions going on between them and man's relationship with this ecological balance.

Conservation in Cornwall

Nature conservation arose tentatively in the middle of the 19th century out of concern for wild birds which were being slaughtered to provide feathers for the fashion industry. As commercial exploitation of land has increased over the intervening century, so too has the conservation movement. It now has a wide sphere of influence throughout the world and its ethos is upheld by international legislation, government agencies and voluntary organisations.

GOVERNMENT AGENCIES AND SCHEMES

Natural England
Natural England is responsible for identifying, establishing and managing National Parks, Areas of Outstanding Natural Beauty (both previously managed by the Countryside Agency), National Nature Reserves, Sites of Special Scientific Interest, and Special Areas of Conservation (all previously managed by English Nature).

The highest level of landscape protection is the designation of land as a **National Park** which recognises the national importance of an area in terms of landscape, biodiversity and as a recreational resource. This designation does not signify national ownership and they are not uninhabited wildernesses, making conservation a knife-edged balance between protecting the environment and the rights and livelihoods of those living in the park. However, there are no national parks in Cornwall.

The second level of protection is **Area of Outstanding Natural Beauty (AONB)** and **Heritage Coasts**. Much of the coast path crosses land covered by these designations. Their primary objective is conservation of the natural beauty of a landscape. As there is no statutory administrative framework for their management, this is the responsibility of the local authority within whose boundaries they fall.

The next level includes **National Nature Reserves (NNRs)** and **Sites of Special Scientific Interest (SSSIs)**. There are 222 NNRs in England of which three are in Cornwall. The coast path passes through the Lizard NNR, an area of 1662 hectares, which was established to protect a rich collection of rare plant species. There are about 4100 SSSIs in England ranging in size from little pockets protecting wild flower meadows, important nesting sites (such as Loe Pool p212), or special geological features, to vast swathes of upland, moorland and wetland. SSSIs are a particularly important designation as they have some legal standing. They are managed in partnership with the owners and occupiers of the land who must give written notice before initiating any operations likely to damage the site and who cannot proceed without consent from Natural England.

Natural England has also established management schemes for **Special Areas of Conservation** (SAC), an international designation which came into being as a result of the 1992 Earth Summit in Rio de Janeiro, Brazil. This European-wide network of sites is designed to promote the conservation of habitats, wild animals and plants, both on land and at sea. At the time of writing 231 land sites in England had been designated as SACs. Every land SAC is also an SSSI.

National Trails

The Cornwall coast path is a section of the South-West Coast Path, one of 15 National Trails in England and Wales. These are Britain's flagship long-distance paths which grew out of the post-war desire to protect the country's special places, a movement which also gave birth to National Parks and AONBs.

National Trails in England are largely funded by the Countryside Agency (Natural England) and are managed on the ground by a National Trail Officer. They coordinate the maintenance work undertaken by either the local highway

---

❏ **Statutory bodies**
● **Cornwall Council** (☎ 01872-322000, 🖳 www.cornwall.gov.uk) The Council acting as Highway Authority manages the coast path.
● **Department for Environment, Food and Rural Affairs** (☎ 020-7238 6951, 🖳 www.defra.gov.uk) Government ministry responsible for sustainable development in the countryside.
● **Natural England** (☎ 0845-600 3078, www.naturalengland.org.uk) See opposite.
● **English Heritage** (☎ 0870-333 1181, 🖳 www.english-heritage.org.uk) Organisation whose central aim is to make sure that the historic environment of England is properly maintained. It is officially known as the Historic Buildings and Monuments Commission for England. Tintagel Castle (see p92) is an English Heritage site.

THE ENVIRONMENT & NATURE

authority, or the National Trust, where it crosses their land, and ensure that the trail is kept up to nationally agreed standards.

CAMPAIGNING AND CONSERVATION ORGANISATIONS

These voluntary organisations started the conservation movement back in the mid-1800s and they are still at the forefront of developments. Independent of governments, they can concentrate their resources either on acquiring land which can then be managed purely for conservation purposes, or on influencing political decision-makers by lobbying and campaigning.

Managers and owners of land include the **National Trust**, the **Royal Society for the Protection of Birds** (RSPB) and the equally important but smaller **Cornwall Wildlife Trust** (see box below).

Lobbying groups such as the **Marine Conservation Society** and **Campaign to Protect Rural England** play a vital role in environmental protection by raising public awareness. A huge increase in membership over the last 20 years and a general understanding that environmental issues can't be left

❏ **Campaigning and conservation organisations**
● **National Trust** (☎ 0870-458 4000, 🖳 www.nationaltrust.org.uk) A charity with 3.4 million members which aims to protect, through ownership, threatened coastline, countryside, historic houses, castles and gardens, and archaeological remains for everybody to enjoy. The trust owns over 40% of the Cornish coastline, as well as sites such as the Old Post Office (see p91) in Tintagel and Godrevy Point (see p148).
● **Royal Society for the Protection of Birds** (RSPB; ☎ 01767-680551, 🖳 www.rspb.org.uk) The largest voluntary conservation body in Europe focusing on providing a healthy environment for birds and wildlife and with over a million members, and 150 reserves in the UK including two on the coast path: Hayle Estuary (p153) and Marazion Marsh (p202).
● The umbrella organisation for the 47 wildlife trusts in the UK is **The Wildlife Trusts** (☎ 0870-036 7711, 🖳 www.wildlifetrusts.org). **Cornwall Wildlife Trust** (☎ 01872-273939, 🖳 www.cornwallwildlifetrust.org.uk) is the largest voluntary organisation (8000 members) in the county concerned with all aspects of nature conservation. They own over 50 nature reserves. See box p69.
● **Marine Conservation Society** (☎ 01989-566017, 🖳 www.mcsuk.org) A national charity dedicated solely to protecting the marine environment and its wildlife (see box p69).
● **Butterfly Conservation** (☎ 01929-400209, 🖳 www.butterfly-conservation.org) For further information contact the Cornwall branch (🖳 www.cornwall-butterfly-conservation.org.uk)
● **Woodland Trust** (☎ 01476-581135, 🖳 www.woodland-trust.org.uk) The trust aims to conserve, restore and re-establish native woodlands throughout the UK.
● **British Trust for Conservation Volunteers** (BTCV; ☎ 01302-572244, 🖳 www.btcv.org) Encourages people to value their environment and take practical action to improve it.
● **Campaign to Protect Rural England** (CPRE; ☎ 020-7981 2800, 🖳 www.cpre.org.uk) A charity whose members care about the countryside and campaign for it to be protected and enhanced.

THE ENVIRONMENT & NATURE

in government hands is creating a new and powerful lobbying group: an informed electorate.

Butterfly Conservation was formed in 1968 by some naturalists who were alarmed at the decline in the number of butterflies, and moths, and who now aim to reverse the situation. They now have 31 branches throughout the British Isles and operate 33 nature reserves and also sites where butterflies are likely to be found.

BEYOND CONSERVATION

As walkers we are among the best placed people to appreciate the natural world and realise just how precious it is. When out on a walk our senses connect us to the complex web of life we call nature and they tell us that it is seriously under threat; we can smell the increase in pollution, we can hear the roar of the traffic drowning out the songbirds, and we can see the ever-increasing urban sprawl.

We need to expand our ideas beyond those of nature conservation. After all, a Nature Reserve or Heritage Coast designation is of little use if we continue to destroy the wider environment: our sky, soil and sea. We now need to take a good hard look at the way each of us live our lives; recycling our glass and making a donation to a conservation organisation simply isn't enough any more.

Our Western society creates huge pressures on the global environment on which we all depend. With ever-increasing demands for material objects and wealth the unsustainable taking of raw materials increases. As we build more and more houses, roads and factories we keep on squeezing the natural world, sending hundreds of species to extinction every day. All of us can play our part in slowing this tidal wave of destruction by making changes to our own lifestyles; choosing to consume less and to live more. At first this may seem insignificant on a worldwide scale, but each small decision is a tiny step which eventually leads to leaps and bounds in the right direction.

Once an area has gone, it has gone forever, and we can do nothing but mourn its loss. Such grieving may be easier to bear in the knowledge that we have done our utmost to prevent it.

Flora and fauna

FLORA

Cornwall is best known for its springtime flora when the cliff tops have spectacular displays of wildflowers. Being the most southerly province flowers tend to come out in Cornwall earlier than in the rest of Britain; **daffodils** (*Narcissus sp.*) and **wild primroses** (*Primula vulgaris*) start to make an appearance as early as February. Trees find it difficult to grow on the coast except in sheltered valleys. **Blackthorn** (*Prunus spinosa*), **gorse** (*Ulex sp.*) and **elder** (*Sambucus nigra*) provide some windbreak.

THE ENVIRONMENT & NATURE

When identifying wild plants it is best to identify the habitat first as this should considerably narrow your search.

Heathland

Heathland once used to stretch right across Cornwall from the Lizard to St Agnes and from Bodmin Moor in the east of the county to the Atlantic coast, covering an area of 80,000ha. Now just 7000ha remain of this internationally important habitat. Much of it has been destroyed by farming but there are still significant tracts around both St Agnes and the Lizard, as well as smaller coastal patches between St Ives and Land's End. Surprisingly, much of this has survived because of the mining industry (see box p172). Heather and other associated species thrive on land contaminated by mine waste, preferring an acidic, nutrient-poor environment where there is little competition from other plants that can tolerate such inhospitable territory. The unique nature of the Lizard is also due to poor soil, caused by the underlying serpentine rock, which has similarly saved much of the area from the plough.

Heathland is at its best in August and September when it is ablaze with pinks, purples and yellow. Of the different types of heather found are **common** (*Calluna vulgaris*), **bell** (*Erica cinerea*), **cross-leaved** (*E. tetralix*) and **Dorset heather** (*E. ciliaris*), as well as **Cornish heath** (*E. vagans*), the Lizard being the only place in the world where it is found. **Common** (*Ulex europaeus*) and **western gorse** (*U. gallii*) often grow amongst the heather. Other plants to look out for are **dyer's greenweed** (*Genista tinctoria*), **dwarf burnet** (*Rosa pimpinellifolia pumila*), **burnet rose** (*Rosa pimpinellifolia*), **betony** (*Betonica officinalis*), **bloody cranesbill** (*Geranium sanguineum*), **milkwort** (*Polygala sp.*), **dropwort** (*Filipendula vulgaris*), **heath-spotted orchid** (*Dactylorhiza maculata*) and **yellow bartsia** (*Parentucellia viscosa*) and **red bartsia** (*Odontites verna*).

Cropped turf

Traditionally farmed land is an important habitat for many wildflowers throughout Britain because the low-intensity grazing controls scrub and trees while allowing less aggressive plants to flourish. Unfortunately, traditional methods are being eroded by intensive farming practices such as heavy grazing and the widespread use of herbicides leading to a reduction, and even loss of, many species. However, in a few places low-intensity grazing has been reintroduced.

Short cropped turf is brilliant with flowers from early spring. The most common ones are **thrift**, or **sea pink** (*Armeria maritima*), **spring squill** (*Scilla verna*), **kidney vetch** (*Anthyllis vulneraria*) and **sea campion** (*Silene maritima*). Other wild flowers to look out for are **dyer's greenweed**, **sheep's bit**

❏ **Lizard flora**

There are a number of rare plants found on the Lizard Peninsula growing in rough grassland and cropped turf. They include **thyme broomrape** (*Orobanche alba*), **fringed rupturewort** (*Herniaria ciliolata*), **hairy greenweed** (*Genista pilosa*), and **green-winged orchid** (*Orchis morio*). **Cornish heath** (*Erica vagans*) is a very special plant as it is unique to the area.

Common Centaury
Centaurium erythraea

Spear Thistle
Cirsium vulgare

Sea Holly
Eryngium maritimum

Lousewort
Pedicularis sylvatica

Bell Heather
Erica cinerea

Heather (Ling)
Calluna vulgaris

Rosebay Willowherb
Epilobium angustifolium

Common Fumitory
Fumaria officinalis

Thrift (Sea Pink)
Armeria maritima

Gorse
Ulex europaeus

Meadow Buttercup
Ranunculis acris

Honeysuckle
Lonicera periclymemum

Tormentil
Potentilla erecta

Birdsfoot-trefoil
Lotus corniculatus

Scarlet Pimpernel
Anagallis arvensis

Common Ragwort
Senecio jacobaea

Primrose
Primula vulgaris

Silverweed
Potentilla anserina

Sea Campion
Silene maritima

Hogweed
Heracleum sphondylium

Yarrow
Achillea millefolium

Dog Rose
Rosa canina

Common Hawthorn
Crataegus monogyna

Germander Speedwell
Veronica chamaedrys

Self-heal
Prunella vulgaris

Bluebell
Endymion non-scriptus

Violet
Viola riviniana

Tree Echium
Echium (species)

Wall Pennywort
Umbilicus rupestris

Mesembryanthemum

Common Vetch
Vicia sativa

Hottentot Fig
Carpobrutus edulis

Herb-Robert
Geranium robertianum

Foxglove
Digitalis purpurea

Heath-spotted Orchid
Dactylorhiza maculata

Red Campion
Silene dioica

Peacock
Inachis io

Small Tortoiseshell
Aglais urticae

Small Pearl-Bordered Fritillary
Boloria selene

Brimstone
Gonepteryx rhamni

Common Blue
Polyommatus icarus

Painted Lady
Vanessa cadui

Small Copper
Lycaena phlaeas

Red Admiral
Vanessa atalanta

Meadow
Brown
Maniola jurtina

Large Garden/
Cabbage White
Pieris brassicae

Clouded Yellow
Colias croceus

Above (clockwise from bottom): **adder** (© Keith Carter), **herring gull**, **great black-backed gull**, **puffin** (all © Bryn Thomas), **black headed gull**, **jackdaws** (© Roderick Leslie), **Atlantic grey seal** (© Edith Schofield). (See pp66-71).

ABOVE (clockwise from bottom left): **shelduck, oystercatcher, common tern, fulmar, manx sheerwater, pied wagtail** (all © Roderick Leslie), **curlew** (© Keith Carter), **wigeon** (© Roderick Leslie). (See pp66-71).

(*Jasione montana*) and **bird's foot trefoil** (*Lotus corniculatus*). Rather unusually you may also come across swathes of **bluebells** (*Endymion non-scriptus*) on the cliff tops. Bluebells are more commonly associated with woodland, but can also be indicators of ancient woods.

Lime-rich grasslands
Soils in Cornwall are generally acidic, although in some areas coastal grasslands are 'limed' by windblown sand consisting of tiny shell fragments. Kelsey Head (Map 32, p135) is a good example of this type of habitat. **Cowslips** (*Primula veris*) grow in abundance and other lime-lovers are **salad burnet** (*Poterium sanguisorba*), **pyramidal** (*Anacamptis pyramidalis*) and **autumn lady's tresses orchids** (*Spiranthes spiralis*), **wild clary** (*Salvia horminoides*), **carline thistle** (*Carlina vulgaris*), **pale flax** (*Linum bienne*), **Cornish gentian** (*Gentianella anglica ssp. Cornubiensis*), and **hairy greenweed**.

Dunes
Dunes are formed by wind action creating a fragile, unstable environment. Among the first colonisers is **marram grass** (*Ammophila arenaria*) which is able to withstand drought, exposure to wind and salt spray and has an ability to grow up through new layers of sand that cover it. Other specialist plants are **sea holly** (*Eryngium maritimum*), **sea spurge** (*Euphorbia paralias*) and **sea bindweed** (*Calystegia soldanella*). The one thing that these seemingly indomitable plants can't tolerate is trampling by human feet; stay on the path which is nearly always well marked through dunes.

Hedges and field margins
Cornish hedges are not your stereotypical neat row of planted trees and shrubs. They are more like a wall than a hedge as they are constructed from stones and earth. In time, they provide a habitat for all types of vegetation ranging from simple mosses and grasses to fully fledged trees which are allowed to grow along the top of the hedges. Along with rough grassland at field edges these habitats provide a wildlife corridor and refuge for many species of wildflowers and small mammals such as voles and shrews.

Some flowers that you may see are **violets** (*Viola riviniana*), **lesser celandine** (*Ranunculus ficaria*), **red campion** (*Silene dioca*), **alexanders** (*Smyrnium olusatrum*), **hogweed** (*Heracleum sphondylium*), **yarrow** (*Achillea millefolium*) and **foxgloves** (*Digitalis purpurea*).

Gardens
The warm climate in Cornwall means that some plants not normally found in the British Isles thrive both in gardens and in sheltered areas in the wild as garden escapees. These include the **tree echium** (from the Canary Islands), succulents such as the **aeonium** (Canary Islands) and **mesembryanthemum** (South Africa) species and purple **agapanthus** lilies, also from South Africa.

(**Opposite**) Red hot poker display in the gardens of St Michael's Mount (see p204). (Photo © Henry Stedman).

THE ENVIRONMENT & NATURE

FAUNA

In and around the fishing villages

The wild laugh of the **herring gull** (*Larus argentatus*) is the wake-up call of the coast path. Perched on the rooftops of the stone villages, they are a reminder of the link between people and wildlife, the rocky coast and our stone and concrete towns and cities. Shoreline scavengers, they've adapted to the increasing waste thrown out by human society. Despite their bad reputation it's worth taking a closer look at these fascinating, ubiquitous birds. How do they keep their pale grey and white plumage so beautiful feeding on rubbish?

Nobel-prize-winning animal behaviourist Nikko Tinbergen showed how the young pecking at the red dot on their bright yellow bills triggers the adult to regurgitate food. In August the newly fledged brown young follow their parents begging for food. Over the next three years they'll go through a motley range of plumages, more grey and less brown each year till they reach adulthood. But please don't feed them and do watch your sandwiches and fish and chips – they are quite capable of grabbing food from your hand, especially in St Ives.

The village harbours are a good place for lunch or an evening drink after a hard day on the cliffs. Look out for the birds who are equally at home on a rocky shore or in villages, such as the beautiful little black-and-white **pied wagtail** (*Motacilla alba*) with its long, bobbing tail.

Also looking black from a distance as they strut the beach are **jackdaws** (*Corvus monedula*). Close up, however, they are beautiful with a grey nape giving them a hooded look and shining blue eyes. They are very sociable: you will often see them high up in the air in pairs or flocks playing tag or performing acrobatic tricks.

Small, dark brown and easy to miss, the **rock pipit** (*Anthus petrosus*) is one of our toughest birds, as it feeds whilst walking on the rocks between the land and the sea. They nest in crevices and caves along the rocky coastline.

❏ Conservation and the fishing industry

Small boats crowding sheltered harbours and the sea dotted with crab pot buoys are constant reminders of this coast's fishing tradition. However, few people now work full time in fishing. The great pilchard shoals are long gone, probably victims of changing ocean currents rather than over fishing, but it is over fishing combined with increasingly sophisticated catching methods that have left Newlyn as the only major deep sea port. Strict quotas and an EU-sponsored scheme to take boats out of service is further reducing the fleet. Controversy between different fishing methods focuses on the damage done by bottom trawling, whilst the accidental catching of seabirds in the miles-long gill nets catching sea bass has led to restrictions on their use in St Ives bay. There is also considerable resentment in Cornwall at the rights of EU partners, especially the Spanish, to what many see as British waters. Now, for the smaller ports crab fishing may be the main business, with many ironically exported to the seafood-hungry Spanish! Day boats fish inshore under the regulation of the Sea Fisheries Committees which make byelaws within the six-mile limit and tourist boats take visitors fishing for the summer shoals of mackerel.

❏ **Birding and birders**
Along with the Scilly Isles, Cornwall is England's rare-bird capital. Coming from North America, Siberia and southern Europe many rarities are pretty boring looking and it takes an expert to tell them from more common species. The best way to find them is to look for a sea of telescopes. Birders are generally pretty friendly people and may well show you the bird, but they can be grumpy if they haven't seen the rarity – 'dipped out' in birder parlance!

Birdline South West (☎ 0906-870 0241) is the premium-rate phone line for up-to-the-minute rare bird news.

Seen on or from the sea cliffs

Walking on the coastal path leads you into a world of rock and sea, high cliffs with bracken-clad slopes, exposed green pasture, dramatic drops and headlands, sweeping sandy beaches and softer country around the estuaries. Stunning **stonechats** (*Saxicola torquata*) with black, white and orange colouring are common on heath and grassy plains where you may hear their distinctive song, which is not dissimilar to two stones being clacked together. Twittering **linnets** (*Carduelis cannabina*) with their bright red breasts and grey heads fly ahead and perch on gorse and fences. **Green hairstreak butterflies** (*Callophrys rubi*) emerge on gorse in May. The vertiginous swoops of the path mean it's often possible to be at eye level or even look down on birds and mammals. Watch for **kestrels** (*Falco tinnunculus*), hovering on sharp brown wings, before plummeting onto their prey – **field voles** (*Microtus arvalis*).

At eye level the black 'moustache' of the powerful slate-grey-backed **peregrine** (*Falco peregrinus*) is sometimes visible. At a glance it can be mistaken for a pigeon, its main prey. But the power and speed of this, the world's fastest bird, soon sets it apart. In the late summer whole families fly over the cliffs. In mid winter look for them over estuaries where they hunt ducks and waders. Despite the remote fastness of the cliffs, peregrine have suffered terribly. Accidental poisoning by the pesticide DDT succeeded where WWII persecution for fear they would kill carrier pigeons failed, and they were almost extinct in Cornwall by the end of the 1960s. Its triumphant return means not only a thriving population on its traditional sea cliffs, but more and more nesting in our cities on man-made cliffs, such as tower blocks and cathedrals.

Cliff ledges, a kind of multi-storey block of flats for birds, provide nesting places safe from marauding land predators such as **foxes** (*Vulpes vulpes;* see also p70) and rats. It's surprising just how close it's possible to get to **fulmars** (*Fulmarus glacialis*), which return to their nesting ledges in February for the start of the long breeding season that goes on into the autumn. Only in the depth of winter are the cliffs quiet. Fulmars are related to albatrosses and like them are masters of the air. You can distinguish them from gulls by their ridged, flat wings as they sail the wind close to the waves with the occasional burst of fast flapping. Fulmars are incredibly tenacious at holding their nesting sites and vomit a stinking oily secretion over any intruders, including rock-climbers! The

THE ENVIRONMENT & NATURE

elegant **kittiwake** (*Rissa tridactyla*), the one true seagull that never feeds on land, is another cliff nester, identified by its 'dipped in ink' black wingtips.

Black above, white below, **manx shearwaters** (*Puffinus puffinus*) make globe-encircling journeys as they sail effortlessly just above even the wildest sea. Small and fast on hard-beating wings black and white **guillemots** (*Uria troile*) and **razorbills** (*Alca torda*) shoot out from their nesting ledges hidden in the cliffs. There are large colonies around the Godrevy–St Austell area. Guillemot have a long thin bill, razorbill a heavy half circle.

Puffins (*Fratercula arctica*) with their unmistakable parrot-shaped bills are a rare prize round these coasts.

Big, rapacious **great black-backed gulls** (*Larus marinus*) cruise the nesting colonies for prey. Star of the sea show, however, has to be the big, sharp-winged, Persil-white **gannets** (*Morus bassanus*) cruising slowly for fish, then suddenly plunging with folded wings into the sea. Their strengthened skulls protect them from the huge force of the impact with the water.

Two birds more familiar from the artificial cliffs of our cities can be seen here in their natural habitat – **house martins** (*Delichon urbica*), steely-blue backed like a **swallow** (*Hirundo rustica*), but with more V-shaped wings and a distinctive white rump, and **rock doves** (*Columba livia*). These are so mixed with town **pigeons** (*Columba livia* domest.) it's hard to say if any 'pure' wild birds remain, but many individuals with the characteristic grey back, small white rump and two black wing bars can be seen.

Where the path drops steeply to a rocky bay, **oystercatchers** (*Haematopus ostralegus*), with their black and white plumage and spectacular carrot-coloured bill, pipe in panic when they fly off. This is also a good spot to get close to **shags** (*Phalacrocorax aristotelis*) and **cormorants** (*Phalacrocorax pygmeus*), common all round the coast, swimming low and black in the water. Shags are smaller and are always seen on the sea – cormorants are also on rivers and estuaries – and in the summer have a crest whilst cormorant have a white patch near their tail and white face. Close up, these oily birds shine iridescently; shags are green, cormorants are purple. They are a primitive species and since their feathers are not completely waterproof both have to dry their bodies after time in the sea; their heraldic pose, standing upright with half-spread wings on drying rocks is one of the special sights of the coast path.

On or in the sea

The high cliffs are also a great place from which to look out over the sea. Searching for seals is an enjoyable and essential part of cliff walking. You'll spot lots of grey lobster-pot buoys before your first seal, but it's worth the effort. **Atlantic grey seals** (*Halichoerus grypus*) relax in the water, looking over their big Roman noses with doggy eyes, as interested in you as you are in them. Twice the weight of a red deer, a big bull can be over 200kg. On calm sunny days it's possible to follow them down through the clear water as they dive, as elegant in their element as they are clumsy on land. Seals generally come ashore only to rest, moult their fur, or to breed. Seals 'haul out' – come up on the rocks – on Godrevy Island (Map 44, p151), the Carracks near Zennor Head (Map 51,

❏ **Reporting wildlife sightings**
Report basking shark sightings to the **Marine Conservation Society** (see box p62) by going to Species the Basking Shark where there is a report form to fill in or send an A5 stamped addressed envelope to receive a basking shark report card. Remember to note any tags you've spotted. Reports are greatly appreciated.

If you see any of the other larger marine creatures such as dolphins, whales, seals and turtles you can report them online through **Seaquest South West Cornwall**, part of the Cornwall Wildlife Trust (see box p62) giving the location, number and the direction they were heading in.

If you come across a stranded marine animal like a dolphin or porpoise, don't approach it but contact either **British Divers's Marine Life Rescue** (☎ 01825-765546) or the **RSPCA hotline** (☎ 0300-123 4999).

p165) and around Land's End (Map 61, p183). Breeding takes place between September and December and the caves below Navax Point (Map 43, p150) are a popular breeding site. It is also possible to see them at the National Seal Sanctuary (see p236) in Gweek.

A cliff-top sighting of Britain's largest fish is also a real possibility, but is more chilling than endearing! **Basking sharks** (*Cetorhinus maximus*) can grow to a massive eleven metres and weigh seven tonnes, and their two fins, a large shark-like dorsal fin followed by a notched tail fin, are so far apart it takes a second look to be convinced it's one fish. But these are gentle giants, cruising slowly with open jaws, filtering microscopic plankton from the sea. You are most likely to see one during late spring and summer when they feed at the surface during calm, warm weather. Look out for coloured or numbered tags, put on for research into this sadly declining species and report them to the address given in the box above.

Taking a longer view and with some good luck, watch the sea for dolphins, porpoises or even a whale. **Harbour porpoises** (*Phocoena phocoena*) and **bottlenose dolphins** (*Tursiops truncatus*) are the most likely to be seen, in places like St Ives Bay, Mount's Bay and Falmouth Bay. Other cetaceans you may catch a glimpse of are **Risso's dolphins** (*Grampus griseus*), **common dolphins** (*Delphinus delphis*), **striped dolphins** (*Stenella coeruleoalba*), **orcas** or killer whales (*Orcinus orca*) and **pilot whales** (*Globicephala melaena*) but, be warned, they are fiendishly difficult to tell apart: a brief glimpse of a fin is nothing like the 'whole animal' pictures shown in field guides.

In pastures, combes and woods
The path rises up onto rich green pasture. **Skylark** (*Alauda arvensis*) soar tunefully – almost disappearing into the spring sky, while in winter small green-brown **meadow pipits** (*Anthus pratensis*) flit weakly, giving a small high-pitched call. Spring also brings migrant **wheatears** (*Oenanthe oenanthe*): they are beautiful with their grey and black feathers above, buff and white below, and unmistakable when they fly and show their distinctive white rump. **Meadow brown** (*Maniola jurtina*) butterflies flap weakly amongst the long grass. **Buzzard** (*Buteo buteo*)

THE ENVIRONMENT & NATURE

soar up with their tilted, broad round wings, giving their high, wild Ke-oow cry. They are probably the most common bird of prey found in Cornwall.

Rabbits (*Oryctolagus cuniculus*) are one of the few mammals you are likely to see. Prey for buzzard and foxes, they also play a vital role maintaining the short turf habitat of a range of cliff-top species, including **small copper** (*Lycaena phlaeas*) butterflies in September and **common blue** (*Polyommatus icarus*) and **small heath** (*Coenonympha pamphilus*) in May and August. **Ravens** (*Corvus corax*) cronk-cronk over the cliffs and are distinguished from more common **carrion crows** (*Corvus corone*) by their huge size and wedge-shaped tail. One of the most exciting birds around the Cornish coast, at the moment on the Lizard only, is the newly returned **chough** (see box below).

Rain and sun, cold and warmth are normal weather for most of us, but on the coast path the walker soon learns the overwhelming importance of the wind. Dip round a corner into a sheltered combe and suddenly the climate changes. Here are warm bracken slopes and small woodlands. Look out for the big holes and dug-out earth of **badger** (*Meles meles*) setts. Sadly the best chance of seeing a badger is dead on the roadside as they are so shy, and mostly nocturnal like **foxes** (see p67) which are equally common, but much shyer than their urban cousins. Both badgers and foxes are now protected from persecution and it is generally accepted that a badger cull is not the best way to fight tuberculosis in cattle, so another threat to these fascinating animals has been removed.

In spring familiar birds such as **robins** (*Erithacus rubecula*), **blackbirds** (*Turdus merula*), **blue** and **great tits** (*Parus major & caeruleus*), **chaffinches** (*Fringila coelebs*) and **dunnocks** (*Prunella modularis*) are joined by the small green **chiffchaff** (*Phylloscopus collybita*); it's not much to look at but is one of the earliest returning migrants and unmistakably calls its own name in two repeated notes. **Grey squirrels** (*Sciurus carolinensis*), which were introduced from North America in the late 19th century, are the other mammal you're most likely to see.

Butterflies such as the **small pearl-bordered fritillary** (*Boloria selene*) come out in May and August in brackeny combes rich in violets. Look out for

❏ **Choughs**
There is one very special and exciting thrill for walkers on The Lizard – against all the odds, Cornwall's emblem bird, the chough (*Pyrrhocorax pyrrhocorax*), has returned to nest! This stunning little crow, jet black with a bright red beak and legs, is packed with charisma; it's superbly agile in the air and charming on the ground as it pecks, in small flocks, for insects. The chough needs tight, low-grazed turf on the cliff edges. Over the years, flatter pastures were improved with fertiliser and the grass grew too long for choughs, and grazing was abandoned on the steep, rough slopes. Now, as you walk the cliff paths there's a good chance of seeing hardy Dartmoor ponies and Dexter cattle grazing the cliff edge. Pioneered by the National Trust, the improved habitat has allowed choughs to return. From April to June there's a chough watchpoint most afternoons at the southerly point on the Lizard, from which choughs can be seen near the crevice in the cliff where they nest. All year-round they can be seen between Mullion and this southerly point.

the spectacular migrants **clouded yellow** (*Colias croceus*), **red admiral** (*Vanessa atalanta*) and **painted lady** (*Vanessa cardui*) in August and September, and the **wall brown** (*Lasiommata megera*) which has declined steeply and is now found almost entirely near the coast.

In and around estuaries

Descending to the long walk round the estuaries is moving into a different, softer world of shelter and rich farmland. Best for birds in winter, they are a welcome refuge from the ferocity of the worst weather for wildlife and people. There are large flocks of ducks – whistling **wigeon** (*Anas penelope*), a combination of grey and pinky brown, with big white wing patches in flight – and waders like the brown **curlew** (*Numenius arquata*) with its impossibly long, down-curved beak and beautiful sad fluting call, evocative of summer moors. The **redshank** (*Tringa totanus*), **greenshank** (*Tringa nebularia*), **golden** and **grey plover** (*Pluvialis sp.*) and **black-tailed** and **bar-tailed godwit** (*Limosa sp.*) can also be seen in winter.

Look out for the big black, white and chestnut **shelduck** (*Tadorna tadorna*), and for the tall **grey heron** (*Ardea cinerea*), hunched at rest or extended to its full 175cm as it slowly, patiently stalks fish in the shallows. A real rarity 10 years ago, another species of heron, the stunning white **little egret** (*Egretta garzetta*) is now unmissable on Cornish estuaries. Here the more common gull is the nimble **black headed gull** (*Larus ridibundus*), with its elegant cap, dark in summer but pale in winter. In summer, terns come: the big **sandwich tern** (*Sterna sandvicensis*) with its shaggy black cap and loud rasping call, and the smaller sleeker aerobatic **common tern** (*Sterna hirundo*).

After near extinction, owing to pollution, **otters** (*Lutra lutra*) are returning to the rivers and estuaries in Cornwall, though they are still very hard to see – look out for a slithering, lithe shape, or a dog-like head poking out from the water as they swim.

On sand dunes and heath and around mines

Sand dunes swarm with butterflies in high summer and the scarce **silver studded blue** (*Plebeius argus*) can be seen at Holywell Dunes west of Newquay in July and August. Dry heathland provides the warmth needed for reptiles such as **adders** (*Vipera berus*), **slow worms** (*Anguis fragilis*), a type of legless lizard that is commonly mistaken for a snake, and the **common lizard** (*Lacerta vivipara*) seen on the heath vegetation of cliff tops. Warming their blood, they sun themselves on rocks or old mining spoil heaps. With their distinctive and beautiful brown, diamond-patterned backs, adders are our only poisonous snake, but they pose little risk to people in walking boots. Except in spring when the cold can make them sluggish, they quickly move off the path when they feel the vibration of feet.

You are very unlikely to see another beneficiary of mining, the **greater horse-shoe bat** (*Rhinolophus ferrumequinum*). Old mine shafts where bats live have been covered with bat-friendly metal grilles rather than capped with concrete so the bats can still come and go. The commonest bat is the smaller **pipistrelle** (*Pipistrellus pipistrellus*), but all bats are hard to tell apart in the dusk light.

THE ENVIRONMENT & NATURE

Using this guide

The trail guide and maps have not been divided into rigid daily stages since people walk at different speeds and have different interests. The **route summaries** below describe the trail between significant places and are written as if walking the coast path from Bude to Falmouth. To enable you to plan your own itinerary, **practical information** is presented clearly on the trail maps. This includes walking times, all places to stay, camp and eat, as well as shops where you can buy supplies. Further service **details** are given in the text under the entry for each place.

For a condensed overview of this information see Itineraries pp32-4.

TRAIL MAPS

Scale and walking times

The trail maps are to a scale of 1:20,000 (1cm = 200m; 3⅛ inches = one mile). Walking times are given along the side of each map and the arrow shows the direction to which the time refers. Black triangles indicate the points between which the times have been taken. **See note below on walking times.**

The time-bars are a tool and are not there to judge your walking ability. There are so many variables that affect walking speed, from the weather conditions to how many beers you drank the previous evening. After the first hour or two of walking you will be able to see how your speed relates to the timings on the maps.

Up or down?

Other than when on a track or bridleway the trail is shown as a dotted line. An arrow across the trail indicates the slope; two arrows show that it is steep. Note that the arrow points towards the higher part of the trail. If, for example, you are walking from A (at 80m) to B (at 200m) and the trail between the two is short and steep it would be shown thus: A— — — >> — — – B. Reversed arrow heads indicate downward gradient.

GPS waypoints

The numbered GPS waypoints refer to the list on pp248-52.

❏ **Important note – walking times**
Unless otherwise specified, **all times in this book refer only to the time spent walking**. You will need to add 20-30% to allow for rests, photography, checking the map, drinking water etc. When planning the day's hike count on 5-7 hours' actual walking.

Accommodation

Apart from in large towns where some selection of places has been necessary, almost every place to stay that is within easy reach of the trail is marked. Details of each place are given in the accompanying text.

Proprietors either quote their **tariffs** on a **per room** basis, assuming two people are sharing, or on a **per person** basis (see pp14-15 for more information on prices); rates are also given for single occupancy of a room.

The number and type of rooms are given after each entry: S = single room, T = twin room, D = double room, Tr = triple room (sleeps three people, usually in a double and a single) and F = family room (usually assumes two adults and two children, in a double and bunk beds or a double and two singles).

Prices for **camping** vary from site to site but for backpackers many sites charge for two people in a small tent although others charge per pitch and per person. There is not a single rule that applies everywhere. It is often the case that owners of quite large sites set aside a small field just for backpackers on a site otherwise occupied by caravans since their main customers are families on their annual holidays, hence backpackers are low down on their list of priorities.

Other features

Features are marked on the map when pertinent to navigation. In order to avoid cluttering the maps and making them unusable not all features have been marked each time they occur.

The route guide

BUDE [MAP p75]

Bude is a small, compact seaside town with plenty of charm and character as well as a sizeable beach. Before setting off on the coast path take time to potter round the streets and maybe have a peek in **The Castle** with its **Heritage Centre** (☎ 01288-357300, 🖳 www.bude-stratton.gov.uk; daily Easter-Oct 10am-6pm, Nov-Easter 10am-4pm; £3.50), which may appeal for its emphasis on shipwrecks and nautical memorabilia. It stands near **Bude Canal** (see box p74), an unexpected relic of an earlier time when they transported sand inland to spread on the fields. Restoration work has tidied it up nicely and a stroll along the tow path can be an agreeable pastime.

Jazz fans should consider being here at the end of August for **Bude Jazz Festival** (see p30); everyone else should be aware of the consequent increased demand for accommodation so if you're planning your walk then remember to book well in advance.

Services

Bude Tourist Information and Canal Centre (TIC; ☎ 01288-354240, 🖳 www .visitbude.info; Mon-Fri 10am-5pm, Sat-Sun 10am-4pm) is located in the car park between the canal and the River Neet. They have a comprehensive listing of accommodation in the area and the enthusiastic staff can help you find somewhere to stay. **Internet access** is available here: £2 for up to half an hour then £1 for each additional quarter hour. You can also use the internet at the *Coffee Pot* (see p76) where the charge is £1 for 20 minutes.

❏ Bude Canal

The Bude Canal was dug to transport mainly sand inland from the seashore so that it could be spread on the fields to improve the soil which was rather poor in parts of north Cornwall. The Canal was the brainchild of one John Endyvean, the intention being to link up with the River Tamar at Calstock, thus providing a waterway between the Bristol Channel and the English Channel, 90 miles of canal to span just 28 miles as the crow flies.

The full scheme was never realised although by 1823 some 35 miles of canal were in operation. Once the railways were built the use of the canal began to decline and by the Second World War it became ineffective as a waterway. Today only a short stretch remains between Bude and Helebridge.

Currently a project to restore the canal is in progress with the aid of £45m grant from the Heritage Lottery Fund. The lock-gates giving access to the open sea suffered damage in the early part of 2008 due to huge storms but it is expected that with the work now in hand the canal will be a great attraction in years to come.

On The Crescent across from the TIC is a sub **post office**; the main one is at the top of Belle Vue, the main shopping street.

For food shopping, **Somerfield** supermarket is at the junction of Belle Vue and Crooklets Rd. There's also a **Co-op** at the end of Burn View and a **Local Plus** on Lansdown Rd. They all open daily from early till late. There are at least three **chemists** including Boots on Belle Vue.

There are also branches of three high street **banks** (Barclays, Lloyds TSB and NatWest), all located at the bottom of Belle Vue and all with cash machines; you will also find **ATMs** at all the town's supermarkets and convenience stores.

Finally, if you should need a **launderette** (8am-8pm weekdays, Sat 9am-5pm and Sun 10am-5pm) this early there's one tucked away just off Lansdown Rd.

Where to stay

Upper Lynstone Caravan and Camping Park (Map 1; ☎ 01288-352017, 🖳 www.up perlynstone.co.uk), about three-quarters of a mile on the road to Watergate Bay, is geared to families but welcomes coast-path walkers. A night for two people in a tent costs £10.50-15.50 depending on the season.

The enthusiastic *North Shore Bude Backpackers* (☎ 01288-354256, 🖳 www .northshorebude.com, 57 Killerton Rd; 32 dorm beds & 3D/1T/1Tr) is open all year, accepts credit/debit cards and has self-cater-

ing facilities. A bed in one of the dorms costs £14-17 and it's £20 per person for two sharing a room; real value for money.

There is a wide choice of **B&Bs** and hotels some with superb views over the spectacular Summerleaze Beach. Several are on Burn View by the golf club including *Palms Guest House* (☎ 01288-353962, 🖳 www.palms-bude.co.uk; 1S/2T/2D/1F), which costs £25-35 per person (single occupancy supplement £3). It's a very friendly establishment with unusual breakfast choices and an airy light ambience. Along the same road *Links Side Guest House* (☎ 01288-352410, 🖳 www.links sidebude.co.uk; 1S/4D/1F), and *Sunrise B&B* (☎ 01288-353214, 🖳 www.sunrise-bude.co.uk; 2S/3D/1Tr/1F), both charge £25-35 per person. *Tee-side* (☎ 01288-352351, 🖳 www.tee-side.co.uk; 1S/2D/3T, all en suite) charges £23-29 (£30-35 single occupancy).

On Summerleaze Crescent there are several hotels to choose from of which the best is *The Edgcumbe* (☎ 01288-353846, 🖳 www.edgcumbe-hotel.co.uk; 2S/5D/3T). It's one of the smartest places in town and at £38-47 per person is good value for superior accommodation. The view alone is worth the cost of the room.

If you prefer to stay in a pub, *The Brendon Arms* (☎ 01288-354542, 🖳 www .brendonarms.co.uk; 1S/5D/3T, all en suite) charges £33-39 per person; it's right next

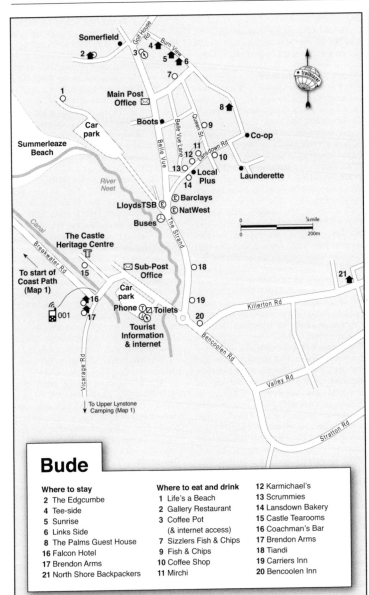

Bude

Where to stay
2 The Edgcumbe
4 Tee-side
5 Sunrise
6 Links Side
8 The Palms Guest House
16 Falcon Hotel
17 Brendon Arms
21 North Shore Backpackers

Where to eat and drink
1 Life's a Beach
2 Gallery Restaurant
3 Coffee Pot
 (& internet access)
7 Sizzlers Fish & Chips
9 Fish & Chips
10 Coffee Shop
11 Mirchi

12 Karmichael's
13 Scrummies
14 Lansdown Bakery
15 Castle Tearooms
16 Coachman's Bar
17 Brendon Arms
18 Tiandi
19 Carriers Inn
20 Bencoolen Inn

ROUTE GUIDE AND MAPS

door to the impressive **Falcon Hotel** (☎ 01288-352005, 🖳 www.falconhotel.com; 4S/25D, all en suite) charging £59 to £74 per person depending on the grade of room.

Where to eat and drink
There is plenty of choice in Bude, almost too much really, although fans of fine dining are going to be disappointed. Starting at the lower end, the town abounds in take-aways, burger bars, chippies, ethnic places and, of course, places selling pasties and cream teas such as the **Coffee Shop** (daily 10am-6pm), on Lansdown Rd, and **Castle Tearooms** (Thur-Tue, 10am-5pm) beside the Canal with outside tables where a cream tea claiming to be 'the best in the West' costs £4.45. Another option is the **Coffee Pot** (☎ 01288-356142; Mon-Sat 10am-4pm but they expect to open more in the main season), Morwenna Terrace, just up the hill from the main post office, a friendly no-frills café doing an all-day breakfast, lunch and afternoon tea. Among the plethora of cafés, **Lansdown Bakery** is the one to head for since they have been serving teas since 1839 so should know how to do it by now.

Karmichael's on Lansdown Rd does pizzas from £5.95 and nearby is **Scrummies** which is essentially a tea shop that becomes a fish restaurant in the evenings. The fish and chip shops do a roaring trade in the season; try the one on Queen St called simply **Fish and Chips**, or **Sizzlers** on Princes St.

Ethnic options include **Tiandi** on The Strand where a Mandarin banquet costs £16.90 a head. Here the décor is 'timelessly decorated with authentic antique screens' which may pull in the crowds on that claim alone. If you prefer a curry, **Mirchi** (☎ 01288-350300; daily 5.30-11.30pm), on Lansdown Rd, serves the usual Asian choices with dishes priced typically from £8.50.

For pub food look no further than the **Carriers Inn** (☎ 01288-352459; food served daily noon-3pm & 6-9pm), on The Strand, which has atmosphere and low beams and you can sit at tables outside and look across the road at the river. The **Brendon Arms** (see Where to stay; food available daily noon-2pm & 6-9pm) is a

lively pub claiming 'the warmest welcome in the West' with Sharp's Doom Bar and IPA on draught. A half lobster salad here costs £10.95.

Just off the main thoroughfare at the corner of Killerton Rd is the **Bencoolen Inn** (☎ 01288-354694; noon-4pm & 6pm to late) with a Spanish restaurant attached although you can eat in the bar or garden if you want. Menu choices include meat platter El Barco (£14.95) and seafood Mediterraneo (£15.45). Among the beers are St Austell Brewery's Tribute at 4.2% and Sharp's real ales.

The Falcon Hotel (see Where to stay) might be the classiest place in town but their **Coachman's Bar** (Sun-Thur noon-2pm & 6.30-9pm, Fri/Sat noon-2pm and 6.30-9.30pm) should not put you off since prices are reasonable: choices include mackerel goujons and deep-fried breaded brie as starters for £5.50 and fishermen's pie at £9.95 or steak and ale pie at £8.95. Watch those calories!

For bistro-style eating, try Edgcumbe's **Gallery** restaurant (see Where to stay; daily 11.30am-4pm & 6-8.30pm except Thur), an imaginatively themed place decorated with local artwork. Where possible their food is from local produce; try their Edgcumbe sausage with creamy mash and home-made gravy (£8.95).

Finally, **Life's a Beach** (☎ 01288-355222; summer daily 10am-10pm) is a stylish and trendy place in which to be seen with a fabulous outlook over Summerleaze Beach. Starters are £5-8 and what they call their 'favourites' cost around £16.

Transport
The main **bus stop** in Bude is at the junction of The Strand, Lansdown Rd and Belle Vue. Western Greyhound's 595 service runs between Bude and Boscastle and the 518 does a circular route with a stop in Widemouth Bay. Hookway's X90 goes to Exeter (nearest **train** station Exeter St Davids), Stagecoach's 85/319 to Bude and First's 76 to Plymouth. See public transport map and table, pp46-50.

For a **taxi**, call Bea-line (☎ 07747-196090, 🖳 www.bea-line.co.uk).

BUDE TO CRACKINGTON HAVEN

The first **ten miles** (**16km, 4-5hrs**) start benignly enough following a grassy cliff-top for about a mile before unexpectedly meeting a road with a small cluster of houses, **Upton**.

The next port of call is **Widemouth Bay** (say 'Widmouth') the first of many beaches popular with surfers and sun-seekers alike and adequately supplied with cafés and places to stay.

Once past these early distractions the hard work begins with a punishing ascent onto **Penhalt Cliff**, the first of several more ups and downs (Millook, Chipman Point and Castle Point) on the trek to **Crackington Haven**. On finally reaching that exciting-sounding destination you'll find a village tucked around a sheltered cove and feel a sense of satisfaction at completing what for most people will have been a strenuous first day's walk.

Despite these testing beginnings there is still time to appreciate the beautiful green cliffs that slope down to the waves below.

(right margin, vertical) ROUTE GUIDE AND MAPS

UPTON [MAP 1, p78]

Upton is a satellite of Bude so it is not surprising to find several places to stay and thus is worth considering, especially if everywhere in Bude is fully booked. The best option for campers is Upper Lynstone Camping (see p74).

At the road, to the left is a smart **B&B** *The Sheiling* (☎ 01288-353128; Easter-Sep; 2D/1T, all with private facilities), a spacious property which is nicely laid out and has a lounge; they charge £28-30 per person (£35 single occupancy).

Advertised on a sign beside the road *Upton Cross Guest House* (☎ 01288-355310, 🖳 www.uptoncrossbedandbreakfast.co.uk; 3D or T, all en suite) is a lovely place with rooms from £25-28 per person; £30-35 for single occupancy. The owner

will run guests into Bude for an evening meal and is used to walkers.

A bit further on, and on the same lane, is *Harefield Cottage* (☎ 01288-352350, 🖳 www.coast-countryside.co.uk; 5 rooms) charging £28-35 per person for B&B. They will pick guests up and drop them off, and can also provide packed lunches.

The fourth choice is up on a hill a quarter of a mile further on but reached from the cliff path. This is *Elements Hotel* (☎ 01288-352386, 🖳 www.elements-life.co.uk; 1S/5D/4T/1F, all en suite) charging £45 per person for B&B and £65 for single occupancy during the season. They have a drying room for walkers as well as a sauna and gym.

WIDEMOUTH BAY [MAP 2, p79]

The village, which gets very busy in the summer, is strung out rather randomly along the main road behind the long beach but it has a **general store and post office** (but this may soon be closed down) selling all the essentials including alcohol. It is open daily.

There are two (seasonal) **cafés** if you need refreshment. At *Café Widemouth* you can get a toasted teacake for £1.10 or toasted paninis for £3.75. Further on is *Black Rock Café* which serves similar fare.

Campers will need to endure the steep climb from the trail to *Penhalt Farm Holiday Park* (Map 3, p80; ☎ 01288-361210, 🖳 www.penhaltfarm.co.uk) where pitches for a two-man tent cost £7-14 depending on the season. They have a small shop for essential foodstuffs and accept Visa, Mastercard and Switch.

Set back from the beach is *The Bay View Inn* (☎ 01288-361273, 🖳 www.bayviewinn.co.uk; 1S/3D/2F, all en suite). Rates are £38-55 per person. *(cont'd on p82)*

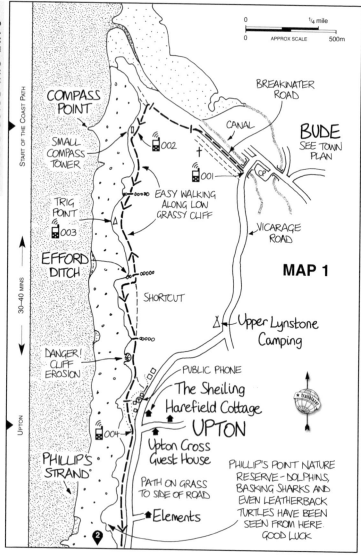

START OF THE COAST PATH

30-40 MINS

UPTON

0   ¼ mile

0   APPROX SCALE   500m

COMPASS POINT

SMALL COMPASS TOWER

002

TRIG POINT
003

EFFORD DITCH

EASY WALKING ALONG LOW GRASSY CLIFF

001

BREAKWATER ROAD

CANAL

BUDE
SEE TOWN PLAN

CP

VICARAGE ROAD

MAP 1

SHORTCUT

Upper Lynstone Camping

DANGER! CLIFF EROSION

PUBLIC PHONE

The Sheiling
Harefield Cottage
UPTON

004

Upton Cross Guest House

PHILLIP'S STRAND

PATH ON GRASS TO SIDE OF ROAD

Elements

2

PHILLIP'S POINT NATURE RESERVE - DOLPHINS, BASKING SHARKS AND EVEN LEATHERBACK TURTLES HAVE BEEN SEEN FROM HERE. GOOD LUCK

★ trailblazer

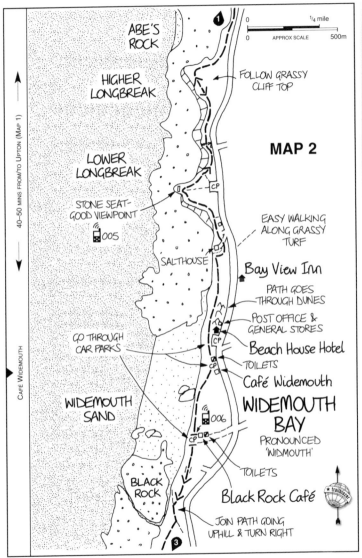

ABE'S ROCK

HIGHER LONGBREAK

LOWER LONGBREAK

MAP 2

FOLLOW GRASSY CLIFF TOP

40–50 MINS FROM/TO UPTON (MAP 1)

STONE SEAT- GOOD VIEWPOINT

005

EASY WALKING ALONG GRASSY TURF

SALTHOUSE

CP

Bay View Inn

PATH GOES THROUGH DUNES

POST OFFICE & GENERAL STORES

GO THROUGH CAR PARKS

Beach House Hotel

TOILETS

CAFÉ WIDEMOUTH

Café Widemouth

WIDEMOUTH SAND

006

WIDEMOUTH BAY

PRONOUNCED 'WIDMOUTH'

CP

TOILETS

BLACK ROCK

Black Rock Café

JOIN PATH GOING UPHILL & TURN RIGHT

1/4 mile

APPROX SCALE 500m

ROUTE GUIDE AND MAPS

MAP 3

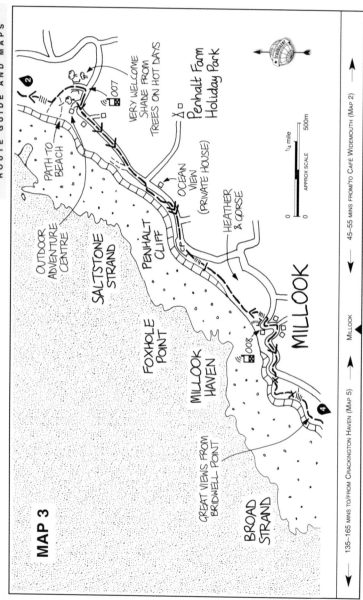

OUTDOOR ADVENTURE CENTRE

PATH TO BEACH

SALTSTONE STRAND

FOXHOLE POINT

PENHALT CLIFF

VERY WELCOME SHADE FROM TREES ON HOT DAYS

⌧ 007

OCEAN VIEW (PRIVATE HOUSE)

Å □ Penhalt Farm Holiday Park

HEATHER & GORSE

MILLOOK HAVEN

⌧ 008

MILLOOK

GREAT VIEWS FROM BRIDWELL POINT

BROAD STRAND

APPROX SCALE

¼ mile

0   500m

0

← 135–165 MINS TO/FROM CRACKINGTON HAVEN (MAP 5) →   MILLOOK   ← 45–55 MINS FROM/TO CAFÉ WIDEMOUTH (MAP 2) →

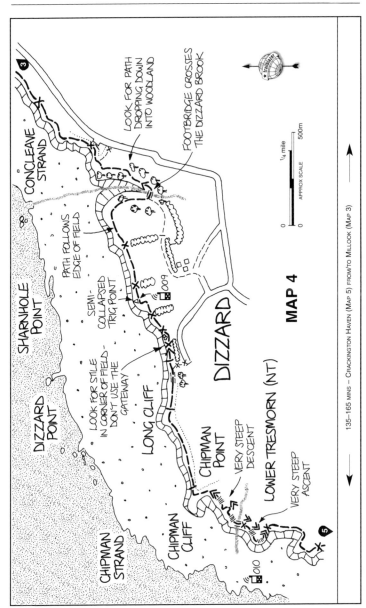

SHARNHOLE POINT

CONCLEAVE STRAND

LOOK FOR PATH DROPPING DOWN INTO WOODLAND

FOOTBRIDGE CROSSES THE DIZZARD BROOK

PATH FOLLOWS EDGE OF FIELD

SEMI-COLLAPSED TRIG POINT

009

DIZZARD POINT

LOOK FOR STILE IN CORNER OF FIELD – DON'T USE THE GATEWAY

LONG CLIFF

DIZZARD

MAP 4

¼ mile   500m
APPROX SCALE
0   0

135–165 MINS – CRACKINGTON HAVEN (MAP 5) FROM/TO MILLOOK (MAP 3)

CHIPMAN STRAND

CHIPMAN CLIFF

CHIPMAN POINT

VERY STEEP DESCENT

LOWER TRESMORN (NT)

VERY STEEP ASCENT

010

(cont'd from p77) The pub is the heartbeat of the surfing community but is happy to welcome walkers. The bar is modern and opens to an extensive area of decking, a good place to sit out and enjoy a pint. Food is served noon-2.30pm & 6-9pm Mon-Sat and noon-8pm Sun.

Next to the general store the *Beach House* (☎ 01288-361256, 🖳 www.beach housewidemouth.co.uk; 1S/6D/1T/2F, all en suite) does B&B from £29 per person plus a £5 single occupancy supplement. Possibly in need of a little modernisation, it's very conveniently situated for the beach and would be fine if you only wanted to stay one night.

Western Greyhound **bus** 518 and 595 stops opposite the post office. See public transport map and table, pp46-50.

CRACKINGTON HAVEN   [MAP 5]

Crackington Haven lies at the head of the cove of the same name and can get busy in summer thanks to its lovely beach, which is ideal for families. The view from *Coombe Barton Inn* (☎ 01840-230345) is fantastic. The restaurant has a menu dominated by seafood including Japanese torpedo prawns (£5.50), lemon sole (£14.95) or whole plaice (£15.50). They also do a takeaway fish (fresh Cornish fish) and chips for £4.99. At the time of writing Coombe Barton did not provide accommodation but they are planning to.

The only other B&B option here is *Lower Tresmorn Farm* (☎ 01840-230667, 🖳 www.lowertresmorn.co.uk; 4D/2F, all with private facilities), a lovely old building, over a mile from the Haven with B&B starting at £28 per person and rising to £36 for a room with a four-poster bed and views to Lundy Island. The single occupancy sup-

plement depends on the length of stay and season. If booked in advance they will do an evening meal for £20 for three courses.

There are two **cafés** competing for your need for a cup of tea and a scone: *Haven Café* and *Cabin Café* stare uneasily at each other across the car park. The latter specialises in home baking and has an amusing line in comments on the black-boards in the window and inside. Their scones are said to be made to a secret recipe of Mum's. They're both perfectly fine so you could try either.

Conveniently, by the bus stop, there's both a **public toilet** and an excellent inter-pretative panel with information on the his-tory and geology of the area which you can read whilst waiting for the **bus**. The service is Western Greyhound's 595 Bude–Boscastle route. See public transport map and table, pp46-50.

CRACKINGTON HAVEN TO BOSCASTLE   [MAPS 5-8]

The cliffs on this **seven-mile (11km, 2¹/₂-3¹/₂ hrs)** stretch are some of the high-est in Cornwall (High Cliff, 731ft, is the highest point on the coast path in Cornwall and the highest sea cliff in the county); the path is careful to keep to the top of them.

If you feel the urge to head for the beach the only access is at **The Strangles** which can be reached by a detour down a steep path. There are some beautiful rugged coves and clefts on the approach to Boscastle, particularly at **Pentargon** where a small waterfall freefalls over a lip into the sea below.

BOSCASTLE   [MAP 8, p87]

Beautiful Boscastle is tucked into a small but deep green valley that ends in a shel-tered natural harbour. During the 18th and 19th centuries roads to the harbour were rough and narrow so the village relied on the sea for trade and transport. Above the harbour is the medieval part of the village, based round the site of the 12th-century

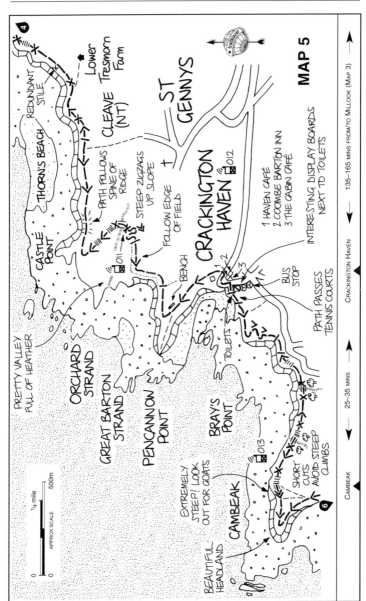

MAP 5

4

Lower
Tresmorn
Farm

THORNS BEACH

REDUNDANT
STILE

CASTLE
POINT

CLEAVE
(NT)

PATH FOLLOWS
SPINE OF RIDGE

ST
GENNYS

STEEP ZIGZAGS
UP SLOPE

FOLLOW EDGE
OF FIELD

O11

CRACKINGTON
HAVEN

O12

BENCH

PRETTY VALLEY
FULL OF HEATHER

ORCHARD
STRAND

GREAT BARTON
STRAND

PENCANNON
POINT

BRAY'S
POINT

TOILETS

1 HAVEN CAFÉ
2 COOMBE BARTON INN
3 THE CABIN CAFÉ

INTERESTING DISPLAY BOARDS
NEXT TO TOILETS

BUS
STOP

PATH PASSES
TENNIS COURTS

EXTREMELY
STEEP! LOOK
OUT FOR GOATS

CAMBEAK

O13

SHORT
CUTS
AVOID STEEP
CLIMBS

6

BEAUTIFUL
HEADLAND

1/4 mile
500m
0
0
APPROX SCALE

← 135–165 MINS FROM/TO MILLOOK (MAP 3) →

▸ CRACKINGTON HAVEN

← 25–35 MINS →

CAMBEAK ▸

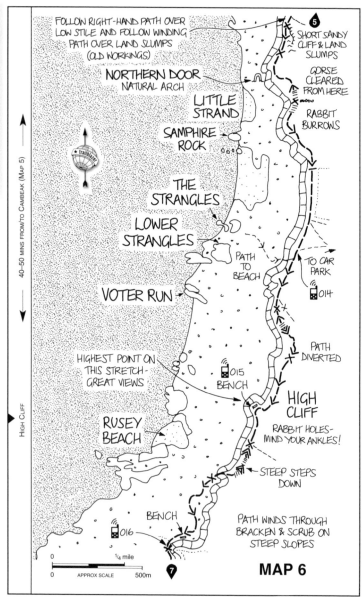

ROUTE GUIDE AND MAPS

40-50 MINS FROM/TO CAMBEAK (MAP 5)

High Cliff

FOLLOW RIGHT-HAND PATH OVER
LOW STILE AND FOLLOW WINDING
PATH OVER LAND SLUMPS
(OLD WORKINGS)

NORTHERN DOOR
NATURAL ARCH

LITTLE STRAND

SAMPHIRE ROCK

THE STRANGLES

LOWER STRANGLES

PATH TO BEACH

VOTER RUN

HIGHEST POINT ON
THIS STRETCH -
GREAT VIEWS

015 BENCH

RUSEY BEACH

BENCH

016

5

SHORT SANDY
CLIFF & LAND
SLUMPS

GORSE
CLEARED
FROM HERE

RABBIT
BURROWS

TO CAR
PARK

014

PATH
DIVERTED

HIGH CLIFF

RABBIT HOLES -
MIND YOUR ANKLES!

STEEP STEPS
DOWN

PATH WINDS THROUGH
BRACKEN & SCRUB ON
STEEP SLOPES

0   1/4 mile
0   500m
APPROX SCALE

7

MAP 6

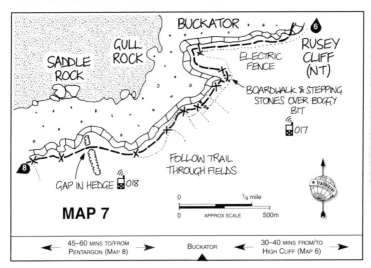

BUCKATOR

GULL ROCK

SADDLE ROCK

RUSEY CLIFF (NT)

ELECTRIC FENCE

BOARDWALK & STEPPING STONES OVER BOGGY BIT

017

FOLLOW TRAIL THROUGH FIELDS

GAP IN HEDGE 018

MAP 7

0   ¼ mile
0   APPROX SCALE   500m

trailblazer

45–60 MINS TO/FROM PENTARGON (MAP 8)   BUCKATOR   30–40 MINS FROM/TO HIGH CLIFF (MAP 6)

Bottreaux Castle from which the village derives its name.

The village achieved headline news in August 2004 when a spectacular and devastating flash flood swept through the streets carrying away houses and cars and creating chaos. A year later most of the buildings had been faithfully restored to their original state and today the village looks smart and spruce.

Worries that the flood would put visitors off have proved unfounded. Indeed many visitors seem to come to Boscastle because of the flood, having seen it unfold on their television screens.

It is a shame if they come only out of curiosity since Boscastle has plenty to offer the visitor the flood notwithstanding. For starters there's **The Museum of Witchcraft** (☎ 01840-250111, 💻 www .museumofwitchcraft.com; Easter to Halloween Mon-Sat 10.30am-6pm, Sun 11.30am-6pm, last entry 5.30pm; admission £3/2 (£10 for naughty children and little monsters!).

The superb new **Visitor Centre** (☎ 01840-250010, 💻 www.visitboscastleand tintagel.com; daily Mar-Oct 10am-5pm, rest of the year 10.30am-4pm) is a triumph with stylish and contemporary graphics and artwork describing the never-to-be-forgotten flood as well as the history and geology of the area and some of the characters who made it famous. It occupies purpose-built premises just up from the harbour and deserves to win awards.

Services
The village is well supplied with shops and places of refreshment all within a small area. There is a **cash machine** in the **newsagent** (Cornish Stores) and one in the Cobweb Inn (see p86) both charging for withdrawals.

The **post office** is up the hill in the upper village along with **Bottreaux Surgery** (☎ 01840-250209; Mon-Fri 8.30am-6pm, closed 1-2pm) although the heart of the village is the lower part with a bakery, cafés and accommodation. There is a **public toilet** at the main car park where the buses stop.

Where to stay
Boscastle Youth Hostel (☎ 0845-371 9006, 💻 boscastle@yha.org.uk; 24 beds), Palace Stables, is open again after having suffered severely in the flood. Adults pay from

£13.95 per night and there are self-catering facilities.

The B&Bs here set a high standard. *Bridge House* (☎ 01840-250011, 🖳 www.cornwall-online.co.uk/bridgehouse-bocastle; 2D/1T, all en suite), right in the heart of the village in a typical stone-built house, charges from £28-32 per person.

Beyond the main car park are two B&Bs equally highly recommended: *Lower Meadows* (☎ 01840-250570, 🖳 www.lowermeadows.co.uk; 4D/1T, all en suite) charges £33-36 per person and, practically next door, *Valency* (☎ 01840-250397, 🖳 www.valencybandb.com; 1D/1T, both en suite) where B&B costs £70-80 per room. They also have a self-catering studio but there is a minimum three-night stay.

Immediately on hitting the harbour from the cliff path, *Pencarmol* (☎ 01840-250435, 🖳 www.pencarmol.co.uk; 2D/1D, T or F, all en suite) presents itself. It has an unrivalled position in an old fisherman's cottage, and is charming, cosy and walker friendly. The tariff is £30-35 per person; single occupancy by arrangement. They have some camp beds which can be put in any of the rooms if necessary. They will transfer luggage and subject to availability can pick walkers up or drop them off.

Next to the bridge, *The Riverside* (☎ 01840-250216, 🖳 www.hotelriverside.co.uk; 1S/7D/3T/2F, all en suite) occupies a building built by Sir Richard Grenville of *Revenge* fame ('At Flores in the Azores Sir Richard Grenville lay'...), extensively refurbished since the flood. The tariff is £32.50-35 per person (single occupancy is £40-50) with a £5 supplement for stays of one night.

The premier hotel in the village is *The Wellington* (☎ 01840-250202, 🖳 www.boscastle-wellington.com; 4S/8D/6T/2F, all en suite). The tariff (per person) is £40-47 for a standard room, £50-57 for a superior cottage room and £60-67 for a superior turret double.

Where to eat and drink

There is a wide choice of sustenance in Boscastle from Cornish cream teas to pasties, fish and chips, pub grub and restaurants: there is something for everyone. If you need supplies for the trail, *Boscastle Bakery* does an excellent quiche for £2.50 as well as filled rolls and sandwiches. *Bridge House* (see Where to stay) has a terrace and tearoom and *Miller's Pantry* (☎ 01840-250223) is a tiny café serving cream teas tucked in beside The Wellington.

The *Cobweb Inn* (☎ 01840-250278; food Mon-Sat 11.30am-2.30pm & 6-10pm, Sun noon-2.30pm & 6.30-10pm) reigns supreme for lovers of pub grub; on Sundays they have a carvery. The pub is open all day in summer and their range of beers includes Sharp's Doom Bar and St Austell's Tribute. The lunchtime menu includes a choice crab sandwich for £3.95 and in the evening you can go for their Cobweb mixed grill for £14.75.

The *Old Manor House* (☎ 01840-250251) serves meals on the terrace with steak and ale pie for £8.50 or simple fish and chips for £4.50.

Riverside Restaurant (see Where to stay) serves locally caught fish including roasted monkfish at £16.95 and crab salad at £12.95.

Finally, at the top end of the market, The Wellington (see Where to stay) has a swanky restaurant, *The Waterloo* (Fri-Wed; booking advisable) but if you don't want to dress up try their *Welly Long Bar* (food served summer daily noon-10pm, winter noon-3pm & 6-9pm) for British cuisine with a twist! The bar is open all day.

Transport

Western Greyhound's 595 **bus** runs between here and Bude and the 594 goes to St Columb Major via Tintagel. See public transport map and table, pp46-50.

For a **taxi**, ring Valency Taxis (☎ 01840-211702).

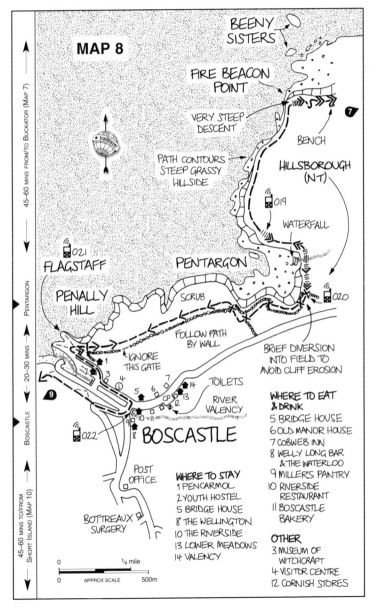

MAP 8

BEENY SISTERS

FIRE BEACON POINT

VERY STEEP DESCENT

PATH CONTOURS STEEP GRASSY HILLSIDE

BENCH

HILLSBOROUGH (NT)

WATERFALL

019

021

FLAGSTAFF

PENTAGON

PENALLY HILL

SCRUB

020

FOLLOW PATH BY WALL

IGNORE THIS GATE

BRIEF DIVERSION INTO FIELD TO AVOID CLIFF EROSION

TOILETS

RIVER VALENCY

BOSCASTLE

022

POST OFFICE

BOTTREAUX SURGERY

WHERE TO EAT & DRINK
5 BRIDGE HOUSE
6 OLD MANOR HOUSE
7 COBWEB INN
8 WELLY LONG BAR & THE WATERLOO
9 MILLER'S PANTRY
10 RIVERSIDE RESTAURANT
11 BOSCASTLE BAKERY

OTHER
3 MUSEUM OF WITCHCRAFT
4 VISITOR CENTRE
12 CORNISH STORES

WHERE TO STAY
1 PENCARMOL
2 YOUTH HOSTEL
5 BRIDGE HOUSE
8 THE WELLINGTON
10 THE RIVERSIDE
13 LOWER MEADOWS
14 VALENCY

45–60 MINS FROM/TO BUCKATOR (MAP 7)

PENTAGON

20–30 MINS

BOSCASTLE

45–60 MINS TO/FROM SHORT ISLAND (MAP 10)

0   1/4 mile
0   APPROX SCALE   500m

ROUTE GUIDE AND MAPS

BOSCASTLE TO TINTAGEL   [MAPS 8-11]

For the next **five miles (8km, 2-2¹/₂hrs)** we leave the high cliffs behind. We start by passing the site of the **Willapark Iron Age fort** before following a convoluted and rugged section of coastline, decorated with small bays, coves and headlands. The walking is not too strenuous and there are plenty of tempting places for a break, not least the sheltered **Rocky Valley**, just before Bossiney, a narrow gorge that provides welcome shade on hot summer days. **Bossiney Mound** is an ancient earthwork and late site of a Norman castle. It is said to be where Arthur's Round Table lies buried.

At the end of this leg are the remains of **Tintagel Castle**, a fittingly mystical spot for a fortress that is reputed to be the birthplace of the legendary King Arthur.

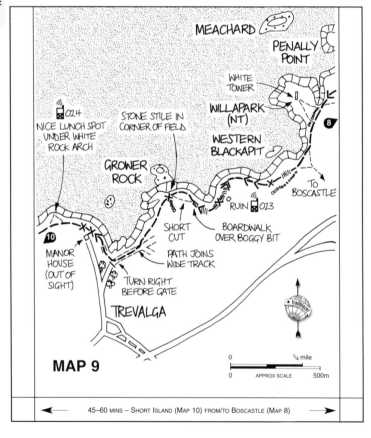

MEACHARD

PENALLY POINT

WHITE TOWER

WILLAPARK (NT)

WESTERN BLACKAPIT

024
NICE LUNCH SPOT UNDER WHITE ROCK ARCH

STONE STILE IN CORNER OF FIELD

8

TO BOSCASTLE

GROWER ROCK

RUIN 023

SHORT CUT

BOARDWALK OVER BOGGY BIT

10

MANOR HOUSE (OUT OF SIGHT)

PATH JOINS WIDE TRACK

TURN RIGHT BEFORE GATE

TREVALGA

trailblazer

0   ¹/₄ mile
0   500m
APPROX SCALE

MAP 9

← 45–60 MINS – SHORT ISLAND (MAP 10) FROM/TO BOSCASTLE (MAP 8) →

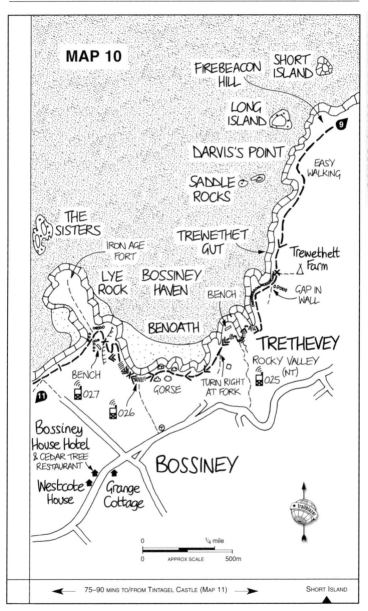

BOSSINEY [MAP 10, p89]

Bossiney is essentially an offshoot of Tintagel and has its footnote in history for having had Sir Francis Drake as its Member of Parliament in the 16th century. However, it is only really worth the detour if you intend staying the night in which case you will take the path that runs off the coast path at Bossiney Haven.

You can't really miss *Trewethett Farm Caravan and Campsite* (☎ 01840-770222; Mar-Oct) right by the path, a Caravan Club site which welcomes overnighters for £6 per person for a single tent. The site has a shop which opens all day during the summer.

Of the B&Bs, *Grange Cottage* (☎ 01840-770487; 1S/2D/1T, all with private facilities) charges £28-32 per person and *Westcote House* (☎ 01840-779194, 🖳 www

.westcote-house.co.uk; 1D/1T) charges £55-60 per room.

The smart-looking hotel standing back from the road is *Bossiney House Hotel* (☎ 01840-770240, 🖳 www.bossineyhouse .com; 10D/6T/3F, most en suite) which is fairly upmarket; the tariff is from £36 to £45 per person (single occupancy supplement £10). Their restaurant, the *Cedar Tree* (daily noon-2.30pm & 6.30-9pm), prides itself on using locally sourced produce including fresh fish direct from Port Isaac. They have a carvery on Sundays.

Western Greyhound's 594 **bus** service between Boscastle and Wadebridge stops here. See public transport map and table, pp46-50.

TINTAGEL [MAP p93]

There has been a settlement at Tintagel since the Iron Age. Recent history is more obvious; the **Old Post Office** (☎ 01840-770024, 🖳 www.nationaltrust.org.uk; daily mid Mar-Sep 11am-5pm, Oct 11am-4pm;

£3) is a medieval 'hall house' with a famously undulating slate roof. It is not now used as a post office.

However, Tintagel is associated in many minds with the legend of King Arthur

---

❏ **The King Arthur myth**

Given the high profile accorded King Arthur in Tintagel where the name is purloined for pubs, pasties and pizzas it is worth pausing for a moment to ask exactly who he was. Sadly the answer is that he is a figure from the imagination.

Whether the saga in Geoffrey of Monmouth's *History of the Kings of Britain* from the 12th century was drawn from legend or not, this dubious work came out hundreds of years after the events described. It was Tennyson who popularised the myth drawing on Malory's Morte d'Arthur and the Victorians lapped it up thanks to its dreamy, romantic imagery and nostalgia for an era when good prevailed over evil but at a terrible cost.

The 20th century re-working of the story brought us *The Sword in the Stone* and *The Once and Future King* by TH White later translated into film versions that help to keep the myth alive. Arthur's adoption by the hippie community ensures that the torch is passed on. Don't be disappointed. Somewhere back in the 6th century a real king called Arthur did actually exist although the stuff about knights and round tables and Merlin the Wizard are fiction. It's a great story and who could fail to be stirred by Tennyson's description of the last battle:

So all day long the noise of battle rolled
Among the mountains by the winter sea
Until King Arthur's table, man by man,
Had fallen in Lyonesse about their Lord.
Alfred, Lord Tennyson, *Morte d'Arthur*, 1885

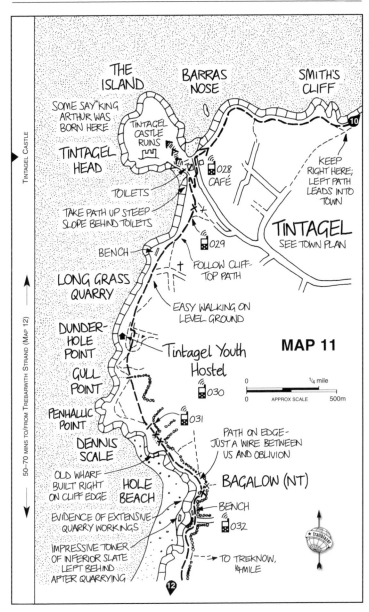

TINTAGEL CASTLE

50–70 MINS TO/FROM TREBARWITH STRAND (MAP 12)

THE ISLAND

BARRAS NOSE

SMITH'S CLIFF

SOME SAY KING ARTHUR WAS BORN HERE

TINTAGEL CASTLE RUINS

TINTAGEL HEAD

10

028 CAFÉ

KEEP RIGHT HERE; LEFT PATH LEADS INTO TOWN

TOILETS

TAKE PATH UP STEEP SLOPE BEHIND TOILETS

029

TINTAGEL
SEE TOWN PLAN

BENCH

FOLLOW CLIFF-TOP PATH

LONG GRASS QUARRY

EASY WALKING ON LEVEL GROUND

DUNDER-HOLE POINT

MAP 11

Tintagel Youth Hostel

0   ¼ mile
0   500m
APPROX SCALE

GULL POINT

030

PENHALLIC POINT

031

DENNIS SCALE

PATH ON EDGE — JUST A WIRE BETWEEN US AND OBLIVION

OLD WHARF BUILT RIGHT ON CLIFF EDGE

HOLE BEACH

BAGALOW (NT)

BENCH

EVIDENCE OF EXTENSIVE QUARRY WORKINGS

032

IMPRESSIVE TOWER OF INFERIOR SLATE LEFT BEHIND AFTER QUARRYING

TO TREKNOW, ¼ MILE

12

★ trailblazer

who is thought to have been born in Tintagel Castle (☎ 01840-770328, 🖳 www .english-heritage.org.uk; daily Apr-Sep 10am-6pm, Oct 10am-5pm, Nov-Mar 10am-4pm; £4.70), which dominates the narrow inlet on its rocky promontory.

There's a *café* (see Map 11; summer daily 10am-5.30pm, winter 11am-3pm), serving locally sourced food, and a shop close by the castle entrance which is down by the cove a longish walk from the village. Luckily there's a Land Rover shuttle service to give you a lift on payment of £1.50 a head. The castle was a stronghold of the dukes of Cornwall but whilst the position is stunning only the walls remain.

There is more to find out about the Arthurian legend at **King Arthur's Great Halls** (☎ 01840-770526, 🖳 www.king arthursgreathalls.com; summer daily 10am-5pm, winter Wed-Sun 11am-3pm; £3.50), which tells the story in detail by a laser light show and you can shop for memorabilia to your heart's content. Dogs are welcome and are free.

Services

Tintagel Visitor Centre (☎ 01840-779084, 🖳 www.visitboscastleandtintagel.com; daily Mar-Oct 10am-5pm, Nov-Feb 10.30am-4pm) has information on just about everything from local wildlife, history, where to go and where to stay and they also have **internet access** charging £1 for 15 minutes.

Both **Londis** (daily 8am-10pm) and **Spar** (daily 7.45am-8pm, to 9pm on Fri and Sat) have ATMs. The only bank in town is now closed although NatWest send a van on Tuesday afternoons to maintain a tenuous service for locals. As well as the **cash machines** at the two supermarkets there's also one outside the **post office** and one inside King Arthur's Arms which is accessible when the pub is open.

Anyone in need of **camping supplies** might find what they are looking for at Camping Sport and Leisure (☎ 01840-770 0600; daily summer 10am-6pm, winter Mon-Sat 10am-5pm). If you need a **launderette** there's one by the big car park on Atlantic Rd and if your feet need attention

Alliance Chemist is on Fore St. For more serious medical needs the **Tintagel Surgery** (☎ 01840-770214; Mon-Fri 8.30am-1pm & 2-6pm) is at the top of the village.

Where to stay

Those intending to stay at *Tintagel Youth Hostel* (Map 11; ☎ 01840-770 6068 or ☎ 0845-371 9145, 🖳 tintagel@yha.org.uk; Apr-Oct, 20 beds, from £11.95, self-catering only) will need to keep going past Tintagel for half an hour to Dunderhole Point. In a fantastic position perched right on the cliff top, the building was once the manager's office for the quarry workings on the cliffs.

Campers should head for *Headland Caravan and Camping Park* (☎ 01840-770239, 🖳 www.headlandcaravanpark.co .uk; Easter/April-Oct); they charge £6-7 per person.

Four Winds (☎ 01840-770300, 🖳 kay 4windsaccom@aol.com; Mar-Nov; 1D/1F en suite) is a modern dormer bungalow with a conservatory and fantastic views north; they charge £28-30 per person for B&B. At the right-angle bend in the road, *Pendrin Guest House* (☎ 01840-770560, 🖳 www.pendrintintagel.co.uk; 1S/4D/2T plus a two-room suite, all with private facilities) offers B&B from £30 to £35 per person; there's a surcharge of £10 for single occupancy. They accept credit and debit cards but no longer do an evening meal. Practically next door is *Bosayne Guest House* (☎ 01840-770514, 🖳 www.bos ayne.co.uk; 3S/2D/1T/2F) open all year and charging £25-30 per person. Some rooms are en suite and some share a bathroom. Both places welcome walkers and cyclists.

Trevenna Lodge (☎ 01840-770264, 🖳 www.trevennalodge.com; 1S/3D/1T/1F) charges from £32.50 per person and is a well-run establishment that likes to source local ingredients for the tempting breakfast menu.

A little nearer town is *The Avalon* (☎ 01840-770116, 🖳 www.avalon-tintagel.co .uk; 5D/2Tr, all en suite) with prices from £64-88 per room, some of which have handcrafted gothic beds. Walkers are welcome

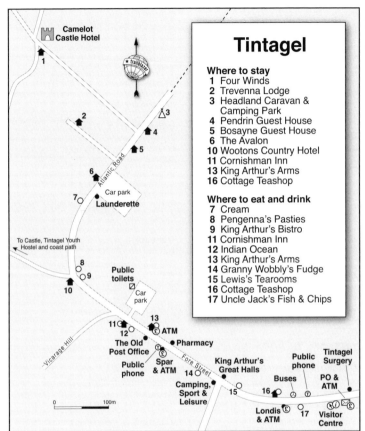

Tintagel

Where to stay
1 Four Winds
2 Trevenna Lodge
3 Headland Caravan &
  Camping Park
4 Pendrin Guest House
5 Bosayne Guest House
6 The Avalon
10 Wootons Country Hotel
11 Cornishman Inn
13 King Arthur's Arms
16 Cottage Teashop

Where to eat and drink
7 Cream
8 Pengenna's Pasties
9 King Arthur's Bistro
11 Cornishman Inn
12 Indian Ocean
13 King Arthur's Arms
14 Granny Wobbly's Fudge
15 Lewis's Tearooms
16 Cottage Teashop
17 Uncle Jack's Fish & Chips

and they also provide luggage transfer. In the town itself *The Cottage Teashop* (☎ 01840-770639; 4D, all en suite) has beds for £26-30 per person. In the heart of things, rooms at *King Arthur's Arms* (☎ 01840-770831; 1S/1T/2F) start at £32.50 per person. The place has been recently renovated but it gets a bit hectic downstairs since it's the only really buzzing pub in the village.

The hotel in Tintagel that aspires to being the classiest is *Wootons Country Hotel* (☎ 01840-770170, 🖳 www.wootons .co.uk; 5D/3T/2F, all en suite) where you'll pay £30-50 per person. Depending on

availability you may be able to do a bit better here so try a little discreet negotiation.

The enormous Camelot Castle Hotel is impossible to miss although it wouldn't be one's first choice for a night's stay being more suitable for tour groups and celebrities.

Where to eat and drink
Tintagel is all about cafés. Just wander along Fore St and take your pick. Among the more traditional teashops is *The Cottage Teashop* (see Where to stay) or you could try *Lewis's Tearooms* or the *Village Tearooms*, all serving cream teas, scones,

teacakes and cakes for a massive carbohydrate overload. *King Arthur's Bistro* also does Cornish cream teas, the price for this ubiquitous delight typically being £3.95. Next door is *Pengenna's Pasties*, a regional chain that crops up all along the coast, where the produce is made and cooked on the premises. They are best bought freshly made so get there early. For fish and chips try *Uncle Jack's*.

Of the pubs, *King Arthur's Arms* (see Where to stay; summer daily 9am-9pm, winter 10am-3pm & 6-9pm) does standard pub fare including their 'famous' big breakfast served all day from 9am onwards with free tea as well. The *Cornishman Inn* (☎ 01840-770238, 🖳 www.cornishmaninn .com; 4D/3T/2Tr/1F, all en suite; food daily 12.30-2.30pm & 6.30-9pm) has daily specials: try the char-grilled tuna steak for £8.95 or the baked aubergine lasagne for £7.95. The main draught beer is Sharp's Doom Bar. B&B costs £50-70 per room and the family room is £120.

For pizzas look no further than the stylish, post-modern *Cream* (☎ 01840-779270; Fri-Wed 3-9pm, closed Nov-Mar), on Atlantic Rd, a long narrow establishment with a small terrace at the back for relaxing on on a warm evening. During the day it transforms itself into yet another teashop to take advantage of the apparently insatiable demand for cream teas (3-5.30pm). Pizzas such as pescatore or their own special (a bit of everything) cost from £8.95. If they are busy they may extend their opening hours.

There's a decent curry house, the *Indian Ocean* (☎ 01840-779000; daily 5-11pm), on Fore St, with a menu that will be familiar to aficionados such as shashlick (£7.95), tandoori king prawn (£10.95) and veggie rogan josh for a reasonable £4.55.

Finally, if you've got a sweet tooth, why not treat yourself to some home-made fudge from *Granny Wobbly's Fudge Pantry* on Fore St. Just follow your nose.

Transport
Western Greyhound's 594 **bus** service between Boscastle and St Columb Major stops here. See public transport map and table, pp46-50.

For a **taxi**, call Camelot Taxis (☎ 01840-770172).

TINTAGEL TO PORT ISAAC   [MAPS 11-15]

This testing **nine-mile (15km, 3^1/$_2$-4^1/$_2$hrs)** section begins with an easy stroll past old tin-mine workings (see box p172) on a level cliff-top. However, once past the attractive hamlet at **Trebarwith Strand** things get decidedly tougher.

Indeed the path between Trebarwith and Port Gaverne is one of the most challenging legs of the whole walk. The trail itself is well-trodden and easy to follow but there is a series of ascents and descents that may have the weak-willed swearing to hang up their boots. If your calf muscles are aching, take comfort in the dramatic views on this lonely coastline, kept hidden from many of the holidaymakers by its inaccessibility.

The hard work is over as soon as you reach the pretty twin villages of **Port Gaverne** and **Port Isaac**.

❑ **Important note – walking times**
Unless otherwise specified, **all times in this book refer only to the time spent walking**. You will need to add 20-30% to allow for rests, photography, checking the map, drinking water etc. When planning the day's hike count on 5-7 hours' actual walking.

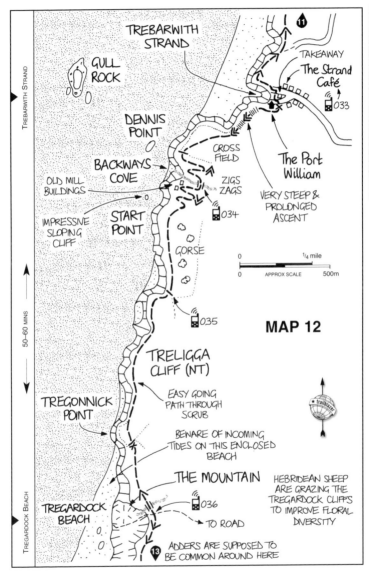

TREBARWITH STRAND

GULL ROCK

TAKEAWAY

The Strand Café

033

DENNIS POINT

CROSS FIELD

BACKWAYS COVE

The Port William

OLD MILL BUILDINGS

ZIGS ZAGS

VERY STEEP & PROLONGED ASCENT

IMPRESSIVE SLOPING CLIFF

START POINT

034

GORSE

0   1/4 mile

0   APPROX SCALE   500m

035

MAP 12

TRELIGGA CLIFF (NT)

EASY GOING PATH THROUGH SCRUB

TREGONNICK POINT

BEWARE OF INCOMING TIDES ON THIS ENCLOSED BEACH

THE MOUNTAIN

HEBRIDEAN SHEEP ARE GRAZING THE TREGARDOCK CLIFFS TO IMPROVE FLORAL DIVERSITY

036

TREGARDOCK BEACH

→ TO ROAD

13 ADDERS ARE SUPPOSED TO BE COMMON AROUND HERE

TREBARWITH STRAND

50-60 MINS

TREGARDOCK BEACH

❏ **Slate quarries on the cliffs**
Between Tintagel and Trebarwith Strand evidence of a once-thriving slate industry can still be seen on the cliffs. Extracting the slate was hazardous and we can well imagine the difficulties faced by the tough men employed here. There were two ways of getting the slate: the first was by digging a hole in the ground in the area of known deposits and winching it to the surface; the other was by getting at the slate that had been exposed by cliff erosion.

Lanterdan and West quarries, both passed on the coastal path, are remarkable for the volume of slate extracted during the three hundred years they are known to have been worked. The isolated pinnacle of Lanterdan is thought to have been left as the fixing point for a cable necessary for winching the slate out of the cliff workings although another explanation is that it contains inferior slate and was left as not worth the effort to extract.

The so-called 'wharf' at Penhallic Point was used as a loading gantry whereby cut slate could be lowered onto ships which were eased close in to the cliffs which would have been trimmed to allow the ships to approach as closely as possible.

Slate was split on the cliff tops by hand and the remains can be seen in the area of the youth hostel (see Map 11) on Glebe Cliff, formerly one of the quarry buildings.

TREBARWITH STRAND
[MAP 12, p95]
This tiny settlement squeezed into a narrow defile overlooks a sandy beach and would be an ideal spot for lunch if it were not within an hour's walk from Tintagel, assuming most walkers will have stayed in the Arthurian realms the previous night.

The Port William Inn (☎ 01840-770230, 🖳 www.smallandfriendly.co.uk; 6D/1T/2Tr; food served daily noon-3pm & 6-9pm, snacks only 3-6pm) sits on an elevated position above the cove. They charge £85-105 for a room and single occupancy is a hefty £85 but special offers are sometimes available. Some rooms are suitable for walkers with dogs. The bar has a certain nautical bias and the menu reflects this with several seafood specials including the catch of the day. Other choices include St Austell beer-battered haddock fillet (£9.25) and vegetarian options (from £8.45). The place is owned by St Austell Brewery so you can guess whose beers are on draught.

The other place for a snack or bacon sandwich is *Strand Café* right on the slipway to the beach.

PORT GAVERNE
[MAP 14, p98]
Port Gaverne is more peaceful than its near neighbour Port Isaac; it consists of a slipway and a hotel with a few cottages scattered nearby.

Port Gaverne Hotel (☎ 01208-880244, freephone ☎ 0500-657867, 🖳 www.port-gaverne-hotel.co.uk; 9D/3T/3F; food served daily bar noon-2pm & 6.30-9pm; restaurant 7-9pm) is the kind of place you look enviously at and think how wonderful it would be to stay there. The tariff is £55 per person; single occupancy attracts a £10 surcharge. The menu is high-end with starters from £5 and mains from £17 unless you go for Port Isaac lobster, grilled or thermidor, which costs £27. Strictly for gastronomes. This is a place with real atmosphere.

Headlands Hotel (☎ 01208-880260: 🖳 www.westcountry-hotels.co.uk; 5S/5T /1F, all en suite and with sea view) charges £72-83 per room for B&B (£54-65 for a single). Their dinner, bed and breakfast tariff is £120-134 per room (£84-98 for a single); their restaurant is open daily 7-10pm.

Western Greyhound's 584 **bus** service stops here. See public transport map and table, pp46-50.

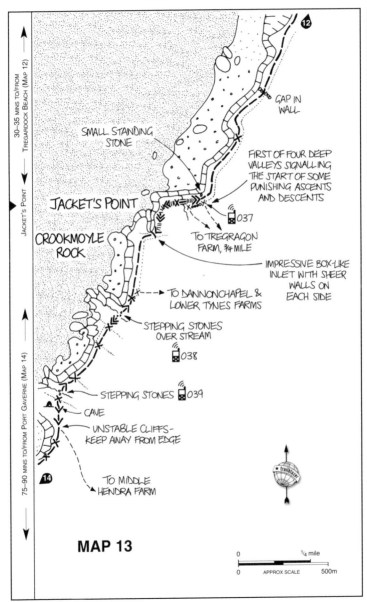

30-35 MINS TO/FROM TREGARDOCK BEACH (MAP 12)

JACKET'S POINT

75-90 MINS TO/FROM PORT GAVERNE (MAP 14)

12

GAP IN WALL

SMALL STANDING STONE

FIRST OF FOUR DEEP VALLEYS SIGNALLING THE START OF SOME PUNISHING ASCENTS AND DESCENTS

JACKET'S POINT

037

CROOKMOYLE ROCK

TO TREGRAGON FARM, ¾ MILE

IMPRESSIVE BOX-LIKE INLET WITH SHEER WALLS ON EACH SIDE

TO DANNONCHAPEL & LOWER TYNES FARMS

STEPPING STONES OVER STREAM

038

STEPPING STONES 039

CAVE

UNSTABLE CLIFFS- KEEP AWAY FROM EDGE

14

TO MIDDLE HENDRA FARM

MAP 13

0   ¼ mile

0   APPROX SCALE   500m

trailblazer

ROUTE GUIDE AND MAPS

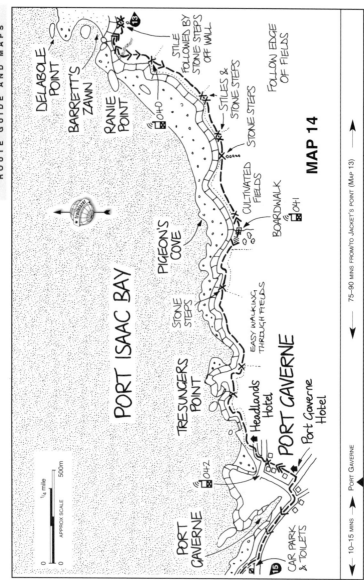

DELABOLE POINT

BARRETT'S ZAWN

RANIE POINT

STILE FOLLOWED BY STONE STEPS OFF WALL

FOLLOW EDGE OF FIELDS

STILES & STONE STEPS

STONE STEPS

CULTIVATED FIELDS

BOARDWALK 041

MAP 14

PORT ISAAC BAY

PIGEON'S COVE

STONE STEPS

EASY WALKING THROUGH FIELDS

TRESUNGERS POINT

Headlands Hotel

PORT GAVERNE

Port Gaverne Hotel

PORT GAVERNE 042

PORT GAVERNE

CAR PARK & TOILETS

15

¼ mile

500m

APPROX SCALE

← 10–15 MINS → Port Gaverne

← 75–90 MINS FROM/TO JACKET'S POINT (MAP 13) →

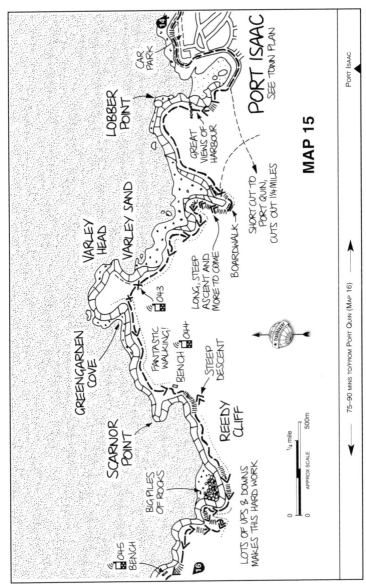

CAR PARK

LOBBER POINT

PORT ISAAC
SEE TOWN PLAN

GREAT VIEWS OF HARBOUR

MAP 15

VARLEY HEAD

VARLEY SAND

☒ 044

BOARDWALK

SHORT CUT TO PORT QUIN, CUTS OUT ¼ MILES

LONG, STEEP ASCENT AND MORE TO COME

GREENGARDEN COVE

FANTASTIC WALKING!

BENCH ☒ 044

SCARNOR POINT

STEEP DESCENT

REEDY CLIFF

BIG PILES OF ROCKS

LOTS OF UPS & DOWNS MAKES THIS HARD WORK

☒ 045 BENCH

0 ¼ mile
0 APPROX SCALE 500m

75–90 MINS TO/FROM PORT QUIN (MAP 16)

PORT ISAAC

Over the hill from Port Gaverne is the picturesque village of Port Isaac. The steep lanes and alleyways are lined on each side by white-washed fishermen's cottages and down by the tiny cove are the still-thriving **fish cellars** and their adjoining **aquarium** where, for £1.50, you can get eye-to-eye with the fish and other creatures that live under the Cornish waves. The harbour area is spoilt to some extent by getting jammed with cars for which it is hopelessly unsuited; the situation is made worse by allowing parking on the beach.

If you are here for a night in the main season go down to The Platt and listen to either St Breward Silver Band (Thursdays) or the Fisherman's Friends (Friday).

Services are confined to shops selling buckets and spades and seaside paraphernalia but there is a **Co-op** in the higher part of the village and a **post office** in the lower. Like other Cornish hideaways, artists have moved in and there are some informal galleries exhibiting their work. Port Isaac is the setting for the TV drama *Doc Martin* starring Martin Clunes.

Where to stay

Port Isaac is a pleasant place to spend a night and for B&B you can't go wrong with *Hathaway Guesthouse* (☎ 01208-880416, 🖳 www.hathawayguesthouse.co.uk; 1D/ 3Tr, most en suite) open from Easter to October and charging £32-40 per person. The view over the harbour from the front is breathtaking.

The *Gallery B&B* (☎ 01208-881032; 2D/1T/1F), on Fore St, charges £55 per room; the rooms are above an artist's studio with work in progress lying about. *Kittiwake Cottage* (☎ 01208-880867, 🖳 www.north-cornwall-accommodation.com;

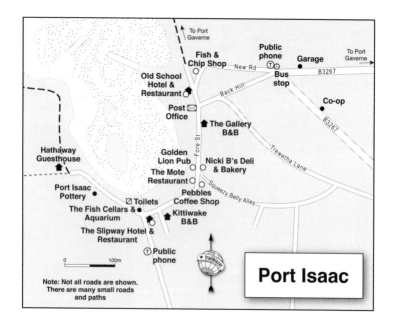

Port Isaac

3D/1T, all en suite), Middle St, is a charming B&B in one of the narrow streets down by the harbour.

The *Old School Hotel & Restaurant* (☎ 01208-880721, 🖥 www.theoldschool hotel.co.uk; 2S/9D/1F, all en suite) charges from £58 per person in high season, £48 in low. The rooms are named after school subjects although how anyone could spend a night in a room called 'Maths' I'll never know. Their restaurant is open daily noon-3pm & 6.30-9.30pm.

The upmarket *Slipway Hotel* (☎ 01208-880264, 🖥 www.portisaachotel.com; 5D/1T, all en suite) is in the very heart of the village with tables under an outside awning. B&B costs £100-120 per room.

Where to eat and drink

Cheap eats are plentiful with a *fish and chip shop*, *Nicki B's* bakery selling pasties and a coffee shop, *Pebbles*, to choose from. For pub food you can decide between the *Golden Lion* (☎ 01208-880336) serving bar meals daily noon-2.30pm and 6-9.30pm

and *The Mote* (☎ 01208-880226, 🖥 www.the-mote.co.uk; Feb-Dec daily 10am-10pm) which has been transformed from its previous incarnation as the Wheel House into a top culinary venue for foodies, the eclectic choices dominated by fish brought in daily from just outside the door. Their menu is seasonal but may include Port Isaac lobster cheesecake (£8.50) as a starter and gurnard with wilted summer leaves and crushed new potato salad (£14).

The *Slipway* (see Where to stay; food served daily noon-2.30pm & from 6.30pm) is the premier place to dine, albeit the most expensive. Food is locally sourced where possible and fish (including crab and lobster and the catch of the day) comes from the fish cellar over the road.

Transport

Western Greyhound **bus** No 584 stops at the Central Garage in the upper village. See public transport map and table, pp46-50.

PORT ISAAC TO PADSTOW   [MAPS 15-20]

This winding **12 miles (19km, 4-5hrs)** of coastline is fairly wild and lonely. It's a strenuous day and you may want to prepare for it by buying a pasty before you set off since the first chance of refreshment is nine miles away in Polzeath. Although there are some long steep sections just after Port Isaac, once past Port Quin the walk poses few difficulties, particularly compared with the previous section. Add to this the pretty beaches tucked between sheer cliffs and the very attractive hamlet of **Port Quin** (only facilities, a tap for drinking water), with its tiny cove housing a sheltered beach, and you have the ingredients for a very enjoyable day's walking. Once past the windswept and beautiful headland at **The Rumps** the path swings by **Pentire Point** and the vast **Padstow Bay** comes into view.

If the tide is out you will be able to marvel at the acres and acres of sand filling the **Camel Estuary** as it sweeps back to **Padstow**. At the holiday town of **Polzeath** you leave the cliffs behind and follow an easy path by the beach and through the dunes to **Rock**, where a passenger ferry leaves regularly for Padstow. It is worth making a detour to **St Enodoc Church** (see Map 18 and box p106) where John Betjeman is buried.

MAP 16

PORT QUIN BAY

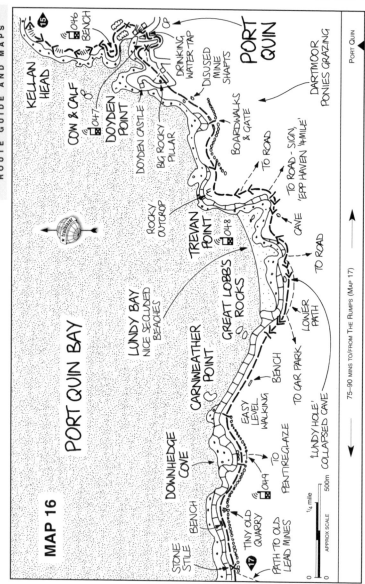

KELLAN HEAD

COW & CALF ■□047

DOYDEN POINT

DOYDEN CASTLE

BIG ROCKY PILLAR

0046 BENCH ■□ ⑮

DRINKING WATER TAP

DISUSED MINE SHAFTS

PORT QUIN

CP

BOARDWALKS & GATE

DARTMOOR PONIES GRAZING

TO ROAD

TO ROAD - SIGN, 'EPP HAVEN ¼MILE'

ROCKY OUTCROP

CAVE

TREVAN POINT ■□048

TO ROAD

LUNDY BAY NICE SECLUDED BEACHES

CARNWEATHER POINT

GREAT LOBB'S ROCKS

LOWER PATH

TO CAR PARK

'LUNDY HOLE' COLLAPSED CAVE

DOWNHEDGE COVE

EASY LEVEL WALKING

BENCH

TO PENTIREGLAZE ■□049

STONE STILE

BENCH

TINY OLD QUARRY

PATH TO OLD LEAD MINES

⑰

¼ mile
500m
APPROX SCALE
0
0

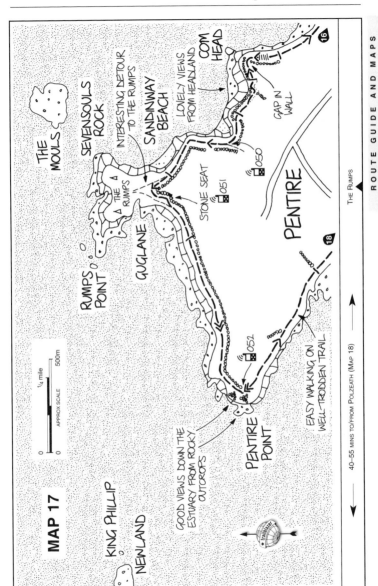

MAP 17

¼ mile
500m
0
0
APPROX SCALE

KING PHILLIP
NEWLAND

THE MOULS

SEVENSOULS ROCK

INTERESTING DETOUR TO THE RUMPS

SANDINWAY BEACH

LONELY VIEWS FROM HEADLAND

COM HEAD

16

GAP IN WALL

RUMPS POINT

THE RUMPS

GUGLANE

STONE SEAT

050

051

PENTIRE

18

052

GOOD VIEWS DOWN THE ESTUARY FROM ROCKY OUTCROPS

PENTIRE POINT

EASY WALKING ON WELL-TRODDEN TRAIL (MAP 18)

40–55 MINS TO/FROM POLZEATH (MAP 18)

THE RUMPS

POLZEATH [MAP 18]

Polzeath is a seaside resort, a place for holiday makers, for families, days on the beach, sand between the toes and rock pools. It is also a place for the surfer and along the strip during the season wetsuits and boards can be hired by the hour, half day or day.

There is little reason for the walker to stop here, in fact every reason to quicken the pace and get away from what seems an alien environment.

All the services are concentrated along the strip facing Hayle Bay including a **post office** and a **Spar** supermarket with an ATM machine.

Campers have two options: *Valley View Caravan Park* (☎ 01208-862391, 🖳 www.valleycaravanpark.co.uk; £18 for a two-man tent in summer), set back from the beach and welcoming walkers, and the sprawling *Tristram Caravan and Camping Park* (☎ 01208-862215, 🖳 www.polzeath camping.co.uk/tristram.htm; Apr to late Oct) which looks out over the beach and charges £15-22 for a two-man tent on a non-bookable pitch; during the season it's absolutely jam-packed so booking in advance is recommended, but it's £23-35 for a bookable pitch though the pitch is larger and comes with electric hook up. The *Salt Water Café* on site is open when the campsite is open, subject to weather – daily in the main season, Tue-Sun only at other times.

Most of the **B&Bs** cater for holiday-makers and tend to turn away walkers during the summer, particularly one-nighters. An exception is *Seaways* (☎ 01208-862382, 🖳 www.seawaysguesthouse.co .uk; 1S/2T or D/1F, most en suite) less than five minutes from the beach and charging from £36 per person.

For **food**, *The Waterfront* (☎ 01208-869655, 🖳 www.thewaterfrontcornwall .co.uk; daily Easter to Sep/Oct 9am-10.30pm, winter Thur-Sun lunch and supper only) has starters from £6.95-8.25 and mains from £13.95-15.95.

Just as you're leaving Polzeath you'll come across *Saltwater Café Bistrot* (sic). It is open daily from 11.45am and serves lunches and teas on the terrace. The breeze is enough to blow the paper serviettes all over the area but hopefully won't spoil the pasta bake of the day at £7.95. The *Beach Café* is open in the main season.

Transport

Western Greyhound **bus** service 584 between Camelford and Wadebridge stops at the beach. See public transport map and table, pp46-50.

ROCK [MAP 19 and map p107]

In recent times Rock has acquired a reputation for being exclusive and pricey, written up in the press as a kind of antidote to Padstow which is perceived in some quarters as having lost a little of its appeal.

Although its snobbish reputation is undeserved, second-homers have snapped up all the available property and in the summer the Porsche-count is high. For the rest of the year, Rock is a quiet residential neighbourhood with a wonderful waterfront.

In my view coast-path walkers should consider making Rock a base for the night whatever time of the year they are walking. It's a short ferry ride (see box p108) from Padstow and is on a bus route with all the services you might require as well as a beautiful beach.

Where to stay

One of the best B&Bs in the area, in fact along the entire North Coast, is the unpronounceable *Tzitzikama Lodge* (☎ 01208-862839, 🖳 www.tzitzikama.co.uk; 2D/1T/3F, all en suite) where two people sharing will pay £70-102 per room.

The double rooms are beautifully appointed and have walk-in showers and comfortable chairs to relax in. This ranch-style property is spacious, open-plan and

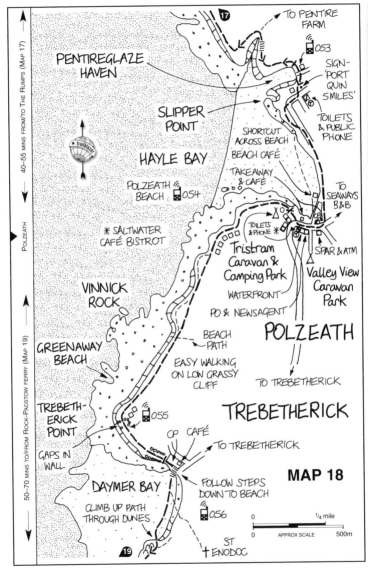

40-55 MINS FROM/TO THE RUMPS (MAP 17)

POLZEATH

50-70 MINS TO/FROM ROCK-PADSTOW FERRY (MAP 19)

TO PENTIRE FARM

053

SIGN-
'PORT
QUIN
5 MILES'

PENTIREGLAZE
HAVEN

TOILETS
& PUBLIC
PHONE

SLIPPER
POINT

SHORTCUT
ACROSS BEACH

BEACH CAFÉ

HAYLE BAY

TAKEAWAY
& CAFÉ

POLZEATH
BEACH   054

TO
SEAWAYS
B&B

* SALTWATER
CAFÉ BISTROT

TOILETS
& PHONE *

SPAR & ATM

Tristram
Caravan &
Camping Park

VINNICK
ROCK

Valley View
Caravan
Park

WATERFRONT

PO & NEWSAGENT

POLZEATH

GREENAWAY
BEACH

BEACH
PATH

EASY WALKING
ON LOW GRASSY
CLIFF

TO TREBETHERICK

TREBETH-
ERICK
POINT

TREBETHERICK

055

GAPS IN
WALL

CP CAFÉ

TO TREBETHERICK

MAP 18

DAYMER BAY

FOLLOW STEPS
DOWN TO BEACH

056

CLIMB UP PATH
THROUGH DUNES

0   1/4 mile

0   500m
APPROX SCALE

ST
✝ ENODOC

19

ROUTE GUIDE AND MAPS

❑ Church of St Enodoc and John Betjeman's grave

A worthwhile and easy detour since it's only a few hundred yards off the coast path, the Church of St Enodoc is named like most Cornish churches after an obscure Celtic saint. The approach from the beach across the golf course brings you to the church path that crosses the fairway, a delightful walk.

Protected now by tamarisk the church is set in a hollow, its 13th-century spire visible above the sand dunes of Daymer Bay. Battered by storms over the centuries it slowly succumbed to the advancing sand which piled high against the walls, blocked the door and began to fill the aisles. By the early 1800s the church had been almost abandoned and the only access was through the roof. Restoration began in the mid-19th century by local craftsmen using as much of

© Philip Thomas

the original stone as possible so it has retained an atmosphere of earliest Christianity even in its final Victorian, basically Norman-style, restoration.

John Betjeman (Poet Laureate 1972-84) is best known for his poetry but he was also a journalist and broadcaster. There is a memorial to his father, his mother is buried here and he had his own grave so placed that the ornate headstone is set looking out to sea over the view he loved.

The Trebetherick area and Betjeman

John Betjeman's love of Cornwall and in particular North Cornwall went back to early childhood when every year his family made the day-long journey by the Great Western Railway from London's Waterloo station to Wadebridge where they'd be met by horse-drawn brake 'out of Derry's stables'; its carriage lamps lighting their uphill way 'past haunted wood and on

© Philip Thomas

> To far Trebetherick by the sandy sea.'
> Soon he'd 'safe in bed' be watching the insects
>   'drawn to the candle flame
> While through the open window came the roar
> Of full Atlantic rollers on the beach.'

> Before breakfast he'd run alone 'monarch of miles of sand
> Its shining stretches satin-smooth and vein'd.
> I felt beneath bare feet the lugworm casts
> And walked where only gulls and oyster-catchers
> Had stepped before me to the water's edge.'

He writes of 'fan-shaped scallop shells, the backs of crabs, bits of old driftwood worn to reptile shapes' and how the sandhoppers leapt around him if he lifted up 'heaps of bladder wrack' left by the outgoing tide. He felt they all welcomed him back and he returned almost annually throughout his life until, staying for longer than usual, he died at Trebetherick in 1984. For further information visit 🖥 www.johnbetjeman.com.

Patricia Major

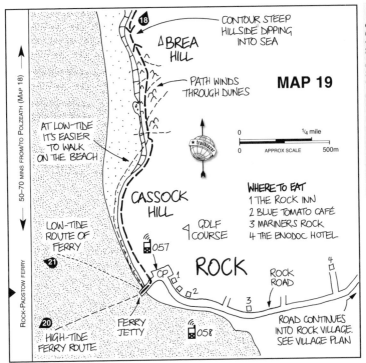

50-70 MINS FROM/TO POLZEATH (MAP 18)

ROCK-PADSTOW FERRY

CONTOUR STEEP HILLSIDE DIPPING INTO SEA

18 △ BREA HILL

PATH WINDS THROUGH DUNES

MAP 19

AT LOW-TIDE IT'S EASIER TO WALK ON THE BEACH

CASSOCK HILL

LOW-TIDE ROUTE OF FERRY

21

GOLF COURSE

📱 057

CP

ROCK

ROCK ROAD

WHERE TO EAT
1 THE ROCK INN
2 BLUE TOMATO CAFÉ
3 MARINERS ROCK
4 THE ENODOC HOTEL

4

20 HIGH-TIDE FERRY ROUTE

FERRY JETTY

📱 058

ROAD CONTINUES INTO ROCK VILLAGE. SEE VILLAGE PLAN

0 — ¼ mile
0 — 500m
APPROX SCALE

furnished with cane furniture rather reminiscent of a hunting lodge. Also recommended is the smaller *Sanderlings* (☎ 01208-862420; 2D, en suite) charging from £70 per room. The beds are king size and so is the breakfast.

Where to eat and drink
Starting at the jetty (see Map 19) where the ferry takes its passengers to Padstow the first place you see is the *Rock Inn* (☎ 01208-863498), which is open all day (food served daily 10am-10pm) and, in the summer, has a **takeaway kiosk** for a quick snack.

The *Blue Tomato* (☎ 01208-863841; daily Apr-Nov 8.30am-7pm, 9am-5pm rest of year) is the place to be seen on the terrace overlooking the estuary. You can get cream teas for £5.95, a knickerbocker glory

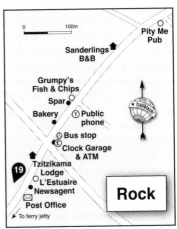

0 — 100m

Pity Me Pub

Sanderlings B&B

Grumpy's Fish & Chips

Spar

Bakery ☎ Public phone

Bus stop

Clock Garage & ATM

Tzitzikama Lodge

L'Estuaire

19 Newsagent

Post Office

To ferry jetty

Rock

❏ **Rock to Padstow ferry**
The Black Tor Ferry (☎ 01841-532239) operates daily (mid Feb to end Oct) between Padstow and Rock, the first one of the day leaves at 8am and the last one at 7.50pm mid July to end August, to 6.50pm June to mid July & September to mid September, to 5.50pm April to end May & mid September to end October; November to mid February Mon-Sat only and to 4.50pm. The fare is £1.50 single, £3 return. In Padstow passengers embark at North Quay when the tide is in but at low tide the ferry operates from the lower beach (see Map 21), clearly signposted. Bicycles (£3 each) can be taken on the ferry.
   Outside the above times the service is maintained by the Rock Water Taxi (☎ 07778-105297, 🖳 www.rock-watertaxi.co.uk; Easter-Oct 7pm-midnight weather and tide permitting, from 7.30pm mid-July to the end of August; £6 return, £4 one-way) so there is enough time to cross to the other side, have a meal and a few drinks, and cross back again before the ferry stops running. In winter the service operates Sundays only 9.30am-4.30pm.

for £4.50 or order a small plate of bouilla-baisse for £11 or a big one for £19.
   Just along Rock Rd is the cheerful *Mariners Rock* (☎ 01208-863679, 🖳 www .marinersrock.com; Easter-Sep food served daily all day) but the menu was changing at the time of writing so contact them for details. There's a restaurant (daily 7-10.30pm) upstairs where booking in advance is recommended.
   The renowned *St Enodoc Hotel* (☎ 01208-863394, 🖳 www.enodoc-hotel.co.uk; food served 12.30-2.30pm & 7-9.30pm) serves superb food but its accommodation is probably out of the average walker's price range.
   About a mile from the ferry is a row of shops (see map p107) that include the **post office**, **newsagent** and the celebrated *L'Estuaire Restaurant* (☎ 01208-862622, 🖳 www.lestuairerestaurant.com; Wed-Sun 12.30-2pm & 7-9.30pm) run by the French

chef Olivier Davoust-Zangari (surely you've heard of him). It's enough to make you say *'zut alors!'*
   Carrying on past the Clock Garage, where there is an **ATM**, *Rock Bakery* (Mon-Sat, 7.30am-3.30pm) is on the left; it's a superb sandwich shop and sells fruit too. Further on we come to the Spar **supermarket** with *Grumpy's* fish and chips next door and if you keep going you'll come to a pub with the curious name of *Pity Me* (☎ 01208-862228; food served daily noon-2pm & 6-9pm). It serves bar meals and has some specials from £8.95. The beers on offer are St Austell's Proper Job at 4.5% and their Tribute at 4.2%.

Transport
Western Greyhound's 584 **bus** stops near the Clock Garage. See public transport map and table, pp46-50. For details of the ferry to Padstow, see box above.

PADSTOW   **[MAP 20, p111]**
Originally Petrocstow after St Petroc established a monastery here in the 6th century, the town clusters round the harbour, cosy and sheltered from the prevailing wind.
   The parish church of **St Petroc's** was built between 1425 and 1450 but the lower part of the tower was built even earlier. The pulpit is decorated with carved scallop shells to honour pilgrims to the shrine of St James in Santiago, Spain.

   Padstow is the most important and the most sheltered port on the north coast although large vessels are prevented from getting in by the **Doom Bar** (see box p110).
   This is definitely a place to dawdle, eat fish and chips and watch the goings-on in the harbour. Boat trips are advertised by men calling out as you pass 'Pay when you come back, if you don't come back you don't pay!'

Padstow has become synonymous with the celebrated TV chef Rick Stein who has made the place his own with (at the time of writing) nine establishments under his name.

For a bit of history visit **Padstow Museum** (☎ 01841 532752, 🖥 www.pad stowmuseum.co.uk; Easter-Oct Mon-Fri 10.30am-4.30pm, Sat 10.30am-1pm; £1.50), an intriguing place with exhibits about Padstow May Day, shipwright's tools, shipbuilding, shipwrecks and other maritime artefacts. It's on the first floor of the Padstow Institute, Market Place.

'**Obby 'Oss day** (see box below) is held here every May, and Carnival Week is in July (see p30).

Services

The town centre is small and compact with everything you need within a few paces of the harbour. You can't miss the invaluable **tourist information centre** (☎ 01841-533449, 🖥 www.padstowlive.com), situated on the North Quay. Their opening hours vary and weren't finalised at the time of writing so phone them for details. However, they expect to be open daily Easter to the end of October. You can get **internet access** (£1 for 15 mins) and they'll find you a room even when the place is at bursting point.

Around Market Place you will find three **banks** (Barclays, Lloyds TSB and HSBC) all with cash machines, a **library** (in Padstow Institute) and a **post office** (Mon-Fri 9am-5.30pm, Sat 9am-1pm).

On a wet afternoon, visit the **cinema** tucked away on Church Lane although not in winter when it's closed. Up the hill above the town is the **Padstow Surgery** (☎ 01841-532346; daily 8.30am-6pm) on Boyd Avenue and a big **Tesco** supermarket (Mon-Sat 8am-8pm, Sun 10am-4pm). There's a **Spar** shop with a cashpoint in town too.

For any camping necessities such as fuel for the stove, the **Sport and Leisure Shop** should have what you need.

Where to stay

You can camp at the excellent *Dennis Cove Camping* (☎ 01841-532349, 🖥 www.den niscove.co.uk) about ten minutes from the harbour and close to the Camel Cycle Trail. Their hiker's rate is £6.50-18.50; it's best to book in advance in July and August though they can usually accommodate walkers with a tent. Leave Padstow along the Camel Trail and after about 200 metres turn right where you see a duckpond on your right. Go down the steps to the duckpond and follow it round (with the pond to your left). You will then reach a small farm track, follow that to the left and you will soon see the campsite through a gate.

There are numerous places to stay since Padstow is an exceedingly busy resort but everywhere gets booked up during the height of the season and one-nighters are not welcomed then. Book well ahead and you may have to plan on a two- or three-night stay, using the buses to take you out to the

---

❏ The Hobby Horse celebration

On May Day bank holiday the 'Obby 'Oss, a man wearing a head mask set on a circular wooden hoop about 6ft in diameter, dances through the town. He is preceded by a Teazer who leads the dance with theatrical movements. The accompanying retinue are dressed in white with added ribbons and flowers.

This celebration has been performed for centuries and there are many theories about its origins. Some say it has pagan roots while others think it began during one of England's numerous wars with France, when the woman of the town dressed up to frighten off an enemy landing while all the men were at sea. Or perhaps it is simply a welcome to the summer, a tradition that has both persisted and changed over the years.

Be aware that if you are passing through Padstow at this time of year you will have to book your accommodation well in advance.

coast path and back again at night. At other times of the year this will not be a problem.

Close to the harbour is *4 Riverside B&B* (☎ 01841-532383; 2D) with one room (the smaller) for £30 per person and the other £39 per person. French and German are spoken here and they offer free internet access. Just up Duke St is the artistic *Trealaw Guest House* (☎ 01841-533161, 🖳 www.trealaw.com; 1S/1D/1D or T, all en suite) with a bijou **tearoom** (summer daily 9am-5pm and open for evening meals in July and August; hours at other times depend on demand) downstairs. They charge £68-70 per room and the single is £35. They can provide packed lunches and evening meals on request.

Another option is *50 Church Street* (☎ 01841-532121, 🖳 www.50churchstreet.co .uk; 2D, en suite), a homely place looking onto St Petroc's Church, where B&B costs £75-80 per room. Also try *10 Treverbyn Road* (☎ 01841-532487 or mobile ☎ 07971-630410; 1S/2D) with rooms (from £30 per person) facing the estuary. *Treverbyn House* (☎ 01841-532855, 🖳 www.treverbynhouse.com, Station Rd; 5D en suite), a lovely turreted house with large rooms and period furniture, charges £37.50 per person. *Pendeen House* (☎ 01841-532724, 🖳 www.pendeenhousepadstow.co .uk; 3D/1F), Dennis Rd, charges £65-90 for two sharing a room and £80-150 for four in the family room.

On Church St there's *Cross House Hotel* (☎ 01841-532391, 🖳 www.cross house.co.uk; 11D) with rooms from £90 or the slightly more upmarket *Tregea Hotel* (☎ 01841-532455, 🖳 www.tregea.co.uk; 8D, all en suite), 16-18 High St, a place with a bleached wood ambience in a lovely creeper-clad building. Single nighters are a no-no here. If you can contemplate staying longer, a room will cost £120 per night. You may prefer to stay in a pub such as *The Old*

Ship Hotel (☎ 01841-532357, 🖳 www .oldshiphotel-padstow.co.uk; 3S/9D/3F, all en suite), Mill Square. It's very central and convenient though not the cheapest at £36-54 per person but it gives discounts for stays of more than one night.

The *London Inn* (☎ 01841-532554; 2D, one en suite), 6 Lanadwell St, does B&B from £55 to £75 per room, and the *Old Custom House* (☎ 01841-532359, 🖳 www.oldcustomhousepadstow.co.uk; 25D or F all en suite), South Quay, charges from £115 per room, single occupancy £95. It couldn't be more central but the bar can get rowdy with drinkers till closing time.

When it comes to expensive places to stay, Rick Stein has a number of options. At what for him is the bottom end of the scale, *Rick Stein's Café* (central reservations ☎ 01841-532700, 🖳 www.rickstein.com; 3D, all en suite), Middle St, charges £88-132 per room; it's very comfortable and tastefully furnished in a *Country Living* way. Visit the website or phone (details as above) for information about other accommodation possibilities.

The *Metropole Hotel* (☎ 01841-532486, 🖳 www.the-metropole.co.uk; 58 rooms, all en suite; food served daily till 9pm) is very traditional and a room costs from £156 for B&B, with a discount for single occupancy; special offers are also available throughout the year. Better still, they have an outdoor heated pool.

Where to eat and drink

Both *Walker's Fish and Chips* (☎ 01841-532915; summer Mon-Sat 8am-10pm, Sun 9am-10pm, winter 9am-4.30pm), on West Quay, or *Chip Ahoy*, on Broad St, are equally good. However, the fish and chip shops in Padstow must feel permanently upstaged by Stein's Fish and Chips (see p112).

For something in the rucksack, there's plenty to choose from. *Doorsteps*

❏ **The Doom Bar**
The Camel Estuary forms a rare natural harbour guarded by a particularly dangerous sand bar across its entrance known as the Doom Bar. Over 300 vessels have been wrecked or stranded on the bar which you can see at low tide.

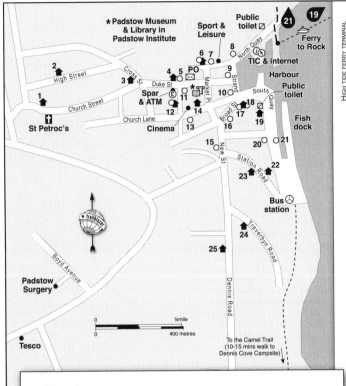

High Tide Ferry Terminal

Public toilet
Ferry to Rock
Sport & Leisure
★ Padstow Museum & Library in Padstow Institute
North Quay
TIC & internet
Harbour
Public toilet
6 7
8
PO
4 5
3 Duke St
2 High Street
1 Church Street
St Petroc's
Cross St
Spar & ATM
11
12
Church Lane
Cinema
9
10
Strand
South Quay
18
17
16
19
Fish dock
13
14
15 New St
20 21
Station Road
22
23
Bus station
24 Treverbyn Road
25
Boyd Avenue
★ trailblazer
Padstow Surgery
Dennis Road
Tesco
0   ¼mile
0   400 metres
To the Camel Trail
(10-15 mins walk to
Dennis Cove Campsite)

Padstow   MAP 20

Where to stay
1 50 Church Street
2 Tregea Hotel
3 Cross House Hotel
4 Trealaw Guest House
6 Old Ship Hotel
12 Rick Stein's Café
14 London Inn
18 Old Custom House
19 4 Riverside B&B
22 Metropole Hotel
23 Treverbyn House
24 10 Treverbyn Road
25 Pendeen House

Where to eat and drink
5 Doorsteps
6 Old Ship Hotel
7 Rojano's
8 Shipwright's Inn
9 Chough Bakery
10 Walker's Fish & Chips and
     Pucelli's (1st floor)
11 Margot's Bistro
12 Rick Stein's Café
13 Chinese Takeaway
15 St Petroc's Bistro
16 Chip Ahoy
17 Pescadou
18 Old Custom House
20 Seafood Restaurant
21 Stein's Fish and Chips

Sandwich Shop (☎ 01841-533443, 12a Duke St; summer Mon-Sat 9am-4pm, winter Mon-Fri 9am-3pm), next door to the post office, offers sandwiches, paninis and jacket potatoes. Alternatively, especially for pasties, try **Chough Bakery** (☎ 01841-532835, 💻 www.thechoughbakery.co.uk, 3 The Strand; Mon-Sat Apr-Oct 8am-5pm Nov-Mar 9am-4pm). An enterprising business with several strings to their bow, they will even send clotted cream, pasties or cream teas to your home by post.

You'll find a **Chinese takeaway** in the town if you can't resist the old sweet and sour but you would do better to eat in **Margot's Bistro** (☎ 01841-533441, 11 Duke St; Tue-Sat noon-2pm & 7-9pm. For a starter try stir-fried squid with ginger, coriander and lemon (£7.50) or for a main course, roast fillet of cod with garlic, anchovies and parsley (£14.50).

There is no shortage of pubs. The **Old Custom House** (see Where to stay; food served daily 10am-9.30pm) is a popular place with a lively clientele and a range of beers on draught from St Austell Brewery. You can eat the usual pub grub here; fresh cod and chips in beer batter (£7.95). The **Shipwright's Inn** (☎ 01841-532451; Mon-Sat 11am-11pm, Sun noon-11pm) serves pub food daily from noon-9pm in the bar and 6-9.30pm in the restaurant.

The **Old Ship Hotel** (see Where to stay; open all day) is another place with a fairly standard menu although helpings are large: their trawler pie costs £10.95 and where possible their food is sourced locally. If you have set your heart on seafood try **Pescadou** (☎ 01841-532359, South Quay; daily noon-2pm & 6-9pm); it's quite a stylish place with bright décor and a Mediterranean feel to it. Mains cost from £16.95 and vegetables are served as side dishes so are an extra cost. They are open from 10am daily for coffee.

Just across the harbour from them is **Pucelli's**, a lively place that occupies an upstairs space above Walker's (see p110). Pucelli's serves pizzas: typically a 9" pizza

costs £6.50 and a 12" one £9.25. **Rojano's** (☎ 01841-532796, 💻 www.rojanos.co.uk, 9 Mill Square; Mar-Nov Tue-Sun 10am-2.30pm & 6pm till late) is another place with Italian tendencies; they offer takeaway as well as eat in.

You would not contemplate a visit to Padstow without giving some thought to visiting one of Rick Stein's restaurants. The central reservation service (☎ 01841-532700, 💻 www.rickstein.com) covers all of them. **Stein's Fish and Chips** (South Quay; Mon-Sat noon-2.30pm & 5-9pm, Sun noon-6pm; eat in or takeaway) is reputedly the best fish and chips you can buy served in cardboard cartons and on scrubbed pine tables in about the least formal surroundings you're likely to find. A meal for two is not going to fall far short of £20. The flagship **Seafood Restaurant** (peak season daily noon-2pm & 6.30-10pm, out of season 7-10pm) is a mecca for foodies but remember you won't escape after a meal for less than £65 per head excluding drinks. At **St Petroc's Bistro** (daily noon-2pm & 7-10pm) you can eat outdoors under awnings in fine weather. The food is superb but even here your bill will leave only small change from £35 per head excluding drinks. The prices at **Rick Stein's Café** (Middle St) are more reasonable (a three-course dinner menu for £22) and the one to choose if you'd love to try at least one of the fabled places whilst in town. The café is open noon-3pm and 6.30-10pm.

Transport

The **bus** terminus is on the South Quay opposite the Lobster Hatchery. Western Greyhound's 555 service goes to Bodmin Parkway station via Wadebridge and the 556 follows the coast road to Newquay. See public transport map and table, pp46-50. See box p108 for details of the Rock to Padstow **Ferry** service. If you need a **taxi** try the following: Padstow Transport Services (☎ 01841-534866), Ocean Taxis (☎ 0798-000-1323) or Call-a-cab (☎ 01841-521184).

PADSTOW TO TREVONE [MAPS 20-23]

It's an easy and enjoyable **five miles (8km, 1³/₄-2¹/₄hrs)** to Trevone with cliff-top scenery at its best without the sharp ascents and descents characteristic of the path up to now.

The path soon leaves Padstow behind and we begin to experience what coastal walking is all about. Past **Stepper Point** we head for a Daymark Tower, an early aid to navigation, and a pause here gives time to take in the Camel Estuary behind and the rugged coastline ahead. Marvellous.

The **Merope Islands**, huge chunks of rock that have split away from the mainland like fragments of broken teeth, and the sudden gaping holes that have opened up in the turf, terrifying to contemplate going near, are two of the strange features of the morning's walk.

Note the increase in the carpet of wild flowers – sea pinks, cornflowers, kidney vetch – particularly during May. Sometimes the flowers reach down the cliffs almost into the sea.

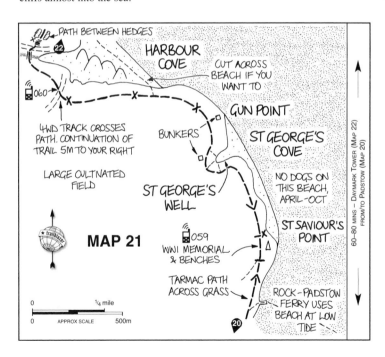

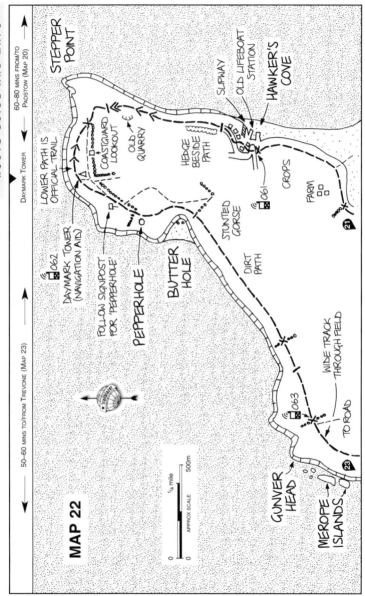

MAP 22

50–60 MINS TO/FROM TREVONE (MAP 23)

DAYMARK TOWER

60–80 MINS FROM/TO PADSTOW (MAP 20)

STEPPER POINT

SLIPWAY

OLD LIFEBOAT STATION

HAWKER'S COVE

COASTGUARD LOOKOUT

OLD QUARRY

HEDGE BESIDE PATH

LOWER PATH IS OFFICIAL TRAIL

062

DAYMARK TOWER (NAVIGATION AID)

FOLLOW SIGNPOST FOR 'PEPPERHOLE'

PEPPERHOLE

BUTTER HOLE

STUNTED GORSE

CROPS

061

FARM

21

DIRT PATH

WIDE TRACK THROUGH FIELD

063

TO ROAD

23

GUNVER HEAD

MEROPE ISLANDS

¼ mile

500m

APPROX SCALE

0

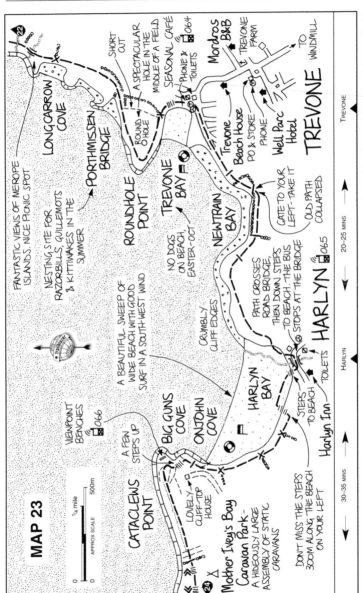

MAP 23

¼ mile

500m

APPROX SCALE

CATACLEWS POINT

Mother Ivey's Bay

Caravan Park –
A HIDEOUSLY LARGE
ASSEMBLY OF STATIC
CARAVANS

DON'T MISS THE STEPS
300m ALONG THE BEACH
ON YOUR LEFT

LOVELY CLIFF-TOP HOUSE

A FEW STEPS UP

VIEWPOINT BENCHES 066

BIG GUNS COVE

ONJOHN COVE

A BEAUTIFUL SWEEP OF
WIDE BEACH WITH GOOD
SURF IN A SOUTH-WEST WIND

HARLYN BAY

Harlyn Inn

STEPS TO BEACH

TOILETS

HARLYN 065

PATH CROSSES
ROAD BRIDGE,
THEN DOWN STEPS
TO BEACH. THE BUS
STOPS AT THE BRIDGE

CRUMBLY CLIFF EDGES

NEWTRAIN BAY

GATE TO YOUR LEFT – TAKE IT

OLD PATH COLLAPSED

NO DOGS ON BEACH, EASTER–OCT

TREVONE BAY

ROUNDHOLE POINT

FANTASTIC VIEWS OF MEROPE
ISLANDS. NICE PICNIC SPOT

NESTING SITE FOR
RAZORBILLS, GUILLEMOTS
& KITTIWAKES IN THE
SUMMER

LONGCARROW COVE

PORTHMISSEN BRIDGE

SHORT CUT

ROUND HOLE

A SPECTACULAR HOLE IN THE
MIDDLE OF A FIELD

SEASONAL CAFÉ

PHONE & TOILETS 064

Mordros B&B

TREVONE FARM

TO WINDMILL

TREVONE

Well Parc Hotel

PO & STORE

PHONE

Trevone Beach House

TREVONE

30–35 MINS   HARLYN   20–25 MINS   TREVONE

ROUTE GUIDE AND MAPS

TREVONE [MAP 23, p115]

This is the first bay after leaving Padstow with seasonal cafés and shops catering for the influx of holidaymakers who populate the place in the season. There is also a **village store** and **post office** (but it may soon be closed down) (Mon-Fri 9am-1pm & 2-5.30pm, closed Wed pm, Sat 9am-12.30pm).

Take the road away from the beach if you want to find accommodation: the first place is *Trevone Beach House* (☎ 01841-520469, 🖳 www.trevonebeach.co.uk; 6D/2T, en suite). It does B&B for £79-100 per room and is a bright, purpose-built establishment with many extras including a teddy bear on each bed. Beyond it in Homer Park Rd, a quiet cul-de-sac off to the left, is *Mordros B&B* (☎ 01841-520769; 1T/1D/1D, T or F, all with private facilities) where you will pay £30-32 for a nice big room, very neatly furnished; it's a relaxed place

and they are welcoming to walkers. There are no surcharges or single-night supplements so it's good value for money. Incidentally, '*mordros*' means the sound of the surf in Cornish.

Well Parc Hotel (☎ 01841-520318, 🖳 www.wellparc.co.uk; 1S/4D/3T/2F, most en suite) charges from £38 to £46 per person. The bar is open daily (11.30am-11pm) for beer and bar meals, food is served daily all day Easter to September, noon-2pm & 7-9.30pm the rest of the year.

The only other place for food is the *seasonal café*.

Western Greyhound's 556 **bus** service between Padstow and Newquay stops at Trevone but not at the beach: you have to walk just over a mile to the junction with the B3278 at Windmill. See public transport map and table, pp46-50.

TREVONE TO TREYARNON [MAPS 23-24]

This section of **five miles (8km, 2-2¹/₂hrs)** is mostly fairly flat with a lovely spot of beach walking at **Harlyn Bay**, perfect for its kind, then out to Trevose Head past the lighthouse. The cliffs above **Mother Ivey's Bay** are great for a long picnic out of season when the hordes have gone.

Booby's Bay and **Constantine Bay** are popular surf beaches with a scattering of houses along the low-lying foreshore. Constantine Bay in particular has a reputation as one of the best surf-pullers in North Cornwall.

HARLYN BAY [MAP 23, p115]

There is a large car park by the bridge at Harlyn Bay and a caravan site but for many walkers *Harlyn Inn* (☎ 01841-520207; 12D, all en suite) will mean a chance of a pint. The bar is serviceable enough but the place lacks style. The food is adequate with mains such as pot-roasted Spanish chicken and chorizo at £10.95. B&B costs from £78 per room but one-nighters have got no chance during the summer. An intact **Iron**

Age cemetery was found on the site of the pub when it was built approximately 40 years ago; it contained over a hundred slate coffins with human remains and bronze and iron ornaments. The finds are in Truro Museum.

Western Greyhound's 556 **bus** service stops at the bridge. See public transport map and table, pp46-50.

MOTHER IVEY'S BAY
[MAP 23 p115 & MAP 24]

The tiny bay is overwhelmed by a massive caravan site that makes the heart quake at the sight of it. *Mother Ivey's Bay Caravan Park* (☎ 01841-520990, 🖳 www.motheriveysbay.com; Apr-Oct) like many campsites around this coastline is a bit of a blot on the landscape but the field for camping in is OK; one tent and two people costs £7.85-20.85. Advance booking is recommended.

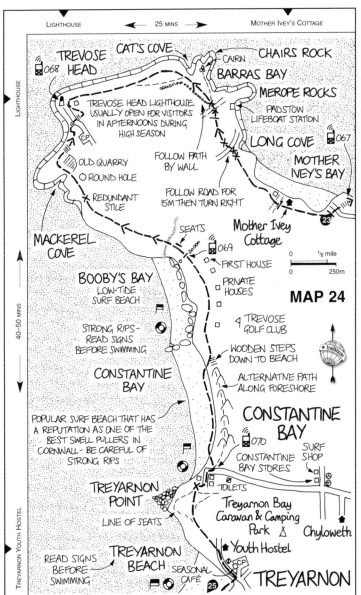

LIGHTHOUSE ← 25 MINS → MOTHER IVEY'S COTTAGE

LIGHTHOUSE

TREVOSE HEAD CAT'S COVE CHAIRS ROCK
068
CAIRN
BARRAS BAY
MEROPE ROCKS
TREVOSE HEAD LIGHTHOUSE, USUALLY OPEN FOR VISITORS IN AFTERNOONS DURING HIGH SEASON
PADSTOW LIFEBOAT STATION
LONG COVE 067
MOTHER IVEY'S BAY
FOLLOW PATH BY WALL
OLD QUARRY
O ROUND HOLE
REDUNDANT STILE
FOLLOW ROAD FOR 15M THEN TURN RIGHT
23

MACKEREL COVE

SEATS
069
Mother Ivey Cottage
FIRST HOUSE
PRIVATE HOUSES

BOOBY'S BAY
LOW-TIDE SURF BEACH

0   1/8 mile
0   250m

MAP 24

STRONG RIPS— READ SIGNS BEFORE SWIMMING

TREVOSE GOLF CLUB

CONSTANTINE BAY

WOODEN STEPS DOWN TO BEACH
ALTERNATIVE PATH ALONG FORESHORE

40–50 MINS

CONSTANTINE BAY

POPULAR SURF BEACH THAT HAS A REPUTATION AS ONE OF THE BEST SWELL PULLERS IN CORNWALL- BE CAREFUL OF STRONG RIPS

070
CONSTANTINE BAY STORES
SURF SHOP

TREYARNON POINT

LINE OF SEATS

TOILETS

Treyarnon Bay Caravan & Camping Park Chyloweth

READ SIGNS BEFORE SWIMMING

TREYARNON BEACH SEASONAL CAFÉ

Youth Hostel

TREYARNON
25

TREYARNON YOUTH HOSTEL

Mother Ivey Cottage (☎ 01841-520329, 🖳 antony@trevosehead.co.uk; 2T en suite) charges £70 per room for B&B; an evening meal (£20) and packed lunches are available if requested in advance. It has a

stunning position on the cliff top but it's miles from anywhere so you'd better get out the Scrabble, there's nothing else to do in the evening. They prefer stays of longer than one night.

CONSTANTINE BAY [MAP 24, p117]

Constantine Bay Stores (**shop**) is a short walk inland. It's also where Western Greyhound's 556 **bus** service between Padstow and Newquay stops. See public transport map and table, pp46-50.

Chyloweth (☎ 01841-521012, 🖳 www.cornwall-online.co.uk/chyloweth-pad

stow; Easter to end Oct; 1T/1D, both en suite) charges from £65 per room for B&B and is highly recommended.

In the summer there is often a **snack kiosk** at the far end of the bay bringing over-priced refreshments to holiday makers.

TREYARNON [MAP 24, p117]

Treyarnon Youth Hostel (☎ 0845-371 9664, 🖳 treyarnon@yha.org.uk) has 68 beds and some of the rooms are en suite. It charges £13.95-21.95 for adults. The cafeteria is open to all Easter to September, for example for coffee and bacon rolls, and they do a lunch-pack for £4.15. Evening meals are available 6-7.30pm. Close by is a seasonal café, *Snak Attack* (May-Sep)

where a breakfast roll (including egg, two sausages, two slices of bacon plus beans and mushrooms) costs £4 and is served until noon.

Behind the YH, *Treyarnon Bay Caravan and Camping Park* (☎ 01841-520681, 🖳 www.treyarnonbay.co.uk; Apr to end Sep) charges £7-11 per night.

TREYARNON TO MAWGAN PORTH [MAPS 24-27]

This **seven miles (11km, 2-2³/₄hrs)** of cliff-top walking is relatively easy with plenty of opportunity to enjoy the impressive scenery.

You first pass **Pepper** and **Warren** coves where weather and the sea have effectively split an **iron-age fort** into three parts. The ditches and ramparts are clearly visible and give you a good idea of what to look for on the numerous other forts and castles along the Cornish coast.

At **Porthcothan** there is a handy shop and bus stop then it's up to one of the most beautiful stretches of coast, **Park Head** and then to **Bedruthan Steps** which gets very crowded in summer. This area was a popular spot with the Victorians who were much taken with the wild sea cliffs.

Just beyond Bedruthan Steps is a National Trust shop and café at **Carnewas**. Leaving the day trippers behind, you're then bound for **Mawgan Porth** where there are plenty of places to take a breather and refreshments.

PORTHCOTHAN [MAP 25]

Porthcothan Stores (daily 7am-7pm in summer; limited hours in the winter) is useful for soft drinks, snacks and crisps etc.

Western Greyhound's 556 **bus** service stops here en route between Padstow and Newquay. See public transport map and table, pp46-50.

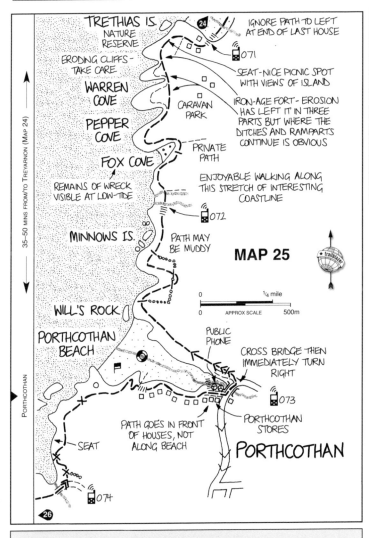

TRETHIAS IS.
NATURE RESERVE

24

IGNORE PATH TO LEFT
AT END OF LAST HOUSE

071

ERODING CLIFFS -
TAKE CARE

WARREN
COVE

PEPPER
COVE

SEAT-NICE PICNIC SPOT
WITH VIEWS OF ISLAND

CARAVAN
PARK

IRON-AGE FORT- EROSION
HAS LEFT IT IN THREE
PARTS BUT WHERE THE
DITCHES AND RAMPARTS
CONTINUE IS OBVIOUS

FOX COVE

PRIVATE
PATH

REMAINS OF WRECK
VISIBLE AT LOW-TIDE

ENJOYABLE WALKING ALONG
THIS STRETCH OF INTERESTING
COASTLINE

072

MINNOWS IS.

PATH MAY
BE MUDDY

MAP 25

35-50 MINS FROM/TO TREVARNON (MAP 24)

0   1/4 mile

0   APPROX SCALE   500m

WILL'S ROCK

PORTHCOTHAN
BEACH

PUBLIC
PHONE

CROSS BRIDGE THEN
IMMEDIATELY TURN
RIGHT

PORTHCOTHAN

073

PORTHCOTHAN
STORES

PATH GOES IN FRONT
OF HOUSES, NOT
ALONG BEACH

PORTHCOTHAN

SEAT

074

26

❏ **Important note – walking times**
Unless otherwise specified, **all times in this book refer only to the time spent walking.** You will need to add 20-30% to allow for rests, photography, checking the map, drinking water etc. When planning the day's hike count on 5-7 hours' actual walking.

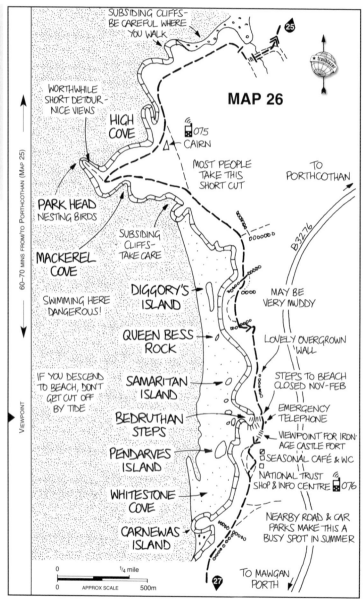

SUBSIDING CLIFFS—
BE CAREFUL WHERE
YOU WALK

25

MAP 26

WORTHWHILE
SHORT DETOUR –
NICE VIEWS

HIGH
COVE

075
CAIRN

MOST PEOPLE
TAKE THIS
SHORT CUT

TO
PORTHCOTHAN

PARK HEAD
NESTING BIRDS

MACKEREL
COVE

SUBSIDING
CLIFFS—
TAKE CARE

B3276

SWIMMING HERE
DANGEROUS!

DIGGORY'S
ISLAND

MAY BE
VERY MUDDY

QUEEN BESS
ROCK

LOVELY OVERGROWN
WALL

IF YOU DESCEND
TO BEACH, DON'T
GET CUT OFF
BY TIDE

SAMARITAN
ISLAND

STEPS TO BEACH
CLOSED NOV-FEB

EMERGENCY
TELEPHONE

BEDRUTHAN
STEPS

VIEWPOINT FOR IRON-
AGE CASTLE FORT

PENDARVES
ISLAND

SEASONAL CAFÉ & WC

NATIONAL TRUST
SHOP & INFO CENTRE   076

WHITESTONE
COVE

CARNEWAS
ISLAND

NEARBY ROAD & CAR
PARKS MAKE THIS A
BUSY SPOT IN SUMMER

VIEWPOINT

60-70 MINS FROM/TO PORTHCOTHAN (MAP 25)

0   ¼ mile

0   500m
     APPROX SCALE

27

TO MAWGAN
PORTH

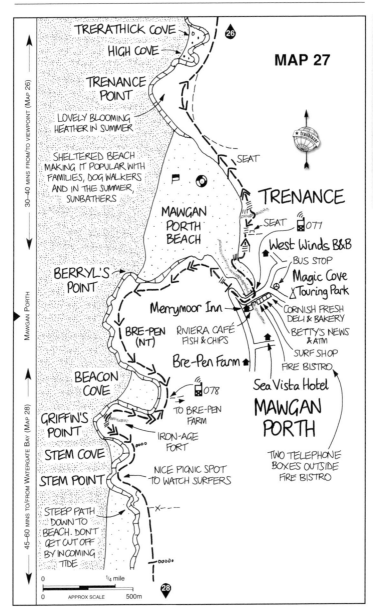

TRERATHICK COVE

HIGH COVE

TRENANCE POINT

LOVELY BLOOMING HEATHER IN SUMMER

SHELTERED BEACH MAKING IT POPULAR WITH FAMILIES, DOG WALKERS AND IN THE SUMMER, SUNBATHERS

MAP 27

26

SEAT

MAWGAN PORTH BEACH

TRENANCE

SEAT 📱077

West Winds B&B

BUS STOP

Magic Cove Touring Park

BERRYL'S POINT

Merrymoor Inn

CORNISH FRESH DELI & BAKERY

BETTY'S NEWS & ATM

BRE-PEN (NT)

RIVIERA CAFÉ FISH & CHIPS

Bre-Pen Farm

SURF SHOP

FIRE BISTRO

BEACON COVE

📱078

Sea Vista Hotel

MAWGAN PORTH

GRIFFIN'S POINT

TO BRE-PEN FARM

IRON-AGE FORT

TWO TELEPHONE BOXES OUTSIDE FIRE BISTRO

STEM COVE

STEM POINT

NICE PICNIC SPOT TO WATCH SURFERS

STEEP PATH DOWN TO BEACH. DON'T GET CUT OFF BY INCOMING TIDE

X---

0   1/4 mile
0   500m
APPROX SCALE

28

30–40 MINS FROM/TO VIEWPOINT (MAP 26)

MAWGAN PORTH

45–60 MINS TO/FROM WATERGATE BAY (MAP 28)

ROUTE GUIDE AND MAPS

MAWGAN PORTH [MAP 27, p121]

Mawgan Porth is a cluster of retail shops and properties around the cove with a large and pleasant beach whose visitors are catered for by shops and places to eat. What was formerly the garage is now *Cornish Fresh Deli and Bakery* (Mon-Sat 8am-6pm, Sun 8.30am-5pm), with a good range of food including filled baguettes and ciabattas. Betty's News has a **cashpoint**.

The beachfront is dominated by *The Merrymoor Inn* (☎ 01637-860258, 🖳 www.merrymoorinn.com; 1S/1T/5D, en suite) where a bed in a room with a sea view costs £35 per person or £32.50 with a country view. It's a no-nonsense pub serving fairly standard food daily all day in summer, winter noon-2pm and 6-9pm. Dogs are welcome: one per room for a £5 charge.

There's a nice B&B up the hill and tucked away in a cul-de-sac, *West Winds* (☎ 01637-860350; 2D/3Tr) charging £22.50 per person with superb views and a homely feel to it, and a little way out of the village *Sea Vista Hotel* (☎ 01637-860276, 🖳 www .seavista.co.uk; 4S/4D/1F, most en suite) charges £30-35 per person.

For farmhouse accommodation, try *Bre-Pen Farm* (☎ 01637-860420, 🖳 www .bre-penfarm.co.uk; 1T/3D, all with private facilities) with rooms from £65 or £37.50 for single occupancy. They do a sideline in aromatherapy if the stress is getting to you.

For campers *Magic Cove Touring Park* (☎ 01637-860263, 🖳 www.magic cove.co.uk) is three hundred yards from the beach along Mawgan Rd. It's a well-appointed site with sparklingly clean toilets and level grassy pitches. The tariff is £9-16 for a tent with two people.

A trendy new place, *Fire Bistro* (☎ 01637-860372; Easter-Oct daily 10am to late), is next door to the pub and serves a full English breakfast for £6.45, and a smaller one for £4.85. Lunch is served from noon to 3pm and dinner from 6pm to late. Their seafood linguine (£7.95) takes some beating or you can go for fish and chips (the posh kind) for £9.50. *Riviera Café Fish & Chips* is open in the main season.

Western Greyhound's invaluable 556 **bus** service stops on Mawgan Rd. See public transport map and table, pp46-50.

MAWGAN PORTH TO NEWQUAY [MAPS 27-30]

The first part of this **six mile (10km, 1½-2hrs)** stretch is perfectly easy once the initial climb out of Mawgan Porth is over with and apart from a minor descent to **Beacon Cove**, a climb to the Iron Age fort at **Griffin's Point** and a short descent to **Stem Cove**, it's plain sailing to Watergate Bay. **Watergate Beach** looks inviting but the path follows the cliffs right the way along above it to arrive at the bay. Where gaps in the gorse permit there are fine views over the beach and if there is a strong swell it is easy to while away an hour watching the crowds of surfers, some flying gracefully with the waves, others spectacularly wiping out. You may also be treated to a fly-past by the RAF who regularly practise manoeuvres over this stretch of coastline from their nearby base and you are likely to hear the planes going to and from Newquay airport.

It would be nice to walk along the beach from Watergate but the tide prevents it so the coast path remains on the cliffs until the first buildings (Sands Resort Hotel) begin to appear. You can walk on the pavement down the hill to **Porth Beach** but it's more pleasant to take the cliff path out to **Trevelgue Head** where a narrow footbridge leads across to the island on which was built one of Cornwall's largest Iron Age forts. As usual there is little of the fort remaining, though the walk to and around it is gentle, with plenty of benches for you to rest

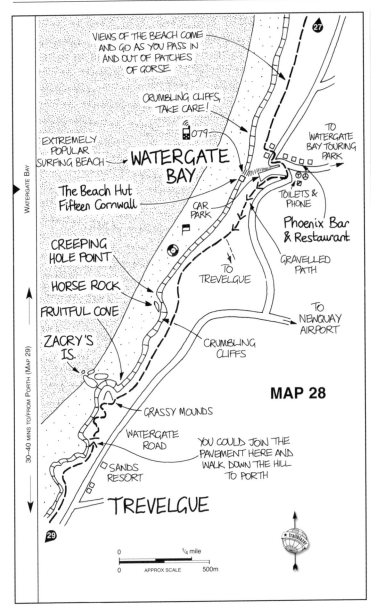

VIEWS OF THE BEACH COME AND GO AS YOU PASS IN AND OUT OF PATCHES OF GORSE

CRUMBLING CLIFFS, TAKE CARE!

079

WATERGATE BAY

TO WATERGATE BAY TOURING PARK

EXTREMELY POPULAR SURFING BEACH

The Beach Hut Fifteen Cornwall

CAR PARK

TOILETS & PHONE

Phoenix Bar & Restaurant

CREEPING HOLE POINT

TO TREVELGUE

GRAVELLED PATH

HORSE ROCK

FRUITFUL COVE

TO NEWQUAY AIRPORT

ZACRY'S IS.

CRUMBLING CLIFFS

MAP 28

GRASSY MOUNDS

WATERGATE ROAD

YOU COULD JOIN THE PAVEMENT HERE AND WALK DOWN THE HILL TO PORTH

SANDS RESORT

TREVELGUE

WATERGATE BAY

30–40 MINS TO/FROM PORTH (MAP 29)

27

29

0   1/4 mile

0   500m
APPROX SCALE

upon, nearly all dedicated to the memory of people 'who loved this spot'. It's not difficult to see why.

From Porth to Newquay is mostly on tarmac. Taking the bus would be a good option though there are some things of interest to look at including the sporting activities on the cliffs above **Lusty Glaze Beach** where groups can be seen abseiling from fixed lines on the cliffs kitted out in safety helmets and harnesses. Once into the town you can take the old tramway, now a pedestrian walkway and work your way along above **Newquay's beaches** – Tolcarne, Great Western Sands and Towan Sands – to the little harbour that's still home to fishing boats.

WATERGATE BAY   [MAP 28, p123]

Watergate Bay is another gastronomic haven with two restaurants for foodies and one that gives great value for money and serves good food too. This is *The Beach Hut* (☎ 01637-860877; summer daily 10am-9pm, winter Mon-Sat 10am-9pm, Sun 10am-5pm) right on the beach with a narrow balcony to sit out on for coffee and cakes. The 'extreme hot chocolate' for £2.95 is a treat. You can have lunch here and may wish to consider the locally caught grilled fish of the day at £10.75 or Fowey River mussels, half a kilo for £7.50 or a whole kilo (respect!) for £14. Ask for plenty of bread and the others can help you mop up the juice.

Right above The Beach Hut is the celebrated *Fifteen Cornwall* (☎ 01637-861000, ▭ www.fifteencornwall.co.uk), part of Jamie Oliver's laudable operation designed to train young people in the catering trade. Booking some way ahead is essential in the summer: bear in mind there is a cancellation charge if you fail to turn up. Open for breakfast 8.30-10am, lunch noon-

2.30pm (to 2pm in winter) and dinner, two sittings, 6.15 & 9.15pm: the five-course tasting menu with coffee starts at £55 a head and is worth it for a special occasion. Alternatively have their three-course set lunch for £25.45.

For those who can't be bothered with fine dining, *Phoenix Bar and Restaurant* (☎ 01637-860353, ▭ www.phoenixwatergate.co.uk; summer daily noon-midnight; winter Fri-Sun noon-midnight) is for you, a no-frills place popular with surfer dudes. It's open all year, is usually busy, and serves food such as fresh seafood, home-made burgers, pizzas and 'flaming woks' from £8.50.

Camping is available at *Watergate Bay Touring Park* (☎ 01637-860387, ▭ www.watergatebaytouringpark.co.uk) which is half a mile out of the bay. The cost for a basic pitch for one tent and two adults is £10-18 depending on the season.

Western Greyhound's 556 **bus** stops opposite the Phoenix Bar. See public transport map and table, pp46-50.

PORTH   [MAP 29]

Porth is an outpost of Newquay but has enough accommodation and eating possibilities to make it a popular choice among walkers reluctant to face the fleshpots of Newquay. It is quiet and has a lovely beach; who could ask for more?

The 556 Padstow to Newquay **bus** service operated by Western Greyhound calls here. See public transport map and table, pp46-50.

Where to stay

Campers need look no further than *Porth Beach Tourist Park* (☎ 01637-876531, ▭ www.porthbeach.co.uk; Mar to end Oct) a site with a stream running down one side of the park. For a small two-man tent the charges are £7.83-18.60 depending on the season. There's a **launderette** on site.

At *The Windward* (☎ 01637-873185, ▭ www.windwardhotel.co.uk; 1S/10D/2T) B&B costs £66-110 per room. At the time

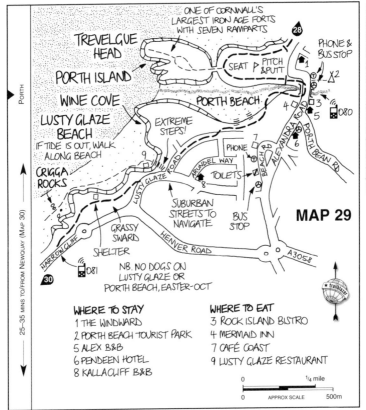

ROUTE GUIDE AND MAPS

MAP 29

ONE OF CORNWALL'S LARGEST IRON AGE FORTS WITH SEVEN RAMPARTS

TREVELGUE HEAD

PORTH ISLAND

WINE COVE

LUSTY GLAZE BEACH
IF TIDE IS OUT, WALK ALONG BEACH

CRIGGA ROCKS

PORTH

PHONE & BUS STOP

SEAT · PITCH & PUTT

PORTH BEACH

EXTREME STEPS!

PHONE

ARUNDEL WAY

TOILETS

SUBURBAN STREETS TO NAVIGATE

BUS STOP

ALEXANDRA ROAD

PORTH BEAN RD

BEACH RD

LUSTY GLAZE ROAD

HENVER ROAD

A3058

GRASSY SWARD

SHELTER

NARROW CLIFF

25-35 MINS TO/FROM NEWQUAY

30

081

NB. NO DOGS ON LUSTY GLAZE OR PORTH BEACH, EASTER-OCT

28

080

trailblazer

WHERE TO STAY
1 THE WINDWARD
2 PORTH BEACH TOURIST PARK
5 ALEX B&B
6 PENDEEN HOTEL
8 KALLACLIFF B&B

WHERE TO EAT
3 ROCK ISLAND BISTRO
4 MERMAID INN
7 CAFÉ COAST
9 LUSTY GLAZE RESTAURANT

0 ..... ¼ mile
0 ..... 500m
APPROX SCALE

of writing they were about to launch a new restaurant; contact them for details.

The breezy *Alex* (☎ 01637-875311, 🖳 www.alexguesthouse.co.uk; 2D/3D, T or F, all en suite) just on the bend above the bay has a cheerful atmosphere and spectacular views and B&B costs £26-34 per person, £35 for single occupancy. *Pendeen Hotel* (☎ 01637-839543, 🖳 www.pendeenhotel .co.uk; 1S/7D/2T/2F, all en suite) charges a reasonable £29 per person. It is part of a group, takes credit cards and you can use the pool at the swanky Porth Veor Manor Hotel nearby.

Overlooking Lusty Glaze Beach before you hit Newquay is a smart B&B that nowhere in the town quite matches: *Kallacliff* (☎ 01637-871704, 🖳 www.kalla cliffhotel.co.uk; 4D/3F, most en suite), Lusty Glaze Rd, charges £33-35 per person for two sharing a standard en suite room going up to £40-45 for a 'premier' room with a sea view.

Their *coffee lounge* (Easter to end Sep, daily open noon-6pm) serves light lunches and cream teas and is open to non residents.

Where to eat and drink

Right on the beach is the colourful local pub, the *Mermaid Inn* (☎ 01637-872954; food served daily 11am-10pm), with Sharp's Doom Bar and Skinner's Betty Stogs on draught. The fare is fairly predictable with some daily specials such as grilled sea bass or home-made steak and ale pie, both of which are £9.95. During the season you might catch a live act here: a popular Elvis impersonator has made Thursday evenings his own. Right across the road from the pub is the *Rock Island Bistro* (☎ 01637-877271, 🖳 www.rock islandporth.co.uk; summer daily 11am-3pm & 6.30pm to late) where the menu includes fish, meat and vegetarian options.

Down at the far end of the beach towards Newquay the enthusiastic *Café*

Coast (☎ 01637-871962; daily Apr-Sep) sells hot and cold drinks, cream teas, cakes, ices and light meals. Opening times depend on whether there are people about. Also consider Kallacliff's coffee lounge (see Where to stay).

For anything from a coffee to a full meal try *Lusty Glaze Restaurant* (☎ 01637-879709, 🖳 www.lustyrestaurant.com; Easter-Oct – daily 10am till late in summer; more limited opening out of the main season so check in advance). The dinner menu includes creamy garlic and woodland mushroom pasta for £10.95 and Cajun swordfish at £13.95. There's a steep flight of steps to get down to the entrance and coming back up with a full stomach is life threatening.

NEWQUAY [MAP 30, p129]

Newquay is the surf capital of Cornwall and the major UK competitions are held on Fistral Beach. Not surprisingly therefore, there are numerous shops selling surfing equipment and the casual gear that surfers like to wear.

Since cheap flights to Newquay Airport became available, Newquay has also become a favourite venue for stag and hen parties to the dismay of many, but the spending power they have brought to the town has led to a burgeoning nightlife.

Services

Sadly the tourist information centre has closed, but information is available from 🖳 www.visitnewquay.org. However, Bank St has branches of **Barclays**, **HSBC**, **NatWest** and **Lloyds TSB** all with cash machines and **Boots**, **WH Smith** and a number of **bakeries** for pasties and filled rolls for the trail. **Pauline's Creamery** does filled baguettes and a 'lunch bag' for £3.20. At 22a Cliff Rd, up towards the railway station, **Newquay Camping and**

❏ Surfing

If you fancy a day walking on water rather than on land there are loads of surf shops up and down the coast offering lessons and equipment hire. If you've never surfed before the best way to begin is with a lesson. They will start you off on a long (7-8ft), soft, foam board which is more buoyant than a normal board and easier to paddle thus making it easier to take-off on a wave. You'll be taught the basics like how to leap to your feet but after that it's practice, and lots of it. Most places charge around £30 for a full day's lesson which includes all equipment and transport to the beach. However, it pays to shop around and ask lots of questions; the price may be for a one-to-one lesson or with a group of twenty people. Alternatively, try body surfing which is much more straightforward and the necessary equipment is also available for hire.

If you prefer to keep your feet dry you may be lucky enough to catch one of the **major surf competitions** held in Newquay each year, such as the English National Surfing Championships which takes place over the May Day bank holiday and the British Cup Surfing over the Spring bank holiday (the last weekend of May).

Leisure (☎ 01637-877619, 💻 www.new quaycampingshop.co.uk; summer daily 9am-9pm, winter Mon-Sat 10am-4pm) stocks everything for walking and the outdoors including camping fuel and there's a **launderette** (daily 8am-8pm) on Beach Rd.

The biggest **supermarket** is Somerfield (Mon-Sat 8am-9pm, Sun 10am-4pm) on Fore St. They have two ATMs with no charge for withdrawing money. There's also a Spar on Tower Rd (daily 8am-10pm).

The main **post office** (Mon-Fri 9am-5.30pm, Sat 9am-12.30pm) is on East St. There's a branch post office on Crantock St with the same opening times. The **internet café** just off Fore St charges 5p per minute.

Where to stay
Camping
The only campsite within walking distance of the town centre is **Trenance Holiday Park** (freephone ☎ 0500-131243, 💻 www .trenanceholidaypark.co.uk) on Edgecumbe Ave close to the zoo and Water World; it's a hectic, popular site and is usually full during the season. They might squeeze in a tent (£7-8.50) but avoid bank holidays when they only take three-night bookings.

Hostels
The scene is changing in Newquay with the old scruffy bear-pit hostels being replaced by trendy, buzzing establishments that could almost be called 'boutique-hostels'. There are two close together on Berry Rd easily recognised by their funky décor and lighting. *Reef Surf Lodge* (☎ 01637-879058, 💻 www.reefsurflodge.info) has 18 rooms sleeping three to ten people and rates of dizzying complexity depending on when you stay and how many of you there are but as a guide you should be prepared to pay £17.50-29.95 per person for room only. A slightly less funky place but no less determinedly modern is *The Escape* (☎ 01637-851736, 💻 www.escape2newquay.co.uk; 24 rooms sleeping 136 people) where again tariffs vary according to when you stay but expect to pay £27.50 for an en suite room or £25 for a 'normal' one. Their appeal is mainly for groups there for the surfing. Breakfast is extra (from £3.75).

One old-style surfer haunt has survived: *Newquay International Backpackers* (☎ 01637-879366, 💻 www.backpackers.co .uk/newquay, 69-73 Tower Rd; 50 beds). A bed in a twin room costs £12.95-17.95 per person but they have a 7-night minimumstay rule at the height of the season. The prices are for accommodation only.

B&Bs and guesthouses
Newquay has a huge variety of places to stay but it is worth remembering that this is a seaside town and the majority of visitors are on holiday. This is the clientele being catered for and although walkers are welcome they are just passing through and their impedimenta of boots, rucksacks and sometimes wet gear can be an inconvenience. Every street in Newquay has at least one B&B. Some streets are lined with them and it should not be difficult to find one with vacancies, the only problem being whether they are prepared to take you for a single night.

The following all offer a reasonable standard of accommodation and say they welcome walkers: *Together Guest House* (☎ 01637-871996; 💻 www.togetherguest house.co.uk, 33 Trebarwith Crescent; 3F) charges from £25 per person and two of the rooms are en suite; *Silver Jubilee* (☎ 01637-874544, 💻 www.silverjubileehotel .co.uk, 13 Berry Rd; 6D/1F, en suite) has hanging baskets and a licensed bar and rooms for £30 to £45 per person depending on the season. They are environmentally aware and are keen on recycling.

Blenheim Hotel (☎ 01637-872921, 💻 www.blenheimhotel.co.uk; 2S/3D/4F, some en suite), 47 Mount Wise, a creeper-clad two-storey house with bright red awnings, does B&B from £20 to £30 per person and an evening meal for £7.50. *Roma Guest House* (☎ 01637-875085, 💻 www.roma guesthouse.co.uk; 2D/1T/2F), 1 Atlantic Rd, overlooks the golf course and has daily rates of £25-28 per person. *Longbeach Hotel* (☎ 01637-874751, 💻 www.long beachhotel.co.uk; 2D/1T/3F), 11 Trevose Avenue, charges £22-30 per person. *Wenden Guest House* (☎ 01637-872604, 💻 www.newquay-holidays.co.uk; 7D en suite) charges £22.50-30 per person but only accepts couples.

Heading up towards the Headland, *Treheveras* (☎ 01637-874079, 🖳 www.tre heveras.co.uk; 3D/1T/3F), 2a Dane Rd, charges £30-35. Some rooms are en suite and they guarantee at least seven items on your breakfast plate. A comfortable, welcoming establishment, walker friendly and right on the trail, this would be a good choice if you wanted an early start the next day.

If you prefer to stay in a pub, *Griffin Inn* (☎ 01637-874067; 1S/6D/6T/1F, all en suite), near the station, does B&B for £32.50 per person but it's in a noisy part of town.

There are lots of hotels to choose from. *Priory Lodge Hotel* (☎ 01637-874111, 🖳 www.priorylodgehotel.co.uk; 2S/10D/15T or F), Mount Wise, is a long-established middle-range hotel efficiently run with large public rooms and a heated pool at the back. Rates are mostly geared to weekly bookings but start at £35-55 per person for one night. The two single rooms are not en suite but the other rooms are. The hotel has a slightly older feel about it but they know their business.

Rather up the scale and beautifully restored, *Harbour Hotel* (☎ 01637-873040, 🖳 www.harbourhotel.co.uk; 5D, all en suite), North Quay Hill, has overlooked nothing in tasteful décor and accommodation. With a superb position it would be a real treat to stay here if only for the Egyptian cotton bedding and brass beds but the tariff of £130-140 per room (£95 single occupancy) might put you off. Food is served daily 10am-9.30pm.

Right up above the town is the impressive *Atlantic Hotel* (☎ 01637-872244, 🖳 www.atlantichotelnewquay.co.uk; 6S/8T/ 40D/6F, all en suite and with sea view), Dane Rd, with deep-pile carpets and mahogany panelling, it breathes affluence and comfort from every pore. The choice of room is complex but a 'classic' room, the cheapest, is £35-80 per person. It would be lovely to indulge yourself for a night here and use the pool, before knuckling down to the trail again.

Where to eat and drink

Approaching from the railway station, the options come thick and fast with Chinese, Indian, Italian, Mexican and fast-food bars following one after the other. On Cliff Rd you can sample *The Maharajah* (☎ 01637-877377, 🖳 www.maharajah-restaurant.co .uk; daily 5.30pm to late) for typical Indian food (eat in or takeaway) or *Jade Garden* (☎ 01637-877953; daily 5-10pm) for Chinese. *La Luna* (☎ 01637-878500; summer daily from 5pm, winter from 7pm five days a week) is for lovers of Italian cuisine and for Thai food where better than *Lotus Thai* (☎ 01637-874994; summer daily noon-11pm, restricted hours at other times): their £15 set menu is a feast.

There are two Mexican restaurants, both on Cliff Rd: *Mexican Cantina* (☎ 01637-851700, 🖳 www.mexican-cantina .co.uk; food served summer daily noon-3pm & 5.30-11pm, winter daily 5.30-11pm; salsa bar open all day) and *Senor Dick's* (☎ 01637-870350, 🖳 www.senor-dicks.co.uk; open daily 6pm to late) with chimichangas for £8.75 and enchiladas for £9.25. Don't forget, Mexican food contains beans!

If you're happy with pub grub, it's in plentiful supply here. *Griffin Inn* (see Where to stay) serves food daily noon-2.30pm and 6-9.30pm. Nearly opposite is the *Towan Blystra* and at the top of Bank St *The Central* (☎ 01637-873810; daily 11am-8pm, or 9pm summer), both busy drinkers' pubs which serve food. The Central is owned by St Austell Brewery. It's probably the main party pub in town: the crowds spill out onto the pavement seating area which has space heaters on colder nights. Smoked ham and eggs costs £6.50, sausage and mash £7.50 and a 10oz rump steak £10.95. Further along Fore St, *Fort Inn* (☎ 01637-875700; daily noon-9pm) is another St Austell Brewery pub. The menu includes homemade vegetable chilli for £8.50 and local Cornish ham salad bowl (£7.25).

Cafés abound but one of the best is *Coast Café* (☎ 01637-854976; Fore St, late Mar-Dec main season daily 8.30am-6pm, low season 10am-4pm) where the little extras make all the difference. Award-

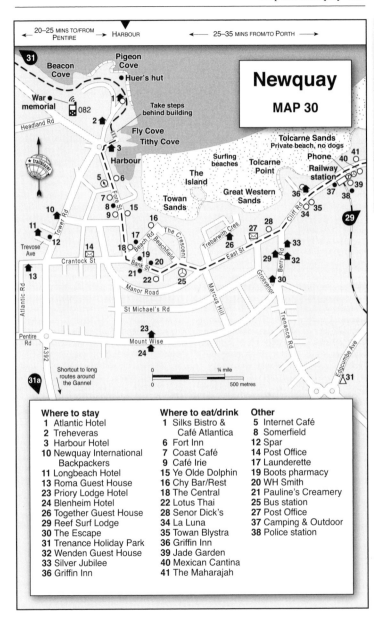

Newquay

MAP 30

20–25 MINS TO/FROM PENTIRE ← → HARBOUR ← 25–35 MINS FROM/TO PORTH →

Pigeon Cove
Beacon Cove
Huer's hut
War memorial
082
Headland Rd
Take steps behind building
Fly Cove
Tithy Cove
Harbour
Tolcarne Sands
Private beach, no dogs
Surfing beaches
Tolcarne Point
Phone
Railway station
The Island
Great Western Sands
Towan Sands
Fore St
Trebarwith Cres
Cliff Rd
Tower Rd
Trevose Ave
Crantock St
Beach Rd
The Crescent
Beachfield
Bank St
East St
Berry Rd
Grosvenor
Atlantic Rd
Manor Road
St Michael's Rd
Marcus Hill
Trenance Rd
Pentire Rd
A392
Mount Wise
Shortcut to long routes around the Gannel
Edgcumbe Ave

0 ¼ mile
0 500 metres

Where to stay	Where to eat/drink	Other
1 Atlantic Hotel	1 Silks Bistro &	5 Internet Café
2 Treheveras	Café Atlantica	8 Somerfield
3 Harbour Hotel	6 Fort Inn	12 Spar
10 Newquay International	7 Coast Café	14 Post Office
Backpackers	9 Café Irie	17 Launderette
11 Longbeach Hotel	15 Ye Olde Dolphin	19 Boots pharmacy
13 Roma Guest House	16 Chy Bar/Rest	20 WH Smith
23 Priory Lodge Hotel	18 The Central	21 Pauline's Creamery
24 Blenheim Hotel	22 Lotus Thai	25 Bus station
26 Together Guest House	28 Senor Dick's	27 Post Office
29 Reef Surf Lodge	34 La Luna	37 Camping & Outdoor
30 The Escape	35 Towan Blystra	38 Police station
31 Trenance Holiday Park	36 Griffin Inn	
32 Wenden Guest House	39 Jade Garden	
33 Silver Jubilee	40 Mexican Cantina	
36 Griffin Inn	41 The Maharajah	

winning scones, Fairtrade coffee, pain au chocolat for £1.50, breakfast special for £3.80, cream tea £3.80, toasted sandwiches/paninis with salad from £2.80/3.30, this is an original and relaxing place to take the weight off your feet. Just nearby is the alternative *Café Irie* (☎ 01637-859200; Easter to end Oct daily 10am-5pm, to 10pm in summer holidays, weekends only in winter) where the dudes chill out. They serve an all-day breakfast, home-made bread and cakes and use local produce where possible. They are expecting to open a deli next door from Easter 2009.

If you want a proper meal, *Ye Olde Dolphin* (☎ 01637-874262; daily 6pm to late, Sun noon-3pm) is one of the oldest established restaurants in Newquay. They claim to have the best wine cellar in town and who can doubt them? Their early birds menu (served daily 6-7pm) has three courses for £14.45.

Several trendy eateries have sprung up close to the beach including one on Lusty Glaze Beach (see p126).

There's plenty going on at *The Chy Bar & Restaurant* (☎ 01637-873415, 🖳 www.the-chy.co.uk; Beach Rd; summer daily 10am-10pm, winter hours variable) offering dishes such as fresh pan-seared scallops with celeriac and chorizo as a starter for £6.50 and herb and horseradish mackerel fillets at £11.50. The veggie options are imaginative – try glazed butternut squash on a puy lentil casserole with garlic croute (£10.50).

Silks Bistro and Champagne Bar (from 11am for coffee, lunch noon-3pm, evening 6-10.30pm at the Atlantic Hotel, see Where to stay) is among the top places to eat here. The ambience is just on the formal side of relaxed and the surfing crowd don't tend to come in here fresh off the beach. The menu choices are comprehensive and interesting and include daily specials biased towards seafood such as Six Falmouth Bay oysters served with a glass of champagne for £13.95 and pan-fried sea bass at £15.95. The hotel's *Café Atlantica* (daily 8.30am-6pm) serves Italian food.

Beyond the Headland on Fistral Beach is *Fistral Blu* (Map 31; ☎ 01637-879444, 🖳 www.fistral-blu.co.uk; daily all day, evening menu 6.30-10pm) overlooking the fabulous Fistral Beach where you can watch the surfers in action. The complex has retail concessions and shops as well as a huge deck to wander about on and watch from when there's a competition in progress. Upstairs in the restaurant you can have an 'out-of-the-blu' salad for £7 or Cornish fish pie for £11. The menu changes seasonally but may include classic moules marinière and piri piri chicken in the evening.

Transport
The **bus station** is right in the centre of town. Western Greyhound operates a number of services from here: the 501 goes to St Ives, the 510 to Exeter, the 556 to Padstow, the 585, 586, 587 & 597 take different routes to Truro, and the 588 operates a circular route to Pentire Head. Summercourt (403) and First (89 & 90) also operate services to Truro; First's 305 service goes to Porth.

Newquay's **railway station**, just off Cliff Rd, has trains to Par from where you can change for Penzance and Bodmin Parkway. First Great Western's ticket office is open Mon-Fri 9.30am-3pm, Sat 8.30am-5pm and Sun 9.30am-4pm. See public transport map and table, pp46-50.

There are two National Express **coach** services (see box p44) a day. **Newquay Airport** (☎ 01637-860600, 🖳 www.newquaycornwallairport.com) has flights from a number of UK airports.

For a **taxi**, call A2B Taxis (☎ 01637-877777) or Wave Taxis (☎ 01637-851123).

NEWQUAY TO CRANTOCK   [MAPS 30-31 & 31a]

This simple **2-mile (3km, 35-45 mins** if using ferry, longer for other options) stretch leaves Newquay by way of the headland, crosses inland of **Fistral Beach** through the dunes and becomes involved with suburban streets, most of them with Pentire in the name; choose your route. The only obstacle of the route is the crossing of the tidal **Gannel River** and how easy this is will depend on the state of the tide. It helps to have picked up a copy of the Tide Tables which are available at the tourist information centre and at many other places such as hotels and some shops.

You can cross by ferry at high tide, by the Penpol footbridge or by walking the long way round by the Trevemper footbridge (see options in detail below).

Once across the Gannel, you may decide to walk the short distance inland to **Crantock** (see pp132-4) for what limited services it has to offer or carry on on the official route, or if it is low tide walk along the beach through the dunes.

Crossing the Gannel River   [MAPS 31 & 31a]

If you haven't already bought a tide table (see box below) you are probably going to need one now. There are four ways to cross the Gannel; which one you take depends on the time of year and the state of the tide. On the Pentire side light refreshments, including sandwiches, cakes and hot drinks, are available at the *Fern Pit Café* (end May-mid Sep, daily 10am-6pm), open whether the ferry is running or not. There is also a seasonal café on the opposite side near the car park. Note: all distances are Newquay–Crantock.

● The official crossing (2 miles/3km) is via the **Fern Pit Ferry (A)** (☎ 01637-873181, 🖥 www.fernpit.co.uk). This is the quickest and easiest option but the ferry (£1 each way) only operates from late May to mid-September, daily 10am-6pm. If the tide is out you can walk across their footbridge (note this is also closed during the winter) for free;

● The second option (3 miles/5km) is to cross the **Penpol Footbridge (B)**. This footbridge is tidal but you should be able to cross two to four hours either side

---

❏ **Tides**

Tides are the regular rise and fall of the ocean caused by the gravitational pull of the moon. They are actually very long waves which follow the path of the moon across the ocean. Twice a day there is a high tide and a low tide and there are approximately $6\frac{1}{4}$ hours between high and low water.

Spring tides (derived from the German word *springan* meaning to jump) are tides with a very large range that occur just after the full- and new-moon phases when the gravitational forces of the sun and the moon line up. High tides are higher and low tides lower than normal. Spring tides occur twice every month. **Neap tides** occur halfway between each spring tide and are tides with the smallest range, so you get comparatively high low tides and low high tides. They occur at the first and third quarters of the moon when the sun, moon and earth are all at right angles to each other, hence the gravitational forces of the sun and moon are weakened.

It is a good idea to carry a tide table with you; they can be purchased for about 90p from newsagents or TICs in coastal areas.

of low tide. If you are in any doubt whatsoever it is very easy to continue walking from here to the next bridge further up the Gannel;
● The third option (5 miles/8km) is the **Laurie Bridge** (**C**; **Map 31a**), which is also a bridleway. The only time it's not possible to cross this bridge is one hour either side of a high spring tide;
● The final option (6 miles/10km) is to follow the **main road** (A392) right around the Gannel. However, this is a long and boring walk with the constant smell of exhaust fumes. You really would do much better to wait for the tides, plan ahead or catch a bus (see public transport map and table, pp46-50).

CRANTOCK   [MAP 31]

Crantock is a traditional Cornish village with thatched cottages clustered round a village green. It's a ten-minute walk uphill from Crantock Beach where there is a barely adequate *seasonal café* so if you need refreshments I would advise going into the village.

There is a curious enclosure known as **Crantock Round Garden** to look at and perhaps sit inside to eat your sandwiches bought at the village shop. It used to be a pound (a place to keep stray cattle in until they could be claimed). You can even check out the **stocks**, last used in the 19th century, round the back of the church.

Londis Store and post office (Mon-Sat 7.30am-8pm, closed Wed pm, Sun 8am-6pm) has a good range of essentials including sandwiches and fruit.

The two pubs stand opposite each other so take your choice. *The Old Albion* (☎ 01637-830243; Easter-Oct bar meals daily noon-2pm & 6.30-9pm; rest of year Sun lunch noon-2pm only) is 400 years old and a traditional village pub. *The Cornishman* (☎ 01637-830869; food served Easter-Oct daily noon-9pm) has bar meals with mains from £6.95, or sandwiches from £2.50 and soup of the day from £3.50.

If pub food doesn't attract you, *Cosynook Tea Gardens* (☎ 01637-830324; Easter-Oct daily 10.30am-5pm & July & Aug Wed-Fri 6.30-8.30pm) besides doing morning coffee, lunches and cream teas opens for evening meals in summer. Booking is essential. The mussels in garlic butter at £7.95 sound enticing.

For campers, *Quarryfield Caravan and Camping Park* (☎ 01637-872792, ☐ www.quarryfield.co.uk) charges £6-9 per person depending on the season and is open from Easter to the end of October.

There are a few **B&Bs** including the recommended *Carden Cottage* (☎ 01637-830806, ☐ cardencottage@btinternet.com; 2D/1T, all en suite), a charming cottage in a quiet location. The rooms have king-size beds and they charge from £34 per person. Walkers are frequent guests here and are made welcome; they also offer baggage transfer. *Tregenna House* (☎ 01637-830222, ☐ www.tregennahouse.co.uk; 1S/3D/1F) charges £65-70 per room (£38.50 for single occupancy), or £75 for the family room including use of the pool in the season; it's great for a dip after a sweaty day on the trail. *Sandbanks* (☎ 01637-830130, ☐ alisonsmithurst@hotmail.com; 2D/1T), Beach Rd, is open March to October and charges from £25 per person. One of the doubles is en suite but the other rooms share facilities.

To the west of the village is a larger establishment, *Fairbank Hotel* (☎ 01637-830424, ☐ www.fairbankhotel.co.uk, West Pentire Rd; 2S/10D/2T, all en suite) where you'll pay £85-95 per room (£40 for a single) for B&B but they are licensed and have a restaurant (open from 7pm).

Ten minutes walk along the coast path up on the left overlooking the bay is the swanky *Crantock Bay Hotel* (Map 32; ☎ 01637-830229, ☐ www.crantockbayhotel.co.uk; mid Feb to end Oct; 8S/14D/10T, all en suite) where dinner, bed and breakfast is from £63 to £122 per person; the higher rates are for a room with a sea view. Deduct £20 for B&B only. Food is served daily noon-2pm and 7-8.30pm. Lunch can be

ROUTE GUIDE AND MAPS

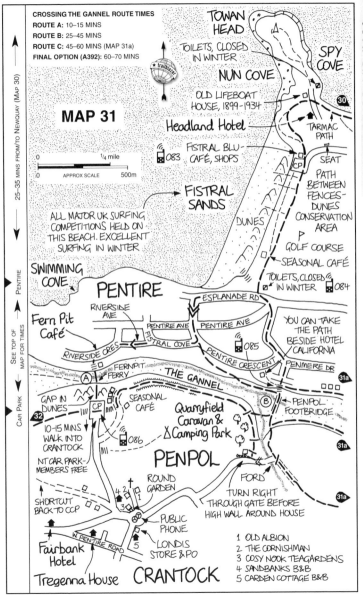

CROSSING THE GANNEL ROUTE TIMES
ROUTE A: 10–15 MINS
ROUTE B: 25–45 MINS
ROUTE C: 45–60 MINS (MAP 31a)
FINAL OPTION (A392): 60–70 MINS

★ trailblazer

25–35 MINS FROM/TO NEWQUAY (MAP 30)

MAP 31

0   ¼ mile
0   500m
APPROX SCALE

TOWAN HEAD

SPY COVE

TOILETS, CLOSED IN WINTER

NUN COVE

OLD LIFEBOAT HOUSE, 1899–1934

Headland Hotel

TARMAC PATH

FISTRAL BLU-CAFÉ, SHOPS   ⌔083

30

CP   SEAT
PATH BETWEEN FENCES-DUNES CONSERVATION AREA

FISTRAL SANDS

ALL MAJOR UK SURFING COMPETITIONS HELD ON THIS BEACH. EXCELLENT SURFING IN WINTER

DUNES

P GOLF COURSE
SEASONAL CAFÉ
TOILETS, CLOSED IN WINTER   ⌔084

SWIMMING COVE

PENTIRE

ESPLANADE RD

RIVERSIDE AVE

PENTIRE AVE   PENTIRE AVE

YOU CAN TAKE THE PATH BESIDE HOTEL CALIFORNIA

Fern Pit Café

RIVERSIDE CRES   FISTRAL COVE

⌔085

PENTIRE CRESCENT   PENMERE DR

SEE TOP OF — PENTIRE — CAR PARK
SEE TOP FOR TIMES

FERNPIT FERRY

A   THE GANNEL

31a

GAP IN DUNES

CP

SEASONAL CAFÉ

Quaryfield Caravan & △ Camping Park

B   PENPOL FOOTBRIDGE

32

10–15 MINS WALK INTO CRANTOCK

⌔086

PENPOL

31a

NT CAR PARK- MEMBERS FREE

SHORTCUT BACK TO CCP

ROUND GARDEN

4 2
3   1

FORD
TURN RIGHT THROUGH GATE BEFORE HIGH WALL AROUND HOUSE

31a

PUBLIC PHONE

Fairbank Hotel

W. PENTIRE ROAD   5

Tregenna House

LONDIS STORE & PO

CRANTOCK

1 OLD ALBION
2 THE CORNISHMAN
3 COSY NOOK TEAGARDENS
4 SANDBANKS B&B
5 CARDEN COTTAGE B&B

eaten on the sun terrace: typically it's £8 for a bowl of moules marinière or £6 for a prawn sandwich. A lovely place but it's pricey.

Western Greyhound's 585 **bus** service stops here as does the 587. See public transport map and table, pp46-50.

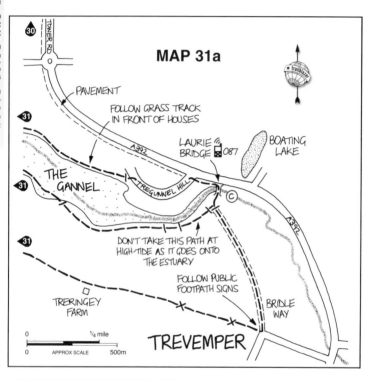

MAP 31a

PAVEMENT

FOLLOW GRASS TRACK IN FRONT OF HOUSES

LAURIE BRIDGE 087

BOATING LAKE

THE GANNEL

TREGUNNEL HILL

DON'T TAKE THIS PATH AT HIGH-TIDE AS IT GOES ONTO THE ESTUARY

FOLLOW PUBLIC FOOTPATH SIGNS

BRIDLE WAY

TRERINGEY FARM

TREVEMPER

0   ¼ mile
0   APPROX SCALE   500m

CRANTOCK TO PERRANPORTH [MAPS 31-34]

The next **8 miles (13km, 2-3hrs)** provide classic cliff-top walking with some sharp ups and downs soon after leaving Crantock including the descent to the secluded beach at **Porth Joke**, accessed only on foot. **Kelsey Head** with its huge expanse of grass is a place to linger and savour so don't keep charging ahead. Slow the pace down a bit and make the most of an exquisite area.

Next comes **Holywell** with two pubs and a large holiday park after which the coast path skirts the scattered installations of **Penhale Camp**, MoD property which is heavily fenced. You imagine that somebody has you under observation as you pass by the concrete barracks and communications masts and hear the noise of small-arms fire from the ranges. Once behind this, a narrow, heart-stopping path brings you by stages to the start of **Perran Beach**, a two-mile

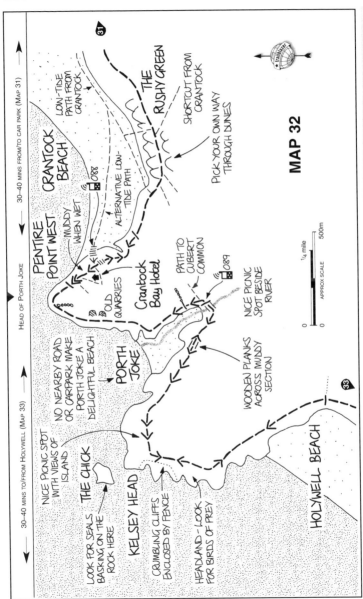

← 30-40 MINS FROM/TO CAR PARK (MAP 31) →

▶ HEAD OF Porth Joke ◀

← 30-40 MINS TO/FROM HOLYWELL (MAP 33) →

31

MAP 32

LOW-TIDE PATH FROM CRANTOCK

THE RUSHY GREEN

SHORTCUT FROM CRANTOCK

PICK YOUR OWN WAY THROUGH DUNES

CRANTOCK BEACH

PENTIRE POINT WEST

ALTERNATIVE LOW-TIDE PATH

MUDDY WHEN WET

☎ 089

OLD QUARRIES

Crantock Bay Hotel

PATH TO CUBERT COMMON

☎ 089

NICE PICNIC SPOT BESIDE RIVER

¼ mile
APPROX SCALE
500m

0   0

PORTH JOKE

NO NEARBY ROAD OR CARPARK MAKE PORTH JOKE A DELIGHTFUL BEACH

WOODEN PLANKS ACROSS MUDDY SECTION

NICE PICNIC SPOT WITH VIEWS OF ISLAND

THE CHICK

LOOK FOR SEALS BASKING ON THE ROCK HERE

KELSEY HEAD

CRUMBLING CLIFFS ENCLOSED BY FENCE

HEADLAND - LOOK FOR BIRDS OF PREY

HOLYWELL BEACH

33

long stretch of golden sand bordered by dunes, the walk along the edge of the tide making a welcome change. You'll see dog walkers, families, horse-riders and, if the wind is up, sand yachts whistling across the beach; you'll probably want to take your boots off.

The approach to Perranporth is exciting, the town coming into sight only as you round the rocky outcrop of **Cotty's Point**. At high tide it will be necessary to leave the beach at the lifeguard station and continue the last leg to Perranporth through the dunes.

Perranporth is the largest settlement between Newquay and St Ives.

HOLYWELL [MAP 33]

Holywell has **seasonal** beach shops, a **grocery** store and two **pubs** though no accommodation. The exact site of the holy well this village is named after is disputed. Some say it's in the caves on the northern end of the beach, others that it's further inland along the road.

Of the two pubs, the *Treguth Inn* (☎ 01637-830248; food served daily noon-2pm & 6-9pm) is the oldest, a converted 13th-century farmhouse with a thatched roof; they are open all day May to October and serve standard pub grub with some vegetarian options. More convenient to walkers is *St Piran's Inn* (☎ 01637-830205, 🖳 www.stpiransinn.co.uk; food served daily all day in summer, rest of year Wed-Sat noon-2pm & 6-9pm, Sun noon-

4pm) nearer the beach. The menu includes crispy Cornish pork belly and creamy mashed potato (£9.50) and St Piran's fish pie (£9.25). The bar is open all day in summer, Tue-Sun in winter.

Holywell Bay Holiday Park (☎ 01637-830227, 🖳 www.parkdeanholidays .co.uk; Mar-Oct) is a site aimed at families during the season so bookings must be for at least a week but out of the busy period you can pitch a small tent here for £13-29 per night.

Western Greyhound's Newquay–Truro 587 **bus** service stops here. The bus stop is five minutes' walk from the beach near Treguth Inn. See public transport map and table, pp46-50.

❏ **St Piran**

St Piran, the patron saint of Cornwall, supposedly arrived in Perranporth having floated from Ireland on a millstone. In his old age he had been captured by pagan Irish and thrown over a cliff with this millstone round his neck. The stone floated and became a raft. He built a small chapel on Penhale Sands (now engulfed by the dunes) and lived there for many years as a hermit performing miracles for the locals. When he died his relics were kept in a shrine nearby and became a major place of medieval pilgrimage.

His popularity among the Cornish lies in the tradition that it was he who first discovered tin. He was cooking on a fireplace of black rock when he saw that the intense heat made a trickle of pure white metal ooze from the stones. He shared this knowledge with the locals and it was on this that the prosperity of Cornwall was based.

St Piran is not only remembered on St Piran's Day on 5 March, but also on the Cornish flag, a white cross on a black background symbolising the white tin seeping from the black rock, the triumph of good over evil and God's light shining out of the darkness.

For further details visit the St Piran's Trust website (🖳 www.st-piran.com).

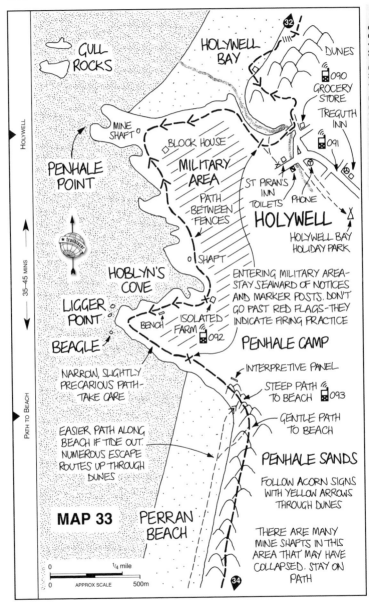

GULL
ROCKS

HOLYWELL
BAY

DUNES

📱090
GROCERY
STORE

TREGUTH
INN

📱091

MINE
SHAFT

BLOCK HOUSE

PENHALE
POINT

MILITARY
AREA

ST PIRAN'S
INN

PATH
BETWEEN
FENCES

TOILETS   PHONE

HOLYWELL

HOLYWELL BAY
HOLIDAY PARK

SHAFT

HOBLYN'S
COVE

ENTERING MILITARY AREA-
STAY SEAWARD OF NOTICES
AND MARKER POSTS. DON'T
GO PAST RED FLAGS-THEY
INDICATE FIRING PRACTICE

LIGGER
POINT

BENCH

ISOLATED
FARM 📱092

PENHALE CAMP

BEAGLE

INTERPRETIVE PANEL

NARROW, SLIGHTLY
PRECARIOUS PATH-
TAKE CARE

STEEP PATH 📱093
TO BEACH

GENTLE PATH
TO BEACH

EASIER PATH ALONG
BEACH IF TIDE OUT.
NUMEROUS ESCAPE
ROUTES UP THROUGH
DUNES

PENHALE SANDS

FOLLOW ACORN SIGNS
WITH YELLOW ARROWS
THROUGH DUNES

MAP 33

PERRAN
BEACH

THERE ARE MANY
MINE SHAFTS IN THIS
AREA THAT MAY HAVE
COLLAPSED. STAY ON
PATH

0   ¼ mile

0   APPROX SCALE   500m

HOLYWELL

35-45 MINS

PATH TO BEACH

trailblazer

PERRANPORTH [MAP 34]

Named after St Piran (see box p136), the patron saint of Cornwall, Perranporth is a small seaside town that depends for its existence on the holiday trade. The beach is superb and a spell of nice weather sees it crowded with sun and fun seekers of all ages.

Perranzabuloe Museum (☎ 01872-573321, Ponsmere Rd; Easter-Oct Mon-Fri 10.30am-1pm & 2-4.30pm, Sat 11am-1pm; free) provides some useful information on the area's industrial past with displays on mining, fishing and farming. **Lowender Peran Celtic Festival** (see p31) is held here in October.

The **Lloyds TSB** has a **cash machine** and there are others in Tywarnhayle Pub and in the **supermarkets** (Spar, Co-op and Premier): the **Co-op** is open daily 7am-10pm. The **post office** (closed Wed afternoons) is on St Piran's Rd, and there's **internet access** at *Hard Drive Café* (☎ 01872-572006; summer Mon-Sat 10am-5pm, Sun 11am-4pm). If you are looking for a **launderette** (daily 8am-10pm in summer, 8am-8pm in winter) there is one on The Gounce. Nearby on Beach Rd is **Perranporth Surgery** with a Boots **Pharmacy** next door. The **information centre** (☎ 01872-575254,

🖳 www.perranporthinfo.co.uk; daily late May to Oct 9am-5pm, rest of year 9am-4pm), staffed by volunteers, is in the little square in the centre of town.

Where to stay

This part of Cornwall is full of holiday parks for caravanners but the best for true campers is *Tollgate Farm Caravan and Camping Park* (off Map 34; ☎ 01872-572130, 🖳 www .tollgatefarm.co.uk; Easter to end Sep), right next door to the massive Perran Sands site. A small backpacker's tent with two adults is £9.50-14.50.

Perranporth Youth Hostel (Map 34; ☎ 0845-371 9755, 🖳 perranporth@yha.org .uk; Apr-Nov; 24 beds) is up on the hill on the cliffs at Droskyn Point, a fantastic location and a prime spot for watching the sunset, brew in hand. The facilities are only self catering; no meals are served. The cost for adults is from £15.95 per night.

B&B accommodation is fairly easy to come by. *Chy an Kerensa* (☎ 01872-572470, Cliff Rd; 3S/1T/2D/3F, all en suite), a cheerful licensed guesthouse minutes from the beach, charges £25-32 per person and would be a good choice.

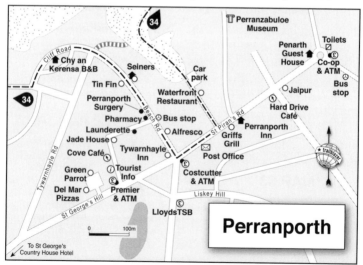

Perranporth

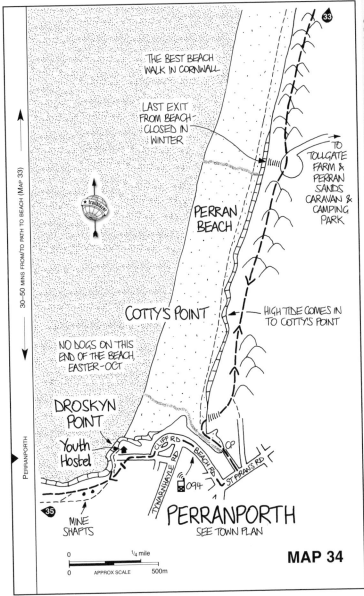

THE BEST BEACH
WALK IN CORNWALL

LAST EXIT
FROM BEACH -
CLOSED IN
WINTER

TO
TOLLGATE
FARM &
PERRAN
SANDS
CARAVAN &
CAMPING
PARK

PERRAN
BEACH

★ trailblazer

30-50 MINS FROM/TO PATH TO BEACH (MAP 33)

COTTY'S POINT

HIGH TIDE COMES IN
TO COTTY'S POINT

NO DOGS ON THIS
END OF THE BEACH,
EASTER-OCT

DROSKYN
POINT

Youth
Hostel

CLIFF RD

CP

PERRANPORTH

TYNARNHAYLE RD

BEACH RD

ST PIRAN'S RD

094

MINE
SHAFTS

PERRANPORTH
SEE TOWN PLAN

0   ¼ mile

0   500m
APPROX SCALE

MAP 34

Penarth Guest House (☎ 01872-573186, 🖵 www.penarthperranporth.co.uk; 3S/3D/1T/1F), 26 St Pirans Rd, welcomes walkers, pet lovers and motorcyclists alike, charging £27.50 per person; deduct £5 for room only. *Perranporth Inn* (☎ 01872-573234, 🖵 www.perranporthinn.co.uk; 5T/10D/1Tr/4F, all en suite), charges from £60 to £80 per room for B&B and £50 for single occupancy. It's clean and well-run.

Seiners (☎ 01872-573118, 🖵 www.sei ners.co.uk; 2S/6T/13D/2F, most en suite) has been reinvented from the former Seiners Arms, a pub with rooms attached; rooms cost £60-80 (£50-55 for single occupancy). It is right on the sea front.

A half-mile trudge out of town on St Georges Hill is *St Georges Country House Hotel* (☎ 01872-572184, 🖵 www.stgeorges countryhouse.co.uk; 7D/2F, all en suite), a fine detached house with dormer windows charging £40-45 per person or £45 for single occupancy. They keep their own hens and bake their own bread so your breakfast will certainly be fresh and local. French and German are spoken and they have a **bistro/bar** attached (food is served all day and they can provide packed lunches).

Where to eat and drink

Perranporth has an Indian Restaurant, *Jaipur* (☎ 01872-573625; Mon-Sat 5-11.30pm, Sun 3-10pm) and a Chinese, *Jade House* (☎ 01872-572880; Tue-Sun 5.30-11.30pm) both with menus familiar to lovers of ethnic fare. For cheap and cheerful food, *Griffs Grill* (☎ 01872-572889; Easter-Oct daily 9am-8.30pm) does a breakfast from £1.80. For an above-average café look for *Alfresco* on Beach Rd; they offer filled baguettes and sandwiches from £2.50.

The choice when it comes to **pubs** is between the *Tywarnhayle Inn* (aka the Tye; ☎ 01872-572215; summer daily noon-8.30pm, winter noon-2pm & 5-7.30pm) for standard pub grub and *Seiners* (see Where to stay; bar serves food daily noon-3pm & 5-9pm, restaurant 6pm to late) which is like the lower deck of a sailing ship inside with a range of piratical beers from Truro Brewery. Try the mackerel fillet wrapped in

Parma ham (£11.50) or an 8oz ribeye steak with fat chips, roasted garlic and shallots (£14.50). They are opening a new restaurant for fine dining in spring 2009.

Tin Fin (☎ 01872-572117, Beach Rd; March to late May Thur-Sun 10am-8.30pm, Jun-Sep daily 10am-8.30pm) is a new enterprise that has gained a good reputation. They source their ingredients locally so the menu varies depending on what they can get but they always have steak (£14.95) on the menu and may have spiced fish stew with spinach and bread for £12.95. They also do cream teas and sandwiches to take away. The *Waterfront Restaurant* (☎ 01872-573167; Easter-Oct daily from 6.30pm to late, from 5pm in July & Aug) serves a crab special for £13.95 with free salad from a help-yourself bar. They also have an early birds menu for the first half-hour (or hour in the summer).

Green Parrot (☎ 01872-573350, 🖵 www.thegreenparrot.co.uk, St Georges Hill; food served summer daily noon-9pm, winter Mon-Sat noon-3pm & 6-9pm, Sun noon-4pm) serves their Original Parrot Burger for £8.95 and a spicy bean burger for £7.95. Sharing the pub's car park is *Del Mar Italian Restaurant and Pizzeria* (☎ 01872-572878, 🖵 www.delmarrestaurant .co.uk; daily noon till midnight during the season, winter daily 5pm to midnight) specialising in pizzas.

Cove Café (☎ 01872 571487, 🖵 www .perranporthcove.co.uk) adjoins the information centre and **internet access** is free as long as something is purchased in the café; they serve toasties, paninis, baguettes and an all-day breakfast (£3.85).

Transport

Western Greyhound's 501, 583 and 587 services stop here as do Summercourt Travel's 403 and First's 85/85A. First's buses leave from outside the fire station just across the road from the Co-op whereas the other buses leave from Beach Rd. See public transport map and table, pp46-50.

For a **taxi**, ring Atlantic Taxis (☎ 01872-572126).

PERRANPORTH TO PORTHTOWAN [MAPS 34-38]

This is another **eight-mile** (**13km, 2½-3hrs**) section and it goes through terrain that is mostly heathland which at one time covered the whole of the west of Cornwall. The walking is relatively easy and you should be able to crack on and make light of the few ups and downs, the most severe of which is down to **Chapel Porth**. It is here that we first begin to encounter the remains of Cornwall's mining industry at **Wheal Coates** and **Towan Roath** mines, the abandoned engine houses lonely relics of a once-thriving period. We also notice the heads of many shafts close to the path, most of them fenced and in some cases topped with a steel-wire pyramid-shaped cage for safety. They have become colonised by the greater horseshoe bat, an endangered species which is unlikely to be seen unless you are passing this way at dusk.

ST AGNES (Trevaunance Cove)
[map p142]

Trevaunance Cove is small and rocky with a sandy beach at low tide. At mid-tide the surf can be powerful. The village of St Agnes itself is a 20- to 25-minute walk inland with houses and cottages dotted along the way. See p30 for details of the **Giant Bolster Festival** held here in May.

A well-known local landmark not to be missed is the **Stippy Stappy**, a row of mine workers' cottages that climb the hill-like steps. **St Agnes Museum** (☎ 01872-553228, Penwinnick Rd; Easter-Oct daily 10.30am-5pm, free) has many exhibits mostly on the area's sea-going connections. There is a **Barclays Bank**, a **post office**

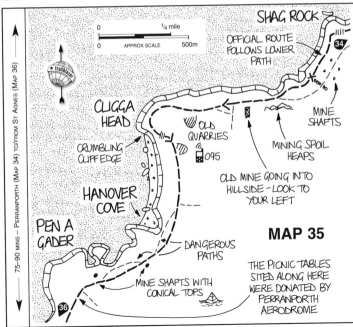

(Mon-Fri 9am-5.30pm, Sat 9am-12.30pm), with an ATM with no charge, and a **pharmacy**. **Costcutter** (Mon-Sat 7.30am-10.30pm, Sun 8.30am-10.30pm) also has an ATM and there's a **Londis** in Peterville.

The **tourist information centre** (☎ 01872-554150, ☐ www.st-agnes.com) is through a gift shop/art gallery (Churchtown Arts Gallery; Mon-Sat 9.30am-5.30pm, Sun 10am-5pm) and is staffed part time (daily 10am-2pm) but is still worth visiting outside these hours because it has loads of helpful leaflets and information about the area. They also produce a booklet (£3) detailing ten local walks.

Where to stay
Campers need to go a little way out of the village to find *Presingoll Farm Caravan and Camping Park* (☎ 01872-552333, ☐ www.presingollfarm.fsbusiness.co.uk, Penwinnick Rd), a working farm where a night for a walker with a small tent costs £6.50. Alternatively, *Beacon Cottage Farm* (Map 37; ☎ 01872-552347, ☐ www.beaconcottagefarmholidays.co.uk, Beacon Drive; Easter-Oct) charges £6 for backpackers; excellent value in a nicely run site.

Driftwood Spars (Map 36; ☎ 01872-552428, ☐ www.driftwoodspars.com, Quay Rd; 1S/9D/1T/4F, all en suite) is a tastefully decorated and enthusiastically run establishment where B&B is £43-51 per person; the single room is £45 (single occupancy of a double or twin costs an extra £15 a night). Wifi access is free.

Further up Quay Rd is a recently renovated house now styling itself *The Aramay* (☎ 01872-553546, ☐ www.thearamay.com; 4D/1T, all en suite) with rooms costing £85-95. Open all year, the place has quality written all over it, from its seclusion to the furniture and fittings. Very chic.

Another option is *Enysvilla* (☎ 01872-552137, ☐ enysvil la@aol.com; 3D, T or F, all with private facilities) charging £25-30 per person. Single occupancy is an extra £5.

Opposite the church, tucked away with its back to the street, is the charming *Churchtown B&B* (☎ 01872-552716, ☐ churchtownb&b@aol.com; 1S/1T/1D, all en suite), with accommodation from £30 per person, while just out of the village on Penwinnick Rd is *Penkerris* (☎ 01872-552262, ☐ www.penkerris.co.uk; 9 rooms most can be D/T or F). It is a lovely detached Edwardian house with Virginia creeper climbing over it and a slightly fading ambience that does not detract from the experience of staying there and it has been run by the same redoubtable lady for the past 20 years; she welcomes walkers and has written a book on local walks. B&B costs from £22.50 to £35 per person with a £5-10 single occupancy supplement. An evening meal is available for £15.

The ever-popular *Malt House* (☎ 01872-553318, ☐ www.themalthousestagnes.co.uk; 1S/3D, share facilities) charges

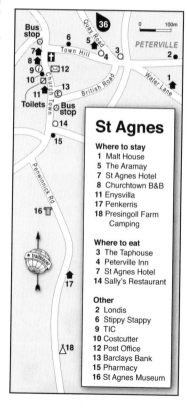

St Agnes

Where to stay
1 Malt House
5 The Aramay
7 St Agnes Hotel
8 Churchtown B&B
11 Enysvilla
17 Penkerris
18 Presingoll Farm Camping

Where to eat
3 The Taphouse
4 Peterville Inn
7 St Agnes Hotel
14 Sally's Restaurant

Other
2 Londis
6 Stippy Stappy
9 TIC
10 Costcutter
12 Post Office
13 Barclays Bank
15 Pharmacy
16 St Agnes Museum

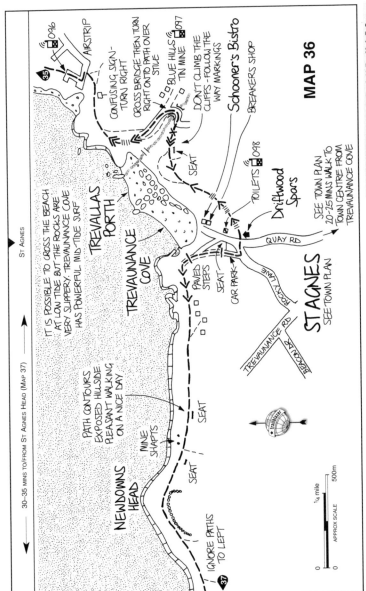

St Agnes

30–35 MINS TO/FROM ST AGNES HEAD (MAP 37)

MAP 36

IT IS POSSIBLE TO CROSS THE BEACH AT LOW TIDE BUT THE ROCKS ARE VERY SLIPPERY. TREVAUNANCE COVE HAS POWERFUL MID-TIDE SURF

AIRSTRIP

096

35

CONFUSING SIGN – TURN RIGHT

CROSS BRIDGE THEN TURN RIGHT ONTO PATH OVER STILE

BLUE HILLS TIN MINE 097

DON'T CLIMB THE CLIFFS – FOLLOW THE WAY MARKINGS

Schooner's Bistro

BREAKERS SHOP

TREVALLAS PORTH

SEAT

TOILETS 098

Driftwood Spars

TREVAUNANCE COVE

ST AGNES
SEE TOWN PLAN

QUAY RD

SEE TOWN PLAN
20–25 MINS WALK TO
TOWN CENTRE FROM
TREVAUNANCE COVE

PAVED STEPS

SEAT

CAR PARK

ROCKY LANE

TREVAUNANCE RD

BEACON RD

PATH CONTOURS EXPOSED HILLSIDE PLEASANT WALKING ON A NICE DAY

SEAT

SEAT

NEWDOWNS HEAD

MINE SHAFTS

SEAT

IGNORE PATHS TO LEFT

37

trailblazer

¼ mile
APPROX SCALE
500m

£25 per person. This is the kind of B&B you seldom find now, a home from home.

St Agnes Hotel (☎ 01872-552307, 🖳 www.st-agnes-hotel.co.uk; 6D, all en suite), opposite the church, is a hostelry of the old sort. B&B costs £80 for two sharing (£45 for single occupancy).

Where to eat and drink

Driftwood Spars (see Where to stay; daily noon-2.30pm & 6.30-9.30pm) has a welcoming feel and the dining room overlooks the sea. Seafood is the obvious choice: south-coast sardines, bruschetta and salsa verde cost £5.25, and fresh pollock and chips £9. Their food is locally sourced and in addition to a well-chosen wine list they stock real ales and 50 malt whiskies. *Schooners Bistro* (Map 36; ☎ 01872-553149, 🖳 www.schoonersbistro.co.uk; food served daily summer 9.30am-9pm, winter Sat & Sun daytime only) serves some irresistible moules frites for £10.95.

In St Agnes itself, *Sally's Restaurant* (☎ 01872-552194, 🖳 www.sallysrestaurant .co.uk; Mar-Jan Thur-Mon 5-10pm) is gaining a reputation locally for good food. Apart from the daily fish specials the menu might include roast breast of barbary duck with potato rosti and cassis, or baked field mushrooms with Welsh rarebit and cauliflower croquettes. Three courses cost £20-25.

In Peterville *The Taphouse* (☎ 01872-553095, 🖳 www.the-taphouse.com; Mon-Sat noon-2pm & 5.30-9pm) is a lively, unconventional place with music some evenings. The menu (steaks, salads and pasta) is similar to that served at *Peterville Inn* (☎ 01872-552406; food served Tue-Sat noon-3pm & 6-9pm, Sun noon-3pm).

St Agnes Hotel (see Where to stay; food served daily noon-3pm & 6.30-9.30pm) has a fairly standard menu using local produce: rack of barbecued ribs with chips (£9.50) or the Aggie burger (£7.95).

Transport

Hopley's 315, Western Greyhound's 501 and First's 85/85A **bus** services call here. See public transport map and table, pp46-50.

If you need a taxi call St Agnes Taxis (☎ 01872-553795 or ☎ 07778-436753).

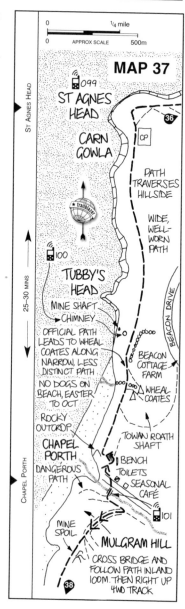

Map 38 (Porthtowan) and Map 39 145

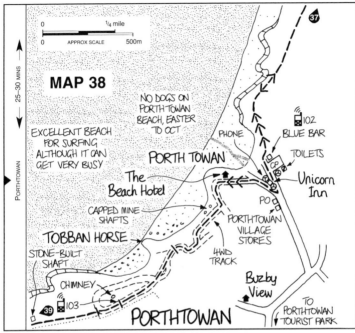

MAP 38

0   1/4 mile
0   APPROX SCALE   500m

25-30 MINS

PORTHTOWAN

EXCELLENT BEACH
FOR SURFING
ALTHOUGH IT CAN
GET VERY BUSY

NO DOGS ON
PORTH TOWAN
BEACH, EASTER
TO OCT

PHONE

PORTH TOWAN

The
Beach Hotel

CAPPED MINE
SHAFTS

TOBBAN HORSE

STONE-BUILT
SHAFT

CHIMNEY

39   103

4WD
TRACK

PORTHTOWAN

BLUE BAR

TOILETS

Unicorn
Inn

PO

PORTHTOWAN
VILLAGE
STORES

Buzby
View

TO
PORTHTOWAN
TOURIST PARK

102

37

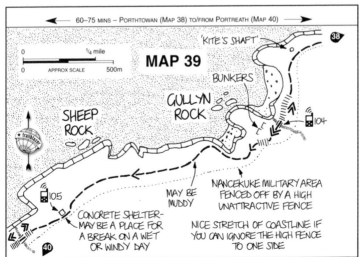

60-75 MINS - PORTHTOWAN (MAP 38) TO/FROM PORTREATH (MAP 40)

0   1/4 mile
0   APPROX SCALE   500m

MAP 39

'KITE'S SHAFT'

BUNKERS

GULLYN
ROCK

SHEEP
ROCK

trailblazer

105

104

38

CONCRETE SHELTER-
MAY BE A PLACE FOR
A BREAK ON A WET
OR WINDY DAY

40

MAY BE
MUDDY

NANCEKUKE MILITARY AREA
FENCED OFF BY A HIGH
UNATTRACTIVE FENCE

NICE STRETCH OF COASTLINE IF
YOU CAN IGNORE THE HIGH FENCE
TO ONE SIDE

PORTHTOWAN   [MAP 38, p145]

Porthtowan is a small settlement, hardly even a village, but it has an enormous car park, a **post office** (Mon-Thurs 9am-1pm and 2-5.30pm, Fri 9am-1pm and Sat 9am-noon), and a Porthtowan **Village Stores** (☎ 01209-891210; Mon-Thur 7.30am-8pm, Fri & Sat 730am-9pm, Sun 8am-8pm, July & Aug daily until 9pm, Sat till 10pm) which stocks basic supplies and is a good place to stock up on bread and pasties.

The nearest campsite to the beach is **Porthtowan Tourist Park** (☎ 01209-890256, 🖳 www.porthtowantouristpark .co.uk; Apr-Oct) where the cost of a basic pitch for two people is £8.50-16 depending on the season. The site has a new toilet block, a laundry room and a **shop** (daily 8.30-10.30am & 4.30-7.30pm) selling a few essentials such as bread, milk, eggs, bacon and some tinned food.

There's one **B&B** *Buzby View* (☎ 01209-891178, 🖳 buzbyview@freenet.co .uk; 1S/1T/2D) a spacious, open-plan place charging a remarkably reasonable £26 per person with no single supplement and a great breakfast. Packed lunches are available on request. The other choice is *The Beach Hotel* (☎ 01209-890228, 🖳 www .thebeachhotel.net; 3T/6D/2F) where B&B starts at £30 per person plus a single occupancy supplement of £7 in summer. The position is stunning but involves a steep climb up to it and steep steps down to the beach. In summer you can enjoy a coffee on their terrace and imagine a week of looking at the view.

The beach café is the lower-case *blue bar* (☎ 01209-890329, 🖳 www.blue-bar .co.uk) which entices walkers off the path and is open daily 10am till late in the summer (food is served noon-3pm & 6-9pm with an afternoon menu featuring pizzas) but you may want to head straight for the bar of the *Unicorn Inn* (☎ 01209-890244; daily noon-9pm) which mostly serves pizzas and grills. They provide a takeaway service between 9pm and closing time.

Western Greyhound's 501 calls here Hopley's 315 **bus** goes to St Agnes and the 304 to Truro. See public transport map and table, pp46-50.

PORTHTOWAN TO PORTREATH   [MAPS 38-40]

For most of these **three miles (5km, 1-1¼hrs)** the walking is alongside heavily fenced MoD land with frequent signs warning of dire penalties for straying from the path. It keeps to the edge of the cliffs and on the sea side the views are spectacular but it is hard to ignore the concrete buildings and chain link fencing of Penhale Camp. You can't escape the uneasy feeling that somebody is keeping you under observation although this may just be paranoia.

PORTREATH   [MAP 40]

Portreath is a small community with most if not all you might need in the way of refreshment or an overnight stop on the way to St Ives.

The row of shops opposite the Portreath Arms (see opposite) consists of the **post office**, a **Londis store** (Mon-Sat 7am-9pm, Sun 7.30am-9pm) with a **cash machine**, the **Portreath Bakery** (☎ 01209-842612; main season Mon-Fri 6.30am-5.30pm, Sat 6.30am-4pm; rest of year to 4.30pm Mon-Fri and to 3pm on Sat) for filled rolls and pasties and the *Harbour Diner* (Tue-Sat 11am-2.30pm & 5.30pm till late, last orders 9pm).

B&B is available at the attractive *Cliff House* (☎ 01209-843847, 🖳 www.cliff houseportreath.com; 2T/3D/1F, some en suite), an ideal stopover and a great favourite with coast-path walkers. In the conservatory at the front of the house there are some fascinating old photos of Portreath when it was a thriving port for sailing ships. A room for the night costs £63 (£38 for single occupancy); they also offer a packed lunch (£6) and luggage transfer.

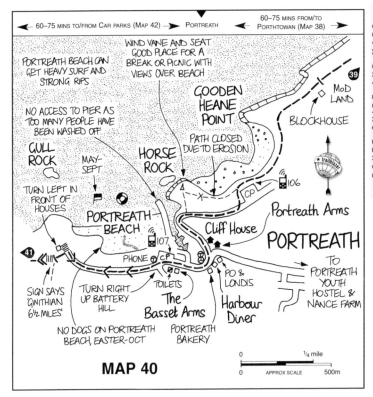

← 60–75 MINS TO/FROM CAR PARKS (MAP 42) → PORTREATH ← 60–75 MINS FROM/TO PORTHTOWAN (MAP 38) →

WIND VANE AND SEAT GOOD PLACE FOR A BREAK OR PICNIC WITH VIEWS OVER BEACH

PORTREATH BEACH CAN GET HEAVY SURF AND STRONG RIPS

GOODEN HEANE POINT

39

MoD LAND

BLOCKHOUSE

NO ACCESS TO PIER AS TOO MANY PEOPLE HAVE BEEN WASHED OFF

PATH CLOSED DUE TO EROSION

GULL ROCK

MAY-SEPT

HORSE ROCK

106

trailblazer

TURN LEFT IN FRONT OF HOUSES

Portreath Arms

PORTREATH BEACH

Cliff House

PORTREATH

107

TO PORTREATH YOUTH HOSTEL & NANCE FARM

41

PHONE CP

PO & LONDIS

SIGN SAYS 'GWITHIAN 6½ MILES'

TURN RIGHT UP BATTERY HILL

TOILETS

The Basset Arms

Harbour Diner

NO DOGS ON PORTREATH BEACH, EASTER-OCT

PORTREATH BAKERY

0 ¼ mile

MAP 40

0 APPROX SCALE 500m

Portreath Youth Hostel (☎ 01209-842244, 🖳 mary.alway@btinternet.com; open all year, 20 beds), Nance Farm, Illogan, is a newly converted barn on a working farm, with a self-catering kitchen and drying room. A bed costs £18. Nance Farm also does B&B (£25 per person) for up to six people. It's 150m from Illogan Churchtown stop on First's 44 bus route (see p50).

Portreath Arms Hotel (☎ 01209-842259; 2D/5T, some en suite) charges £60 per room for B&B for two people sharing; £35 single occupancy. They will transport walkers' luggage charging for example £15

to go to Hayle, £20 to St Ives. They can also provide packed lunches. Food is served daily noon-2pm & 6-9pm. The place is friendly but the interior needs some tender-loving care.

The **Basset Arms** (☎ 01209-842077; food served Mon-Sat noon-2pm & 6-9pm, Sun roast noon-5pm) also serves fairly standard fare.

Transport

Western Greyhound's 501 and and First's 44 bus services stop here See public transport map and table, pp46-50.

PORTREATH TO GWITHIAN [MAPS 40-44]

This **eight-mile (13km, 2-2³/4hrs)** leg is nearly all on the cliff top through gorse and shrub with only a narrow path to walk on. Once you reach Hudder Cove and the spectacularly named **Hell's Mouth** you are well rewarded as the cliffs are filled with nesting birds while grey seals breed in the caves below Navax Point. The path here has been surfaced to suit the heavy use that it now gets from dog walkers and joggers who are able to park in the car parks close to the cliff edge. There is a *seasonal café* here.

Godrevy Point is in the care of the National Trust and is a popular place for picnics and recreation. The offshore lighthouse was the inspiration for Virginia Woolf's classic novel, *To the Lighthouse*. Written in 1927, it drew on her memories of holidays with her parents in St Ives; the lighthouse in the book

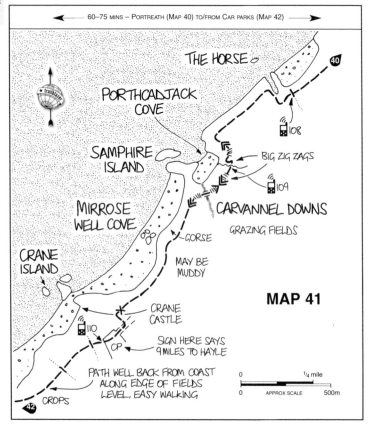

← 60–75 MINS – PORTREATH (MAP 40) TO/FROM CAR PARKS (MAP 42) →

THE HORSE

40

PORTHCADJACK COVE

📱108

BIG ZIG ZAGS

SAMPHIRE ISLAND

📱109

MIRROSE WELL COVE

CARVANNEL DOWNS

GRAZING FIELDS

GORSE

CRANE ISLAND

MAY BE MUDDY

MAP 41

CRANE CASTLE

📱110

CP

SIGN HERE SAYS 9 MILES TO HAYLE

PATH WELL BACK FROM COAST ALONG EDGE OF FIELDS LEVEL, EASY WALKING

0   ¹/4 mile
0   APPROX SCALE   500m

CROPS

42

is merely a device for the development of the plot. Plans to switch off the light permanently were shelved after vocal protests by fishermen and Virginia Woolf fans.

From the NT car park at Godrevy the path cuts off the coast and follows a long stretch of road into Gwithian so you may need a refreshment break at Godrevy Beach Café or Sandsifter Restaurant (see p152) both on the road into Gwithian.

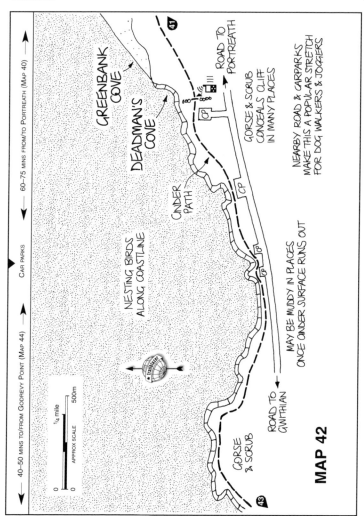

MAP 42

GREENBANK COVE

DEADMAN'S COVE

ROAD TO PORTREATH

CINDER PATH

NESTING BIRDS ALONG COASTLINE

GORSE & SCRUB CONCEALS CLIFF IN MANY PLACES

NEARBY ROAD & CARPARKS MAKE THIS A POPULAR STRETCH FOR DOG WALKERS & JOGGERS

MAY BE MUDDY IN PLACES ONCE CINDER SURFACE RUNS OUT

ROAD TO GWITHIAN

GORSE & SCRUB

60-75 MINS FROM/TO PORTREATH (MAP 40)

CAR PARKS

40-50 MINS TO/FROM GODREVY POINT (MAP 44)

CP

¼ mile

500m

APPROX SCALE

Trailblazer

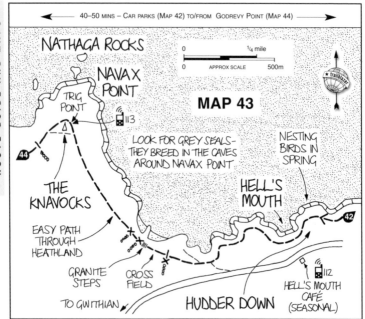

NATHAGA ROCKS

NAVAX POINT

TRIG POINT

MAP 43

LOOK FOR GREY SEALS–
THEY BREED IN THE CAVES
AROUND NAVAX POINT

NESTING
BIRDS IN
SPRING

THE KNAVOCKS

HELL'S MOUTH

EASY PATH
THROUGH
HEATHLAND

GRANITE
STEPS

CROSS
FIELD

HUDDER DOWN

HELL'S MOUTH
CAFÉ
(SEASONAL)

TO GWITHIAN

ROUTE GUIDE AND MAPS

GWITHIAN   [MAP 44]

Gwithian is a sandy sort of place just inland from the dunes with the main road running through it bordered by a few houses.

The best choice for campers is ***Gwithian Farm Campsite*** (☎ 01736-753127, 🖥 www.gwithianfarm.co.uk), a clean, efficient and well-run site with a shop, laundry and spotlessly clean toilet block. A pitch for a single tent for the night costs £8-16 depending on the season. They claim never to turn walkers away.

Up the mile-long track at ***Nanterrow Farm*** (☎ 01209-712282, 🖥 www.nanterrowfarm.co.uk; 1D/1F, shared bathroom) you will find a lovely welcome and have an unforgettable stay in this beautiful farmhouse where B&B costs £29-35 per person (single occupancy supplement £20).

As you enter the village there is a house advertising B&B. The accommodation advertised is at ***Godrevy House*** (☎ 01736-756560, 🖥 www.gwithianholidays.com; four apartments sleeping two to five people) but the rooms are all suites and they are let by the week only between mid July and early September. However, stays of one night are possible at other times of the year: £58-65 for two sharing. A more traditional B&B is the imposing ***Calize Country House*** (☎ 01736-753268, 🖥 www.calize.co.uk; 1S/2D/1T, all en suite) where the single is £55 and for two sharing a double/twin it's £90. Packed lunches (£5) are available if booked in advance and they will also do baggage transfer. The proprietor has herself walked the entire South West Coast Path with her dog so don't try to exaggerate your achievements.

Godrevy Beach Café (Map 44; ☎ 01736-757999; Easter-Nov daily 10am-5pm, summer holidays 6-8.30pm; winter 10am-4pm) is an enterprise run by three ladies with lots of imagination and good ideas. How does the thought of Mediterranean fish stew (£8.95) grab you?

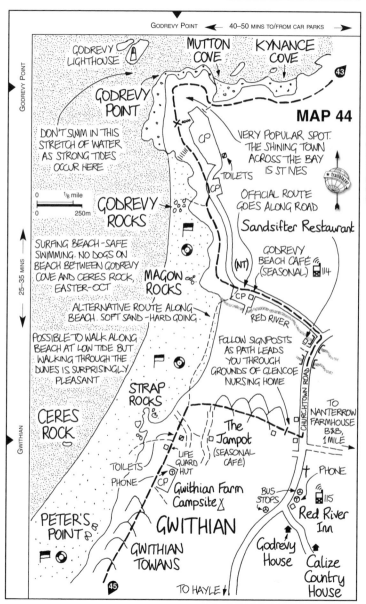

GODREVY POINT ← 40–50 MINS TO/FROM CAR PARKS →

GODREVY LIGHTHOUSE

MUTTON COVE

KYNANCE COVE

GODREVY POINT

GODREVY POINT

43

MAP 44

DON'T SWIM IN THIS STRETCH OF WATER AS STRONG TIDES OCCUR HERE

CP

VERY POPULAR SPOT. THE SHINING TOWN ACROSS THE BAY IS ST IVES

TOILETS

CP

OFFICIAL ROUTE GOES ALONG ROAD

GODREVY ROCKS

Sandsifter Restaurant

SURFING BEACH - SAFE SWIMMING. NO DOGS ON BEACH BETWEEN GODREVY COVE AND CERES ROCK, EASTER-OCT

(NT)

GODREVY BEACH CAFÉ (SEASONAL) 114

ALTERNATIVE ROUTE ALONG BEACH. SOFT SAND - HARD GOING

MAGOW ROCKS

CP

RED RIVER

POSSIBLE TO WALK ALONG BEACH AT LOW TIDE BUT WALKING THROUGH THE DUNES IS SURPRISINGLY PLEASANT

FOLLOW SIGNPOSTS AS PATH LEADS YOU THROUGH GROUNDS OF GLENCOE NURSING HOME

CERES ROCK

STRAP ROCKS

The Jampot (SEASONAL) CAFÉ

CHURCHTOWN ROAD

TO NANTERROW FARMHOUSE B&B, 1 MILE

LIFE GUARD HUT

TOILETS

PHONE

CP

PHONE

Gwithian Farm Campsite

BUS STOPS

115

PETER'S POINT

GWITHIAN

Red River Inn

GWITHIAN TOWANS

Godrevy House

Calize Country House

TO HAYLE

45

At the time of research **Sandsifter Bar & Restaurant** (Map 44) served freshly prepared food with tasty snacks such as Latin eggs – scrambled eggs with salsa and chorizo on a tortilla (£5.50). However, new owners were taking over in April 2009 so the menu may change.

In the evening most people gravitate to the **Red River Inn** (☎ 01736-753223, 🖳 www.red-river-inn.co.uk; Mon-Sat noon-3pm & 6-9pm, Sun noon-9pm). The lunch menu includes jacket potatoes and ciabattas; in the evening try their bean and capsicum stew (£7.95) or sea bass (£12.25). The beers include Fullers London Pride (4.1%) and Sharps Eden (4.3%). Nearer the beach **The Jampot** is a seasonal café serving home-made cakes, snacks and drinks.

Western Greyhound's 501 & 515 **bus** services stop at the entrance to Gwithian Farm Campsite. See public transport map and table, pp46-50.

GWITHIAN TO HAYLE   [MAPS 44-46]

For these **four miles (6km, 1-1¹/₄hrs)** you have the choice of either walking along the beach or taking the official coast path through the dunes. Although it is continually up and down the walk through the dunes is actually quite pleasant.

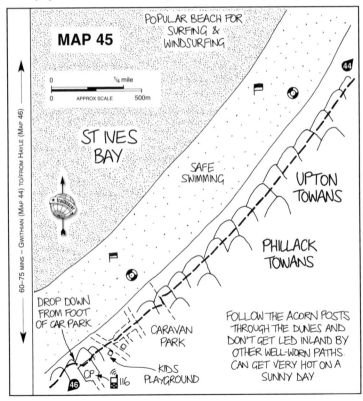

MAP 45

POPULAR BEACH FOR SURFING & WINDSURFING

0   ¹/₄ mile
0   APPROX SCALE   500m

ST IVES BAY

SAFE SWIMMING

UPTON TOWANS

PHILLACK TOWANS

trailblazer

60-75 MINS – GWITHIAN (MAP 44) TO/FROM HAYLE (MAP 46)

DROP DOWN FROM FOOT OF CAR PARK

CARAVAN PARK

CP   116   KIDS PLAYGROUND

46

44

FOLLOW THE ACORN POSTS THROUGH THE DUNES AND DON'T GET LED INLAND BY OTHER WELL-WORN PATHS. CAN GET VERY HOT ON A SUNNY DAY

It's a game of connect the dots as you follow the acorn posts with their yellow arrows from dune to dune and the sleepy undemanding scenery allows your mind to wander. Though the posts are not always easy to find, if you keep to a roughly straight line you shouldn't go far wrong. Be aware, however, that if the sun is out, the dunes trap the heat and shelter you from the breeze; it can get very hot so take plenty of water. The last section, from Hayle Towans to Hayle, is through an industrial area.

HAYLE [MAP 46, p155]

Hayle (*heyl* meaning estuary in Cornish) is recorded as having supplied tin as early as 1500BC and the Romans sailed their ships up as far as St Erth. Today the estuary is home to lobster boats, their catch going mostly to the continent.

For keen birdwatchers the muddy flats are good twitching territory and the RSPB (see p62) owns a **nature reserve** on the estuary. Autumn and winter are particularly good for migrating and wintering wild fowl such as widgeon, teal, shelduck and waders, including dunlin, curlew and grey plover.

Hayle has two centres: Copperhouse, and Foundry Square around the railway station. It is a bustling town where walkers can find all the services they need including branches of two **banks** (Lloyds TSB and Barclays), both with cash machines, and a **post office** (Mon, Thur 8.30am-5.30pm, Tue, Wed, Fri 9am-5.30pm, Sat 9am-1pm) at 13 Penpol Terrace (see below). The **tourist information centre** (☎ 01736-754399; Easter-Oct Mon, Tue, Wed, Fri 9am-6pm, Sat 9.30am-12.30pm, closed Thurs and Sun) is in the **library** (same hours as TIC but year-round) where **internet access** is available for £1.80 for 30 minutes for visitors.

There are numerous small shops along Penpol Terrace including **Martins Newsagents** with a free ATM machine and the post office. There is also a **Spar** supermarket and a **pharmacy**.

One surprise for walkers coming out of the dunes is the open-air **swimming pool** (☎ 01736-755005; late May to late Sep, daily 11am-6pm), on East Quay, which charges £2.50 for adults and £1.60 for seniors and juniors. There's a **launderette** (Mon-Sat 8am-6pm, Sun 9am-1pm, last wash an hour before closing) next door to Barclays Bank on Foundry Square.

The **Heritage Festival** (see p30) is held here every summer.

Where to stay

B&Bs include the *Mad Hatter* (☎ 01736-754241, 🖳 www.cornwall-online.co.uk/madhatter; 2D/2T or D/1F), 73 Fore St. One room is en suite but the others share facilities; they charge £25 per person all year (£32.50 per person for the en suite room). There is a **tearoom** (see p154) downstairs.

Another option is *Fernleigh* (☎ 01736-752166, 🖳 mikelynreffold@fernleigh.fsbusiness.co.uk; 2D/1T, all en suite), 26 Commercial Rd, with rooms costing £30 per person or £35 for single occupancy in a welcoming and friendly place that is immediately appealing. They are happy to collect guests from the station in Hayle to save them the half-mile walk along the pavement; they will also do luggage transfers, eg to St Ives, but will charge for that.

Cornubia Hotel (☎ 01736-753351; 2D/3F/2T), 35 Fore St, is actually a pub with rooms; it does B&B for £20-25 per person. Some rooms are en suite but the others share facilities. Alternatively try the slightly more upmarket and certainly larger *White Hart Hotel* (☎ 01736-752322, bookings@whiteharthayle.demon.co.uk; 2S/15D/5T/2F, all en suite), Foundry Square, in an elegant Regency building. They charge £60 for two sharing a twin or double room with a continental breakfast and £65 for a room with a full English breakfast. A single room costs £45 or £40 if you are happy to settle for a continental breakfast.

One other B&B worth a try is the small but hospitable *54 Penpol Terrace* (☎ 01736-752855, 🖳 jacoop@talktalk.net; 1S/1D/1T shared facilities) charging £30 per person, £35 for single occupancy.

Where to eat and drink

There is an abundance of fast food in Hayle such as *Pizza Patio* (☎ 01736-753745, 🖳 www.pizzapatio.co.uk; daily July & Aug noon-3pm & 5.30pm till late; rest of year daily 5.30pm till late) and *Balti King* Indian Takeaway or *Eastern Empire*, both open daily 5.30-11pm. *Hubbard's Fish and Chips* (Tue, Wed, Fri 11.45am-1.30pm, Tue-Sat 4.45-7.30pm) is on Penpol Terrace.

A place that is constantly busy is *Philp's Bakery* (☎ 01736-755661; Mon-Sat 8.30am-6pm, Sun 11am-4.30pm), on East Quay, reckoned by many to bake the best pasties in Cornwall although this disputable honour will never be resolved owing to personal preference. Try their Premier Standard, a meal in a bag for £2.05.

Food is available in *White Hart Hotel*'s restaurant (daily noon-2pm & 6-9pm) and also at *Cornubia Hotel* (Apr-Oct daily noon-2pm & 6-9pm; Sunday lunch is available year-round). *Mad Hatter* (see p153; Apr-Oct Mon-Sat 10am-5.30pm) has a tearoom: Cornish cream teas are available all day.

Public transport

Bus services stopping here include Western Greyhound's 501 & 515, First's 14/14B & 18/X18/18B as well as Williams 401. Hayle is a stop on the **railway** line to Penzance.

See public transport map and table, pp46-50. For a **taxi** ring Hayle Taxis (☎ 01736-753000), or St Erth & Hayle Cars (☎ 0770-604 0400).

HAYLE – MAP KEY

Where to stay, eat and drink
1 The Cornubia Hotel
2 Balti King
3 Mad Hatter
4 Fernleigh
6 Pizza Patio
7 Eastern Empire
8 Philp's Bakery
9 54 Penpol Terrace
10 Hubbard's Fish & Chips
17 White Hart Hotel

Other
 5 Tourist Information, library & internet access
11 Pharmacy
12 Martin's Newsagent & Post Office
13 Spar
14 Barclays
15 Launderette
16 LloydsTSB

HAYLE TO ST IVES   [MAPS 46-49]

The **five-mile (8km, 1³/₄-2hrs)** stretch leaves Hayle along the busy Carnsew Rd and The Causeway crossing to the other side of the estuary. The path crosses the railway line – a branch line between St Erth and St Ives (see box p50); it's a delightful excursion in a stunning seascape.

From here the official route follows the A3074 through Lelant, an unpleasant highway with hardly any pavement and many cars. To avoid this, walk through the quiet suburban streets on the outskirts of **Lelant**. From **St Uny Church** the coast path follows the railway line into St Ives, firstly through more dunes then past **Carbis Bay**. The path beyond Carbis Bay winds its way through wooded cliffs to arrive at the broad sands of **Porthminster Beach** where there is an upmarket beach café (see p162) complete with decking.

LELANT & CARBIS BAY
                              [MAP 47, p156]
About a mile out of Hayle, en route to Lelant, is *Old Quay House Inn* (☎ 01736-753988, 🖳 www.theold-quayhouse.co.uk;

4D/3Tr/2F, all en suite). The doubles cost £100 per room, the triples (called friends' rooms because they have three single beds) and the family rooms cost £150 per room.

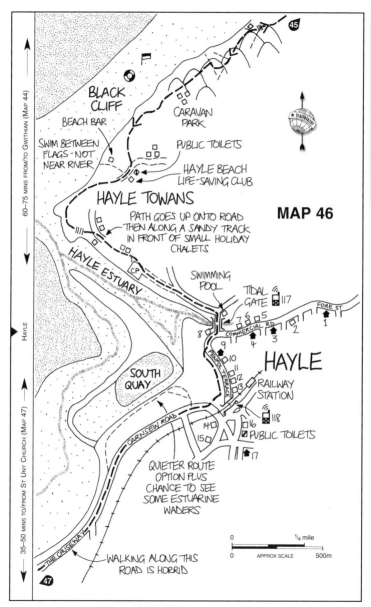

60-75 MINS FROM/TO GWITHIAN (MAP 44)

HAYLE

35-50 MINS TO/FROM ST UNY CHURCH (MAP 47)

BLACK CLIFF

BEACH BAR

SWIM BETWEEN FLAGS - NOT NEAR RIVER

CARAVAN PARK

PUBLIC TOILETS

HAYLE BEACH LIFE-SAVING CLUB

HAYLE TOWANS

PATH GOES UP ONTO ROAD THEN ALONG A SANDY TRACK IN FRONT OF SMALL HOLIDAY CHALETS

MAP 46

HAYLE ESTUARY

CP

SWIMMING POOL

TIDAL GATE 117

FORE ST

7 6 5

COMMERCIAL RD

8

4 3

2

1

9

SOUTH QUAY

10

HAYLE

11

12

PENPOL TERRACE

13

RAILWAY STATION

118

CARNSEW ROAD

14

15

16

PUBLIC TOILETS

17

QUIETER ROUTE OPTION PLUS CHANCE TO SEE SOME ESTUARINE WADERS

THE CAUSEWAY

WALKING ALONG THIS ROAD IS HORRID

0   1/4 mile

0   APPROX SCALE   500m

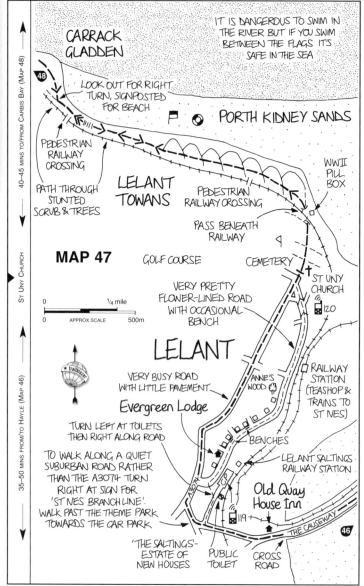

ROUTE GUIDE AND MAPS

40–45 MINS TO/FROM CARBIS BAY (MAP 48)

ST UNY CHURCH

35–50 MINS FROM/TO HAYLE (MAP 46)

48

CARRACK GLADDEN

IT IS DANGEROUS TO SWIM IN THE RIVER BUT IF YOU SWIM BETWEEN THE FLAGS IT'S SAFE IN THE SEA

LOOK OUT FOR RIGHT TURN, SIGNPOSTED FOR BEACH

PORTH KIDNEY SANDS

PEDESTRIAN RAILWAY CROSSING

WWII PILL BOX

PATH THROUGH STUNTED SCRUB & TREES

LELANT TOWANS

PEDESTRIAN RAILWAY CROSSING

PASS BENEATH RAILWAY

MAP 47

GOLF COURSE

CEMETERY

ST UNY CHURCH

120

VERY PRETTY FLOWER-LINED ROAD WITH OCCASIONAL BENCH

0   1/4 mile
0   APPROX SCALE   500m

trailblazer

LELANT

VERY BUSY ROAD WITH LITTLE PAVEMENT.

Evergreen Lodge

ANNE'S WOOD

RAILWAY STATION (TEASHOP & TRAINS TO ST IVES)

TURN LEFT AT TOILETS THEN RIGHT ALONG ROAD

BENCHES

LELANT SALTINGS RAILWAY STATION

TO WALK ALONG A QUIET SUBURBAN ROAD RATHER THAN THE A3074 TURN RIGHT AT SIGN FOR 'ST IVES BRANCH LINE'. WALK PAST THE THEME PARK TOWARDS THE CAR PARK

Old Quay House Inn

119

THE CAUSEWAY

46

'THE SALTINGS' ESTATE OF NEW HOUSES

PUBLIC TOILET

CROSS ROAD

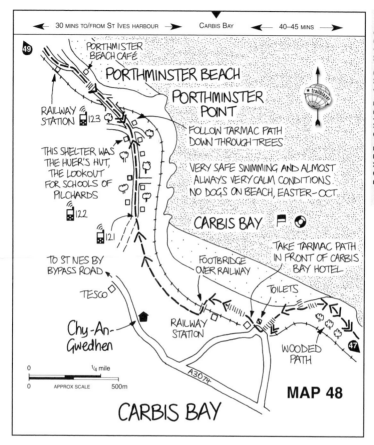

← 30 MINS TO/FROM ST IVES HARBOUR →   CARBIS BAY   ← 40-45 MINS →

PORTHMISTER BEACH CAFÉ

PORTHMINSTER BEACH

PORTHMINSTER POINT

FOLLOW TARMAC PATH DOWN THROUGH TREES

RAILWAY STATION 123

THIS SHELTER WAS THE HUER'S HUT, THE LOOKOUT FOR SCHOOLS OF PILCHARDS 122

VERY SAFE SWIMMING AND ALMOST ALWAYS VERY CALM CONDITIONS. NO DOGS ON BEACH, EASTER-OCT.

CARBIS BAY

121

TO ST NES BY BYPASS ROAD

FOOTBRIDGE OVER RAILWAY

TAKE TARMAC PATH IN FRONT OF CARBIS BAY HOTEL

TOILETS

TESCO

Chy-An-Gwedhen

RAILWAY STATION

WOODED PATH

47

0   ¼ mile

0   APPROX SCALE   500m

A3074

MAP 48

CARBIS BAY

They also serve standard pub fare (daily noon-2.30pm & 6-9pm).

In Lelant itself *Evergreen Lodge* (☎ 01736-755035, 🖳 www.evergreenlodge .biz; 1S/1D/1F), 12 Estuary View, charges £30-35 per night. The double room is en suite and has a four-poster bed. There is a seasonal *teashop* at Lelant station.

In **Carbis Bay** there's a Tesco and a very smart B&B with the tongue-twisting name of *Chy-an-Gwedhen* (☎ 01736-798684, 🖳 www.chyangwedhen.com; 4D/ 1T, all en suite) charging £30-38 per per-

son. They are planning to start serving **cream teas** (daily noon-5 or 6pm) in summer 2009.

You might find it convenient to stay in Carbis Bay but most walkers will push on to St Ives where food, drink and accommodation are plentiful.

Western Greyhound's 501, First's 14/ 14B, 17/17A/17B and 300 as well as Williams's 401 **bus** service call at Lelant and/or Carbis Bay. See public transport map and table, pp46-50.

ST IVES [MAP 49, p163]

St Ives is a major milestone on the coast path coming roughly halfway between Bude and Falmouth. The trouble is it gets so crowded and for a visit it is certainly preferable to come off-season to experience the unique character of its harbour and tightly packed fishermen's cottages. If you have to come in the main season (particularly July and August) book your accommodation well in advance.

St Ives has attracted artists for years and is definitely a place in which to chill out and take your time exploring and soaking up the atmosphere.

The flagship gallery is **Tate St Ives** (see box below; ☎ 01736-796226, 🖳 www.tate.org.uk/stives; Mar-Oct daily 10am-5.20pm, last admission 5pm, Nov-Feb Tue-Sun 10am-4.20pm, last admission 4pm; £5.65), Porthmeor Beach. It's well worth a visit if only for the excellent *café*. If you're interested in art you should also put an hour aside to visit the **Barbara Hepworth Museum** (☎ 01736-796226, 🖳 www.tate.org.uk/stives/hepworth). The opening hours are the same as the Tate. The entry charge is £4.65 but a joint ticket to both the Tate and Barbara Hepworth Museum costs £8.55. There are also numerous small **galleries** in St Ives with art on display but also usually for sale with prices ranging from moderately expensive to ludicrous.

Your perambulations round the town might bring you to the doors of the **St Ives Museum** (☎ 01736-796005; Easter to late Oct Mon-Fri 10am-5pm, Sat 10am-4pm, last admission half an hour before closing time; £1.50), Wheal Dream, on the harbour front. The exhibits include memorabilia of local significance such as the fishing industry, shipwrecks, lighthouses and lifeboats.

In addition to all this several **festivals** (see pp30-1) are held here every year.

Services

The **tourist information centre** (☎ 01736-796297, 🖳 www.visit-westcornwall.com; year-round Mon-Fri 9am-5pm, Jun-Sep Sat 10am-4pm & Sun 10am-2pm, rest of year Sat 10am-1pm) in the Guildhall is helpful and has a good range of material on what to see and do locally.

The **banks** in town are Barclays, HSBC and Lloyds TSB, all on High St and with cash machines; NatWest is on Tregenna Hill.

The **main post office** (Mon-Fri 9am-1pm & 2-5.30pm, closed Thurs pm, Sat 9am-12.30pm) is at the end of Fore St on the harbour front. The **sub post office** (Mon-Fri 9am-5.30pm, Sat 9am-12.30pm), on Tregenna Hill, is more accommodating as it stays open at lunchtime, and on Thursday afternoon.

❏ Art in St Ives

It was the quality of the light and the landscape which first attracted artists to St Ives and is still inspiring them today. Most modern art histories of Cornwall begin with Turner's visit in 1811; however, 1928 is when the development of St Ives as an artists' colony really began with a meeting of Alfred Wallis, Ben Nicholson and Christopher Wood.

Tate St Ives was built on the site of the town's old gas works. The gallery has no static collection and instead displays exhibitions of selected works from the national Tate collection. Even if you are not a supporter of modern art you are bound to find something of interest; whether you find it intriguing or more along the lines of, 'my five-year-old could paint that,' is another debate.

Barbara Hepworth was a well-known sculptress who worked mainly with stone and bronze. Some of her sculptures are big enough to walk inside and around so that you can study every angle. Her studio has been preserved exactly as it was when she died in 1975 and there is a collection of her sculptures in the garden; a very peaceful place to spend a morning or afternoon watching each work change with the movement of the sun.

On The Stennack is a **launderette** (daily 8.30am-8.30pm) and further up a **medical centre** (Stennack Surgery; ☎ 01736-795237). The Edward Hain **Hospital** (off Map 49; ☎ 01736-576100) has a minor injuries unit (Sun-Fri 10am-3pm) and there are several **pharmacies** including Leddra Chemists on Fore St. There are also several **convenience stores** including two branches of the Co-op, one on The Stennack and the other on Tregenna Hill, both of which are open 8am-11pm, closing half an hour earlier on Sunday evenings.

The **Harbour Bookshop** has a good choice including lots of local interest books on Cornish themes. The **library** (☎ 01736-795377, 🖳 www.cornwall.gov.uk/library; Tue 9.30am-9.30pm, Wed-Fri 9.30am-8pm in summer, to 6pm Oct-June, Sat 9.30am-12.30pm), on Gabriel St, offers **internet access** (£1.80 for 30 mins).

The **cinema** is near the venue used by an enterprising drama company Kidz-R-Us, **St Ives Theatre** (☎ 01736-797007, 🖳 www.kidzrus.net), Lower Stennack, where you can certainly spend an enjoyable evening.

There is a good deli on Fore St, **Fore Street Deli** (Mon-Sat 8am-6pm, Sun 'some time in the morning till 4-ish') selling fresh fruit and vegetables. Pasties are everywhere but look no further than the **Cornish Bakehouse** on Fore St. Their medium traditional pasty for £2 is excellent.

Where to stay

For **campers**, *Ayr Holiday Park* (☎ 01736-795855, 🖳 www.ayrholidaypark.co.uk) is about 10-15 minutes' walk from the harbour. It's open all year and you'll pay £5.75-8.75 (depending on the season) per person in a small tent. Alternatively, consider Trevalgan Touring Park, see p166.

Hostel accommodation is available at *St Ives International Backpackers* (☎ 01736-799444, 🖳 www.backpackers.co.uk/st-ives/index.html; 70 beds). It looks a bit of a barracks from the street but it's clean and the staff are friendly. A bed in a dorm costs £11.95-17.95 depending on the season. Bedding is supplied and they have a communal self-catering kitchen.

The B&Bs in St Ives are many and varied but bear in mind that prices can vary depending on the weather, demand and how long you plan to stay. This means the prices quoted may differ from those stated below.

There are several B&Bs and guesthouses round the bus terminus at The Malakoff, near Porthminster Beach, including *The Rookery* (☎ 01736-799401, 🖳 www.rookerystives.com; 5D/1Tr/1F; all en suite), 8 The Terrace, hosted by the Rook family. Most of the rooms (£30-45 per person) have a sea view; the family room has a four-poster bed. A few doors down, at No 5, *The Belmont* (☎ 01736-793401; 1S/4D, all en suite) is a tidy, well-run house with B&B at £70-90 for two sharing a double and £35-45 for the single. Credit cards are not accepted and guests staying only one night must pay in cash.

Sunrise (☎ 01736-795407, 🖳 sunrise@talktalk.net; 2S/3D/1T, all en suite), just across the way in The Warren, charges £30-35 per person. In addition to en suite shower facilities in the rooms they also have a number of bathrooms. However, they are very popular so you will need to book early but don't expect to be able to book a one-night stay for the main season months ahead: only bookings for three or four nights will be accepted.

Also on The Warren, *Blue Mist* (☎ 01736-793386, 🖳 www.blue-mist.co.uk; 1F/4D/1T or Tr) have quite small but perfectly adequate rooms costing £40 per person based on two sharing with a £15 surcharge for single occupancy. All the rooms have sea views and private facilities.

A couple of streets inland we find a Victorian villa, *Rivendell* (☎ 01736-794923, 🖳 www.rivendell-stives.co.uk; 1S/5D/1T), 7 Porthminster Terrace, charging £30-40 per person. The single has a private bathroom but the other rooms are en suite. The house was used in the final episode of a TV series, *Wycliffe*, set in Cornwall. Next door, at No 9, *Carlill* (☎ 01736-796738, 🖳 www.visitcornwall.co.uk/carlillguesthouse; 1S/2D/1T/1F, all with private facilities) is a comfortable, licensed guesthouse with all the usual amenities; the tariff is from £35 per person.

In the old part of town down by the harbour there are a number of lovely, intimate, converted fisherman's cottages offering B&B. For example, on Bunker's Hill just off Fore St is *Grey Mullet* (☎ 01736-796635, 🖳 www.touristnetuk.com/sw/grey mullet; 1S/5D/1T, all en suite) with hanging baskets festooning the front door; it's a pleasure to stay in with rooms costing £30-38 per person. Immediately opposite is *The Anchorage* (☎ 01736-797135,🖳 www .anchoragestives.co.uk; 3D/1D, T or F) charging £70-82 per room for two sharing or £35-60 for single occupancy. One double has a private shower room; the other rooms have en suite facilities. A lovely place, beautifully restored.

The *Sloop Inn* (☎ 01736-796584, 🖳 www.sloop-inn.co.uk; 12D/3T/4F) has a variety of rooms in the pub and around the Sloop. The family rooms sleep three to four people and most rooms are en suite. Rates are £44-46 per person plus a £20 supplement for single occupancy.

Further round the harbour on Fish St we find *Nancherrow Cottage* (☎ 01736-798496, 🖳 www.nancherrow-cottage.co .uk; 3D, all en suite), a former sail loft now restored to a high standard. They charge £75-90 per room in high season but book early as they are popular; they don't take credit cards. Another old, whitewashed cottage in the same part of town is *Downlong Cottage* (☎ 01736-798107, 🖳 downlong cottage@btopenworld.com; 3D/1T/1F) at 95 Back Rd East. The rooms are all en suite except for one which has private facilities. Expect to pay £60-90 per room or £60-70 for single occupancy.

In spite of such a wide choice of accommodation you might still prefer a hotel and there is no shortage. *The Western Hotel* (☎ 01736-795277, 🖳 www.western hotel-stives.co.uk; 2S/7D/2T/3Tr), Royal Square, chages £35 to £42 per person; the rooms are en suite apart from the twins which have private facilities. They have free internet access. The bar is the lively Kettle 'n' Wink known as the 'Kidleywink'

where anyone who likes music congregates either to listen or play. You can expect a good night in here.

Next to the bus station is *Regent Hotel* (☎ 01736-796195, 🖳 www.regenthotel .com; 2S/5D/2T/1Tr). Its two singles, which share a bathroom, cost £35, or it's £36.50-48.50 per person in one of the other rooms which are en suite. They don't do meals but take all credit cards except Diners.

Close by, down the steps to The Warren, is a lovely hotel, *Pedn-Olva* (☎ 01736-796222, 🖳 www.pednolva.co.uk; 3S/19D/4T/2Tr/3F, all en suite), which is owned by St Austell Brewery and has a bar/restaurant looking out over the bay. A single room costs £65-85 and single occupancy of a double costs an eye-watering £105-145; rates for two sharing a room are £120-60.

Where to eat and drink

It is said that you could easily eat at a different restaurant here every day for a fortnight and still miss some of the best. For this reason it's a good idea to wander where your feet take you to 'case the joint' before deciding where you are going to eat.

Of course, with fresh fish being brought in daily all along the coast, Cornwall is where you can get seafood at its best and it would be madness to go home without having tried any or all from a list that includes langoustine, crab, line-caught bass, bream, monkfish and scallops. On the harbour frontage, Wharf Rd and The Wharf, there are at least a dozen places to eat starting with simple fish and chips from the fryer, eaten in a polystyrene carton with a plastic fork from *Kingfisher Fish and Chips* whilst beating off the seagulls to the finest of fine dining. Yet elsewhere in the town away from the hubbub you'll come across brilliant little eateries with well-thought-out menus and prices that won't break the bank. It would be best to book especially during July and August and as well as deciding where to eat you might ask if they do a cheaper meal before 7pm since many of them do.

(Opposite) Top: The vast empty expanse of Perran Beach (see p136). **Bottom**: The harbour at St Ives. (Photos © Henry Stedman).

Rajpoot (☎ 01736-795307, 5-6 Gabriel St; daily 5.30-11pm), just up from the library, has tandoori dishes from £7.95 and house specialities from £9.50. Practically next door is *The Mex* (☎ 01736-797658; daily 5.30pm-9.30pm, Mon-Sat only in winter). Far Eastern cuisine is available at *New World Chinese Restaurant* (☎ 01736-797341; daily from 6pm), centrally located on Market Place, where a meal consisting of a starter, main course and a glass of wine will cost about £17. Try the noodle dishes, they're good.

If you'd rather have a takeaway, *Hong Kong Kitchen* (daily 5-11.30pm), on Chapel St, will do nicely. For pizzas or pasta, try *Peppers* (☎ 01736-794014, 💻 www.peppers-stives.co.uk, 22 Fore St; daily from 5.30pm), or *On Shore* (☎ 01736-796000, Wharf Rd; daily 9am-10pm in summer, though food is not served between 4 and 5pm, daily 9am-3pm & 6-8pm in winter) for an informal, quick meal.

There are many pubs in the town. Most people gravitate to the harbour for an evening stroll and the *Lifeboat Inn* is right at the heart of things with lots going on but it's short on atmosphere. The *Sloop Inn* (see Where to stay; daily noon-3pm & 5-10pm) has more character with low beams, slate floors and wooden benches. The food is tasty and filling, for example seafood chowder (£8.95), or a simple plate of grilled fish, locally caught, with new potatoes and a salad for £7.95.

An absolute gem is *Blas Burger Works* (☎ 01736-797272, 💻 www.blasburgerworks.co.uk, The Warren; Feb-Nov Tue-Sat 6-10pm; main season daily noon-2pm & 6-10pm) an intimate restaurant with only a limited number of tables. Local organic produce is where they're at and their philosophy shines through. Try the Cornish beefburger (£7.50) or the Beet Burger (£9.50) and tell me you've ever tasted burgers as good. Close by is *The Wave* (☎ 01736-796661, 17 St Andrews St; Mon-Sat from 6pm till people stop coming), a

modern, trendy place which also does a cheap meal (two courses for £13.95/three courses £16.95) if ordered before 7.15pm.

Down on Wharf Rd opposite the lifeboat station check out *Alba* (☎ 01736-797222, 💻 www.alba-restaurant.co.uk; daily summer noon-2.30pm & 5.30-9.30pm, winter noon-2pm & 6-9pm) a glass-fronted restaurant on two floors offering fine dining. Their early-birds' menu is £13 for two courses or £16 for three courses. The à la carte is tempting although the prices are less so – eg monkfish cassoulet with chorizo, smoked pancetta and haricot blanc costs £15.95.

Alfresco Café Bar (☎ 01736-793737; Apr-Oct daily from 10am for coffee, noon-2.45pm & 6-9.30pm; winter Wed-Sun only but same hours), further along the harbour front, is an open-fronted continental-style restaurant with a seafood bias. The menu has starters such as pan-seared local scallops (£6.95) and mains including seafood marinière; in the evening this costs £19.95 and would easily feed two adults, at lunch is £9.95. The menu at *Hobblers House* (☎ 01736-796439, 💻 www.hobblers.co.uk; Easter to end Nov, Tue-Sun 6-10.30pm) is fish orientated but the menu also includes steak dishes: steak on a spit costs £11.95.

Ocean Grill (☎ 01736-799874; summer daily 9am-2.30pm & 6-10pm, winter daily 9am-2.30pm & Wed-Sat 6-10pm) is a first-floor restaurant that's always lively. The cooking can be described as Mediterranean and the view over the harbour from the outdoor tables when the weather is fine adds a touch of magic to a meal. Continuing along the harbour front, *Café Coast* (☎ 01736-794925; daily 9am-4pm & 5.30pm till late) is yet another place with a first-floor position, very much in the St Ives style. They do an early special menu before 7pm for £10.95.

On Fore St, seek out *Seafood Café* (☎ 01736-794004, 💻 www.seafoodcafe.co.uk; daily noon-3pm & 6-9pm, often later in summer), a relaxed and energised venue with a

---

(Opposite) **Top**: Godrevy Lighthouse (see p148), inspiration for Virginia Woolf's *To the Lighthouse*. **Middle**: The Old Post Office in Tintagel (see p90) dates back to the 14th century. **Bottom**: Sunny but surf's hardly up at Harlyn Bay (see p116). (Photos © Jim Manthorpe).

ST IVES – MAP KEY

Where to stay
1 Downlong Cottage
4 Nancherrow
   Cottage
5 Sloop Inn
6 Grey Mullet
7 The Anchorage
19 St Ives International
   Backpackers
20 The Western Hotel
23 Rivendell
24 Carlill

25 Belmont
26 The Rookery
27 Regent Hotel
28 Blue Mist
29 Sunrise
30 Pedn-Olva Hotel

Where to eat & drink
2 Café Coast
3 Ocean Grill
5 Sloop Inn
8 Seafood Café

9 Hobbler's House
10 Peppers and Pasta
11 Alfresco Café Bar
12 Kingfisher Fish & Chips
13 Lifeboat Inn
14 On Shore
15 Alba
16 New World Chinese
17 Blas Burger Works
18 Hong Kong Kitchen
21 Rajpoot
22 The Mex

real buzz. Among the choices available are shark, swordfish and weaverfish steaks (£13.45-14.95) and you can choose from a range of sauces and potatoes or noodles.

That's probably enough restaurants but there is one more that genuine foodies must not miss: ***Porthminster Beach Café*** (Map 48; ☎ 01736-795352, 💻 www.porthminster cafe.co.uk; summer daily 9am-10pm, winter Tue-Sun noon-3pm Fri & Sat 6-9pm) which is frequently mentioned in the media as being the best beach café along the coast. You can have a coffee on the decked area right on the beach or dine inside looking out over St Ives Bay on something more substantial: the lunch menu features lighter and larger options with something for everyone. The evening menu was changing at the time of writing but is sure to be worth checking out. The café is open all day in summer but

lunch is served noon-4pm and evening meals 6-10pm.

Transport
The **bus station** at The Malakoff has regular buses to most places of interest to the walker: Services include: Western Greyhound 501, 504, 516, First's 14/14B, 17/17A/17B and 300), and Williams 401. The **railway station** is at Porthminster Beach. Trains run to St Erth where you must change for mainline services but the ride to Lelant Saltings is a delightful short journey. Many folk do the trip both ways for the sheer fun of it but you could walk to Lelant and get the train back in an afternoon, a great little excursion for £4.50 one way. See public transport map and table, pp46-50.

For a **taxi**, AB Cars (☎ 01736-797799) have an office next door to the bus station.

ST IVES TO ZENNOR HEAD   [MAPS 49-52]

Although this is the toughest **six miles (10km, 1³/₄-2¹/₂hrs)** of the coast path it is also amongst the most stunning. The path hugs the contours of the coastline sending you on an endless series of ups and downs as it travels through boggy fields and across rough and rocky terrain.

While the weathered and windblown landscape is reward enough, there's also much evidence of its ancient occupation, if you care to venture a little inland, in the form of ancient stone circles and quoits (see box on p164). It is little wonder that many artists found inspiration here.

The village of **Zennor** is a 10- to 15-minute walk inland. You will need to take this into consideration if you plan to visit. You may prefer to pack a picnic lunch and sit on the rocks above the sea for an hour or two instead, although the museum at Zennor is well-worth checking out.

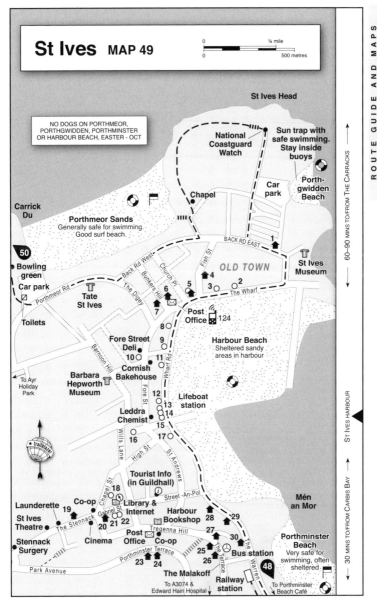

St Ives MAP 49

0 — ¼ mile
0 — 500 metres

St Ives Head

NO DOGS ON PORTHMEOR, PORTHGWIDDEN, PORTHMINSTER OR HARBOUR BEACH, EASTER - OCT

National Coastguard Watch

Sun trap with safe swimming. Stay inside buoys

Car park

Porth- gwidden Beach

Chapel

Carrick Du

Porthmeor Sands
Generally safe for swimming. Good surf beach.

BACK RD EAST

OLD TOWN

St Ives Museum

50
Bowling green
Car park

Back Rd West

Church Pl

Fish St

The Digey

Bunker's Hill

Porthmeor Rd

Tate St Ives

4
6 5
3 2
The Wharf

Toilets

7

8

Post Office 124

To Ayr Holiday Park

Fore Street Deli

Barnoon Hill

9

10 11

Harbour Beach
Sheltered sandy areas in harbour

Barbara Hepworth Museum

Cornish Bakehouse

Fore St

Wharf Rd

12
13
14

Lifeboat station

Leddra Chemist

15

trailblazer

16 17

Wills Lane

High St

St Andrews

Tourist Info (in Guildhall)

Street -An-Pol

Mén an Mor

Launderette

Co-op

19

Chapel St

18

Library & Internet

Gabriel St

Harbour Bookshop

28

29

St Ives Theatre

The Stennack

20 21 22

Post Office

Co-op

27

30

The Terrace

Porthminster Beach
Very safe for swimming, often sheltered

Stennack Surgery

Cinema

Tregenna Hill

26

Bus station

48

Park Avenue

Porthminster Terrace

23 24

25

Warren

The Malakoff

To A3074 & Edward Hain Hospital

Railway station

To Porthminster Beach Café

60–90 MINS TO/FROM THE CARRACKS

ST IVES HARBOUR

30 MINS TO/FROM CARBIS BAY

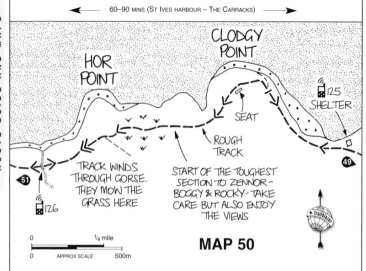

60–90 MINS (ST IVES HARBOUR – THE CARRACKS)

CLODGY POINT

HOR POINT

125 SHELTER

SEAT

ROUGH TRACK

49

51

TRACK WINDS THROUGH GORSE. THEY MOW THE GRASS HERE

126

START OF THE TOUGHEST SECTION TO ZENNOR – BOGGY & ROCKY-TAKE CARE BUT ALSO ENJOY THE VIEWS

0   ¼ mile
0   APPROX SCALE   500m

MAP 50

❏ **Ancient Cornwall**
The history of Cornwall goes back a lot further than its churches and the arrival of the saints. There is another history which is far less tangible and more mysterious with most of its secrets yet to be unlocked by modern man.

Mesolithic nomadic hunters and gatherers were the first settlers after the Ice Age but they left few remains. Neolithic man arrived from across the Atlantic in 3500BC, bringing both the skills to rear crops and raise flocks *and* the art of building *quoits*, the stone chambers used for communal burials. **Zennor Quoit** is relatively easy to visit from the coast path and is signposted from Zennor church (see Map 52 p167).

In 2000BC the Beaker Folk arrived and many believe it was they who erected the stone circles and standing stones; enigmas to modern science and thinking. The **Merry Maidens** and the **Pipers** (see box p189 and Map 65 p188) are worth visiting.

It was Bronze-Age man, 1500-700BC, who made the discovery of adding tin to copper. **Ballowal Barrow** (see Map 58 p176), right on the coast path, is thought to be late bronze age or early iron age. Its purpose is unknown, but one speculation is that the *barrows* were used for religious ceremonies.

The Iron Age Celts, 700BC, introduced the iron-making process from north-west Europe. They organised themselves into clans and formed alliances under kings. As you walk the coast path you pass many signs of Celtic occupation in the form of hillforts and cliff castles. It has even been suggested that the name Cornwall was derived from the Cornish word *cornovii*, meaning cliff castles.

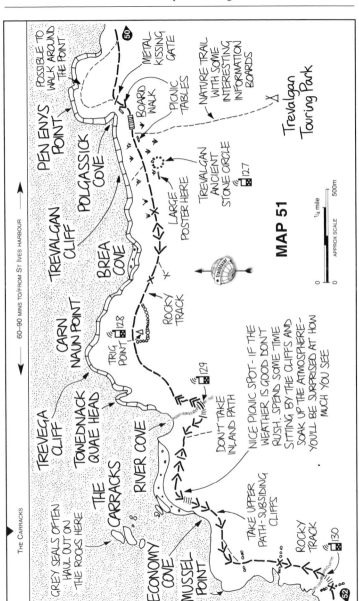

THE CARRACKS

← 60–90 MINS TO/FROM ST IVES HARBOUR →

POSSIBLE TO WALK AROUND THE POINT

PEN ENYS POINT

METAL KISSING GATE

NATURE TRAIL WITH SOME INTERESTING INFORMATION BOARDS

BOARD WALK

PICNIC TABLES

Trevalgan Touring Park

POLGASSICK COVE

TREVALGAN ancient STONE CIRCLE

LARGE POSTER HERE

TREVALGAN CLIFF

BREA COVE

CARN NAUN POINT

MAP 51

APPROX SCALE

ROCKY TRACK

TRIG POINT

TREVEGA CLIFF

TOWEDNACK QUAE HEAD

THE CARRACKS

RIVER COVE

DON'T TAKE INLAND PATH

GREY SEALS OFTEN HAUL OUT ON THE ROCKS HERE

ECONOMY COVE

MUSSEL POINT

TAKE UPPER PATH - SUBSIDING CLIFFS

NICE PICNIC SPOT - IF THE WEATHER IS GOOD DON'T RUSH. SPEND SOME TIME SITTING BY THE CLIFFS AND SOAK UP THE ATMOSPHERE - YOU'LL BE SURPRISED AT HOW MUCH YOU SEE

ROCKY TRACK

50

127

128

129

130

52

ROUTE GUIDE AND MAPS

ZENNOR [MAP 52]

Zennor seems to emerge from the rocky landscape itself, surrounded as it is by granite tors and outcrops, boulder-strewn fields with their high stone walls and the slate and granite cliffs of the coastline.

The village has attracted its share of outsiders for centuries, not least the author DH Lawrence and his wife Frieda who lived at Higher Tregerthen Farm, near Zennor, for a period during the First World War. Their story can be read at the brilliant **Wayside Museum** (☎ 01736-796945; Easter/Apr & Oct Mon-Fri 10.30am-5pm May-Sep 10am-5.30pm, plus Sat summer hols and bank holiday weekends; £3.50 adults). It is the oldest privately owned museum in Cornwall and houses a collection of photographs, information and relics of people who have lived in the area, from stone tools dating back to 3000BC to some stuff on DH Lawrence from 1916. The museum is closed Saturdays and Sundays except during public and school holidays. There is a small shop selling souvenirs, books and some confectionery.

Zennor is a tiny place with the few houses clustered together round the granite **church of St Senara** and the pub (the Tinners Arms), neither of which should on any account be missed. Walkers who fail to visit Zennor, just ten minutes inland from the coast path, are missing a treat. Take a moment to look inside the church and find the **Mermaid's Chair**, an ancient carved chair whose dark wood is polished by time. The mermaid is a pagan superstition and it's remarkable that its depiction in a Christian church should have been tolerated to the present day.

There are no services in Zennor such as shops or a post office but there is a telephone box, though it only accepts credit cards and phone cards. A reverse charge call costs a painful £7.

The **bus stop** is on the main road, a sharp sprint from the pub if you have lingered too long over your pint. Western Greyhound's 508 service between St Ives and Penzance stops here as does First's 300 Penzance to Land's End circular route. See public transport map and table, pp46-50.

Where to stay, eat and drink

You can camp at **Trevalgan Touring Park** (Map 51; ☎ 01736-795855, 🖳 www.ayr holidaypark.co.uk; May-Sep) for £4.75-6.75 per person with a small tent depending on the season. It is reached from the cliff path by a series of signposts in the form of notices describing the flora and fauna of the area and by following them you come to the campsite which has twice been voted Park of the Year by *Camping Magazine*.

Hostel accommodation is available at **Old Chapel Backpackers** (☎ 01736-798307, 🖳 www.zennorbackpackers.co.uk; 32 beds) which also has a busy *café* (Easter-Oct daily 11am-5pm) open to the public as well as serving meals for hostellers. The dorms sleep six and are unisex if they get too busy; they also have a family room. The showers are segregated and the cost for a night is £15 with bedding supplied but not towels. You can **camp** at the back for £5 and use the facilities indoors.

The famous **Tinners Arms** (☎ 01736-796927, 🖳 www.tinnersarms.com; 2S/2D) has accommodation in the White House adjoining the pub. Recently renovated, the lovely, simple bedrooms are a pleasure with crisp white linen and plain white walls. The doubles have en suite facilities but the singles share a bathroom. In the main season you will pay £50 for a single and £90 for two in a double. They serve great food (daily noon-2.30pm & 6.30-9.15pm); the menu changes frequently with choices such as sea bass with chorizo risotto and vanilla cream (£13.50), or root vegetable mixed nut crumble (£9.50). The stone-flagged floors, oak benches and Cornish beer make this a pub to include in your top ten favourites. On Thursday nights musicians gather (outside in summer) and sessions begin with fiddles, guitar and penny whistle until closing time; a unique experience.

Trewey Farm (☎ 01736-796936; Feb-Nov; 1S/1D/1D or T/2F) charges £35 per person; the rooms have washbasins but share bathroom facilities.

About half a mile along the road, in the direction of Gurnard's Head (Treen),

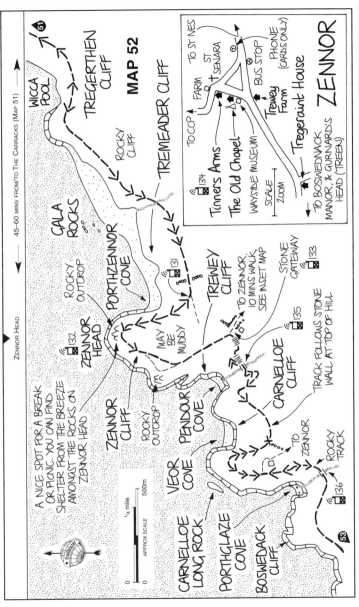

ZENNOR HEAD

← 45-60 MINS FROM/TO THE CARRACKS (MAP 51) →

WICCA POOL

51

TREGERTHEN CLIFF

MAP 52

ROCKY CLIFF

TREMEADER CLIFF

CALA ROCKS

ROCKY OUTCROP

PORTHZENNOR COVE

ZENNOR HEAD 📷 132

MAY BE MUDDY

ZENNOR CLIFF

ROCKY OUTCROP

PENDOUR COVE

📷 131

TRENEY CLIFF

TO ZENNOR, 10 MINS WALK, SEE INSET MAP

STONE GATEWAY 📷 133

CARNELLOE CLIFF

📷 135

TRACK FOLLOWS STONE WALL AT TOP OF HILL

VEOR COVE

TO ZENNOR

CARNELLOE LONG ROCK

PORTHGLAZE COVE

BOSWEDACK CLIFF

ROCKY TRACK

📷 136

53

A NICE SPOT FOR A BREAK OR PICNIC. YOU CAN FIND SHELTER FROM THE BREEZE AMONGST THE ROCKS ON ZENNOR HEAD

Inset:

TO ST IVES

ST SENARA

FARM

TO CCP

Tinners Arms 📷 134

The Old Chapel

WAYSIDE MUSEUM

SCALE 200M

PHONE (CARDS ONLY)

BUS STOP

Trewey Farm

Tregerant House

ZENNOR

TO BOSWEDNACK MANOR & GURNARD'S HEAD (TREEN)

APPROX SCALE

0 — ¼ mile

0 — 500m

★ trailblazer

Tregeraint House (☎ 01736-797061, 🖥 www.cornwall-online.co.uk/tregeraint-house; 1D/1T/1F) is a lovely B&B, artistically decorated in a secluded setting. The rooms have washing facilities but share a bathroom; they charge £35 per person or £40 single occupancy. Perhaps one night in this delightful place is not enough to appreciate the unique beauty of the area.

Further along the road to Gurnard's Head, *Boswednack Manor* (☎ 01736-794183, 🖥 www.boswednackmanor.co.uk;

1S or D/2D or Tr en suite/1T/1F) is open between April and October and is a spacious, granite farmhouse. They charge from £23.50 per person in the rooms with shared facilities (£24 for single occupancy) and from £26.50 per person in an en suite room. The owners are doing their bit to save the planet and have installed solar panels and recycle their waste. They serve a vegetarian breakfast with organic food where possible.

ZENNOR HEAD TO PENDEEN WATCH   [MAPS 52-56]

For the next **seven miles (11km, 2¼-3hrs)** the going is sometimes rocky along this quite challenging stretch with some boggy places unless there has been a particularly dry spell. The path cuts across the long, graceful neck of **Gurnard's Head**. The small settlement here, lying ten minutes inland, is technically Treen but is generally referred to as Gurnard's Head.

The route-finding is easier now with improved waymarking across the boulder-strewn cliffs of **Bosigran**, a favourite haunt for rock-climbers.

Approaching the lighthouse of **Pendeen Watch** you meet a tarmac road which leads to the limited facilities at Pendeen village, a half-mile walk inland.

GURNARD'S HEAD (TREEN) [MAP 53]
This Treen should not be confused with the Treen (Map 63, p185) on the south coast. It is possible that this is why it is commonly referred to as Gurnard's Head.

There are two much-talked-about places here: for B&B, *Cove Cottage* (☎ 01736-798317, 🖥 www.cornwall-online .co.uk/cove-cottage; 2D shared facilities) occupies one of the most remarkable and romantic positions not just on the coast but anywhere in the world, right on the cliff edge with the waves crashing on to the rocks below. What a location! The room rate of £100 is well worth it but be advised they get booked up a long way ahead and walkers should also be aware that in the summer months they do not accept bookings for less than two nights, nor do they accept children or dogs. However, I rate this as one of the best B&Bs along the coast path.

Up the slope into Treen is *Treen Farm* (☎ 01736-796932; 1D/1T) where you will

pay from £60 per room or from £30 for single occupancy. The rooms are not en suite and the owner does not take payment by credit card or do an evening meal but dogs are welcome and they also offer luggage transfer up to St Just (£15), but not towards St Ives.

At the road junction we come to *The Gurnard's Head* (☎ 01736-796928, 🖥 www.gurnardshead.co.uk; 3T/7D/1F, all en suite; food served daily 12.30-2.30pm & 6.30-9.30pm), which has won awards for its food. Rooms cost £85-150 for two sharing and £65 for single occupancy. The menu changes regularly but features local produce and may include grey mullet (£13.50), or grilled polenta, asparagus, spinach and taleggio (£10.50). The wine list is sophisticated and easily the best on the coast. Booking is essential for dinner.

Western Greyhound's invaluable 507 and 508 and First's 300 **buses** stop here. See public transport map and table, pp46-50.

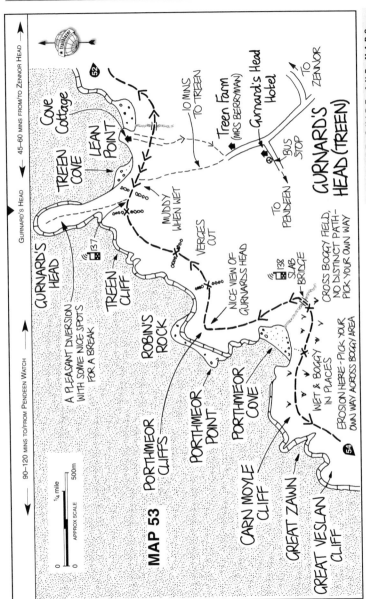

← 90–120 MINS TO/FROM PENDEEN WATCH → GURNARD'S HEAD 45–60 MINS FROM/TO ZENNOR HEAD →

MAP 53

¼ mile

APPROX SCALE

0   500m

GREAT VESLAN CLIFF

GREAT ZAWN

CARN MOYLE CLIFF

PORTHMEOR CLIFFS

PORTHMEOR POINT

PORTHMEOR COVE

ROBIN'S ROCK

TREEN CLIFF

GURNARD'S HEAD

A PLEASANT DIVERSION WITH SOME NICE SPOTS FOR A BREAK

TREEN COVE

COVE COTTAGE

LEAN POINT

52

MUDDY WHEN WET

VERGES CUT

NICE VIEW OF GURNARDS HEAD

SLAB BRIDGE

CROSS BOGGY FIELD, NO DISTINCT PATH– PICK YOUR OWN WAY

WET & BOGGY IN PLACES

EROSION HERE– PICK YOUR OWN WAY ACROSS BOGGY AREA

54

10 MINS TO TREEN

TREEN FARM (MRS BERRYMAN)

GURNARD'S HEAD HOTEL

TO ZENNOR

BUS STOP

TO PENDEEN

GURNARD'S HEAD (TREEN)

Trailblazer

☐ 137

☐ 138

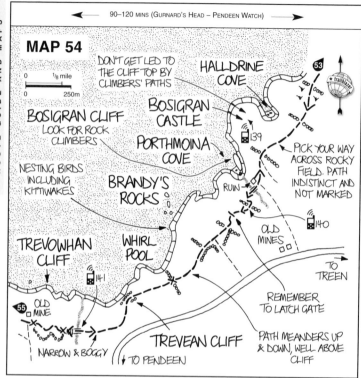

90–120 MINS (GURNARD'S HEAD – PENDEEN WATCH)

MAP 54

0   ⅛ mile
0   250m

BOSIGRAN CLIFF
LOOK FOR ROCK
CLIMBERS

DON'T GET LED TO
THE CLIFF TOP BY
CLIMBERS' PATHS

HALLDRINE
COVE

53

trailblazer

BOSIGRAN
CASTLE

PORTHMOINA
COVE

139

PICK YOUR WAY
ACROSS ROCKY
FIELD. PATH
INDISTINCT AND
NOT MARKED

NESTING BIRDS
INCLUDING
KITTIWAKES

BRANDY'S
ROCKS

RUIN

140

TREVOWHAN
CLIFF

WHIRL
POOL

OLD
MINES

141

TO
TREEN

55 OLD
MINE

REMEMBER
TO LATCH GATE

TREVEAN CLIFF

PATH MEANDERS UP
& DOWN, WELL ABOVE
CLIFF

NARROW & BOGGY

TO PENDEEN

MORVAH   [MAP 55]

This is one of the smallest parishes in
Cornwall with about 70 residents but this
does not mean that nothing happens here.
This is a community bursting with energy
and at the heart of it is **The Schoolhouse**, a
gallery, meeting-place, activity centre and
coffee shop (☎ 01736-787808, 🖥 www
.morvah.com; summer Tue–Sun 10.30am–

5pm, winter Thur–Sun 11.30am-4pm).
Have a look at the stained-glass door which
the community created depicting scenes
from daily life in the area.

Western Greyhound's 507 **bus** service
calls here as does First's 300: see public
transport map and table, pp46-50.

PENDEEN & TREWELLARD
                          [MAP 56, p173]
Pendeen

Pendeen has a **post office** (Mon-Wed & Fri
9am-1pm & 2-5.30pm, Thur 9am-1pm, Sat
9am-12.30pm) on The Square and a **convenience store** (Boscaswell Stores, Mon-
Sat 7am-7pm, Sun 7am-1pm).

B&B is available at the ivy-clad *Old
Count House* (☎ 01736-788058, 🖥 www
.cornwall-online.co.uk/old-count-house;
2D, shared facilities), open May-Oct,
which charges £50 per room and £35 for
single occupancy. *The North Inn* (☎
01736-788417, 🖥 www.thenorthinnpen

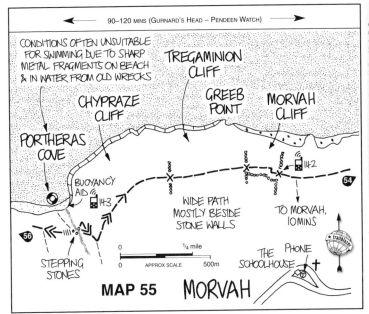

90–120 MINS (GURNARD'S HEAD – PENDEEN WATCH)

CONDITIONS OFTEN UNSUITABLE
FOR SWIMMING DUE TO SHARP
METAL FRAGMENTS ON BEACH
& IN WATER FROM OLD WRECKS

TREGAMINION
CLIFF

CHYPRAZE
CLIFF

GREEB
POINT

MORVAH
CLIFF

PORTHERAS
COVE

BUOYANCY
AID

WIDE PATH
MOSTLY BESIDE
STONE WALLS

TO MORVAH,
10 MINS

STEPPING
STONES

0   1/4 mile
0   APPROX SCALE   500m

THE
SCHOOLHOUSE

PHONE

MAP 55   MORVAH

deen.co.uk; 3D or T/1D, all en suite; daily noon-2.30pm & 6-8.30pm) charges £30 per person; it's a delightful local with real ale and a large beer garden. You can **camp** in their field with a shower block for a trifling £4 per person. The **food** in the bar leads with a selection of curries, their speciality, and is reasonably priced at £9. They also accept dogs and have an **ATM** though it costs £1.75 to withdraw cash.

St John's House (☎ 01736-787435, 📧 tim.hichens@tesco.net; 1S/1D/1T/1F) charges £30 with no single supplement. Guests share the two bathrooms but they do have baths. They accept credit cards and have a small **café**, *Mood Indigo* (Easter-Sep daily 10am-5pm, limited hours in winter) for lunches and teas and will do you an evening meal by arrangement. They do open for dinner on Friday and Saturday evenings and are popular with locals out of season. They will also transfer your luggage (£15 to places within a day's walk).

Radjel Inn (☎ 01736-788446; 1S/1D/1T/1F) is a St Austell Brewery pub where the rate is £27.50 per person regardless of the time of year. The bathroom has to be shared but it does have a bath and a shower. The bar is open daily 11am-11pm and meals in the bar are served daily 11am-8.30pm.

Western Greyhound's 507 calls here en route between St Just and Gurnard's Head: see public transport map and table, pp46-50.

Trewellard

Trewellard has three places worth noting: for B&B *The Old Manse* (☎ 01736-787790, 📧 oldmanse.pendeen@google mail.com; 2D/1T all with private facilities) charges £62-68 for two sharing a room or £50-55 for single occupancy.

Trewellard Arms Hotel (☎ 01736-788634; daily noon-2.30pm & 6-9pm) is planning to offer accommodation but at the time of writing it was not available. The menu changes regularly but the food (standard pub fare) is good: try the Trewellard platter (£16.95) if it's on the specials menu; it's guaranteed to fill you up. There are up to five real ales including the ever-popular Doom Bar.

For a meal you could try the gothic *Trewellard Meadery* (☎ 01736-788345; summer daily 6.30-9.30pm, winter Fri-Sun 7-9.30pm). The menu includes mead (honey wine) which is the kind of drink you tend to order once, just to try it. Food is eaten off wooden platters and with fingers so it is called 'in the rough': (half a) chicken in the rough costs £7.85.

First's 300 **bus** service stops at Boscaswell Stores. See public transport map and table, pp46-50.

❏ Mining in Cornwall

For at least two thousand years tin, copper and lead have been extracted from the Cornish peninsula. Tin found in streams was first utilised by Bronze-Age people. As these sources became exhausted miners began to dig out veins of ore from solid rock. It wasn't until the early 19th century that the technology of steam-driven pumps allowed mines to be worked below the water table. With the invention of dynamite, mining literally exploded. Shafts could be constructed to depths of over 300m (1000ft) and could even be extended below the seabed. At Levant Mine it is said that miners could hear the rumble of boulders being rolled across the seabed during bad storms.

Life in the mines was tough. Poor pay and extreme conditions such as constant dampness and the intense heat given off by the rock itself led to an average life expectancy of less than forty years. When the market collapsed due to cheaper sources being discovered in South America and Australia many Cornishmen emigrated, taking their knowledge to these countries.

Today all that can be seen of this once huge industry are the engine houses left on the surface. The hundreds of miles of underground galleries and shafts lie forgotten, destined to become yet another secret clutched to the bosom of the earth.

Between Pendeen Watch and Cape Cornwall are two popular mining attractions. The first you pass is **Geevor Tin Mine** (Map 56; ☎ 01736-788662, 🖳 www .geevor.com, Easter-Oct Sun-Fri 9am-5pm, Nov-Easter Sun-Fri 10am-4pm, admission £8.50) which closed as a mine in 1990 and is now a museum where you can don a helmet to be guided on a half-hour underground tour. There's also a small *café* (open same hours as the mine) here.

The second place, well worth a visit, is the National Trust's **Levant Engine House** (Map 57, p175; ☎ 01736-786156, Apr-May Wed & Fri, June Wed-Fri & Sun, Jul-Sep Tue-Fri & Sun, Bank Hol Sun and Mon 11am-4.30pm, admission £5.80) where the cliff-top engine house and steam-powered beam engine have been restored to their former glory. The engine, which from 1840 to 1930 lifted copper and tin ore to the surface, is now steamed up for the public in the main season; phone beforehand to check opening. The Levant Mine was the site of a tragic disaster in 1919 when the lift collapsed killing 31 miners. For a mind-boggling insight into the harsh realities of life in the mines join one of the free tours here which really help to make sense of all the mines you see on your walk.

Cornwall and West Devon's industrial heritage is of international importance. For several centuries the region was the world's largest producer of tin and copper providing some of the main raw materials for the industrialisation of the world. In recognition of the importance of this, the mining sites of the region were granted World Heritage site status by UNESCO in July 2006 .

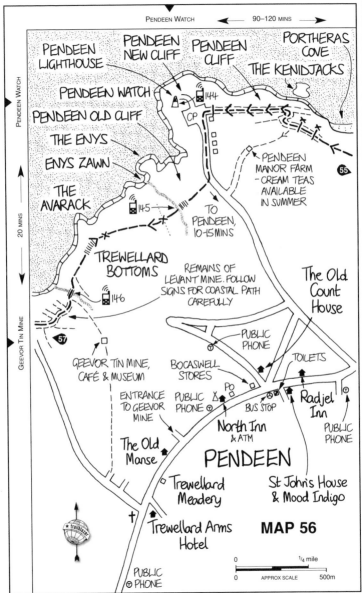

PENDEEN WATCH ← 90–120 MINS →

PENDEEN LIGHTHOUSE

PENDEEN NEW CLIFF

PENDEEN CLIFF

PORTHERAS COVE

THE KENIDJACKS

PENDEEN WATCH

PENDEEN OLD CLIFF

THE ENYS

ENYS ZAWN

THE AVARACK

PENDEEN WATCH

20 MINS

GEEVOR TIN MINE

📱144

CP

55

PENDEEN MANOR FARM – CREAM TEAS AVAILABLE IN SUMMER

📱145 ← TO PENDEEN, 10-15 MINS

TREWELLARD BOTTOMS

REMAINS OF LEVANT MINE. FOLLOW SIGNS FOR COASTAL PATH CAREFULLY

The Old Count House

📱146

57

GEEVOR TIN MINE, CAFÉ & MUSEUM

ENTRANCE TO GEEVOR MINE

PUBLIC PHONE

PUBLIC PHONE

BOCASWELL STORES

PO

BUS STOP

North Inn & ATM

PUBLIC PHONE

TOILETS

Radjel Inn

PUBLIC PHONE

The Old Manse

Trewellard Meadery

PENDEEN

St John's House & Mood Indigo

Trewellard Arms Hotel

MAP 56

0   ¼ mile

0   APPROX SCALE   500m

PUBLIC PHONE

trailblazer

PENDEEN WATCH TO CAPE CORNWALL [MAPS 56-58]

There is a lot to see on this **four-mile (6km, 1¹/₂-1³/₄hrs)** section with views from the cliff tops all the way. Just off the path and signposted from it are the remains of **Geevor Tin Mine** (see box p172) closed in 1990 and now a museum where you can get a coffee and a tour underground if you have the time. The surroundings here are post-industrial and offer a fascinating insight into what it must have been like here when the mine was in full production. The path passes through the remains of **Levant Mine** and then, further on, the eyrie cliff-top location of the **Crown Mine**.

The backdrop changes again by the time you reach the site of the Iron Age fort known as **Kenidjack Castle**, a nice place to take a break and admire the views towards Cape Cornwall. Once thought to be the most westerly point in the British Isles, **Cape Cornwall** is often referred to as 'the connoisseur's Land's End'. It is certainly everything that Land's End could have been in different hands. A cape is defined as a headland where two oceans or channels meet, here the English Channel and St George's Channel. There's a **snack caravan** in the car park during the season, open all day depending on the weather.

The coast path doesn't actually go out to the very point of the Cape but there's nothing to stop you from making the short diversion just to say you've done it and perhaps get a photo of the remains of the tiny **St Helen's chapel**.

The thriving community of **St Just** is another resort popular with artists and it is well worth the detour even if you're not scheduled to stay there. Take the road out of the car park – it should take you 15-20 minutes on foot. You can rejoin the path near Land's End Youth Hostel.

BOTALLACK [MAP 57]

There's a good campsite here, ***Trevaylor Caravan and Camping Park*** (☎ 01736-787016, 🖥 www.trevaylor.com) charging £4-7 a night for a tent plus £3 per person, though between September and June they have a backpacker rate of £5 for a tent and one person. They have an on-site bar and restaurant and a shop selling most of the essentials including camping gas; both are open daily in season but not all day long.

If you need B&B, there's ***The Black Well*** (☎ 01736-787461; 1T/1Tr/1D, T or F) where the tariff is from £25 per person, £35 single occupancy. However, they only accept bookings of two nights or more.

The ***Queen's Arms*** (☎ 01736-788318, 🖥 www.queensarms-botallack.co.uk; daily noon-2.30pm & 6-9pm) is a lively place for an evening and the food is great. The menu includes seafood broth (£5.95 as a starter or £8.95 as a main) and if requested in advance they can serve Botallack Bay lobster. They have Press Gang (4.8%) cider and real ales such as Tallack Tipple (4.2%) and Sharp's Doom Bar (4%) so you're sure of a good time. They also have a self-catering cottage (1D or T) at the back but a two-night booking (a week in the main season) is the minimum.

Western Greyhound's 507 and First's 17A/17B and 300 **bus** services stop right outside the pub. See public transport map and table, pp46-50.

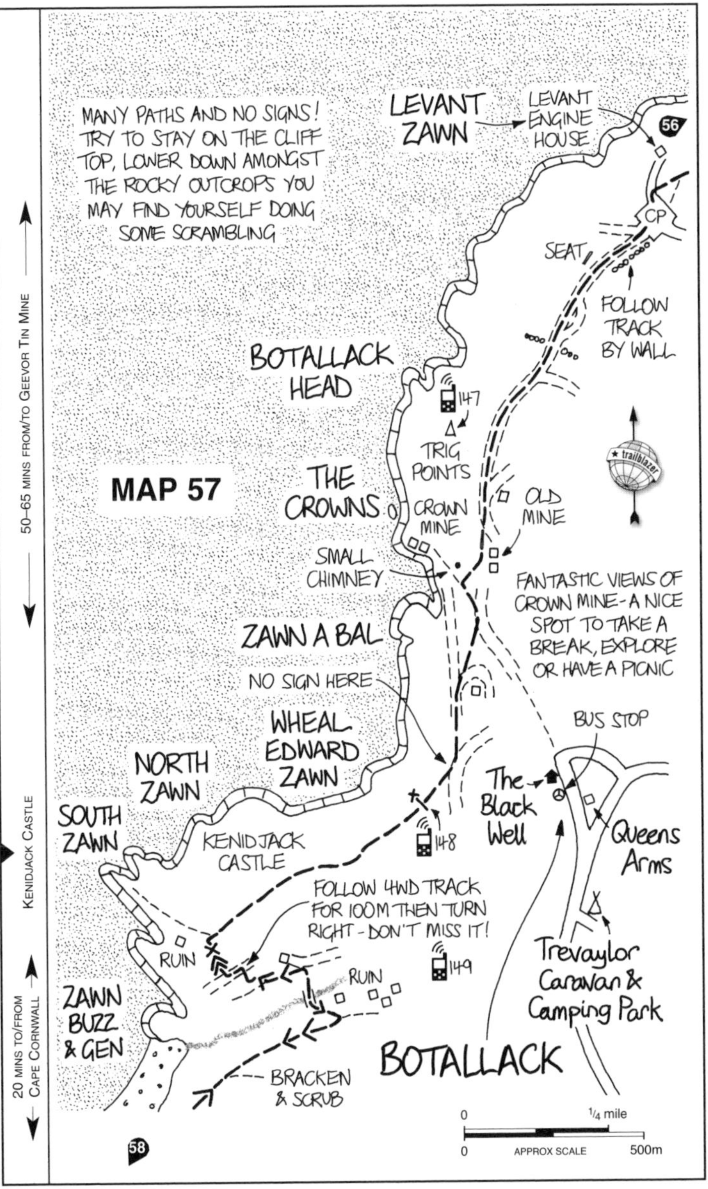

MANY PATHS AND NO SIGNS!
TRY TO STAY ON THE CLIFF
TOP, LOWER DOWN AMONGST
THE ROCKY OUTCROPS YOU
MAY FIND YOURSELF DOING
SOME SCRAMBLING

LEVANT ZAWN

LEVANT ENGINE HOUSE

56

CP

SEAT

FOLLOW TRACK BY WALL

BOTALLACK HEAD

147

TRIG POINTS

OLD MINE

MAP 57

THE CROWNS

CROWN MINE

SMALL CHIMNEY

FANTASTIC VIEWS OF CROWN MINE - A NICE SPOT TO TAKE A BREAK, EXPLORE OR HAVE A PICNIC

ZAWN A BAL

NO SIGN HERE

WHEAL EDWARD ZAWN

BUS STOP

NORTH ZAWN

The Black Well

Queens Arms

SOUTH ZAWN

KENIDJACK CASTLE

148

RUIN

FOLLOW 4WD TRACK FOR 100M THEN TURN RIGHT - DON'T MISS IT!

149

Trevaylor Caravan & Camping Park

ZAWN BUZZ & GEN

RUIN

BOTALLACK

BRACKEN & SCRUB

58

50-65 MINS FROM/TO GEEVOR TIN MINE

KENIDJACK CASTLE

20 MINS TO/FROM CAPE CORNWALL

trailblazer

| 0 | | | 1/4 mile |
| 0 | APPROX SCALE | | 500m |

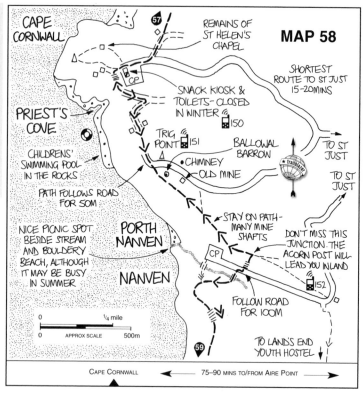

MAP 58

CAPE CORNWALL

REMAINS OF ST HELEN'S CHAPEL

SHORTEST ROUTE TO ST JUST 15-20 MINS

CP

SNACK KIOSK & TOILETS-CLOSED IN WINTER 150

PRIEST'S COVE

TRIG POINT 151

BALLOWAL BARROW

TO ST JUST

CHILDRENS' SWIMMING POOL IN THE ROCKS

CHIMNEY

OLD MINE

TO ST JUST

PATH FOLLOWS ROAD FOR 50M

STAY ON PATH - MANY MINE SHAFTS

DON'T MISS THIS JUNCTION. THE ACORN POST WILL LEAD YOU INLAND

NICE PICNIC SPOT BESIDE STREAM AND BOULDERY BEACH, ALTHOUGH IT MAY BE BUSY IN SUMMER

PORTH NANVEN

NANVEN

CP

152

FOLLOW ROAD FOR 100M

0   ¼ mile
0   APPROX SCALE   500m

TO LAND'S END YOUTH HOSTEL

CAPE CORNWALL ◄— 75-90 MINS TO/FROM AIRE POINT —►

❏ Cape Cornwall

Cape Cornwall is a headland four miles north of Land's End which was thought at one time to be the most westerly point in mainland Britain. It turned out later not to be so after calculations proved Land's End to have that distinction. It is a place of stunning beauty once the crowds have left. The cape is the point at which the current splits, going south into the English Channel and north into St George's Channel. There is an old chimney at the highest point left over from the days when tin mining dominated the area and shafts extended right out under the sea. The chimney dates from 1850 and served the Cape Cornwall Mine extracting tin and copper from beneath the sea bed between 1836 and 1879 when the mine merged with the St Just United Mine further south.

In the early 20th century the Cape was owned by Captain Francis Oates: he had started work at 12 years old and worked his way up to become owner of the Cape and managing director of de Beers in South Africa. On retirement he returned to Cornwall and built Porthledden House near St Just in 1909 as his family home.

ST JUST

*Dear Lord, we hope that there be no ship-
wrecks, but if there be, let them be in St Just
for the benefit of the inhabitants.*

Spoken in St Just Church by
Parson Amos Mason, 1650

St Just is the most westerly town in England
and, as if in deference to the Atlantic weather, built from granite arranged in a charm-
ingly rugged way. Despite its isolated location St Just is a surprisingly cosmopolitan
place with art shops and an active social life
throughout the year. Whereas most of the
villages round about have only a weekend
of events for their annual carnivals, St
Just's Lafrowda Festival (see p30) lasts a
whole week.

More than 50 artists have made St Just
their home and their work is to be seen at
the many **galleries** around the town. The
church is worth a visit for its two splendid
medieval frescoes, *St George* and *Christ of
all Trades*. Also note the wooden plaque

near the door listing all the vicars and rec-
tors since 1297.

Services

Tourist information (☎ 01736-788165, 💻
stjusttourist@cornwall.gov.uk; May-Sep
Mon-Fri 10am-1pm & 2-5pm, Sat 10am-
1pm) is based at the **library** (☎ 01736-
788669; Mon-Wed 10am-1pm & 2-5pm, Fri
10am-1pm & 2-6pm, Sat 10am-1pm, closed
Thursday) where **internet access** is available at £1.80 per half hour for visitors. The
medical centre (☎ 01736-788306) is
behind the library; the village also has a
pharmacy. The **Co-op** (daily 8am-10pm),
in the Square, doesn't have a cash machine
but you can get cashback if you buy something. The **post office** (Mon-Fri 9am-
5.30pm, Sat 9am-12.30pm, closed Thurs
pm) has a **cash machine** with no charge for
withdrawing cash.

Yasmin's Deli (☎ 01736-785933; Tue-
Sat Easter-Sep 10am-5.30pm; rest of year

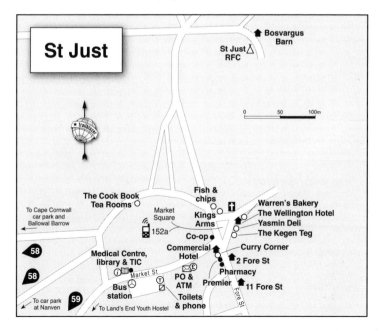

St Just

Bosvargus
Barn

St Just ⌂
RFC

0   50   100m

Fish &
chips

The Cook Book
Tea Rooms ○

Warren's Bakery
The Wellington Hotel
Yasmin Deli
The Kegen Teg

To Cape Cornwall
car park and
Ballowal Barrow

Market
Square

Kings
Arms

152a

Co-op ●

Commercial
Hotel

Curry Corner

2 Fore St

58

Medical Centre,
library & TIC

58

Market St

PO &
ATM

Pharmacy

Premier

11 Fore St

To car park
at Nanven

59

Bus
station

Toilets
& phone

To Land's End Youth Hostel

Fore St

10am-2pm) serves pizza slices and other interesting items with which to create a packed lunch.

Where to stay, eat and drink

The only budget accommodation around here is at Land's End Youth Hostel (see opposite). **B&B** can be found easily. Try the tiny *11 Fore Street* (☎ 01736-786767, 🖳 www.11forestreet.co.uk; 2D) where prices start at £55 per room or from £35 for single occupancy; one double is en suite and the other shares a bathroom with the owners. Next to the Star Inn, *2 Fore Street* (☎ 01736-787784, 🖳 www.stjustbandb.com; 1T/1D or F, shared facilities) charges £60 per room and £35 for single occupancy.

There are two larger establishments, both on the Square: *Commercial Hotel* (☎ 01736-788455, 🖳 www.commercial-hotel.co.uk; 1T/5D/5F, all en suite) charging £60 to £75 per room, single occupancy for £35-45, with nice airy rooms and access to broadband at no cost; and *Wellington Hotel* (☎ 01736-787319, 🖳 www.wellington-hotel.co.uk; 2T/5D/4F, all en suite) where two sharing a twin pay £60 each or single occupancy for £40. They take credit and debit cards and you can eat in the bar (daily noon-2pm & 6-9pm, to 8.30pm in winter).

North of the village, in Tregeseal Valley, is *Bosvargus Barn* (☎ 01736-787356, 🖳 www.bosvargusbarn.co.uk, 1T/2D, all en suite). It's an attractive converted riverside barn where breakfast is served in the conservatory. They charge £65-69 for two sharing a room, or £60 for single occupancy.

St Just Rugby Football Club (☎ 01736-788593; 🖳 www.stjustrfc.co.uk) offers **camping** from mid May to the end of August, with full use of the club's facilities, including showers. They charge £5 per tent; pay at the bar.

There are numerous **places to eat** in St Just. Starting with the cafés, *Kegen Teg* (☎ 01736-788562; daily 9am-5pm, to 9pm in the main season) is a great little place right on the square where all the food is freshly prepared and home made. You can get all-day breakfasts, either veggie or carnivorous, for £7, and burgers made from locally sourced meat though a lot of the items on their menu are vegetarian; they also serve Cornish cream teas for £4.20. Another equally brilliant café is *The Cook Book* (☎ 01736-787266, 🖳 www.thecookbookstjust.co.uk; daily 10am-5pm, to 4pm in winter) for morning coffee or afternoon tea before a long browse among the books, which are all second hand.

There is a **fish and chip shop** (Mon-Sat noon-8pm), *Curry Corner* (daily 5pm-midnight) and for your regular pasty fix, *Warren's Bakery*.

Transport

St Just is served by several **bus** services: First's 17/17A/17B & 300 and Western Greyhound's 504, 507 & 509. Buses stop at the large car park opposite the library. See public transport map and table, pp46-50.

❏ National Coastwatch

Modern technology such as accurate positioning systems has made coastal waters much safer, but it can still fail in distress situations close to shore. The **National Coastwatch Institution** (🖳 www.nci.org.uk) was reformed in 1994 to re-instate a visual lookout along the British coastline and is manned by volunteers. If they see anybody in distress including yachtsmen, divers, walkers, climbers or people in difficulty the watchkeeper immediately informs the nearest HM Coastguard Rescue Centre to alert the rescue services. There are now 23 stations operating around the coast. The NCI is funded entirely by public donations and company sponsorships.

CAPE CORNWALL TO SENNEN COVE [MAPS 58-61]

This is a fine walk of **five miles (8km, 1³/4-2hrs)** along the cliffs, gradually flattening out to provide a gentle approach through the dunes to **Whitesand Bay**. Practically everyone will find this walk a real pleasure and as a day walk it is very popular. The cliffs are honeycombed with old mine workings so it is best to keep to the path. Leaving Cape Cornwall the path climbs to the trig point on **Ballowal Barrow** then it wanders through fields to descend into the **Cot Valley** where a tarmac road leads to a car park for people going to the tiny beach of **Porth Nanven**.

The views back to Cape Cornwall are great and if you keep an eye on the rocks you may see seals popping their heads up for a look around. Dolphins are a not unusual sighting and basking sharks are occasionally seen. Zig-zag paths take you round **Gribba Point** from whence the path is quite easy and level with one down and up at **Maen Dower**. **Sennen Cove** comes into sight and you may like to take to the beach as an alternative to the official route through the dunes.

If you are planning to camp **Trevedra Farm** (off Map 60; ☎ 01736-871818) is a working farm with a campsite open between Easter and the end of October. It costs £5-5.50 per person and £1 per pitch and their **shop** (daily all day in peak season; limited hours at other times) has fresh bread, milk and pasties. The campsite is about a mile inland: take the steps off the beach (Gwnver Beach) climb up, cross a lane, a stile and two fields. The walk takes about 20 minutes to get there and 10 minutes back down in the morning.

KELYNACK [MAP 59, p180]

The only **budget accommodation** between St Just and Land's End is the **Land's End Youth Hostel** (☎ 01736-788437, 🖳 lands end@yha.org.uk; 36 beds), St Just-in-Penwith, where the rate for adults is between £11.95 and £17.95 depending on the season. **Camping** (Apr-Sep) is available; the rate is half the adult overnight cost so in high season you could pay as much as £9 to camp, more if you are not a member. Meals are available: mains cost from £5.95 and desserts from £2.95. Understandably, given its location, the hostel gets booked up weeks ahead in the season with groups and school parties so if you are hoping to stay here, don't leave it to chance.

An alternative place to camp is **Kelynack Caravan and Camping Park** (☎ 01736-787633, 🖳 www.kelynackcaravans .co.uk) but it's a slightly tiresome walk inland. However, a range of accommodation is available from **camping** (Apr-Oct; £5.50-6.50 per person) to a **bunk barn** (10 beds; £12-14 per person depending on the kind of bedding you have) or **B&B** (2D,

both en suite; £30 per person). The whole complex is very well run with a **shop** (daily in season 8.30-10am & 5.30-7pm) selling groceries including fresh milk and fruit and a sparkling clean toilet block. At peak times they have a breakfast bar (serving bacon baps, coffee etc) and will provide packed lunches on request; in 2009 they expect also to offer evening meals.

Nearby on the B3306 road is an excellent B&B, **Bosavern House** (☎ 01736-788301, 🖳 www.bosavern.com; 1S/2T/3D/ 2F, all with private facilities). The family rooms are in an annexe and the other rooms in the main house. The rate is £31-37 but single occupancy in the season will mean you have to pay the full price (£60-70) for a room. It's a super place, run with just the right attention to detail and the eggs at breakfast are from their own hens – if laying.

Western Greyhound's 504 **bus** service calls here as do some of First's 300 services. See public transport map and table, pp46-50.

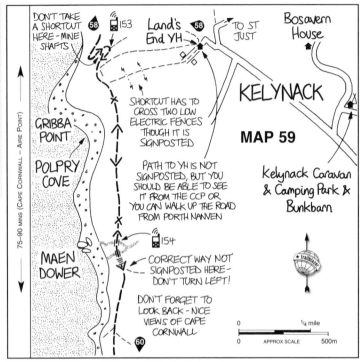

DON'T TAKE A SHORTCUT HERE – MINE SHAFTS

58 153 Land's End YH 58 TO ST JUST Bosavern House

KELYNACK

GRIBBA POINT

SHORTCUT HAS TO CROSS TWO LOW ELECTRIC FENCES THOUGH IT IS SIGNPOSTED

MAP 59

POLPRY COVE

PATH TO YH IS NOT SIGNPOSTED, BUT YOU SHOULD BE ABLE TO SEE IT FROM THE CCP OR YOU CAN WALK UP THE ROAD FROM PORTH NANVEN

Kelynack Caravan & Camping Park & Bunkbarn

154

MAEN DOWER

CORRECT WAY NOT SIGNPOSTED HERE – DON'T TURN LEFT!

DON'T FORGET TO LOOK BACK – NICE VIEWS OF CAPE CORNWALL

60

0   1/4 mile
0   APPROX SCALE   500m

MAYON/SENNEN   [MAP 60]

Mayon is the small settlement on top of the hill above Sennen Cove cheek by jowl with the village of Sennen itself so it's difficult to know where Sennen ends and Mayon begins. For the walker you might as well treat them as all one place.

You might want to buy food for the day at **First and Last Stores** (Mon-Sat 8am-5.30pm, Sun 8am-10.30pm) or go across the road to the **post office** (Mon-Fri 8.30am-5.30pm, Sat 8.30am-12.30pm).

The First and Last Inn (☎ 0871-720 0066, 🖥 www.firstandlastinn.co.uk; food served May-Sep daily noon-9pm; rest of year daily noon-2pm & 6-9pm) is a traditional pub with the usual menu choices. It is a famous old smugglers' haunt with a fascinating history so you may want to check it out if you are in the area.

Whitesands Lodge (☎ 01736-871776, 🖥 www.whitesandslodge.co.uk) is a well-known independent **hostel** with a loyal following particularly among the surfing crowd. It provides self-catering hostel and tipi accommodation as well as camping facilities for backpackers, families and groups. The hostel has 18 beds and the rate is £21 per person for a one-night stay dropping to £15 per night for bookings of a week. There are two **tipis** each sleeping four people (£16 for one night and £10 per night for stays of a week). Tipis can be booked by groups of four people or shared by individuals/couples. **Camping** is from £10 per person. Under the same management, *Whitesands Hotel* (tel as above; 🖥 www .whitesandshotel.co.uk; 1S or D/3D/1T/1F, all en suite) provides B&B accommodation. Again rates reflect the length of stay and the season: £31-55 per person for one night and £25-49 per person for a week's booking. From summer 2009 food will be available daily from 8.30am to 9.30pm; the menu includes an all-day breakfast and features local produce.

Sunnybank Hotel (☎ 01736-871278; 🖳 sunnybank-hotel@btconnect.com; 1S/3D/1T/1Tr) is a nice place to stay with rooms from £30 for the single, £35-37.50 each for two sharing a room and a £15 supplement for single occupancy of a double. The doubles are en suite, the triple has a private bathroom and the single and twin share a bathroom. *Treeve Moor House* (☎ 01736-871284, 🖳 www.firstandlastcottages.co.uk; 1D/1T, both with private facilities) charges £30-35 going up to £40-45 for single occupancy. It's the last B&B before Land's End so is in demand from cyclists about to start the end-to-end cycle ride to John O'Groats. Booking in advance is essential.

The hill down to the cove is mighty steep and the bus has to engage low gear. Don't forget if you go down to the Cove for a drink or meal, the trudge back up again will be hard work.

First's 1 and 300 **buses** stop at the First and Last as does Western Greyhound's 504. See public transport map and table, pp46-50.

SENNEN COVE [MAP 61, p183]

Sennen Cove is a small community where fishing and the tourist trade are the only source of employment. The winter weather is too wild for the boats to go out so from November onwards the quay is piled high with lobster pots and the fishermen spend their time maintaining their boats and nets.

The *Old Success Inn* (☎ 01736-871232, 🖳 oldsuccess@staustellbrewery.co.uk; 1S/2T/8D/1F, all en suite) charges from £60 to £90 per room and £45-55 for single occupancy. Taken over by St Austell Brewery, the inn was being refurbished at the time of writing and should be finished by spring 2009. The beers are St Austell's Tribute, HSD and Proper Job. Food is served daily noon to 2pm and 6-9pm.

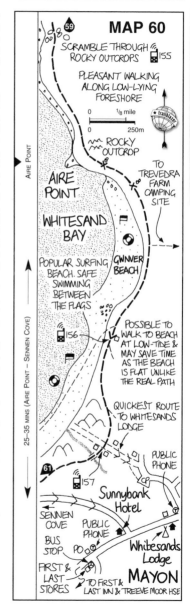

Myrtle Cottage (☎ 01736-871698; 1T/2D) is a small B&B just back from the sea front charging £64 for the en suite double and £60 for the other rooms which share a bathroom. Single occupancy is from £40. It was up for sale in 2009 so do ring to check the situation.

There is a top-notch restaurant in Sennen Cove: *The Beach Restaurant* (☎ 01736-871191, 💻 www.thebeachrestaurant.com; summer daily 9am to late) in the car park right on the beach. Check their website for their winter opening hours as they are variable but in the summer they are open all day for coffee, snacks and teas and in the evening serve a tempting menu – try the crab soup with aioli and toast (£7.25) followed by lemon sole with herb butter and capers (£17.45). Alternatively, try their barbecue (daily 6.30-10.30pm). It's a place of genuine quality.

The *Blue Lagoon* (daily noon-8pm) is a no-frills café and *Breakers Café*, across the road from the lifeboat station, does pasties, baguettes and cream teas.

First's 1 and 300 **buses** stop at the First and Last as does Western Greyhound's 504. See public transport map and table, pp46-50.

If you want a **taxi** ring Prowse Cars (☎ 01736-871786).

SENNEN COVE TO PORTHCURNO [MAPS 61-63]

This **six-mile** (**9.5km, 1³/4-2¹/2hrs**) section includes some spectacular cliff-top walking including the rounding of Land's End, a big milestone on the coast path. The mile from Sennen Cove to Land's End is an easy walk on a hard-packed path, virtually a stroll in the park, used by the whole spectrum of humanity. However, in bad weather it can be very exposed, particularly across Land's End and **Gwennap Head**, as there is barely a rock or bush to shelter behind. **Dr Syntax's Head** is the true most westerly point of mainland England.

When you arrive at the **Land's End** complex you feel as if you have just had an out-of-body experience. You come across a theme park to rival any seaside resort in the land. Over the coach parties and day trippers you can hear the regular sound of the helicopters on their scheduled flights to the Isles of Scilly. There is nothing to do but ignore it all and keep the eyes on the stunning coastal scenery.

Along this stretch the cliff architecture is full of arches and holes, such as the natural land-bridge of **Tol-Pedn-Penwith**, or holed headland, which you can walk across, created by the ceaseless battering of the sea. If you keep on the alert, your chances of seeing grey seals is high, slowing your pace as you watch for them to pop up then disappear again. The path passes through **Porthgwarra** where there is a *seasonal café*, phone and toilets.

LAND'S END [MAP 61]

Land's End stirs all sorts of emotions in us. No one who comes here can be unaffected by the beauty of the rugged coastline and the windswept heath. However, the development of the West Country Shopping Village does tend to dispel one's sense of wonder. The **Visitor Centre** (☎ 0871-720 0044, 💻 www.landsend-landmark.co.uk) is more of a ticket office for the attractions, some of which are quite interesting (the RSPB has a Wildlife Discovery Centre here), than a place for tourist information, but since walkers are usually keen to continue on the path they will probably give them a miss. There are several places for refreshments of the tea, coffee and ice-cream type including the *Old Bake House* for pasties and jacket potatoes. (cont'd on p186)

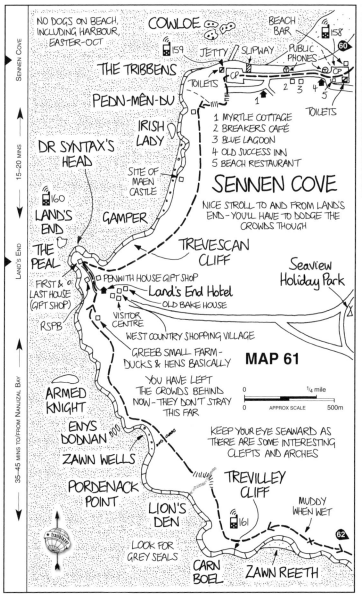

SENNEN COVE

15-20 MINS

LAND'S END

35-45 MINS TO/FROM NANJIZAL BAY

NO DOGS ON BEACH, INCLUDING HARBOUR, EASTER-OCT

COWLOE

BEACH BAR

158

60

159

JETTY SLIPWAY

PUBLIC PHONES

THE TRIBBENS

TOILETS

CP

CP

PEDN-MÊN-DU

2   3   4   5

1

IRISH LADY

1 MYRTLE COTTAGE
2 BREAKERS CAFÉ
3 BLUE LAGOON
4 OLD SUCCESS INN
5 BEACH RESTAURANT

TOILETS

DR SYNTAX'S HEAD

SITE OF MAEN CASTLE

SENNEN COVE

160

NICE STROLL TO AND FROM LAND'S END - YOU'LL HAVE TO DODGE THE CROWDS THOUGH

LAND'S END

GAMPER

THE PEAL

TREVESCAN CLIFF

Seaview Holiday Park

FIRST & LAST HOUSE (GIFT SHOP)

PENWITH HOUSE GIFT SHOP

Land's End Hotel

OLD BAKE HOUSE

RSPB

VISITOR CENTRE

WEST COUNTRY SHOPPING VILLAGE

GREEB SMALL FARM - DUCKS & HENS BASICALLY

MAP 61

ARMED KNIGHT

YOU HAVE LEFT THE CROWDS BEHIND NOW - THEY DON'T STRAY THIS FAR

0   ¼ mile

0   APPROX SCALE   500m

ENYS DODNAN

ZAWN WELLS

KEEP YOUR EYE SEAWARD AS THERE ARE SOME INTERESTING CLEFTS AND ARCHES

PORDENACK POINT

LION'S DEN

161

TREVILLEY CLIFF

MUDDY WHEN WET

62

trailblazer

LOOK FOR GREY SEALS

CARN BOEL

ZAWN REETH

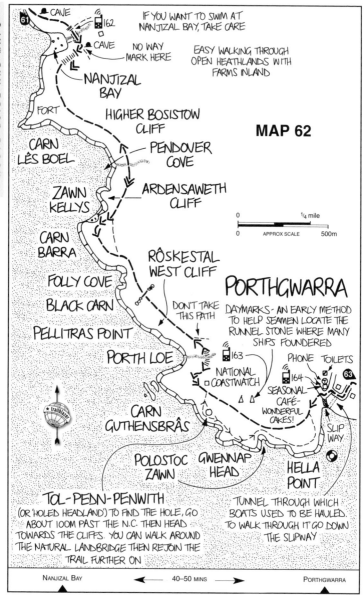

MAP 62

IF YOU WANT TO SWIM AT NANJIZAL BAY, TAKE CARE

EASY WALKING THROUGH OPEN HEATHLANDS WITH FARMS INLAND

CAVE

162

CAVE

NO WAY MARK HERE

NANJIZAL BAY

FORT

HIGHER BOSISTOW CLIFF

CARN LÊS BOEL

PENDOVER COVE

ZAWN KELLYS

ARDENSAWETH CLIFF

CARN BARRA

RÔSKESTAL WEST CLIFF

FOLLY COVE

PORTHGWARRA

BLACK CARN

DON'T TAKE THIS PATH

DAYMARKS - AN EARLY METHOD TO HELP SEAMEN LOCATE THE RUNNEL STONE WHERE MANY SHIPS FOUNDERED

PELLITRAS POINT

PORTH LOE

163

PHONE TOILETS

NATIONAL COASTWATCH

164

SEASONAL CAFÉ - WONDERFUL CAKES!

CARN GUTHENSBRÂS

SLIP WAY

POLOSTOC ZAWN

GWENNAP HEAD

HELLA POINT

0   1/4 mile
0   APPROX SCALE   500m

TOL-PEDN-PENWITH
(OR 'HOLED HEADLAND') TO FIND THE HOLE, GO ABOUT 100M PAST THE N.C. THEN HEAD TOWARDS THE CLIFFS. YOU CAN WALK AROUND THE NATURAL LANDBRIDGE THEN REJOIN THE TRAIL FURTHER ON

TUNNEL THROUGH WHICH BOATS USED TO BE HAULED. TO WALK THROUGH IT GO DOWN THE SLIPWAY

NANJIZAL BAY   ◄——— 40–50 MINS ———►   PORTHGWARRA

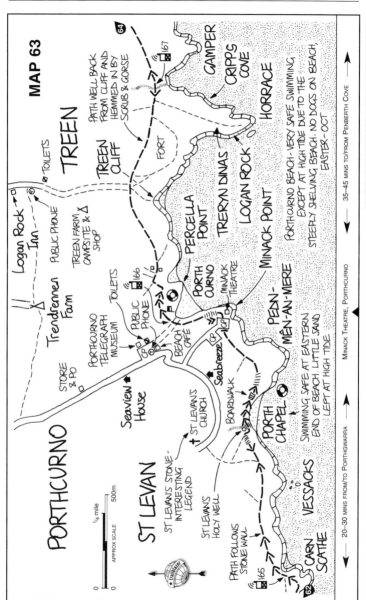

MAP 63

TREEN

TOILETS

Logan Rock
Inn

PUBLIC PHONE

TREEN FARM
CAMPSITE & SHOP

Trendrennen
Farm

PORTHCURNO
TELEGRAPH
MUSEUM

STORE & PO

PUBLIC PHONE

TOILETS

166

PORTHCURNO

Seaview
House

ST LEVAN'S
CHURCH

ST LEVAN

St Levan's Stone-
Interesting
Legend

ST LEVAN'S
HOLY WELL

PATH FOLLOWS
STONE WALL

165

¼ mile

500m

APPROX SCALE

Trailblazer

PATH WELL BACK
FROM CLIFF AND
HEMMED IN BY
SCRUB & GORSE

167

TREEN
CLIFF

FORT

CAMPER

CRIPPS
COVE

PERCELLA
POINT

TRERYN DINAS

LOGAN ROCK

HORRACE

MINACK POINT

PORTH
CURNO

MINACK
THEATRE

BEACH
CAFE

Seabreeze

BOARDWALK

PENN-
MÊN-AN-MERE

PORTH
CHAPEL

PORTHCURNO BEACH - VERY SAFE SWIMMING
EXCEPT AT HIGH TIDE DUE TO THE
STEEPLY SHELVING BEACH. NO DOGS ON BEACH,
EASTER-OCT

SWIMMING SAFE AT EASTERN
END OF BEACH. LITTLE SAND
LEFT AT HIGH TIDE

VESSACKS

CARN
SCATHE

← 20-30 MINS FROM/TO PORTHGWARRA →   MINACK THEATRE, PORTHCURNO   ← 35-45 MINS TO/FROM PENBERTH COVE →

(cont'd from p182) **Land's End Hotel** (☎ 01736-871844, 🖳 www.landsendhotel.co .uk; 2S/8D/14T/2F) would be a great venue for a celebration but is a little over-the-top for a simple overnight stay. Two sharing a room pay £45-85 per person; there is a £10 supplement for either a single or single occupancy of a room. They prefer a minimum stay of two nights. The restaurant is open for bar meals (daily noon to 8pm) and evening meals (7-9pm) with a rather uninspiring menu but a fabulous view.

PORTHCURNO [MAP 63]

A visit to the spectacular open-air **Minack Theatre** (☎ 01736-810181, 🖳 www.min ack.com; May-Sep Mon-Tue, Thur, Sat-Sun 9.30am-5.30pm, Wed & Fri 9.30am-noon) is essential even if you are unable to see a performance. It is open for visits throughout the year but the hours vary so check in advance. Admission is £3.50 for adults. The programme includes anything from musicals to Shakespeare and tickets cost £7-8.50. This remarkable place was built virtually single handed by one woman, Rowena Cade, and a few helpers, using picks and wheelbarrows to shift the granite.

Another interesting place to visit is the **Porthcurno Telegraph Museum** (☎ 01736-810966, 🖳 www.porthcurno.org.uk; daily Mar/Apr-Nov 10am-5pm, Nov-Mar/ Apr Sun & Mon only 10am-5pm; adults £5.50). Porthcurno is the departure point for the first transatlantic cable and the museum tells the remarkable story of the men who overcame the obstacles to lay undersea telegraph cables, many of which come ashore here at Porthcurno.

Another side trip can be to **St Levan's Church** with its 12th-century font and medieval carvings in the Celtic style. On the pew ends are figures such as the bishop, eagles, fishes and a shepherd and in the churchyard is a large stone said to have been split in half by St Levan himself, done

For **Land's End Youth Hostel** see p179. **Camping** is available at **Seaview Holiday Park** (☎ 01736-871266, 🖳 www .seaview.org.uk; Apr-Oct); a tent costs £7-10 plus an additional charge of £3 per adult. Book in advance in July and August.

Buses (First's No 1 and 1A) ply regularly between Penzance and Land's End but using different routes. Their 300 service also calls here as does Western Greyhound's 504. See public transport map and table, pp46-50.

so that people would have something by which to remember him. Opinions vary as to its true origin but its supposed pagan significance was neutralised by the stone cross standing close by.

There is a **general store** and a **post office** (Mon-Fri 9am-1pm & 2-5.30pm, Sat 9am-12.30pm) but the walk inland to the village may put walkers off.

Sea Breeze (☎ 01736-810796; 🖳 philip crow@tiscali.co.uk; 1D, private facilities) has a self-contained cottage and provides B&B for £50-70 per person. However, in July and August they have a three-night minimum stay. *Sea View House* (☎ 01736-810638, 🖳 www.seaviewhouseporthcurno .com; 1S/2D/2T, all with private facilities) charges from £34-36 per person, single occupancy is £60.

Porthcurno Beach Café (☎ 01736-810834; Easter-Oct daily 9am-5.30pm, to 7.30pm main season) is a real gem. They serve a selection of cakes, flapjacks and scones (all home made), pasties, Cornish ice cream and drinks much the same as many other places of a similar type but they do it better. They also serve Lavazza coffee. It's a good idea to stop here because there is not much else before Lamorna.

First's No 1A and Western Greyhound's 504 **buses** call here. See public transport map and table, pp46-50.

PORTHCURNO TO LAMORNA [MAPS 63-66]

The next **five miles (8km, 2-2¹/₂hrs)** of coastline are sometimes described as sub-tropical. The undergrowth is denser than previously, in some places growing overhead to provide a shady tunnel through which to walk.

❏ **The Logan Rock**
Right out on the headland of **Treryn Dinas** sits a massive 70-tonne boulder that could once be rocked by pushing it gently. That is until Lieutenant Goldsmith succeeded in pushing it right off its perch in 1824. Local villagers were incensed as two people had been employed as local guides to the stone. The lieutenant promised to restore it to its original position, but despite help from Admiralty lifting equipment, was unable to restore its fine balance, although it can still be rocked with some difficulty.

After passing the turn-off to **Treen** you may like to make the short detour to the **Logan Rock** (see box above). From here you make gazelle-like progress, one moment walking up high amongst the scrub and gorse, the next dipping down for a taste of the sea at numerous exquisite little coves, all tempting you to stop and explore.

The cove at **Penberth** is a tourist-free zone and to pass through it seems almost an intrusion on the people who make their living here from the sea. Dogs are discouraged and dog-owners are asked to take a diversion inland to keep them from fouling the slipway.

Beyond **Trevedran Cliff** the path crosses an area of heathland with rough, dry-stone walls before turning down to the verdant valley of **St Loy**. Here nestles *Cove Cottage* (Map 65; ☎ 01736-810010, 💻 www.cornwall-online .co.uk/covecottage-stloy; 1D en suite, mid-Feb to Nov), a luxury hideaway in a stunning setting where the minimum stay is for two nights. However, you will need to book very early. They charge £50 per person: cold suppers are available and can be eaten in the room or in the delightful garden.

The path crosses the beach on boulders before regaining the cliffs and passing the lighthouse of **Tater-du** down to the right. When the fog siren sounds it's quite intrusive but that's normal and no one takes any notice of it locally. The name comes from the Cornish, meaning 'black loaf', after the rocks hereabouts. The lighthouse is not open to the public.

TREEN   [MAP 63, p185]

Not to be confused with Treen near Gurnard's Head (Map 53, p169) on the north coast, this Treen is a tiny hamlet with a few farmhouses and the warm and homely *Logan Rock Inn* (☎ 01736-810495), owned by St Austell Brewery. The bar is open from Easter to October daily 10am-midnight and for the winter months daily 10.30am-2.30pm and 5-11pm. Food is served daily 10.30am-2.30pm & 5-9pm; the menu is standard pub fare but also includes locally sourced fish.

Treen Farm Campsite (☎ 01736-810273, 💻 www.treenfarmcampsite.co.uk)

charges £6.50 for an adult with a small tent. They are open Easter to October but don't take advance bookings. Run by an organic dairy farmer, their **shop** (open daily in season) sells homemade pasties, bread and milk.

There's a **B&B** nearby, *Trendrennen Farm* (☎ 01736-810585, 💻 andreasem mens@hotmail.com; 3D) where you'll pay £30-35 per person or £12.50 for single occupancy. One room is en suite but the others share a bathroom. Sit out in the enormous garden and admire the view.

About two miles (3km) further on, just past Porthguarnon, is another campsite at

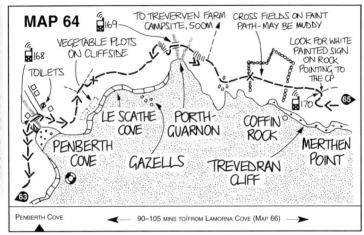

MAP 64

📱169
TO TREVERVEN FARM CAMPSITE, 500M
CROSS FIELDS ON FAINT PATH - MAY BE MUDDY

VEGETABLE PLOTS ON CLIFFSIDE

📱168
TOILETS

LOOK FOR WHITE PAINTED SIGN ON ROCK POINTING TO THE CP

📱170 ←65

LE SCATHE COVE

PORTH-GUARNON

COFFIN ROCK

PENBERTH COVE

GAZELLS

TREVEDRAN CLIFF

MERTHEN POINT

63

PENBERTH COVE ← 90–105 MINS TO/FROM LAMORNA COVE (MAP 66) →

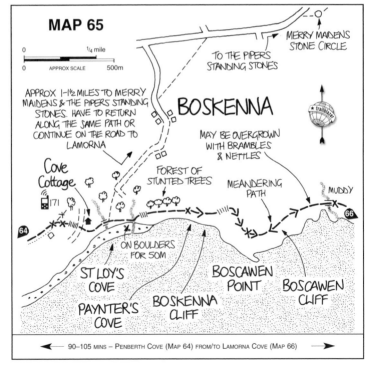

MAP 65

0 ——— ¼ mile
0 APPROX SCALE 500m

MERRY MAIDENS STONE CIRCLE

TO THE PIPERS STANDING STONES

APPROX 1-1½ MILES TO MERRY MAIDENS & THE PIPERS STANDING STONES. HAVE TO RETURN ALONG THE SAME PATH OR CONTINUE ON THE ROAD TO LAMORNA

BOSKENNA

MAY BE OVERGROWN WITH BRAMBLES & NETTLES

MEANDERING PATH

MUDDY

Cove Cottage
📱171

FOREST OF STUNTED TREES

64

66

ON BOULDERS FOR 50M

ST LOY'S COVE

PAYNTER'S COVE

BOSKENNA CLIFF

BOSCAWEN POINT

BOSCAWEN CLIFF

← 90–105 MINS – PENBERTH COVE (MAP 64) FROM/TO LAMORNA COVE (MAP 66) →

ROUTE GUIDE AND MAPS

Treverven Farm (off Map 64; ☎ 01736-810200, Easter-Oct), which is signposted from the coast path. They charge £8-12 for a tent pitch with two adults.

First's 300 **bus** service stops in Treen as does their 1A; Western Greyhound's 504 also calls here. See public transport map and table, pp46-50.

ROUTE GUIDE AND MAPS

❏ **Merry Maidens and Pipers**
Inland from the coast are two ancient sites, the **Merry Maidens** stone circle and the **Pipers**, two large standing stones nearby. According to legend the Merry Maidens were nineteen young girls dancing in the fields to the tunes of the two nearby Pipers when they should have been attending vespers on the Sabbath. For their sins they were all turned to stone. (See also box p164).

It is possible to visit these sites by walking inland (see Map 65) and then staying on the road and walking to Lamorna (see Map 66) but this may not be that enjoyable as it involves walking along narrow roads which can be busy in the summer. The alternative is to return on the same path.

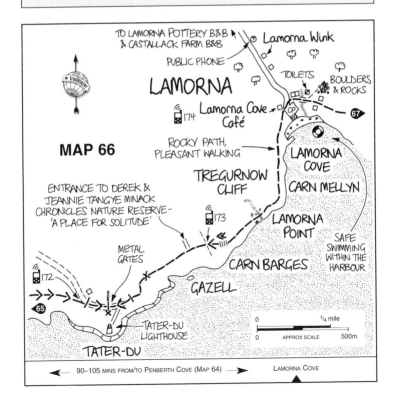

MAP 66

TO LAMORNA POTTERY B&B & CASTALLACK FARM B&B

Lamorna Wink

PUBLIC PHONE

LAMORNA

TOILETS

BOULDERS & ROCKS

📱174 Lamorna Cove Café

67

ROCKY PATH, PLEASANT WALKING

LAMORNA COVE

TREGURNOW CLIFF

CARN MELLYN

ENTRANCE TO DEREK & JEANNIE TANGYE MINACK CHRONICLES NATURE RESERVE- 'A PLACE FOR SOLITUDE'

📱173

LAMORNA POINT

SAFE SWIMMING WITHIN THE HARBOUR

METAL GATES

CARN BARGES

📱172

GAZELL

65

TATER-DU LIGHTHOUSE

TATER-DU

0 ¼ mile
0 APPROX SCALE 500m

← 90–105 MINS FROM/TO PENBERTH COVE (MAP 64) →   LAMORNA COVE

ROUTE GUIDE AND MAPS

LAMORNA [MAP 66, p189]

Lamorna is one of the few wooded coves along the coast path. It hasn't got much in the way of services but walkers will be glad to discover *Lamorna Cove Café*, with ice-cream, teas, pasties, crab and fish soup served on the decking opposite. If your water bottle needs filling don't ask here. Even if you have spent money in the café they will refuse and point to the stern 'We do not give out tap water' sign.

Two B&Bs are worth a look. *Lamorna Pottery* (☎ 01736-810330; 2D/1T/1F) charges £35 for single occupancy and £55-65 for two sharing. The family room is en suite but the other rooms share facilities. Evening meals are available by arrangement. They have a *café* (daily 10am-5pm) with a tasty lunchtime menu that includes salads, quiches and homemade soup.

Castallack Farm B&B (☎ 01736-731969, 🖳 www.castallackfarm.co.uk;

2D/1T, all with private facilities) charges from £30 per person (£44 for single occupancy). They have paid a lot of attention to detail here with corkscrews in the room and facilities for drying wet gear.

The pub on the cove road is the *Lamorna Wink* (☎ 01736-731566; food served daily 11am-2pm); the name goes back to a time when spirits were banned but smuggled brandy could be had with a wink to the publican. The author Martha Grime's murder mystery *The Lamorna Wink* is set in the area and is a good read.

First's No 1/1A and 300 **buses** stop at what they call the Lamorna Turn – in other words it doesn't go down to the cove or it wouldn't get back up. Western Greyhound's 504 stops at Lamorna Wink. See public transport map and table, pp46-50.

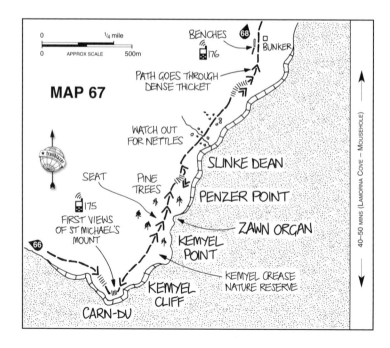

LAMORNA TO MOUSEHOLE   [MAPS 66-68]

This simple **2-mile (3km, 40-50 mins)** stretch passes through the pine forest of the **Kemyel Crease Nature Reserve**, then heads inland through scrub to arrive at the top of the hill above Mousehole. On reaching the road you turn right and walk down into the tiny village acclaimed by Dylan Thomas as 'the loveliest village in England'.

MOUSEHOLE   [MAP 68 & map p192]

Pronounced 'mowzell', possibly from the Cornish *mouz hel* or 'maiden's brook' or alternatively because the entrance to the harbour was so tight that getting through it was like trying to sail through a mouse hole. A former pilchard-fishing village, the old stone quay and cottages are hardly equal to the volume of visitors that crowd in during the season. Traffic is the bane of the village and the time will have to come when cars are banned, leaving the narrow streets to pedestrians. The village is like a film-set, a romantic notion of what a Cornish village should look like and one of the most appealing on the coast path.

There are plenty of services available to the walker although with Penzance only five miles away, a couple of hours on foot or fifteen minutes on the bus, many will push on to the much-bigger destination. Anyone walking the coast path in December may like to be here for **Mousehole Lights**, when

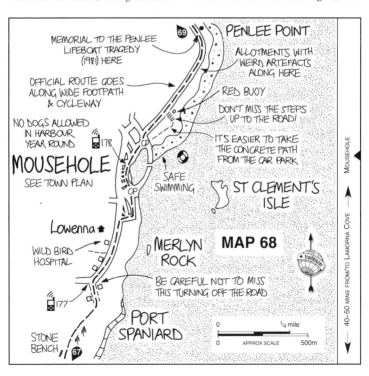

the village is illuminated by a display of Christmas lights, and **Tom Bawcock's Eve** (see p31) on the 23rd.

Coming down the hill into the village you pass the **Wild Bird Hospital** (Map 68; ☎ 01736-731386; daily 10am-4.30pm) for injured, orphaned or oiled birds, which you might decide to visit. Entry is free although donations are, of course, always appreciated.

In the centre of the village is the **post office** (Mon-Fri 9am-5.30pm, Sat 9am-12.30pm, closed Tues pm), and a **newsagent** with some limited groceries.

Where to stay

There are several **B&Bs**. *Lowenna* (Map 68; ☎ 01736-731077, 🖳 mm4lowenna@aol.com; 1D/1T or F, both en suite), on Raginnis Hill near the Bird Hospital, charges £65 for a room. It is convenient because the coast path goes right past the door but they rarely take bookings for one night. At *Renovelle* (☎ 01736-731258; Easter-Oct; 1S/2D), 6 The Parade, you'll pay £20 for the single and £20-25 per person. One double is en suite but the other rooms share a bathroom. The lady who runs it has been in the business for 50 years so has a fair idea of what walkers want. She takes cash and cheques only.

Alternatively, on the opposite side of the road from The Old Coastguard Hotel, *The Dolphins* (☎ 01736-731828, 🖳 www.dolphins-mousehole.co.uk; 1T/1D/1F, all en suite) is a very nice, friendly place; they take walkers regularly and remain open all year. Two sharing a room pay £30-35 each; there is no single occupancy rate in the main season.

Tremayne (☎ 01736-731214; Easter-Oct; 2D/1F, all en suite), 1 The Parade, charges £60-65 per room (£45 for single occupancy) but only does a continental breakfast so this is a good place for those fed up with a full English! One-nighters are welcome. For those who prefer a pub, *The Ship Inn* (☎ 01736-731234, 🖳 www.ship

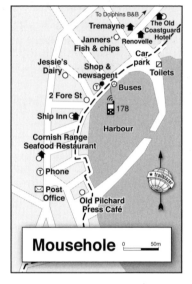

Mousehole 0 ___ 50m

To Dolphins B&B ↗
Tremayne
The Old Coastguard Hotel
Janners' Fish & chips
Renovelle
Jessie's Dairy
Shop & newsagent
Car park
Toilets
2 Fore St
Buses
178
Ship Inn
Harbour
Cornish Range Seafood Restaurant
Phone
Post Office
Old Pilchard Press Café
★ trailblazer

mousehole.co.uk; 7D/1F, all en suite) does B&B from £40 to £100 per room depending on the time of year and whether the room has a sea view or not; single occupancy is £50-60. This old inn celebrates Tom Bawcock's Eve (see p31) on 23rd December.

For hotel-style accommodation, *The Old Coastguard Hotel* (☎ 01736-731222, 🖳 www.oldcoastguardhotel.co.uk; 14D, all en suite) is a traditionally opulent place where the prices are as steep as Mousehole's lanes and alleyways. A solo traveller staying one night is likely to part with over £90 for B&B, even in low season; for two sharing expect to pay £120-210 for a room depending on the season and whether the room has a sea view or not. Free internet access is available.

For a restaurant with rooms consider *Cornish Range Seafood Restaurant* (see Where to eat; 3D, all en suite) which charges £80-110 per room.

(Opposite) Top: Land's End (see p182) with Sennen Cove just visible to the north. (Photo © Bryn Thomas). **Bottom**: Old mine buildings above Porthtowan. The importance of the mining landscape of Cornwall was officially recognised when it was granted World Heritage site status (see p172). (Photo © Jim Manthorpe).

Where to eat and drink

The upmarket **Cornish Range Seafood Restaurant** (☎ 01736-731488, 💻 www.cornishrange.co.uk; summer daily 10am-2.30pm & 6-9.30pm; evenings only in winter) styles itself as a 'restaurant with rooms'. Their early starter menu, between 6 and 7pm, is good value: two courses cost £14.95 and one course £10.95.

Another chic place to eat is **2 Fore Street** (☎ 01736-731164; Feb-Dec daily from 10am, lunch noon-3.30pm, evening meals 6-9.30pm). Food is available most of the day and can either be eaten inside at the plain wooden tables (with artwork by local artists adorning the walls), or in the garden if the weather is good. The owner-chef trained under Raymond Blanc and his deft touch is apparent in the predominantly fish-based menu. Why not try the starter of scallops with rosemary, hazelnuts and pancetta (£6.25), followed by a main (£11-15) and washed down with a nice crisp Muscadet?

Up the hill at **The Old Coastguard's Restaurant** (see Where to stay) the food is what I think is known as *á la mode* and features locally sourced fish and meat (mains

cost around £17.50); the Cornish cheese platter is mouth-watering.

If all this fine dining puts you off try the pub or **Janners Fish and Chips** (☎ 01736-732211; daily Easter-oct noon-1.30pm & 5-8.30pm, though hours can vary depending on demand; in winter Wed, Fri & Sat 5-7.30pm). The menu at **The Ship Inn** (see Where to stay; daily noon-3pm & 6-9pm in summer, daily noon-2.30pm & 6-8.30pm in winter) includes standard Cornish pub fare such as a home-made fish pie (£8.50) as well as meat and vegetarian options. **Old Pilchard Press Café** (☎ 01736-731154, 8 Old Quay St; Easter-Dec daily 8.30am-6pm, Jan-Mar closes earlier) does breakfasts, cream teas, ploughman's, and salads.

Jessie's Dairy is difficult to pass by on a hot day. They have all sorts of ice cream including gooseberry and wild cherry. They also serve pasties.

Transport

Buses (First's No 5A & 6 and Western Greyhound's 504) to Penzance run throughout the day. See public transport map and table, pp46-50.

MOUSEHOLE TO PENZANCE [MAPS 68-70]

The **four-mile (6km, 1-1¼hrs) section** between Mousehole and Penzance is all on tarmac. From the harbour car park the path stays close to the shore on the concrete sea wall but soon leaves it to join a cycle path all the way through **Newlyn** to **Penzance**. The options are to stay on this, which is preferable to being on the road, and walk it, or catch a bus (see public transport map and table, pp46-50) and save yourself some foot slogging. However, there's always something to see and we pass the memorial to the Penlee lifeboat, the *Solomon Browne*, lost with all hands in 1981 whilst trying to rescue the crew of the *Union Star*, an event of national importance at the time.

NEWLYN [MAP 69, p195]

Newlyn is a working fishing port and there is plenty to look at for those who like to lean on stone jetties watching the boats. It is a place that doesn't fit the Cornish mould

having none of the 'Poldark' effect like St Ives for example. There is a danger that outsiders will try to turn Cornwall into a nostalgia trip that bears no relation to the

---

(Opposite) The Minack Theatre, Porthcurno (see p186), dramatically situated right beside the sea. (Photo © Edith Schofield).

living, working area that it is. The Fish Festival (see p30) is held here in August.

Newlyn is famous in the art world for having given its name in the nineteenth century to a colony of artists who came here attracted by the seascapes and its similarity to Brittany, France. Most of their names will be unfamiliar to those not interested in art but in their day the work of Stanhope Forbes, Walter Langley and Edwin Harris was widely applauded. Their paintings can best be appreciated by a visit to Penlee House Gallery (see p196) in Penzance whilst **Newlyn Art Gallery** (☎ 01736-363715, ☐ www.newlynartgallery.co.uk; Easter-Oct Mon-Sat 10am-5pm, Nov-Easter Tue-Sat 10am-5pm, bank hols 11am-4pm; entry free) is a small but beautifully laid-out showcase for work by contemporary artists of local provenance. *The Exchange Café* is open Mon/Tue-Sat 10am-4.30pm; 11am-3.30pm on bank holidays.

Among the services available the **Co-op** (daily 8am-10pm) is well stocked with groceries including fruit and sandwiches and they have a **cash machine** with no charge for withdrawing cash. There's even a branch of **Barclays Bank** (Mon-Thurs 10am-12.30pm, Fri 10am-1pm) and close by is the **post office** (Mon-Tue 8.45am-5.30pm, Wed-Fri 9am-5.30pm, Sat 9am-noon).

Where to stay
There are two B&Bs as you walk in to Newlyn from Mousehole, both overlooking the teeming fish dock and beyond across the curve of Mount's Bay to Penzance. *Harbour View* (☎ 01736-350976; 1T/2D) charges from £25 for B&B but the bathroom is shared. Nearly next door, *The Smugglers* (☎ 01736-331501, ☐ http://smugglersnewlyn.co.uk; 3D, all en suite) is arguably one of the best B&Bs along the Cornwall part of the coast path. Recently renovated, the rooms, named after Newlyn artists, are large and comfortable with king-size beds but sadly the one I stayed in didn't have a view. Rates are £60-80 per room and single occupancy is £55. They are open all year and have an excellent restaurant (see Where to eat).

You could also try the *Swordfish Inn* (☎ 01736-362830, ☐ www.swordfish inn.co.uk; 4D) for en suite accommodation. The cost is £45 a room or £25 for single occupancy. Just near Newlyn Art Gallery is a house on a row, *An Treveth* (☎ 01736-368434, ☐ www.cornwall-online.co.uk/an trevethnewlyn; 1S/1D), 20 New Rd, with B&B for £28.

Where to eat and drink
There are several options in Newlyn including **fish and chips** and *China Garden*, a Chinese takeaway. Pasties are to be had at *Warren's Bakery* by the old bridge. There's a new pizza place, *Pizza Patio* (☎ 01736-363446, ☐ www.pizzapatio.co.uk) under the same ownership as the place of the same name in Hayle where, apart from the usual pizzas, the specials are worth a look. The crab and prawn bake on a linguine base for £9.95 was superb and their home-baked bread a triumph.

The *Red Lion Inn* (☎ 01736-362012; daily noon-2pm & 6-9pm in summer, lunchtime only in winter) is renowned for its crab soup (£5.95). The other pub in the village with food is the *Tolcarne Inn* (☎ 01736-363074; food served daily noon-2.30pm & 6.30-9pm).

The Smuggler's Restaurant (see Where to stay; summer daily 7-9.30pm, contact them for their winter days/hours) has a wonderful view of the harbour, the very boats you are watching have probably brought in the fish you are eating. Try their cod fillet on rosemary sauté potatoes with chorizo, capers and prawns (£16.75). They keep Camel Valley wines too.

On the bridge, *Newlyn Seafood Café* (☎ 01736-367199; Easter to end Sep 6pm to late) is a charming contemporary eatery with an inventive menu: for example try their seafood-tasting plate for £11.95 or naked Newlyn crab at £7.50.

Transport
First's 1/1A, 5 and 300 services stop at Newlyn Bridge. Western Greyhound's 504 service and First's 6 stop at the bridge and at the Red Lion pub. See public transport map and table, pp46-50.

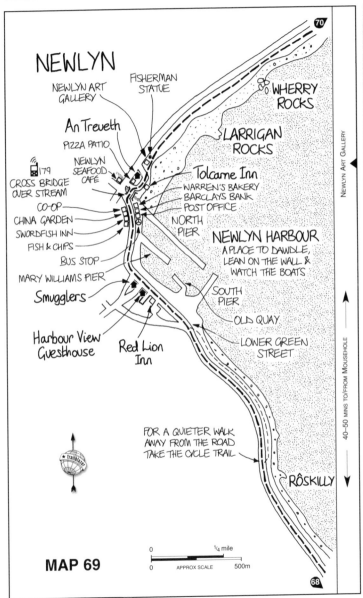

NEWLYN

NEWLYN ART GALLERY

FISHERMAN STATUE

An Treveth

PIZZA PATIO

📱179

NEWLYN SEAFOOD CAFE

CROSS BRIDGE OVER STREAM

CO-OP

CHINA GARDEN

SWORDFISH INN

FISH & CHIPS

BUS STOP

MARY WILLIAMS PIER

Smugglers

Harbour View Guesthouse

Red Lion Inn

WHERRY ROCKS

LARRIGAN ROCKS

Tolcarne Inn

WARREN'S BAKERY

BARCLAYS BANK

POST OFFICE

NORTH PIER

NEWLYN HARBOUR

A PLACE TO DAWDLE, LEAN ON THE WALL & WATCH THE BOATS

SOUTH PIER

OLD QUAY

LOWER GREEN STREET

FOR A QUIETER WALK AWAY FROM THE ROAD TAKE THE CYCLE TRAIL

RÔSKILLY

NEWLYN ART GALLERY

40-50 MINS TO/FROM MOUSEHOLE

70

68

★ trailblazer

0   ¼ mile

0   APPROX SCALE   500m

MAP 69

❏ Cornwall's fishing industry

One of Cornwall's oldest fishing industries is that of fishing for pilchard. Shoals containing millions of fish would appear seasonally off the Cornish coast and a lookout man, called a *huer*, would be stationed on top of the cliffs to alert the community of a sighting.

When the pilchards were spotted he would cry 'hevva' (shoal) and then direct the waiting fishermen with semaphore signals using branches so that they could surround the fish with their nets.

Over-fishing brought the industry to an end by the 1920s, although recently pilchards have once again been caught off Cornwall. Pressing and salting of pilchards is still carried out by traditional methods in Newlyn with the end product being exported to Italy as was traditionally done.

Nowadays in Cornwall there are about 850 fishing vessels of which some 200 are over ten metres in length. About 2000 fishermen are directly employed on board and there are considerably more related jobs onshore.

In the smaller harbours most of the fishing boats you see are landing crabs and lobsters using various types of crab pots, although they may also use nets to fish for spider crabs, ray and anglerfish depending on the season. These vessels tend not to work more than five to ten miles away from their respective ports.

PENZANCE [MAP 70, p199]

Penzance is a busy, bustling town whose heyday was in the nineteenth century when it was the commercial centre of the tin-mining industry. A statue of **Sir Humphry Davy**, born in the town and inventor of the miners' safety lamp, stands outside the Market House.

Penzance is a happy hunting ground for those who love galleries, rivalling St Ives in its artistic prominence. The flagship is **Penlee House Gallery** (☎ 01736-363625, 🖳 www.penleehouse.org.uk, Morrab Rd; Easter Sat-Sep Mon-Sat 10am-5pm, Oct-Good Fri Mon-Sat 10.30am-4.30pm, also open on bank holidays; admission £3 but free to all on Sats); it's in a fine Victorian house and has a wide-ranging collection from archaeology to photography documenting the life and history of west Cornwall, as well as an art collection from the late 19th century painted by well-known Newlyn artists. Last admission is half an hour before the closing time. There's a nice café, *The Orangery* (see p200), and a shop with a great selection of cards.

A close second is **The Exchange** (☎ 01736-363715, 🖳 www.theexchangegallery.co.uk, Princes St; Easter-Oct Mon-Sat 10am-5pm, Nov-Easter Tue-Sat 10am-

5pm, bank hols 11am-4pm; entry free) in the town's former telephone exchange, showcasing the best of contemporary art. Of the many other galleries in Penzance there is sure to be something that appeals and a couple of hours mooching about looking at artwork can pass the time agreeably.

Penzance has an energy that is infectious, apparent for example on the occasion of the **Golowan Festival** (see p30) in June, a celebration of the arts that includes theatre, music, carnival and fireworks.

Services

The **tourist information centre** (☎ 01736-362207, 🖳 www.visit-westcornwall.com; Easter-Sep Mon-Fri 9am-5pm, Sat 10am-4pm, July & Aug Sun 10am-2pm, Oct-Easter Mon-Fri 9am-5pm) is located at the bus station. Take heed, the tourist information office does not give out bus times! However, right next to it is the **bus information office** (Mon-Fri 8.30am-4.45pm, Sat 8.30am-1.30pm) which does.

The main shopping street is Market Jew St. On it you will find the **Co-op** (Mon-Fri 8.30am-10pm, Sat 8.30am-9pm, Sun 10am-4pm) and the main **post office** (Mon-Fri 9am-5.30pm, Sat 9am-12.30pm); there is another post office on Morrab Rd but it may soon be closed down. Millets Outdoor Shop has plenty of **camping supplies** including camping gas and Jessops stocks **camera film** and of course digital cameras if you've dropped yours on the trail. There are several High Street **banks** including Lloyds TSB, in a building that would not disgrace London's Cheapside, HSBC and NatWest, all with ATMs and on Alverton Rd.

For **internet access**, Penzance Library (☎ 01736-363954, Morrab Rd; Mon-Fri 9.30am-6pm, Sat 9.30am-4pm) charges £1.80p for 30 minutes for visitors.

There are some good bookshops including **Books Plus** (Mon-Sat 9am-5.30pm), 23 Market Jew St, which is strong on topics of local interest such as shipwrecks, tin mining and fishing.

There's a **laundrette** (daily 8am-7pm) near the railway station. The pedestrian-only Causeway Head is the best place to find fruit and vegetables; there's also a small **cinema** on this street. Down Morrab Rd there's a **medical surgery** (☎ 01736-363866; Mon-Fri 8.30am-5.30pm) with a **dental surgery** next door and there is a **pharmacy** at the top of New St.

Where to stay

Penzance Youth Hostel (☎ 0845-371 9653, ☐ penzance@yha.org.uk; 100 beds) is a Georgian manor house overlooking Mount's Bay. At the time of writing the hostel was closed but it was expected to reopen in May 2009: the whole place is being refurbished and the number of beds increased from 80 to 100; internet access will also be available. Adult members pay between £11.95 and £17.95 per night. Meals are available: mains cost from £5.95 and desserts from £2.95. You can **camp** (£8.50 per person) in the grounds: campers have their own shower block but can use the other facilities in the hostel. However, it is best to book in advance. The hostel is about 1¹/₂ miles from the bus and train stations.

There is also an independent hostel, *Blue Dolphin Penzance Backpackers* (☎ 01736-363836, ☐ www.pzbackpack.com, Alexandra Rd; 24 beds; 1T/1D/1F) charging £15 a night for a bed in a dorm (most of the dormitory accommodation is en suite). The rooms share a bathroom and cost from £32 per room. They also have self-catering facilities. Another option is the *YMCA* (☎ 01736-334820, ☐ www.cornwall.ymca.org.uk; 52 beds), Alverton Rd, costing from £15.40. Broadband access is available free and the advantage it has over the YH is that it is open 24 hours a day. They do a light breakfast for £3 but other meals are only provided for large groups. At the time of writing they didn't have a self-catering kitchen but it is possible this will change by the end of 2009.

When it comes to **B&Bs** you have a very wide choice. However, be aware that many places do not accept advance bookings for one night only in the main season.

Coming in along the prom from the direction of Newlyn you can start looking once you have passed Alexandra Rd which is itself lined with guesthouses of which the following are all of a reasonable standard: *Torwood House* (☎ 01736-360063, ☐ www.torwoodhousehotel.co.uk; 1S/1T/4D/2F) charges £26.50-28.50 per person, though there is a £14 supplement for single occupancy in the summer months; they also offers an evening meal from £18. One double and the single share a bathroom but the other rooms are en suite. A nice cheerful place, they have free internet access and are open all year.

Glencree House (☎ 01736-362026, ☐ www.glencreehouse.co.uk; 2S/4D/2T or F, all have private facilities), 2 Mennaye Rd, charges £20-39 per person depending on the season. At *Keigwin House* (☎ 01736-363930, ☐ www.keigwinhouse.co.uk; 2S/1T/1T or D/1Tr/2D/1F) B&B is £25-40 per person with a warm welcome for walkers as the manageress is also a keen walker. The rooms are en suite other than the two singles and one of the twins. Guests may use the microwave and toaster. Note that credit cards are not accepted.

On the Promenade is the smart-looking *Beachfield Hotel* (☎ 01736-362067, ☐ www.beachfield.co.uk; 5S/4T/4D/2Tr/2F, all en suite); rooms with sea view cost from £54.50 in low season rising to £119 (£79.50 for single occupancy in the main season). A three-course evening meal with coffee is available for £22.95, less for fewer courses. For those on a tighter budget they have rooms (10D/1F, all en suite) without a sea view in an adjacent building; rates here are £49 per double or £89 for the family room. Online bookings are given a 5% discount.

Morrab Rd also has plenty of accommodation possibilities. On the corner is *The Corner House* (☎ 01736-351324, 🖥 www .thecornerhousepenzance.co.uk; 5D, all en suite), 20 Marine Terrace, a two-storey house with palm trees at the front and a summery look to it. B&B costs from £25-35 per person; £30-45 single occupancy. At *Con Amore* (☎ 01736-363423, 🖥 www .con-amore.co.uk; 3S/2T/2D/2F), 38 Morrab Rd, the rates are similar and the two singles share a bathroom but the other rooms are en suite. *Lynwood* (☎ 01736-365871, 🖥 www.lynwood-guesthouse.co .uk; 2S/3T/ 2D), at No 41, charges £25-35 per person; some rooms are en suite but the others share a bathroom. Dressing gowns are provided for standard rooms and they also have drying facilities. *Woodstock* (☎ 01736-369049, 🖥 www.woodstockguest house.co.uk; 2S/1S or D/2D/1T/1F), at No 29, charges £26-34 depending on room type

(some are en suite and the others share bathroom facilities) and season. Further up Morrab Rd, next to the library, is the bright and cheerful *Richmond Lodge Guest House* (☎ 01736-365560, 🖥 www.rich mondlodge.net; 1S/1T/2D/2F, with private facilities) charging £29 per person, £26 for the single or £35 for single occupancy of a double/twin.

Continuing along Western Promenade you come to Regent Terrace with several guesthouses to choose from. *Lombard House* (☎ 01736-364897, 🖥 www.lombard househotel.com; 2S/4D or Tr/2F, all en suite), at No 16, charges £40 to £45 but doesn't take cheques. They accept single occupancy bookings out of the main season. *Camilla House Hotel* (☎ 01736-363771, 🖥 www.camillahouse-hotel.co.uk; 2S/6D or T, all with private facilities), at No 12, with prices from £35-42.50 per person; *Warwick House* (☎ 01736-363881, 🖥 www.warwickhousepenzance.co.uk; 2S/ 3D/2T, all en suite), at No 17, charges £42 for a single and £42 per person for two sharing with a one-night booking. They also have a walker' package where the rate is £38 per person for a minimum three-night booking. They will pick guests up at

PENZANCE MAP KEY

Where to stay
1 Youth Hostel
2 YMCA
3 Keigwin House
4 Torwood House
5 Blue Dolphin
   Backpackers
6 Glencree House
7 Beachfield Hotel
10 The Corner House
12 Woodstock
13 Con Amore
14 Lynwood
16 Richmond Lodge
27 Cornerways Guest
   House
29 Whiteways
43 Penzance Arts Club
44 Camilla House Hotel
45 Warwick House
46 Lombard House
47 Blue Seas

Where to eat & drink
8 Chinese Emperor
9 Fish & chips
15 Orangery Café
20 Penzance Buttery
21 Alverne Restaurant

Where to eat (cont)
22 New Hong Kong
24 Archie Brown's
37 Curry Corner
38 Harris's Restaurant
39 The Bakehouse
40 Turks Head
41 Admiral Benbow
42 Ganges Balti

Other
11 Post Office
15 Penlee Gallery
17 Surgery
18 Library & internet
   access
19 Pharmacy
23 Cinema
25 Jessops
26 Books Plus
28 Launderette
30 Tourist Information
31 Post Office
32 Millets
33 Co-op
34 Sir Humphrey Davy
   statue
35 Peasgood's Pharmacy
36 The Exchange

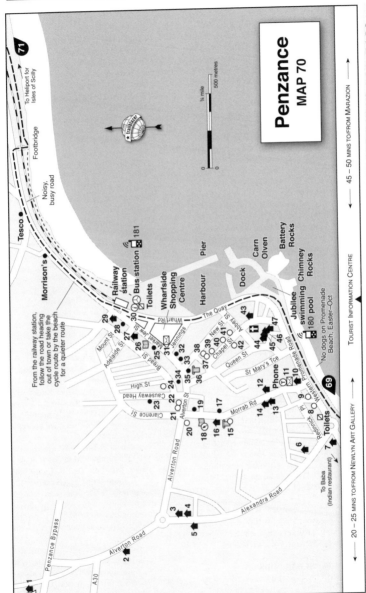

the end of the day but are not able to drop them off in the morning, however public transport is good. On the final day they will take your luggage to the next B&B for a flat charge of £10 per trip. They offer broadband access free. *Blue Seas Hotel* (☎ 01736-364744, 🖳 www.blueseashotel-pen zance.co.uk; Mar to mid-Dec; 1S/5D/2T, all en suite), at No 13, has green credentials and free use of a computer; rates are from £38-42 per person.

When you come to the Thirties-style Yacht Inn, turn up Chapel St and find yourself in the Chelsea of Penzance with the imposing building housing the *Penzance Arts Club* (☎ 01736-363761, 🖳 www.pen zanceartsclub.co.uk; 4D/3D, T or F, all with shower facilities) on the corner. Some rooms are fully en suite but the others share a toilet. This establishment has an unusual and arty interior with a proliferation of artwork on every available wall space. The rooms are large and rather neglected but intriguing. Rates depend on the length of stay, the kind of room and whether you are a member or not. Expect to pay £40-55 per person for one night, and £25-40 per night for a four-night stay. Guests become temporary members so can attend events. They have a garden and bar but do not serve meals. Unfortunately at the time of writing the Club is on the market; it is to be hoped that any new owners keep the atmosphere.

Cornerways Guest House (☎ 01736-364645, 🖳 www.penzance.co.uk/corner ways; 2S/1T/1D, all en suite), 5 Leskinnick St, has rooms for £30-35. There's a 2% surcharge if you want to pay by credit card. They are next door to a launderette. Close by is *Whiteways Guest House* (☎ 01736-366198, 🖳 www.whitewaysguesthouse .com; 2S/2D/1D or F, all en suite), 1 East Terrace, charging £25-27 per person per night and £30-35 for single occupancy of a double room though this is not offered in the main season. They run a *café* (in season daily 8am-7pm); evening meals (5-7pm) are also available in the guesthouse.

Where to eat and drink

There are lots of tea shops and coffee houses in the town including the stylish *Orangery* (☎ 01736-361325; Mon-Sat summer daily 10am-4.45pm, winter 10.30am-4.15pm, lunch served noon-3pm), at Penlee House Gallery, which serves hot paninis and jacket potatoes with a choice of fillings and *Penzance Buttery*, at the top of Morrab Rd, which has Cornish cream teas on the menu as well as coffee and light bites.

Perhaps the most environmentally friendly café in town is *Archie Brown's* (☎ 01736-362828; 🖳 www.archiebrowns.co .uk, Mon-Sat 9am-5pm), on Bread St, a mecca for the green army. Vegetarians need look no further: try the homity pie and mixed salad for £6.95, or mushroom and hazelnut burger for £7.50.

There are lots of **fish and chip shops** in Penzance – and plenty of ethnic options too. The *Chinese Emperor* (daily 5.30-11pm) advertises an all-you-can-eat buffet for £13.99 while the *New Hong Kong* (☎ 01736-362707, Alverton Rd; Sun-Thur 5.30-11pm, Fri & Sat 5.30pm to midnight, Sun noon-2.30pm) have buffet-style eating for £12.80 (Sun-Thur) and £14.50 (Fri & Sat). For Indian food try *Baba* (off Map 70; ☎ 01736-330777; Tue-Sun noon-2pm & 5-10.30pm), The Promenade, Wherrytown, where they have some tasty vegetarian options.

Ganges Balti House (☎ 01736-333002; daily 5.30-11.30pm), 18 Chapel St, has a buffet night on the last Monday of the month when you pay £9.95 for all you can eat. At the top of the street, *Curry Corner* (☎ 01736-331558; daily noon-2pm & 5pm-midnight) offers a set meal for only £8.95 including naan bread.

The menu at *Alverne Restaurant* (☎ 01736-366007; summer Mon-Sat 9.30am-9pm, winter Mon & Tue 9.30am-4pm, Wed-Sat 9.30am-9pm), Alverton St, changes regularly but try the slow-cooked marinated pork on a warm potato salad and caramelised onions (£12.95) if it is on the menu. They also have a specials board with fish dishes.

There are two wonderful old pubs: the swashbuckling *Admiral Benbow* (☎ 01736-363448; food served daily noon-2.3pm, Mon-Sat 6-9.30pm Sun 6-9pm) is named after a 17th-century seafarer whose story is told in notes included with the menu. The beams are low and revellers spill out onto the street outside so you have to push your way through them to get to the bar. The food is great for its kind, like the seafood pie, a medley of fish and shellfish cooked in a sauce made from white wine and cream with chunky chips for £11.25. The ale on draught varies but may include Sharp's Doom Bar and St Austell's Tribute. Slightly quieter but no less nautical and with similar food is the nearby *Turks Head* (☎ 01736-363093; daily 11.30am-2pm & 9pm).

The *Bakehouse* (☎ 01736-331331, 🖥 www.bakehouserestaurant.co.uk; summer daily (winter Mon-Sat) from 6.30pm till they close; summer Tue-Sat (winter Wed-Sat) 10am-2pm), on Chapel St, is an intimate but *trés chic* little restaurant with a well-devised menu.

Harris's Restaurant (☎ 01736-364408, 🖥 www.harrissrestaurant.co.uk; Mon-Sat 7-9.30pm, summer Tue-Sat noon-2pm), 46 New St, is bedecked with hanging baskets outside and is held by some to be the best restaurant in Penzance. The menu includes such culinary delights as scallops on salad leaves with a herb dressing (£8.50) followed by noisettes of Cornish lamb with fennel and rosemary sauce (£18.95) and fresh berries in a biscuit basket with white chocolate ice cream (£7.25) for dessert.

Transport

Penzance is served by National Express **coaches** (see box p44) as well as by **trains** (see pp42-3) from all over the UK. Train services run roughly hourly to St Erth (change for St Ives), Par (for Newquay), Bodmin Parkway, Plymouth, Truro and Falmouth. The Sunday service is limited so be sure to check in advance.

The **bus** network in West Cornwall is excellent. First (1/1A, 2/2A/2B, 5/5A, 6, 17/17A/17B, 18/X18/18B & 300) and Western Greyhound (504, 508, 509, 513, 515 & 516) have routes to and from here. See public transport map and table, pp46-50.

For a **taxi**, try Jolly Rogers (☎ 0780 892 0606, or ☎ 01736-763400).

❏ Visiting the Isles of Scilly

Penzance is one of the gateways to the Isles of Scilly, an archipelago of five inhabited islands and numerous small rocky islets with a population of just over 2000. They are promoted for their peace and tranquillity. If you fancy a romantic getaway it is easy to visit for a few days or even just one.

You can travel to the Isles of Scilly either by sea or air with **Isles of Scilly Travel** (☎ 0845-710 5555, 🖥 www.ios-travel.co.uk). *Scillonian III* sails from Penzance to the main island of St Mary's between late March and late October. Services operate Mon-Sat except for the first and last two weeks of the season and during the World Pilot Gig Championships (early May). The journey takes 2hrs 40 mins but departure times can vary depending on the tides. Period return fares cost from £80 to £95 and a day return is £35.

The Skybus services operate from Land's End, Newquay, Exeter, Southampton and Bristol airports; return fares cost from £140-340. Since flights to/from Land's End Airport only take 20 minutes it might be worth considering sailing one way and flying the other: a day air/sea return costs £70.

British International Helicopter Travel Service (☎ 01736-363871, 🖥 www.islesofscillyhelicopter.com) can fly you across to St Mary's or Tresco from the Penzance heliport (Mon-Sat) throughout the year. The journey takes 20 minutes and a day return costs £96, or it's £140 for a saver return (conditions apply) or £170 for a normal return. Online bookings get a £1.50 discount per sector.

Note that flights (both helicopter and fixed-wing plane) do not operate if the weather conditions are bad.

PENZANCE TO MARAZION

[MAPS 70-72]

The walk to Marazion (**3 miles/5km, 45-50 mins**) is on a cycle path between the railway line and the beach and makes for quite a pleasant stroll with the whole prospect of Mount's Bay to add to the enjoyment.

On the way in to Marazion you pass two places serving food: *The Station House* (Map 71; ☎ 01736-350459; meals served daily 11am-2pm & 5-9.30pm) is open all day and serves cakes and teas during the afternoon. *Jordan's Café* (Map 71; ☎ 01736-360502; summer daily 9.30am-5.30pm, winter 10am-4pm) serves food that can be eaten in or taken away and also offers Wifi internet access.

However, those who don't wish to walk along totally flat cycle tracks can always catch the **bus**: Western Greyhound's 513 and 515 (see public transport map and table, pp46-50) go to Marazion.

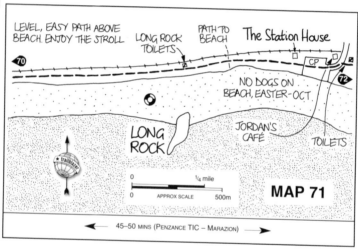

LEVEL, EASY PATH ABOVE BEACH. ENJOY THE STROLL

LONG ROCK TOILETS

PATH TO BEACH

The Station House

70

NO DOGS ON BEACH, EASTER-OCT

CP

72

LONG ROCK

JORDAN'S CAFÉ

TOILETS

trailblazer

0 ___ ¼ mile

0 ___ APPROX SCALE ___ 500m

MAP 71

← 45-50 MINS (PENZANCE TIC – MARAZION) →

MARAZION

[MAP 72]

The name derives from the Cornish *marghas byhgan* or small market from the days when the village held two markets, the marghas byghan and the *marghas yow* or Thursday market. Over time these have become Marazion and Market Jew, the latter now the main street in Penzance.

The impressive off-shore island of **St Michael's Mount** (see box p204) attracts huge numbers of visitors every year. The village itself is quaint and has much to satisfy the curious happy to wander about aimlessly. The little **Marazion Museum** (admission £1) was once the jail and a typical cell has been reconstructed. Of interest to nature lovers is the **RSPB Nature Reserve** (☎ 01736-711682; open all the time, free but donations welcome) on Marazion Marsh, which has Cornwall's largest reed bed.

There is a **post office** (Mon-Fri 9am-5.30pm, Sat 9am-12.30pm) with a **cash machine**, Cobble Corner Newsagents and shop, a **pharmacy**, and **Philp's Pasty**

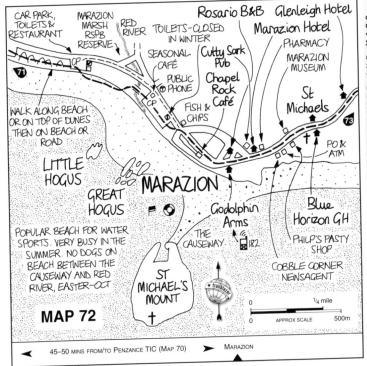

ROUTE GUIDE AND MAPS

CAR PARK,
TOILETS &
RESTAURANT

MARAZION
MARSH
RSPB
RESERVE

RED
RIVER

TOILETS-CLOSED
IN WINTER

Rosario B&B Glenleigh Hotel

Marazion Hotel

SEASONAL
CAFÉ

PUBLIC
PHONE

Cutty Sark
Pub

Chapel
Rock
Café

PHARMACY

MARAZION
MUSEUM

St
Michaels

WALK ALONG BEACH
OR ON TOP OF DUNES
THEN ON BEACH OR
ROAD

FISH &
CHIPS

PO &
ATM

LITTLE
HOGUS

MARAZION

GREAT
HOGUS

Godolphin
Arms

Blue
Horizon GH

POPULAR BEACH FOR WATER
SPORTS. VERY BUSY IN THE
SUMMER. NO DOGS ON
BEACH BETWEEN THE
CAUSEWAY AND RED
RIVER, EASTER-OCT

THE
CAUSEWAY

182

PHILP'S PASTY
SHOP

COBBLE CORNER
NEWSAGENT

MAP 72

ST
MICHAEL'S
MOUNT

0   ¼ mile
0   APPROX SCALE   500m

◄ 45-50 MINS FROM/TO PENZANCE TIC (MAP 70) ►   MARAZION

Shop. Pasty fans will remember Philp's from Hayle: they're simply the best.

The **bus** service includes Western Greyhound's 513 and 515 services as well as First's 300. See public transport map and table, pp46-50.

Where to stay and eat

The nearest place to **camp** is *Wheal Rodney Holiday Park* (Map 73; ☎ 01736-710605, 🖳 www.whealrodney.co.uk; Easter-Oct) a short walk inland from the coast where the charge for a night is £10-15 per tent with up to two people. They have a **shop** (daily 9am-8pm) and an indoor pool on this nicely appointed site.

There are several options if you want to stay in Marazion. *Rosario B&B* (☎ 01736-711998; 1S/2D/1T, all with private

facilities), The Square, is a charming establishment charging £35 per person but take cash or your cheque book as they don't accept cards. They will do luggage transfer though. *St Michaels* (☎ 01736-711348, 🖳 www.stmichaels-bedandbreakfast.co.uk; 1T/4D/1F, all en suite), Fore St, charges £40 per person and £65 for single occupancy. At the time of writing they also did not accept credit cards.

Blue Horizon (☎ 01736-711199, 🖳 www.holidaybreaksmarazion.co.uk; 1S/3D/2T, all with private facilities), Fore St, is a brightly decorated place with rooms from £34 for the single or £58-68 for two sharing a room. Further along, *Glenleigh Hotel* (☎ 01736-710308, 🖳 www.marazionhotels.com; 2S/3D, all en suite) charges £34-35 per person a night. One of

❑ St Michael's Mount

St Michael's Mount (☎ 01736-710507, or for tide and ferry information ☎ 01736-710265, 🖳 www.stmichaelsmount.co.uk) is steeped in history. In one of the earliest written records of Cornwall, Diodorus Siculus, a Greek historian wrote that in the 1st century BC tin was taken on wagons to Ictis (St Michael's Mount) at low tide, thence by sea to Brittany, France, and from there overland to the Mediterranean. Much later, in 1645 during the Civil War, it was one of the last Royalist strongholds and was only eventually taken after a long siege. The spectacular 14th-century castle surmounting the Mount was originally a Benedictine Priory dating from the 12th century, the daughter-house of the famous Mont St Michel in Normandy, France. It is now the home of the St Aubyn family.

The island with its castle is open late March to early November, Sun-Fri, 10.30am-5pm and to 5.30pm during July and August but is closed on Saturday. The gardens are open May-June Mon-Fri 10.30am-5pm, July-October Thurs, Fri 10.30am-5pm, last admission 45 minutes before closing time.

Entry to the castle is £6.60 and to the gardens £3 (NT members get in free). The island has a **shop** and *café* and the *Sail Loft Restaurant* (☎ 01736-710748), all are open the same hours as the castle.

To get to the island you can walk across the causeway from Marazion at low tide or catch one of the regular ferry boats which ply back and forth during the summer months. They charge £1.50 each way and leave from one of three slipways depending on the state of the tide. All visits are also subject to the weather.

Be prepared for a steep climb on cobbles.

the doubles can be converted into a family room if required. An evening meal is available and they are open from Easter to the end of October.

Rather more up-market is the *Marazion Hotel* (☎ 01736-710334, 🖳 www.marazionhotel.co.uk; 2S/3T/5D, all en suite) with single rooms for £50-65 and the rate for two sharing a room is £65-115. You can eat next door at the *Cutty Sark* pub where garlic bread is king or at *The Godolphin Arms* (☎ 01736-710202, www.godolphinarms.co.uk; 6D/2T/2F, all en suite; food served summer daily all day winter noon-2.30pm & 6-8.30pm) looking out over the causeway to St Michael's Mount, a fabulous vista in the setting sun. Locally caught fish are well-represented on the menu, for example Newlyn crab salad for £12.95 with the usual pub standards such as bangers and mash for £7.95. B&B costs £65-110 per person for single occupancy and £42.50-72.50 per person for two sharing a room.

For snacks and quick bites, there's a **fish and chip** shop and *Chapel Rock Café* (☎ 01736-719468; summer daily 9am-5pm, rest of year 10am-4pm) serves paninis, cream teas, coffee, cakes and more.

❑ Prussia Cove (see Map 75)

Prussia Cove derives its name from the former King of Prussia Inn which stood on the cliff. It was run by the notorious Carter family whose smuggling exploits have guaranteed them a place in local folklore. The size of their operation was of such a scale that they needed to mount a small battery of guns to ward off the customs men. More recently, in 1979, a smuggling racket was busted by Customs and Excise who confiscated three million pounds worth of marijuana.

MARAZION TO PRAA SANDS [MAPS 73-76]

The first half of this **six miles (10km, 1¾-2hrs)** provides fairly uninteresting walking on low-lying cliffs devoted to market gardening and requires close attention in following the waymarker posts to avoid straying inland.

Prussia Cove (see box opposite), however, makes the effort worthwhile with Pixies Cove and Bessy's Cove below, a real smugglers' landing place. From here good cliff-top walking takes you to the impressive beach at Praa Sands.

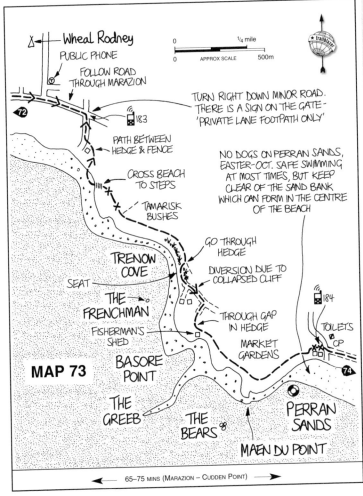

Wheal Rodney

PUBLIC PHONE

FOLLOW ROAD THROUGH MARAZION

0 ¼ mile

0 APPROX SCALE 500m

TURN RIGHT DOWN MINOR ROAD. THERE IS A SIGN ON THE GATE- 'PRIVATE LANE FOOTPATH ONLY'

72

183

PATH BETWEEN HEDGE & FENCE

NO DOGS ON PERRAN SANDS, EASTER-OCT. SAFE SWIMMING AT MOST TIMES, BUT KEEP CLEAR OF THE SAND BANK WHICH CAN FORM IN THE CENTRE OF THE BEACH

CROSS BEACH TO STEPS

TAMARISK BUSHES

GO THROUGH HEDGE

TRENOW COVE

DIVERSION DUE TO COLLAPSED CLIFF

184

SEAT

THE FRENCHMAN

THROUGH GAP IN HEDGE

TOILETS

CP

FISHERMAN'S SHED

MARKET GARDENS

MAP 73

BASORE POINT

74

THE GREEB

THE BEARS

PERRAN SANDS

MAEN DU POINT

◄— 65-75 MINS (MARAZION – CUDDEN POINT) —►

ROUTE GUIDE AND MAPS

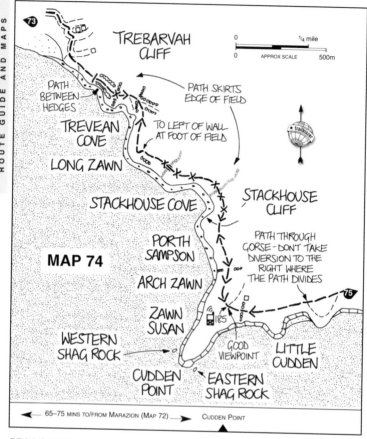

MAP 74

TREBARVAH CLIFF

0   ¼ mile

0   APPROX SCALE   500m

PATH SKIRTS EDGE OF FIELD

PATH BETWEEN HEDGES

TO LEFT OF WALL AT FOOT OF FIELD

TREVEAN COVE

★ trailblazer

LONG ZAWN

STACKHOUSE CLIFF

STACKHOUSE COVE

PORTH SAMPSON

PATH THROUGH GORSE - DON'T TAKE DIVERSION TO THE RIGHT WHERE THE PATH DIVIDES

ARCH ZAWN

75

185

ZAWN SUSAN

WESTERN SHAG ROCK

GOOD VIEWPOINT

LITTLE CUDDEN

CUDDEN POINT

EASTERN SHAG ROCK

← 65–75 MINS TO/FROM MARAZION (MAP 72) →   CUDDEN POINT

PRAA SANDS   [MAP 76, p208]

Praa Sands is a mini holiday resort that gets very busy in the summer and is stone dead in winter when it seems almost to go in to hibernation. There is a Londis **convenience store** (Mon-Fri 7.30am-6pm, Sat 8am-8pm, Sun 9am-1pm) with an adequate stock of groceries but no cash machine and a **post office** (Mon-Fri 9am-5.30pm, Sat 9am-12.30pm) on Pengersick Lane.

If you want to **camp**, *The Old Farm* (☎ 01736-763221, 🖳 www.theoldfarm praasands.co.uk; end May to early Sep) is a beautifully run site; the tariff is £12 per pitch for two people and £16 in the main season (from July).

Mzima (☎ 01736-763856, 🖳 marian foy@prussia-cove-holiday.com; 1T/1F shared bathroom) about half a mile inland, uphill, charging a reasonable £25 per person for B&B (£28 single occupancy). For a 50p charge they will drive walkers to the local pub for a meal. *Dingley Dell* (☎ 01736-763527, 🖳 www.dingleydell.eu; 1T/1D or F, en suite), Pengersick Lane, charges £30

MAP 75

0   1/4 mile

0   APPROX SCALE   500m

trailblazer

PRUSSIA COVE

PATH MEANDERS
UP AND DOWN

TURN LEFT JUST
186 PAST COTTAGE.
STEPS GO TO BEACH

KENNEGGY
CLIFF

NICE SOFT GRASS
MAKES A COMFY
SPOT FOR A BREAK

TAKE PATH
BETWEEN
HEDGES

187

WATCH OUT
FOR NETTLES 76

KENNEGGY
SANDS—RELATIVELY
SAFE FOR SWIMMING,
ACCESS TO BEACH BY
VERTICAL LADDER

74

PESTREATH
COVE

KING'S
COVE

HOE
POINT

BESSYS
COVE
CROSS BEACH AT
LOW TIDE ONLY

THE ENYS

← 40–50 MINS (CUDDEN POINT – PRAA SANDS) →

per person or £40 for single occupancy.

At the western end of the beach cricket lovers will be intrigued to see *Chris Old's Clipper Restaurant* (☎ 01736-763751, 🖥 www.chrisold.co.uk; May-Oct daily 10.30am-7pm, Nov-Apr Fri-Sun 10.30am-5.30pm) which, in addition to fish and chips, serves fresh crab sandwiches, vegetarian dishes, cream teas and a roast on Sundays. Opposite is the seasonal *Sandbar Café*, slogan 'the beach at your feet', serving hot and cold drinks and light bites and on Sunday lunchtimes 'the roast on the coast'.

First's Nos 2 and 2A **bus** stops outside the post office. See public transport map and table, pp46-50.

PRAA SANDS TO PORTHLEVEN [MAPS 76-79]

This **four-mile (6km, 1½-2hrs)** stretch of harder walking returns you to the cliff-tops again after the lower-level terrain between Marazion and Praa Sands. This is another area of old copper workings and you pass some weathered spoil tips that have begun to blend with their surroundings. As you get nearer to **Porthleven** some of the cliffs are subsiding and the path has been fenced off to keep it well back from what is at present the edge. On the last headland there is a **memorial** (see box p208) to the many mariners drowned off these coasts.

❑ **Important note – walking times** Unless otherwise specified, **all times in this book refer only to the time spent walking**. You will need to add 20-30% to allow for rests, photography, checking the map, drinking water etc. When planning the day's hike count on 5-7 hours' actual walking.

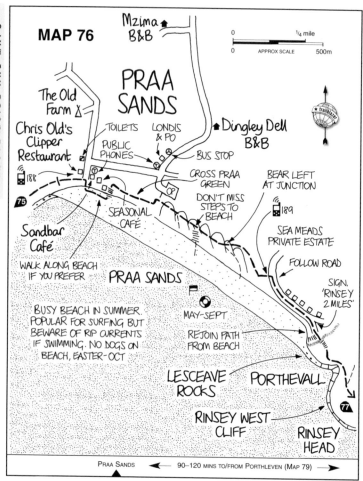

MAP 76

Mzima B&B

0 ¼ mile

0 APPROX SCALE 500m

PRAA SANDS

The Old Farm

Chris Old's Clipper Restaurant

TOILETS

LONDIS & PO

Dingley Dell B&B

PUBLIC PHONES

BUS STOP

188

CROSS PRAA GREEN

BEAR LEFT AT JUNCTION

189

Sandbar Café

SEASONAL CAFÉ

DON'T MISS STEPS TO BEACH

SEA MEADS PRIVATE ESTATE

FOLLOW ROAD

WALK ALONG BEACH IF YOU PREFER

PRAA SANDS

SIGN, 'RINSEY 2 MILES'

BUSY BEACH IN SUMMER. POPULAR FOR SURFING BUT BEWARE OF RIP CURRENTS IF SWIMMING. NO DOGS ON BEACH, EASTER–OCT

MAY–SEPT

REJOIN PATH FROM BEACH

LESCEAVE ROCKS

PORTHEVALL

RINSEY WEST CLIFF

RINSEY HEAD

PRAA SANDS ← 90–120 MINS TO/FROM PORTHLEVEN (MAP 79) →

❏ Gryll's Act
Passed in 1808, the Gryll's Act allowed bodies washed up by the sea to be buried in the nearest consecrated ground. Before this all bodies were buried on the cliff tops as it was not possible to distinguish between Christians and non-Christians. The memorial (see Map 79, p211) marks the passing of this Act.

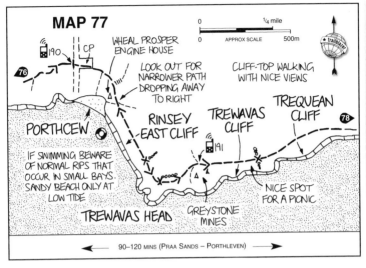

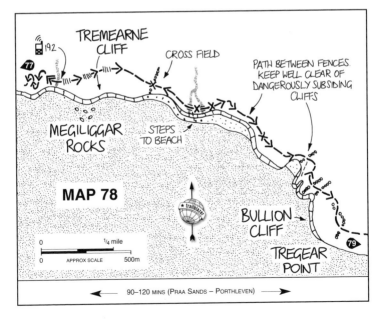

PORTHLEVEN [MAP 79]

Porthleven Harbour was built using prisoners from the Napoleonic wars and at one time housed a fishing fleet which harvested the huge shoals of pilchards and mackerel in the bay. Today its prosperity depends on tourism and the winters have to be endured. The coast is subject to ferocious storms and waves have been known to crash right over the harbour wall to wreck the boats sheltering within. What few fishing boats are left work the local reefs for crab and lobster during the summer months, some of the catch going to local restaurants and the rest to Newlyn for export abroad.

The shops are reasonably up to date with a Costcutter **convenience store** with a cash machine and a Boots **pharmacy** close to the harbour. There is also a self-service **launderette** and further up Fore St is the **post office** (Mon-Fri 9am-5.30pm, Sat 9am-12.30pm) in Premier Shop, a convenience store.

Where to stay

The town has its share of B&Bs starting with the friendly *Fisherman's Cottage* (☎ 01326-573713; 1S or D/1D/1F), 1 Harbour View, right on the harbour with prices from £25-30. The family room is en suite but the other rooms share a bathroom. The *Copper Kettle* (☎ 01326-565660, 🖳 www.cornish copperkettle.com; 1S/2T/2D, all en suite) is at 33 Fore St. The single, and one twin and a double are in the house. The other twin and double are in an annexe which is a self-contained flat with a small kitchenette. The rate is £65-75 for two sharing a room and the single is £37. They accept one-night bookings. All rooms have Sky TV and internet access. They also have special rates for group bookings.

Up on Peverall Terrace there are two B&Bs close to each other. *Seefar* (☎ 01326-573778, 🖳 www.seefar.co.uk; 1S/1T/1D, all with private facilities) charging £24 per night for the single and £28 per person for two sharing a room, and the larger *An Mordros* (☎ 01326-562236, 🖳 www.anmordroshotel.com; 5D/1D, T or Tr, all en suite) with B&B from £31 per person for two sharing, £45-62 for single occupancy.

You can also find accommodation at *Harbour Inn* (☎ 01326-573876, 🖳 www .smallandfriendly.co.uk; 1S/1T/7D/1F, all en suite) one of St Austell Brewery's top houses. They also have a self-contained flat (1D and a sofabed) for longer stays. Rooms cost £75-90 for two sharing and £55 for the single. On the harbour, a restaurant with rooms *Kota* (☎ 01326-562407, 🖳 www .kotarestaurant.co.uk; 1D/1D or F, both en suite) charges £20-40 per person (£40-50 single occupancy); enquire about their special deals. To wake up in the sea-view room and look out of the window would be an unforgettable experience.

Where to eat and drink

It would be hard to go hungry in Porthleven. From chippies to bakeries, pub grub to fine dining, it's got them all. *Roland's Happy Plaice* (☎ 01326-562723; Apr-Aug Tue-Sat noon-8pm, rest of year Wed-Sat noon-7pm) is famous hereabouts, the owners having brought their Yorkshire fish-frying skills to show the Cornish how to do it properly. If your taste is for far eastern cuisine, *Moonflower* (☎ 01326-562973; daily 5.30-11.30pm) does either sit-down meals or takeaways.

Of the three pubs, the *Ship Inn* (☎ 01326-564204; daily noon-2pm & 6.30-9pm) has the most atmosphere. If it's on the menu don't pass up on the bowl of crab claws for £13.95 although you may need to ask to be sponged down afterwards. The Cornish fish pie is another guaranteed winner at £10.95. The beers include Doom Bar and Courage Bitter.

Up on Peverall Terrace, the *Atlantic Inn* (☎ 01326-562439; daily noon-2pm & 6-9pm) serves pub fare 'at realistic prices' or so they claim whilst down at the *Harbour Inn* (see Where to stay; daily noon-9pm) there's always plenty of people dining on the bar meals including St Austell's pie (£6.95; steak and ale pie by any other name would taste the same) and fish and chips at £7.95. The beers are St Austell's Tribute and the nutty Proper Job at 4.5%.

Nauti but Ice (☎ 01326-573747; summer daily 8am-10pm, winter 9am-5pm) is a

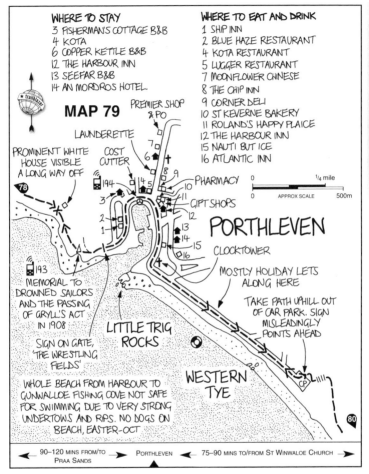

WHERE TO STAY
3 FISHERMAN'S COTTAGE B&B
4 KOTA
6 COPPER KETTLE B&B
12 THE HARBOUR INN
13 SEEFAR B&B
14 AN MORDROS HOTEL

WHERE TO EAT AND DRINK
1 SHIP INN
2 BLUE HAZE RESTAURANT
4 KOTA RESTAURANT
5 LUGGER RESTAURANT
7 MOONFLOWER CHINESE
8 THE CHIP INN
9 CORNER DELI
10 ST KEVERNE BAKERY
11 ROLAND'S HAPPY PLAICE
12 THE HARBOUR INN
15 NAUTI BUT ICE
16 ATLANTIC INN

MAP 79

PREMIER SHOP & PO

LAUNDERETTE

COST CUTTER

PROMINENT WHITE HOUSE VISIBLE A LONG WAY OFF

78

194

3

2

1

4 5

6 7

8 9

10

PHARMACY

11 GIFT SHOPS

12

13

14

15

16

PORTHLEVEN

CLOCKTOWER

0   1/4 mile
0   APPROX SCALE   500m

193
MEMORIAL TO DROWNED SAILORS AND THE PASSING OF GRYLL'S ACT IN 1908

SIGN ON GATE, 'THE WRESTLING FIELDS'

LITTLE TRIG ROCKS

WHOLE BEACH FROM HARBOUR TO GUNWALLOE FISHING COVE NOT SAFE FOR SWIMMING DUE TO VERY STRONG UNDERTOWS AND RIPS. NO DOGS ON BEACH, EASTER-OCT

MOSTLY HOLIDAY LETS ALONG HERE

TAKE PATH UPHILL OUT OF CAR PARK. SIGN MISLEADINGLY POINTS AHEAD

WESTERN TYE

CP

80

← 90-120 MINS FROM/TO → PORTHLEVEN ← 75-90 MINS TO/FROM ST WINWALOE CHURCH →
PRAA SANDS

classy sandwich shop which does a great ham sandwich with coleslaw and salad in a box to go, at £3.95. They serve light lunches and cream teas (£4.10), and are also an ice-cream parlour.

Two establishments offer fine dining and they are located next to each other facing the harbour. *The Lugger Restaurant* (☎ 01326-562761, 🖳 www.thelugger.co.uk; daily 10am-2pm & 6-10pm, Tue-Sat 6-

9pm) has an enticing menu. I would start with crab bisque (£5) followed by seafood risotto with mussels, calamari and prawns (£12). It is a place that does not try to fool us with silly prices. Next door, *Kota* (see Where to stay; summer Mon-Sat 5.30-9pm, Fri & Sat noon-2pm; winter Wed-Sat 5.30-9pm) has an exotic twist to the food; mains are usually around £11-15 but the roast monkfish with saffron costs £18.25.

However, if you eat between 5.30pm and 7pm they do two courses for £14, which is good value. The restaurant is closed on Sundays except on bank holiday weekends.

Finally one other choice for a tasty meal is *Blue Haze* (☎ 01326-564424; daily noon-2pm, Mon-Sat 6.30-9.30pm) across the harbour near the Ship Inn where the menu is described as Asian fusion and continental. An example of this eclectic mix is seafood thermidor (£17.95).

The Corner Deli (☎ 01326-565554; daily 9am-6pm for the deli) has a wide range of rolls and sandwiches including **takeaway pizzas** (summer daily 6-9pm, winter Wed-Sat 6-9pm).

Transport
First's No 2 & 2A bus services operate to Penzance. See public transport map and table, pp46-50.

PORTHLEVEN TO MULLION COVE [MAPS 79-82]

This is an enjoyable **six-mile (10km, 2-2¹/₂hrs)** walk with lots of diversity. You leave Porthleven past the iconic clock tower over which heavy seas sometimes crash in winter storms and climb the hill past all the holiday cottages to the open spaces high above Western Tye beach.

Next you come to **Loe Bar**, a shingle bank that cuts off the sea from the fresh water lagoon known as The Loe (see box below). Keen birdwatchers passing The Loe in winter will want to spend some time here and it is possible to walk around the lake itself.

It was on Loe Bar that *HMS Anson* was wrecked in 1807; this is commemorated by a bright, white-painted cross which you pass as you climb up onto the cliffs again.

There is a seasonal beach café at Gunwalloe Fishing Cove. The coastal path meanders along to the tiny beach at **Gunwalloe** where the church of St Winwaloe (see box p214) huddles in the dunes. The next cove you come to is **Poldhu** which has historic significance in the development of radio signals (see box p216), followed by **Polurrian Cove** before the huge edifice of Mullion Cove Hotel announces your arrival at perhaps the quintessential Cornish harbour, **Mullion Cove**. The coast path doesn't go into **Mullion village** (see pp216-7) which is about a mile inland but it's worth the diversion if you need any of the many services on offer or a wider variety of accommodation than available at the Cove.

❑ The Loe
The Loe (Loe Pool; see Map 80) is Cornwall's largest natural freshwater lake. Originally the Loe was the estuary of the river Cober but it was dammed by the shingle bar around 800 years ago. The National Trust owns all the land surrounding the Loe and it has been designated a Site of Special Scientific Interest (see p61).

It is mostly known for its bird population and over-wintering wildfowl but such a place inevitably attracts legends of its own. One of which is that Sir Bedivere cast Excalibur, the sword of the dying King Arthur, into this lake.

The walk around the Loe is about five miles (8km), mostly along the water's edge. The path is easy to follow but be warned that it can get muddy on the eastern side.

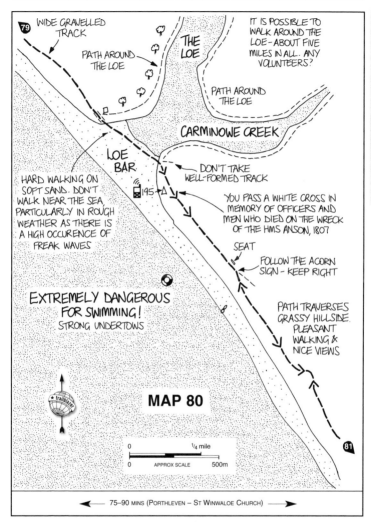

79 WIDE GRAVELLED TRACK

PATH AROUND THE LOE

THE LOE

IT IS POSSIBLE TO WALK AROUND THE LOE - ABOUT FIVE MILES IN ALL. ANY VOLUNTEERS?

PATH AROUND THE LOE

CARMINOWE CREEK

LOE BAR

DON'T TAKE WELL-FORMED TRACK

195 ▵

YOU PASS A WHITE CROSS IN MEMORY OF OFFICERS AND MEN WHO DIED ON THE WRECK OF THE HMS ANSON, 1807

HARD WALKING ON SOFT SAND. DON'T WALK NEAR THE SEA, PARTICULARLY IN ROUGH WEATHER AS THERE IS A HIGH OCCURENCE OF FREAK WAVES

SEAT

FOLLOW THE ACORN SIGN - KEEP RIGHT

EXTREMELY DANGEROUS FOR SWIMMING! STRONG UNDERTOWS

8

PATH TRAVERSES GRASSY HILLSIDE. PLEASANT WALKING & NICE VIEWS

★ trailblazer

MAP 80

0	1/4 mile
0	APPROX SCALE 500m

81

← 75–90 MINS (PORTHLEVEN – ST WINWALOE CHURCH) →

❏ **Warning (Map 80)**
Although the sea may look innocuous on a calm day there are powerful undertows here and the geology of the sea floor on Mount's Bay causes unusually high numbers of freak waves to occur; please **don't consider swimming** and in rough weather it is not advisable to walk near the sea.

ROUTE GUIDE AND MAPS

❑ St Winwaloe Church, Gunwalloe

The setting of this tiny church is truly remarkable. The present church has been restored over the generations but there has been a church here since the 14th century or even earlier. Some of the carved woodwork in the porch has been dated to the 13th century although storms have caused havoc periodically resulting in restoration work by the community determined to keep the faith alive in this inhospitable spot. The burial registers dating from 1716 record shipwrecks and drownings along the coast – a Spanish ship with a cargo of silver dollars was wrecked just to the north in the 1780s – and these have been the object of many searches ever since, so far without success. Dollar Cove (also known as Jangye Ryn) preserves the legend, or truth, of the incident. St Winwaloe, whose statue greets the visitor to the church, was an abbot who came from Brittany, France, in the 6th century and founded the first sacred place on this site which has come to be known as the Church of the Storms.

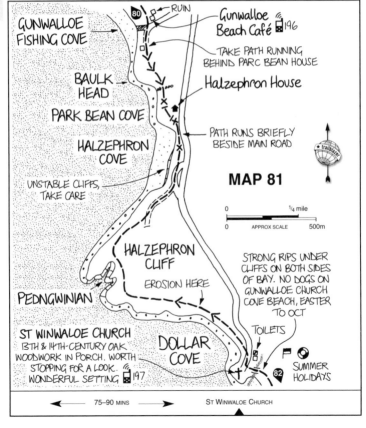

GUNWALLOE FISHING COVE

BAULK HEAD

PARK BEAN COVE

HALZEPHRON COVE

UNSTABLE CLIFFS, TAKE CARE

RUIN

Gunwalloe Beach Café 196

TAKE PATH RUNNING BEHIND PARC BEAN HOUSE

Halzephron House

PATH RUNS BRIEFLY BESIDE MAIN ROAD

MAP 81

0   1/4 mile
0   APPROX SCALE   500m

HALZEPHRON CLIFF

EROSION HERE

PEDNGWINIAN

ST WINWALOE CHURCH
13TH & 14TH-CENTURY OAK WOODWORK IN PORCH. WORTH STOPPING FOR A LOOK. WONDERFUL SETTING 197

DOLLAR COVE

STRONG RIPS UNDER CLIFFS ON BOTH SIDES OF BAY. NO DOGS ON GUNWALLOE CHURCH COVE BEACH, EASTER TO OCT

TOILETS

82

SUMMER HOLIDAYS

◄──── 75–90 MINS ────►   ST WINWALOE CHURCH

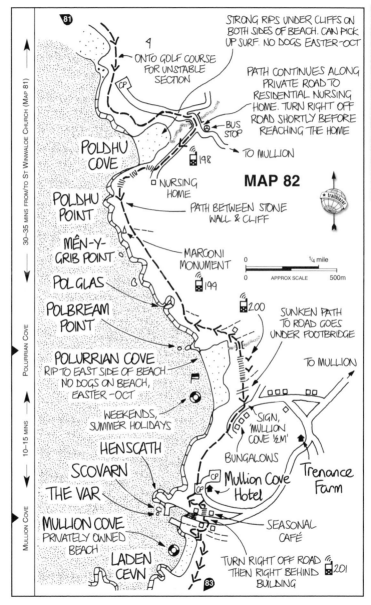

81

ONTO GOLF COURSE FOR UNSTABLE SECTION

STRONG RIPS UNDER CLIFFS ON BOTH SIDES OF BEACH. CAN PICK UP SURF. NO DOGS EASTER-OCT

PATH CONTINUES ALONG PRIVATE ROAD TO RESIDENTIAL NURSING HOME. TURN RIGHT OFF ROAD SHORTLY BEFORE REACHING THE HOME

BUS STOP

TO MULLION

POLDHU COVE

📱 198

MAP 82

NURSING HOME

POLDHU POINT

PATH BETWEEN STONE WALL & CLIFF

MÊN-Y-GRIB POINT

MARCONI MONUMENT

📱 199

POL GLAS

0   ¼ mile

0   APPROX SCALE   500m

POLBREAM POINT

📱 200

SUNKEN PATH TO ROAD GOES UNDER FOOTBRIDGE

POLURRIAN COVE
RIP TO EAST SIDE OF BEACH. NO DOGS ON BEACH, EASTER-OCT

TO MULLION

WEEKENDS, SUMMER HOLIDAYS

SIGN, 'MULLION COVE ½M'

BUNGALOWS

HENSCATH

SCOVARN

Trenance Farm

THE VAR

Mullion Cove Hotel

MULLION COVE
PRIVATELY OWNED BEACH

SEASONAL CAFÉ

LADEN CEVN

TURN RIGHT OFF ROAD THEN RIGHT BEHIND BUILDING

📱 201

83

30-35 MINS FROM/TO ST WINNWALOE CHURCH (MAP 81)

POLURRIAN COVE

10-15 MINS

MULLION COVE

ROUTE GUIDE AND MAPS

HALZEPHRON   [MAP 81, p214]

Right on the cliffs the coast path passes a wonderful white building, *Halzephron House* (☎ 07899-925816, ☐ www.halze phronhouse.co.uk; 2T/2D/1F) which has recently been converted into a house providing self-catering accommodation for groups. However, when the house is not booked they offer B&B: in addition to the rooms in the main house there is accommodation in the observatory (self-catering or B&B) and cabin (1D, en suite) in the grounds. They charge £90-120 per room or £75 for single occupancy but the setting is so outstanding as to make it worthy of a visit.

❏ The Marconi monument

Walkers passing the stone obelisk (see Map 82, p215) on the cliffs near Poldhu might do well to pause and consider what it commemorates. Guglielmo Marconi chose this spot from which to transmit the very first message ever to cross the Atlantic by wireless. On December 12th 1901, a morse signal sent from a station on Angrouse Cliff was received by Marconi in Newfoundland. Twenty years later the world's first shortwave beam signals were transmitted from the same spot and history was made. Poldhu became a research centre and when it closed in 1934 Marconi gave the site to the National Trust and erected the memorial.

  The other significant radio station, Marconi's Lizard Wireless Station (see Map 86, p221) was also bought by the NT and can be seen along the coast path just north of the Lizard lighthouse.

MULLION COVE   [MAP 82, p215]

The upscale place in the area is *Mullion Cove Hotel* (☎ 01326-240328, ☐ www .mullion-cove.co.uk; 11T/12D/3F, all en suite) with an unsurpassable location and a reputation for hospitality; it would be a great place for a special break. They run some courses from the hotel including a Coastal Walking week in October with daily walks to places like the Lizard and Porthleven led by an experienced guide which would be a good introduction for anyone nervous about tackling the coast path. B&B in a standard room costs £50-75 per person, in sea-view rooms £75-100, and in premier sea-view rooms £95-135 but you do get the use of a towelling robe and slippers. Food is available in *The Cove Bistro* (daily noon-9pm), which serves lunch noon-2.30pm, pizzas and snacks 2.30-6pm and has an á la carte menu in the evening (6-9pm) and *The Atlantic View Restaurant* (daily 7-8.45pm), which serves a set menu (£32). There is also a *seasonal café* at the cove.

  En route to Mullion Village, *Trenance Farm* (☎ 01326-240639, ☐ www.trenance farmholidays.co.uk; 1T/2D, all en suite; Apr-Oct) charges £30-32 per person; there is a £5 single occupancy supplement in the main season. They offer luggage transfer (£10) and can provide packed lunches if requested in advance.

MULLION

Mullion Mini Market **convenience store** on Nansmellyon Rd is well stocked and has a cash machine for which the charge is £1.78 and **post office** (Mon-Sat 9am-6.30pm), also in the centre of the village a **Spar** shop (daily 6am-9pm) which also has a cash machine (£1.50) and a bakery with a lovely selection of warm pasties and freshly baked bread. There's a **pharmacy** and you can get **internet access** at the Community Centre (☎ 01326-241552; Mon-Fri 9.30am-12.30pm).

Where to stay

B&B choices include the spacious *Old Vicarage* (☎ 01326-240898, ☐ www.corn wall-online.co.uk/mullionoldvicarage; 2D/

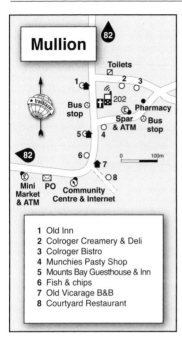

1 Old Inn
2 Colroger Creamery & Deli
3 Colroger Bistro
4 Munchies Pasty Shop
5 Mounts Bay Guesthouse & Inn
6 Fish & chips
7 Old Vicarage B&B
8 Courtyard Restaurant

2F, all with private facilities) a lovely old house in the heart of the village with rooms from £35 for two sharing rising to £45 in high season; single occupancy £35-45. Credit/debit cards are not accepted but single-night bookings are. It is said that Sir Arthur Conan Doyle stayed here and the house is mentioned in the Sherlock Holmes story *The Devil's Foot*.

The rooms at *Old Inn* (☎ 01326-240240; 1T/3D/1F, all en suite) are light and airy; the tariff is £30-37 per person. *Mounts Bay Guesthouse* (☎ 01326-241761, ☐ www.mountsbayguesthouse.co .uk; 1T/3D/1F, all en suite) is a pleasant, welcoming place charging £29 each for two sharing a twin or £34 each if you want a sea view; there is a £10 single occupancy supplement in the main season. The owners provide a drop-off/pick-up service for guests for which there may be a small charge.

Coming down to earth again after such flights of fancy you could always camp. If

this is your intention you should head for *Tenerife Farm Caravan and Camping Park* (Map 83; ☎ 01326-240293; Mar-Jan) about a mile beyond Mullion Cove where the charge for two people and a small tent is £10.

Where to eat and drink
There are two pubs in Mullion. *Mounts Bay Inn* (☎ 01326 240221, ☐ www .mountsbaymullion.co.uk; food served daily noon-2.30pm & Mon-Sat 6-9pm, 6-8.30pm on Sun, winter daily noon-2.30pm & 6.30-8.30pm), below the guesthouse (see Where to stay) is a lively place and is popular with both locals and holidaymakers. Some of the specials are intriguing such as large greenlip mussels (£6.95) and Cornish smoked seafood platter (£9.95).

The *Old Inn* (see Where to stay; summer daily noon-9pm, winter daily noon-2.30pm & 6-9pm) is equally busy and has an interesting menu of daily specials and standards such as cajun chicken (£9.95) or the curry of the day (£8.95). The beers on draught are St Austell's Tribute, HSD, Proper Job and IPA.

Colroger Creamery and Deli (☎ 01326-240833; summer Mon-Sat 9am-5pm, Sun 10am-3pm, winter Mon-Sat 10am-3pm) is a traditional café which will also do you a picnic for the trail; if you ring in advance they can prepare one for you to collect. *Colroger Bistro* (☎ 01326-241007; daily 9am-4pm & 7pm to late) offers home-cooked food starting with breakfast and then light lunches. The evening menu consists of specials which will change daily but they also have fish nights.

If pizza or pasta is your preference, try *Courtyard* (☎ 01326-241556; main season Wed-Mon 6.30-9pm, Fri-Mon 7-9pm the rest of the year), just off Nansmellyon Rd on a side turning.

The village also boasts a **fish and chip** shop and a **pasty** shop (Munchies).

Transport
First's No 33 **bus** service between Helston and the Lizard stops here. See public transport map and table, pp46-50.

MULLION COVE TO LIZARD POINT [MAPS 82-86]

The next **six miles** (**10km, 2½-3¼hrs**) are along exposed cliff tops giving some of the best coastal walking in South Cornwall with superb views of the treacherous rocks on which so many ships have been wrecked.

The terrain under foot can get boggy at times due to poor drainage and it is likely that this will get worse unless something is done to improve the path in these places. You might spot the New Forest ponies brought in by the National Trust to crop the gorse, clearing the ground to allow unique and fragile plant species to come through.

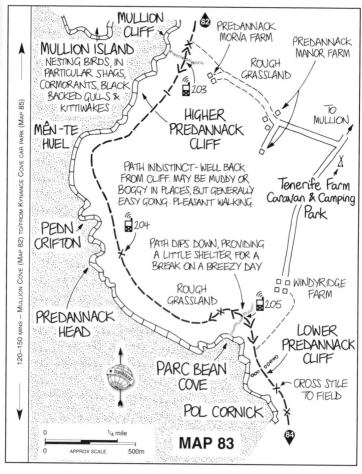

MAP 83

120-150 MINS – MULLION COVE (MAP 82) TO/FROM KYNANCE COVE CAR PARK (MAP 85)

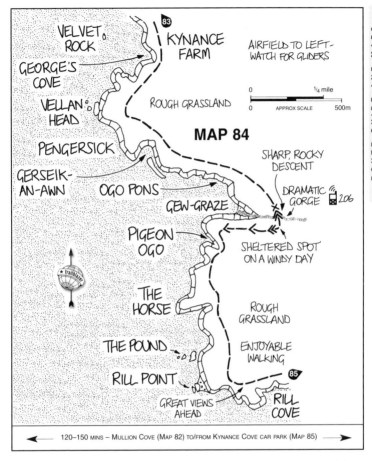

VELVET ROCK

KYNANCE FARM

83

GEORGE'S COVE

VELLAN HEAD

AIRFIELD TO LEFT - WATCH FOR GLIDERS

ROUGH GRASSLAND

0   1/4 mile
0   APPROX SCALE   500m

MAP 84

PENGERSICK

GERSEIK- AN-AWN

OGO PONS

GEW-GRAZE

SHARP, ROCKY DESCENT

DRAMATIC GORGE 206

PIGEON OGO

SHELTERED SPOT ON A WINDY DAY

trailblazer

THE HORSE

ROUGH GRASSLAND

THE POUND

ENJOYABLE WALKING

RILL POINT

85

GREAT VIEWS AHEAD

RILL COVE

ROUTE GUIDE AND MAPS

← 120–150 MINS – MULLION COVE (MAP 82) TO/FROM KYNANCE COVE CAR PARK (MAP 85) →

Kynance Cove is a delightful spot where the intrusion of summer visitors has not spoiled a unique cove that deserves a longer stay than walkers allow it. *Kynance Café* is open in the main season.

As you get nearer to Lizard Point the coastline becomes increasingly spectacular and if this is your first visit you cannot fail to be impressed by its wildness and beauty. **The Lizard** has been called Cornwall's big toe dipped into the ocean. Rare clovers and heathers grow here and nowhere else and some exotics such as gunneras and tree ferns flourish in the sub-tropical conditions.

After **Pentreath Beach** several paths lead away from the coast to Lizard Village where you may have decided to spend the night or get a pasty. The temptation would be to take the first path in and the last path out but this would mean missing Lizard Point. The shortest route into Lizard village is from Housel Cove but it's only about 15 minutes along the path leading in from near Shag Rock. Alternatively, there's a pretty walk from Church Cove past thatched-roofed houses.

LIZARD VILLAGE [MAP 86]

The village has all the services you are likely to need and is an active community.

There is a **post office** (Mon-Thur 9am-noon & 1-5pm, Fri 9am-noon, Sat 9am-12.30pm) and the Premier **convenience store** is the main grocery shop in the village. It has a **cash machine** but it costs £1.65 to make a withdrawal. There's a nice **deli-cum-greengrocers** and everyone gets their pasties from Ann Muller at the **Lizard Pasty Shop** (☎ 01326-290889; Easter-Oct Mon-Sat 9.30am-2pm, Nov-Easter Tue-Sat

9.30am-2pm). However, they stay open if there are customers but it is best to order a pasty in advance, especially if you think you will arrive later than 2pm.

Where to stay

Campers are ideally suited with *Henry's Campsite* (☎ 01326-290596, 🖳 www.henryscampsite.co.uk), an ideal enclave with fire baskets for lighting fires and wood available from Henry himself; it's £5 for logs and a basket. The charge of £7 applies

MAP 85

0 ———— ¼ mile
0 ———— APPROX SCALE ———— 500m

GREAT VIEWS OF THE ISLAND

KYNANCE CLIFF

AT HIGH TIDE WHEN YOU CAN'T CROSS THE BEACH, TAKE THE ROAD – IT'S ONLY A SHORT DIVERSION

Kynance Café (SEASONAL)

TOILETS

GRAVELLED PATH

84

THE BELLOWS

CP 207

ASPARAGUS ISLAND

GREAT VIEWS

NANTIVET ROCK
LOOK FOR GREEN SERPENTINE ROCK

GULL ROCK

KYNANCE COVE

ENYS YEAN

86

THE BISHOP

LION ROCK

AT LOW TIDE IT'S POSSIBLE TO EXPLORE THE ISLANDS AND CAVES. ALWAYS BE AWARE OF THE INCOMING TIDE, PARTICULARLY IF ON THIS SIDE - CAN HAVE VERY DANGEROUS SURF & RIPS

NO DOGS ON BEACH, EASTER-OCT

← 120–150 MINS FROM/TO MULLION COVE (MAP 82) → | KYNANCE COVE CAR PARK | ← 35–45 MINS TO/FROM LIZARD POINT (MAP 86) →

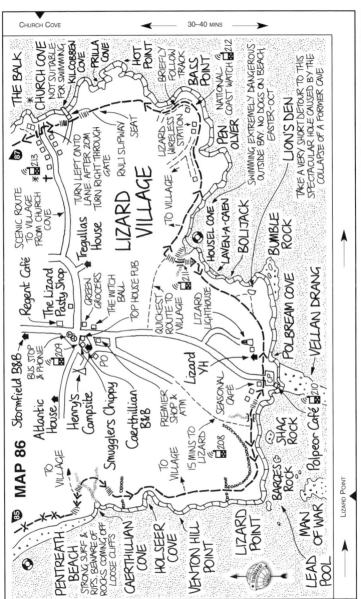

MAP 86

CHURCH COVE ← 30–40 MINS →

THE BALK

CHURCH COVE
NOT SUITABLE
FOR SWIMMING

KILCOBBEN COVE

PRILLA COVE

HOT POINT

BRIEFLY
FOLLOW
TRACK

BASS POINT

NATIONAL
COAST WATCH 212

PEN
OLVER

LIZARD
WIRELESS
STATION

SWIMMING EXTREMELY DANGEROUS
OUTSIDE BAY. NO DOGS ON BEACH
EASTER–OCT

LION'S DEN

TAKE A VERY SHORT DETOUR TO THIS
SPECTACULAR HOLE CAUSED BY THE
COLLAPSE OF A FORMER CAVE

87 213

SCENIC ROUTE
TO VILLAGE
FROM CHURCH COVE

Tregullas
House

TURN LEFT ONTO
LANE AFTER 2CM
TURN RIGHT THROUGH
GATE

RNLI SLIPWAY
SEAT

TO VILLAGE

LIZARD
VILLAGE

Regent Café

The Lizard Pasty Shop

GREEN
GROCERS

THE WITCH
BALL

TOP HOUSE PUB

QUICKEST
ROUTE TO
VILLAGE

LIZARD
LIGHTHOUSE

HOUSEL COVE

LAVEN-A-CAEN

BOLJACK

BUMBLE
ROCK

211

POLBREAM COVE

VELLAN DRANG

Stormfield B&B

Atlantic
House

Henry's
Campsite

BUS STOP
& PHONE 209

PO

Smugglers Chippy

Caerthillian
B&B

PREMIER
SHOP &
ATM

TO
VILLAGE

15 MINS TO
LIZARD

Lizard YH

SEASONAL
CAFÉ

208

SHAG ROCK

Polpeor Café 210

TO VILLAGE

85

PENTREATH
BEACH

STRONG SURF &
RIPS. BEWARE OF
ROCKS COMING OFF
LOOSE CLIFFS

CAERTHILLIAN
COVE

HOLSEER COVE

VENTON HILL POINT

LIZARD POINT

BARGES
ROCK

MAN
OF WAR

LEAD
POOL

LIZARD POINT

trailblazer

ROUTE GUIDE AND MAPS

❏ **Geology of The Lizard**
Even the most ungeologically minded can't miss the colourful serpentine rock around the Lizard; great streaks of green cliffs reminiscent of a snake's skin giving the stone its name. Local sculptors still carve ornaments from the serpentine rock which reached their height of popularity during the Victorian era, although they're probably a little too heavy to carry away in your pack.
Lizard Point isn't just famed as the most southerly point of mainland Britain. The offshore islets from Lizard Point are 500 million years old, a leftover crumb of the collision between the super-continents of Gondwanaland and Euramerica.

all year and you can get eggs and milk as well as a much more popular product – cider – at £2 a pint. Stock up on Alka Seltzer!
Lizard Youth Hostel (☎ 0845-371 9550, 🖳 lizard@yha.org.uk; 30 beds) occupies the buildings of a former Victorian hotel. There is a self-catering kitchen and meals are also provided. A bed costs £13.95. In the winter of 2008-9 the hostel closed for a period for redecoration so expect it to look very smart. One thing to watch for though – it gets heavily booked throughout the season and your chances of turning up and getting a bed are practically nil.
Stormfield (☎ 01326-290806, 🖳 alison.b60@btinternet.com; 1T/1D) is a comfortable bungalow on the Helston Rd where £30-35 will get you B&B. The rooms may not be en suite but they share a bathroom, a rare occurrence in Cornwall, and the water is really hot. The owner ran me to Coverack when the bus times didn't fit in and they'll take your baggage forward for a small fee.
The Caerthillian (☎ 01326-290019, 🖳 www.thecaerthillian.co.uk; 1S/1T/3D; all with private facilities) is a lovely blue and white painted house in the heart of the village where you'll pay £30 or £35 for single occupancy of a double.
Atlantic House (☎ 01326-290399, 🖳 www.atlantichouselizard.co.uk; Feb-Nov; 1D or T/4D, all with private facilities), Pentreath Lane, is a double-fronted Edwardian villa with a lovely open aspect offering exceptional quality in terms of comfort and amenity. The tariff is £35-60 per person (single occupancy is 10% off the full room rate) but, be advised, they don't take single-night bookings in the summer months unless there is a gap in their book-

ings. Walkers are just as welcome as anyone else but the owners prefer their guests to enjoy the area by using them as a base, not a whistle-stop. Fair enough.

Where to eat and drink
For a meal, head for the *Top House* (☎ 01326-290974; summer daily noon-2.30pm, to 2pm in winter, & 6-9pm, 7-8.30pm in winter) which does standard pub grub with a few specials on the blackboard including seafood choices. The garlic bread (£3.50) is out of this world and their cottage pie (£8, £6.50 at lunchtime) is a good plateful. The beers are Betty Stoggs', Sharp's Doom Bar and Greene King IPA.
The Witchball (☎ 01326-290662, 🖳 www.witchball.co.uk; Mar-Dec daily noon-3pm & 7-9.30pm, Jan & Feb Thur-Sun noon-3pm & 7-9pm) is an unusual eatery serving imaginative dishes on a changing menu. Regulars go for the home-made lasagne (£8.50) and for lunch you must try half a pint of shell-on prawns served with lime mayonnaise and crusty bread (£3.95). On Sundays they do a roast. The beers are different, for example they have their own organic Witch Ball at 4.7% and, in the summer, Lizard Point at 4%. A witch ball is a hollow sphere of glass hung in a cottage window to ward off evil spirits.
The most southerly café in the British Isles, *Polpeor Café* (open summer daily 8am-6pm but close earlier if no one is around) at Lizard Point has one of the best terraces anywhere with a view over the rocks and sea that is second to none. Try sitting there to catch the last rays of the setting sun and imagine anywhere more evocative. Fresh crab sandwiches (£6.80), crab salad

(£10.90), or a genuine Cornish cream tea (£4.30) with lashings of jam add to the enjoyment and if like me you have walked twelve miles before sitting down, you'll never forget it.

Smugglers (☎ 01326-290763; summer daily 4.30-8pm; winter Mon-Sat 4.30-8pm) is the place to go for fish and chips and it is also licensed; the *Regent Café* caters for coach parties.

Transport
First's 33 **bus** service calls here. See public transport map and table, pp46-50.

For a **taxi**, ring Goodfellas (☎ 0777-330494).

LIZARD POINT TO CADGWITH COVE [MAPS 86-87]

This **four-mile (6km, 1^1/$_2$-1^3/$_4$hrs)** stretch is so popular that you are hardly likely to wander lonely as a cloud. It must be one of the most heavily used parts of the entire coast path and no wonder, given the superb views back to the lighthouse. The blue-ish rock is serpentine which can be seen on the path and on the slabs used for the stiles. It becomes quite slippery when wet and even on dry days where there has been constant polishing by boots it is easy to slip. Serpentine provides the craftsmen with the raw material for their ashtrays and lighthouse ornaments that you can buy in the gift shops in the area and in the Lizard Village you can watch them at work.

CADGWITH [MAP 87, p224]
This tiny village is a collection of lobster pots, fishing floats and boats clustered around the one pub, *Cadgwith Cove Inn* (☎ 01326-290513, 🖥 www.cadgwithcoveinn .com; 1T/4D) an intriguing survivor from a simpler age before the coming of Sky TV and laptops. If you arrive on a Friday you could be in for a sing-song since the Cadgwith Singers meet to work on their sea shanties. The food (daily noon-2pm & 7-9pm) is standard pub fare and the cost of a night's stay is £41.25 per person for a double en suite and £30.25 per person in a standard room; there is a £15 single occupancy supplement. The beers are the usual Betty Stoggs, Doom Bar and Otter.

The nearest campsite is two miles further on at Kennack Sands (see p225).

The **bus** does not visit Cadgwith and the best option if you need to catch one is to walk to Ruan Minor and get First's 33 which runs between The Lizard and Helston. See public transport map and table, pp46-50.

CADGWITH COVE TO COVERACK [MAPS 87-91]

The next **seven miles (11km, 2^1/$_2$-3hrs)** are over a mixed terrain that makes for varied walking from quite dull to exhilarating. After you leave Cadgwith the cliffs are relatively low-lying and the path traverses country thick with blackthorn, gorse and bracken. You cross the rather untidy beach at **Kennack Sands** and continue with a sharp descent at **Downas Cove** followed by the inevitable climb up out of it.

A further descent has to be tackled at **Beagles Hole** where for the first time hands may be needed as well as feet to scramble down this rocky defile. Once past **Chynhalls Point** Coverack comes into view and an easy path leads into this secretive little harbour village.

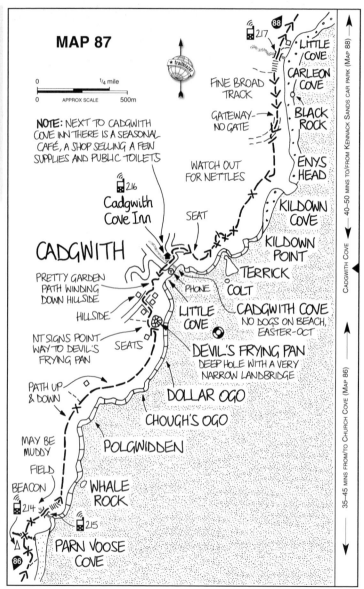

MAP 87

0   1/4 mile
0   APPROX SCALE   500m

NOTE: NEXT TO CADGWITH COVE INN THERE IS A SEASONAL CAFÉ, A SHOP SELLING A FEW SUPPLIES AND PUBLIC TOILETS

★ trailblazer

FINE BROAD TRACK

GATEWAY- NO GATE

WATCH OUT FOR NETTLES

217

88

LITTLE COVE

CARLEON COVE

BLACK ROCK

ENYS HEAD

216

Cadgwith Cove Inn

SEAT

KILDOWN COVE

KILDOWN POINT

CADGWITH

TERRICK

COLT

PHONE

PRETTY GARDEN PATH WINDING DOWN HILLSIDE

HILLSIDE

LITTLE COVE

CADGWITH COVE NO DOGS ON BEACH, EASTER-OCT

NT SIGNS POINT WAY TO DEVIL'S FRYING PAN

SEATS

DEVIL'S FRYING PAN DEEP HOLE WITH A VERY NARROW LANDBRIDGE

PATH UP & DOWN

DOLLAR OGO

CHOUGH'S OGO

POLGWIDDEN

MAY BE MUDDY

FIELD

BEACON

214

WHALE ROCK

215

86

PARN VOOSE COVE

ROUTE GUIDE AND MAPS

40–50 MINS TO/FROM KENNACK SANDS CAR PARK (MAP 88)

CADGWITH COVE

35–45 MINS FROM/TO CHURCH COVE (MAP 86)

(Opposite): Mullion Cove (see p216). (Photo © Edith Schofield).

KENNACK SANDS   **[MAP 88]**
Silver Sands Camp Site (☎ 01326-290631,
🖥 www.silversandsholidaypark.co.uk;

early Apr to mid Sep) charges £12-17 for
two people sharing a small tent. Coastal
walkers are always welcome.

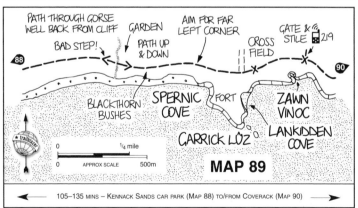

MAP 88

Silver Sands Holiday Camp ⚑

FOLLOW DOG-WALKERS SIGNS

CRUMBLING CLIFFS

EASTERN CLIFF

🏕 218 TOILETS

CROSS CAR PARK. PATH RUNS IN FRONT OF TOILETS

NARROW PATH

SIGN, 'COVERACK 6M'

CARAVAN PATH

PITCH & PUTT GOLF COURSE

PATH SKIRTS EDGE OF GOLF COURSE

THORNY CLIFF

SEASONAL CAFÉ

KENNACK SANDS

GREEN SADDLE

CAERVERRACKS

ONE OF CORNWALL'S SCRUFFIER BEACHES

RIPS CAN OCCUR DURING MID-LOW TIDE. BEACHES PICK UP STRONG EASTERLY WINDS. NO DOGS ON BEACH, EASTER-OCT

89
87

0 — ¼ mile
0 — 500m   APPROX SCALE

← 40-50 MINS →   KENNACK SANDS CAR PARK   ← 105-130 MINS TO/FROM COVERACK (MAP 90) →

PATH THROUGH GORSE WELL BACK FROM CLIFF

BAD STEP!

GARDEN

PATH UP & DOWN

AIM FOR FAR LEFT CORNER

CROSS FIELD

GATE & STILE 🏕 219

88
90

BLACKTHORN BUSHES

SPERNIC COVE

FORT

CARRICK LÛZ

ZAWN VINOC

LANKIDDEN COVE

0 — ¼ mile
0 — 500m   APPROX SCALE

MAP 89

← 105-135 MINS – KENNACK SANDS CAR PARK (MAP 88) TO/FROM COVERACK (MAP 90) →

(Opposite) Top: St Winwaloe Church, Gunwalloe (see p214), in a wonderful setting right beside the coast path. **Bottom**: Boats of all sizes at Falmouth. (Photos © Keith Carter).

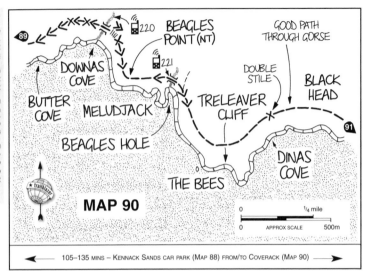

DOWNAS COVE
BUTTER COVE
MELUDJACK
BEAGLES HOLE
BEAGLES POINT (NT)
220
221
GOOD PATH THROUGH GORSE
DOUBLE STILE
BLACK HEAD
TRELEAVER CLIFF
DINAS COVE
THE BEES
89
91
trailblazer

MAP 90

0   ¼ mile
0   APPROX SCALE   500m

◄──── 105–135 MINS – KENNACK SANDS car park (MAP 88) FROM/TO COVERACK (MAP 90) ────►

COVERACK [MAP 91]

The foreshore at Coverack has an unusual claim to fame according to an information board telling the story. It is one of only three places in Britain where you can see the *moho*, what was once the junction between the earth's crust and the mantle. Just exactly what this signifies in geological terms needs some hours on Google but suffice it to say that it is very important. Actually Coverack goes about its business in blissful ignorance of such matters, concerning itself more with coping with the huge influx of holidaymakers in the summer and a total lack of anything to do in the winter. It is in fact one of the nicest little villages in the whole of this part of the coast and has avoided the seaside commercialisation of many other places.

The **post office** (Mon, Wed-Fri 9am-12.30pm & 1.30-5pm, Tues & Sat 9am-12.30pm) also sells a few groceries and has a box of second-hand books outside on the pavement. The **Village Store** (daily 10am-5pm) is better stocked and you can get pasties, sandwiches and fruit for the trail.

The nearest **campsite** is *Little Trevothan* (off Map 91; ☎ 01326-280260,

🖳 www.littletrevothan.co.uk, Easter-Oct) where a hiking tent with two people is £7 in low season, £8 in high. They also have a **yurt** that sleeps four, minimum booking one week (£200-270) in the main season, three nights possible subject to availability at other times.

Coverack Youth Hostel (☎ 01326-280687, 🖳 coverack@yha.org.uk; 30 beds) stands high up on School Hill; it's well-run and welcoming. The hostel closed in the winter of 2009 for new facilities to be added: three en suite rooms were created, though the number of beds overall was reduced from 35 to 30; a new bar; a self-catering kitchen and laundry area were also added; and the capacity for campers was increased from 15 to 35 people. Adults in the hostel pay £11.95-19.95 and **campers** £6.95: campers can use the facilities indoors. The bar has organic wine and local Cornish beer and cider.

For B&B, just down the hill from the hostel is *Boak House* (☎ 01326-280608; 1T/3D) charging £25 per person. The rooms share a bathroom and the place has a slightly faded appearance but is economically priced and adequate. The view from

COVERACK – MAP KEY

Where to stay
1 The Bay Hotel
3 Fernleigh
4 Coverack Youth Hostel
5 Boak House
9 Paris Hotel

Where to eat and drink
6 The Wave Café
8 Archie's Loft

Other
2 Village store
7 Post Office

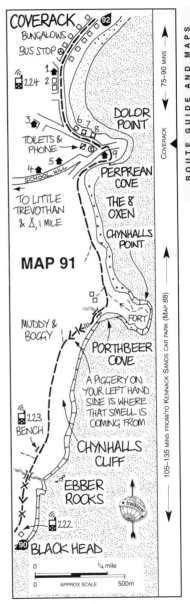

the front of the house is fantastic. Credit/debit cards are not accepted here.

Fernleigh (☎ 01326-280626, 🖳 www .coverack.org.uk; 1T/2D/1F, all with private facilities), Chymbloth Way, is up the scale a bit at £35, a nicely appointed establishment with the added appeal of an evening meal (£15 for three courses), if requested in advance.

At the top of the scale, overlooking the beach. is the charming *Bay Hotel* (☎ 01326-280464, 🖳 www.thebayhotel.co.uk; 12D, 1 suite, all en suite; Mar-Nov) where comfort and a good welcome are assured. Everyone stays in for dinner, attracted by the nice dining room: B&B with dinner is £66-93 per person for a double and £97-112 for the suite. There is a single occupancy supplement of 25-50%. They get lots of walkers.

The only pub in the village is the *Paris Hotel* (☎ 01326-280258, 🖳 www.pariscove rack.com; 1T/3D en suite; daily noon-2pm & 6-9pm) named after a liner, the *SS Paris*, wrecked on the headland in 1899. B&B costs £35 per person. The menu changes regularly but seafood, including paella or mussels and chips for £8.95, is the natural choice for a meal here.

The Wave Café (☎ 01326-281526; daily Feb-Oct 10am-4pm, Nov-Feb 10am-2pm) does a good cream tea (£4.25) as well as light lunches. They have a fish evening on Friday but only for people with advance bookings. *Archie's Loft* is a tiny tea room with Roskilly's ice cream, toasted sandwiches and freshly ground coffee, just right for a quick snack before hitting the trail.

First's 32 **bus** service calls here. The bus turns at the bend north of the village, right on the coast path. See public transport map and table, pp46-50.

COVERACK TO PORTHALLOW [MAPS 91-94]

This **four-mile (6km, 1³/4-2¹/4hrs)** section leaves Coverack along a lane lined with bungalows with gardens full of sub-tropical plants that you won't see at home. You then follow the shore through fields to the monstrous obstacle that is **Dean Quarry** where they dig out gabbro for roadstone. The way through the quarry is well signposted and when I was there the quarry showed no sign of life: in fact, the wind was blowing through the gantries like a scene from a post-apocalyptic movie. Once past the quarry the path is taken inland to avoid more of the same.

Porthoustock has no services other than toilets and there's little in **Porthallow** if the pub hasn't reopened.

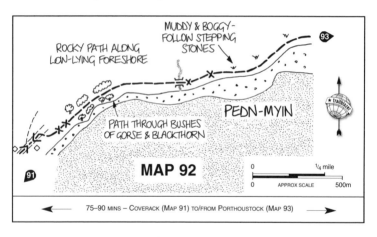

MUDDY & BOGGY – FOLLOW STEPPING STONES

ROCKY PATH ALONG LOW-LYING FORESHORE

PEDN-MYIN

★ trailblazer

PATH THROUGH BUSHES OF GORSE & BLACKTHORN

MAP 92

0   ¹/4 mile
0   APPROX SCALE   500m

75–90 MINS – COVERACK (MAP 91) TO/FROM PORTHOUSTOCK (MAP 93)

❑ The Manacles

This treacherous reef (see Map 93) lies a mile out to sea from Dean Quarry, dangerously close to the shipping lanes in and out of Falmouth. Hundreds of people have lost their lives here. In 1809 two ships were wrecked on the same night: *HMS Dispatch*, which was carrying troops, and *HMS Primrose*. Only eight survived the tragic night. Many shipwreck victims are buried in the churchyard at St Keverne.

On a lighter note, The Manacles provide good fishing grounds for boats from Porthallow and Porthoustock who mainly use handlines to catch bass here.

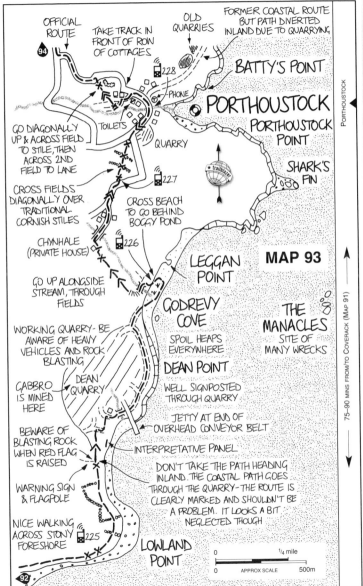

OFFICIAL ROUTE

94

TAKE TRACK IN FRONT OF ROW OF COTTAGES

OLD QUARRIES

FORMER COASTAL ROUTE BUT PATH DIVERTED INLAND DUE TO QUARRYING

BATTY'S POINT

228

PHONE

PORTHOUSTOCK

TOILETS

GO DIAGONALLY UP & ACROSS FIELD TO STILE, THEN ACROSS 2ND FIELD TO LANE

QUARRY

PORTHOUSTOCK POINT

SHARK'S FIN

CROSS FIELDS DIAGONALLY OVER TRADITIONAL CORNISH STILES

227

★ trailblazer

CROSS BEACH TO GO BEHIND BOGGY POND

CHYNHALE (PRIVATE HOUSE)

226

LEGGAN POINT

MAP 93

GO UP ALONGSIDE STREAM, THROUGH FIELDS

GODREVY COVE

THE MANACLES

SITE OF MANY WRECKS

WORKING QUARRY - BE AWARE OF HEAVY VEHICLES AND ROCK BLASTING

SPOIL HEAPS EVERYWHERE

DEAN POINT

GABBRO IS MINED HERE

DEAN QUARRY

WELL SIGNPOSTED THROUGH QUARRY

JETTY AT END OF OVERHEAD CONVEYOR BELT

BEWARE OF BLASTING ROCK WHEN RED FLAG IS RAISED

INTERPRETATIVE PANEL

WARNING SIGN & FLAGPOLE

DON'T TAKE THE PATH HEADING INLAND. THE COASTAL PATH GOES THROUGH THE QUARRY - THE ROUTE IS CLEARLY MARKED AND SHOULDN'T BE A PROBLEM. IT LOOKS A BIT NEGLECTED THOUGH

NICE WALKING ACROSS STONY FORESHORE

225

LOWLAND POINT

92

0   1/4 mile
0   APPROX SCALE   500m

75-90 MINS FROM/TO COVERACK (MAP 91)

PORTHALLOW   [MAP 94]

Porthallow can seem quite a deserted place if you arrive gasping for a drink mid-afternoon on a weekday. The post office has closed and there isn't even a seasonal café but at the time of writing new owners were hoping to take over *The Five Pilchards Inn*

(☎ 01326-280256, 💻 www.fivepilchards .co.uk) and were planning to offer accommodation as well as morning coffee, afternoon teas and meals. Contact them for opening hours and accommodation/food details.

PORTHALLOW TO HELFORD   [MAPS 94-96]

The next **six miles (10km, 1¾-2¼hrs)** are quite tricky. The path crosses sloping ground and even in the dry means walking on the side of the feet for some distance. Once past **Nare Point** where there is a National Coastwatch Station manned by volunteers the path encounters a new obstacle, the inlet of **Gillan Creek**. Here you are faced with a choice. Because the creek is only fordable one hour either side of low tide you will either have to wait for the tide to go out or take the path round the estuary, a walk of 40-45 mins. There is one other possibility. An enterprising boatman (☎ 01326-231357) in St Anthony's will sometimes respond to a telephone call to get you across. You might be lucky.

Across the creek, **St Anthony's in Meneage** is simply some cottages, mostly holiday lets, grouped round the church but it gives you something to aim for when wading across. Beyond **Dennis Head** the sweep of the Helford River offers great views across to Falmouth. The end is in sight. Large ships can be seen standing off until a berth becomes available in the docks. The path meanders through wooded scrub, passes **Ponsence Cove** and **Bosahan Cove** and enters the riverside village of Helford by the back door, through a car park.

HELFORD   [MAP 96, p233]

Helford is a picture-postcard village beside an inlet of the Helford River, the houses stretched out along the creek which drains completely at low tide. The **Village Store** and **post office** (Mon-Tue & Thur-Fri 8.30am-5.30pm, Wed and Sat closed at 1pm, Sun 9am-noon) has a good stock of groceries and you can get fresh hot pasties,

confectionery, fruit and a delicious local apple juice.

The pub, the *Shipwright's Arms* (☎ 01326-231235; summer daily noon-2pm & 7-9pm; winter daily noon-2pm, Wed-Sat 7-9pm) is a lovely old inn with a thatched roof and a garden right beside the creek. The food is standard pub grub.

HELFORD TO HELFORD PASSAGE   [MAPS 96 & 96a-d]

The most convenient crossing of the Helford River is by the **Helford Ferry** (☎ 01326-250770, 💻 www.helford-river-boats.co.uk) which runs Good Friday/ Apr-late June & Sep-Oct daily 9.30am-5.30pm, late June to Aug daily 9.30am-9.30pm, apart from an hour either side of low tide when all you can do is wait; a tide table is essential and is on sale in post offices, many shops and some pubs. The ferry operates on request and if you arrive at the slipway with no sign of it you have to display a yellow disc erected on the jetty for the purpose of alerting the ferryman. Adults pay £4 single, £5 return. See pp233-8 for details of how to get around the Helford River if walking the coast path out of season.

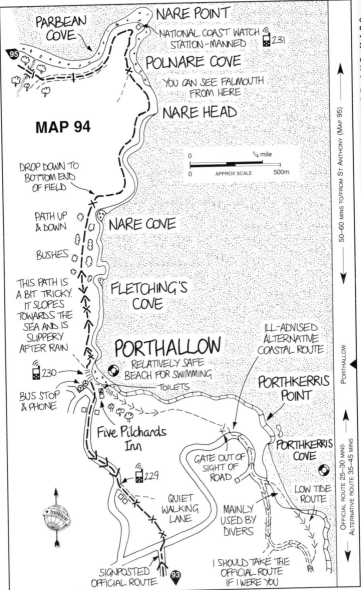

PARBEAN COVE

NARE POINT

NATIONAL COAST WATCH STATION – MANNED 📱231

POLNARE COVE

YOU CAN SEE FALMOUTH FROM HERE

NARE HEAD

MAP 94

0   ¼ mile
0   APPROX SCALE   500m

DROP DOWN TO BOTTOM END OF FIELD

PATH UP & DOWN

NARE COVE

BUSHES

THIS PATH IS A BIT TRICKY. IT SLOPES TOWARDS THE SEA AND IS SLIPPERY AFTER RAIN

FLETCHING'S COVE

📱230

PORTHALLOW

RELATIVELY SAFE BEACH FOR SWIMMING

TOILETS

BUS STOP & PHONE

Five Pilchards Inn

📱229

GATE OUT OF SIGHT OF ROAD

QUIET WALKING LANE

ILL-ADVISED ALTERNATIVE COASTAL ROUTE

PORTHKERRIS POINT

PORTHKERRIS COVE

LOW TIDE ROUTE

MAINLY USED BY DIVERS

I SHOULD TAKE THE OFFICIAL ROUTE IF I WERE YOU

SIGNPOSTED OFFICIAL ROUTE

93

★ trailblazer

50–60 MINS TO/FROM ST ANTHONY (MAP 95)

PORTHALLOW

OFFICIAL ROUTE 25–30 MINS
ALTERNATIVE ROUTE 35–45 MINS

95

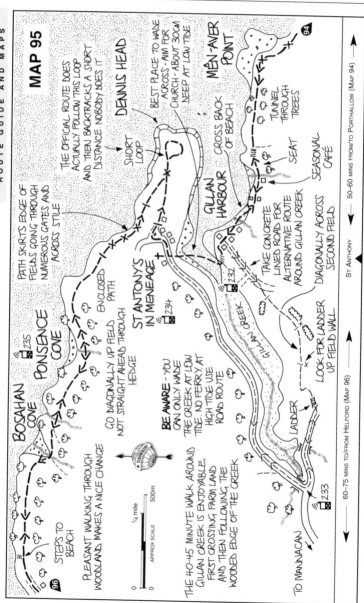

MAP 95

THE OFFICIAL ROUTE DOES ACTUALLY FOLLOW THIS LOOP AND THEN BACKTRACKS A SHORT DISTANCE. NOBODY DOES IT

PATH SKIRTS EDGE OF FIELDS GOING THROUGH NUMEROUS GATES AND ACROSS STILE

BEST PLACE TO WADE ACROSS - AIM FOR CHURCH - ABOUT 30CM DEEP AT LOW TIDE

DENNIS HEAD

SHORT LOOP

MÊN-AVER POINT

TUNNEL THROUGH TREES

ENCLOSED PATH

CROSS BACK OF BEACH

GILLAN HARBOUR

SEAT

SEASONAL CAFÉ

BOSAHAN COVE

PONSENCE COVE

🏠 235

GO DIAGONALLY UP FIELD NOT STRAIGHT AHEAD THROUGH HEDGE

ST ANTONY'S IN MENEAGE

🏠 234

TAKE CONCRETE LINED ROAD FOR ALTERNATIVE ROUTE AROUND GILLAN CREEK

DIAGONALLY ACROSS SECOND FIELD

🏠 232

LOOK FOR LADDER UP FIELD WALL

BE AWARE - YOU CAN ONLY WADE THE CREEK AT LOW TIDE. NO FERRY. AT HIGH TIDE USE ROAD ROUTE

GILLAN CREEK

LADDER

STEPS TO BEACH

PLEASANT WALKING THROUGH WOODLAND MAKES A NICE CHANGE

THE 40-45 MINUTE WALK AROUND GILLAN CREEK IS ENJOYABLE, FIRST CROSSING FARM LAND AND THEN FOLLOWING THE WOODED EDGE OF THE CREEK

🏠 233

TO MANNACAN

¼ mile

500m

0

APPROX SCALE

0

94

96

50-60 MINS FROM/TO PORTHALLOW (Map 94)

St Anthony

60-75 MINS TO/FROM HELFORD (Map 96)

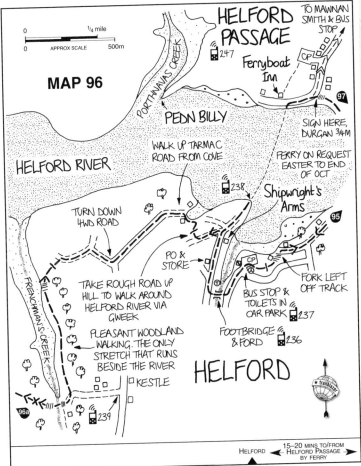

GETTING AROUND THE HELFORD RIVER IN WINTER

On foot (see Map 96 and 96a-96d, pp234-7) It is a **ten-mile (16km, 3-4hrs)** walk around the Helford River. The walk starts off promisingly along the wooded Frenchman's Creek but from Mudgeon Farm to Gweek it's all on tarmac with only tantalising glimpses of the river. However, in winter there won't be many cars and the pretty country lanes can provide some enjoyable walking away from the sea. *Gear Farm* (Map 96a; ☎ 01326-221364) offers **camping** (£8 per person; June-Sep or earlier if the weather is good) and also has a small **café/shop** (daily 9.30am-4.30pm) *(cont'd on p238)*

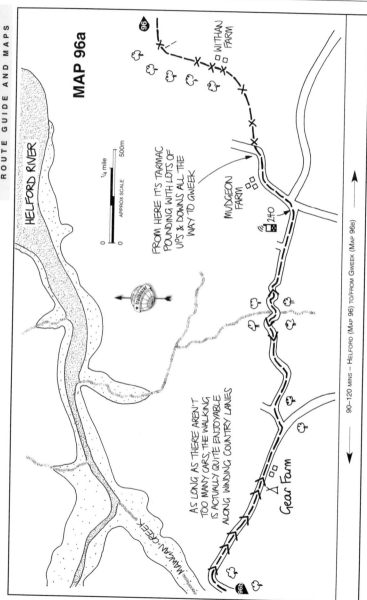

MAP 96a

HELFORD RIVER

WITHAN FARM

FROM HERE IT'S TARMAC POUNDING WITH LOTS OF UP'S & DOWNS ALL THE WAY TO GWEEK

MUDGEON FARM

¼ mile

500m

APPROX SCALE

AS LONG AS THERE AREN'T TOO MANY CARS, THE WALKING IS ACTUALLY QUITE ENJOYABLE ALONG WINDING COUNTRY LANES

MAWGAN CREEK

Gear Farm

90-120 MINS – HELFORD (MAP 96) TO/FROM GWEEK (MAP 96a)

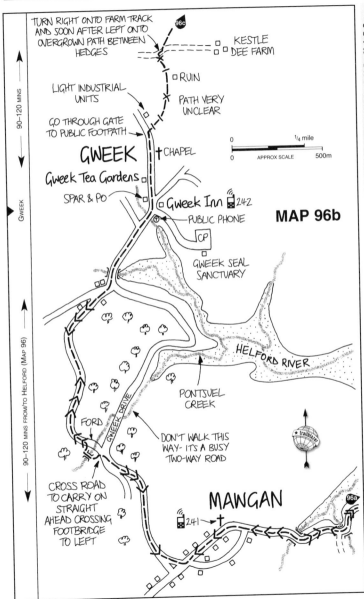

TURN RIGHT ONTO FARM TRACK
AND SOON AFTER LEFT ONTO
OVERGROWN PATH BETWEEN
HEDGES

96c

KESTLE
DEE FARM

RUIN

LIGHT INDUSTRIAL
UNITS

PATH VERY
UNCLEAR

GO THROUGH GATE
TO PUBLIC FOOTPATH

90–120 MINS

GWEEK

GWEEK

† CHAPEL

Gweek Tea Gardens

SPAR & PO

Gweek Inn 📱242

PUBLIC PHONE

CP

MAP 96b

GWEEK SEAL
SANCTUARY

0   ¼ mile
0   APPROX SCALE   500m

HELFORD RIVER

PONTSUEL
CREEK

GWEEK DRIVE

FORD

DON'T WALK THIS
WAY- IT'S A BUSY
TWO-WAY ROAD

★ trailblazer

CROSS ROAD
TO CARRY ON
STRAIGHT
AHEAD CROSSING
FOOTBRIDGE
TO LEFT

MAWGAN

📱241 → †

90–120 MINS FROM/TO HELFORD (MAP 96)

96a

GWEEK [MAP 96b, p235]

Gweek can provide some rest and relaxation although the services are limited. Those who failed to spot a single seal on their coastal wanderings may like to visit the **National Seal Sanctuary** (☎ 01326-221361, 💻 www.sealsanctuary.co.uk; daily 10am-5pm, to 4pm in winter). Last admission is an hour before closing and they charge £11.95.

The **Spar** (Mon-Sat 8am-8pm, Sun 10am-5pm) may be useful for cut sandwiches and fruit and the **post office** (Mon-Fri 9am-1pm, Mon & Wed-Fri 2-5.30pm).

Across the road from the Spar *Gweek Inn* (☎ 01326-221502, 💻 www.gweekinn.co.uk) has a wide selection of real ales. The usual bar meals are enlivened by some specials including Mediterranean goats' cheese tart for £8.75. *Gweek Tea Gardens* (☎ 01326-221635; Feb-Nov coffee daily from 11am, food noon-5pm) serve cream teas and lunches, and evening meals by request.

First's 35 Helston–Falmouth **bus** stops here. See public transport map and table, pp46-50.

HELFORD PASSAGE [MAP 96 p235, & 97 p239]

Helford Passage is directly opposite Helford on the north bank of the wide river mouth. It is alive with the boating set in summer but rather dead out of season.

The only amenity is the *Ferryboat Inn* (☎ 01326-250625). However, at the time of writing the pub was under new management (💻 www .wrightbros.eu.com) and was being refurbished. It was expected to reopen in spring 2009. Since Wright Brothers specialise in oysters expect them on the menu.

Some of First's 35 **buses** between Falmouth and Helston stop here. See public transport map and table, pp46-50.

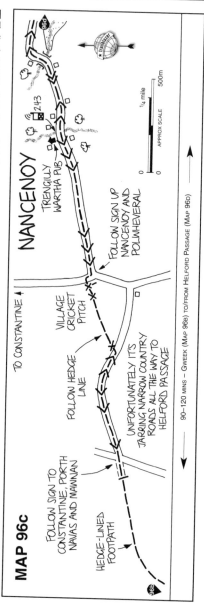

MAP 96c

NANCENOY

TRENGILLY WARTHA PUB

243

FOLLOW SIGN UP NANCENOY AND POLWHEVERAL

TO CONSTANTINE

VILLAGE CRICKET PITCH

FOLLOW HEDGE LINE

UNFORTUNATELY IT'S JARRING NARROW COUNTRY ROADS ALL THE WAY TO HELFORD PASSAGE

FOLLOW SIGN TO CONSTANTINE, PORTH NAVAS AND MAWNAN

HEDGE-LINED FOOTPATH

90-120 MINS – GWEEK (MAP 96B) TO/FROM HELFORD PASSAGE (MAP 96D)

¼ mile

500m

0

APPROX SCALE

96b

96d

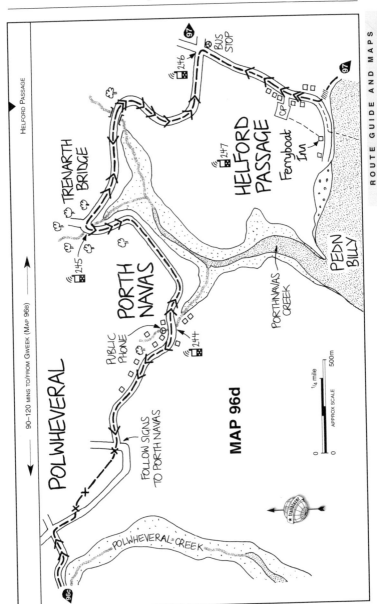

HELFORD PASSAGE

90–120 MINS TO/FROM GWEEK (MAP 96e)

POLWHEVERAL

POLWHEVERAL CREEK

FOLLOW SIGNS
TO PORTH NAVAS

PUBLIC PHONE

PORTH NAVAS

244

TRENARTH BRIDGE

245

PORTHNAVAS CREEK

HELFORD PASSAGE

Ferryboat Inn

247

PEDN BILLY

246

BUS STOP

97

97

CP

MAP 96d

APPROX SCALE

¼ mile

500m

96e

(cont'd from p233) The café serves organic produce such as pasties and pizzas. **Gweek** (see p236 and Map 96b) is a pleasant halfway point. If you are getting tired of walking it is possible to go by bus (First's No 35) from Gweek to Helford Passage (see public transport map and table, pp46-50).

Between Gweek and Helford Passage (see p236) there are a few shortcuts across fields taking you briefly off the roads. You pass through Nancenoy (Map 96c) where you might like to drop in to the *Trengilly Wartha* (☎ 01326-340332, 🖳 www.trengilly.co.uk; food served daily 11am-2.15pm, 6.30-9.30pm), well-known and a favourite locally. The menu may include scallops with pancetta (£7.60) and a fillet of red mullet (£13.20). They also offer B&B (5D/1T/2D or F, all en suite) for £80-96 for two sharing a room or £50 for single occupancy. You rarely see the river but instead are teased every now and again by a steep descent down to a connecting creek and an equally steep climb away from it; the two creeks are Polwheveral and Porth Navas.

By taxi If you decide to choose the **taxi** option, try Autocabs (☎ 01326-573773 or 01326-573131) or Cove Cars (☎ 07980-814058).

HELFORD PASSAGE TO FALMOUTH [MAPS 97-100]

The last **10 miles (16km, 2-2³/₄hrs)** to Falmouth provide wonderful gentle walking. On leaving the foreshore at Helford Passage the path climbs a grassy bank to lead by narrow ways to **Trebah Beach** where American troops embarked for the D-Day landings. **Trebah Gardens** (see box below) come right down to the shore and the path passes below them as it does **Glendurgan Gardens** a little further on. There are wide views across the mouth of the picturesque Helford River.

Before the rocky promontory of **Toll Point** there are a couple of paths leading inland to Mawnan Smith (see p240): after Toll Point the path enters steep woodland and another path leads inland to **Mawnan** which has an interesting church dedicated to St Maunanus, a Celtic saint. Then it loops out to **Rosemullion Head**, a superb viewpoint. A series of little beaches follows

---

❑ **Trebah and Glendurgan Gardens** [MAP 97]

For garden and plant lovers there are two beautiful gardens slightly inland between Helford Passage and Mawnan Smith which would make an exceptionally pleasant and relaxing day of gentle wandering. Both are virtually next door to each other and can be reached by walking up the lane from Helford Passage.

● **Trebah Garden** (☎ 01326-250448, 🖳 www.trebah-garden.co.uk; daily 10am-5pm) descends 200ft down a steeply wooded ravine to a private beach. The stream meanders through ponds containing giant Koi (carp) and runs through two acres of blue and white hydrangeas before spilling onto the beach. Admission is £3 (Nov-Feb) to £7.50 (Mar-Oct). There is a licensed restaurant that sells home-made lunches and cream teas.

● **Glendurgan Garden** (☎ 01326-250906; mid-Feb to end Oct Tue-Sat 10.30am-5.30pm) is owned by the National Trust. The valley garden was created in the 1820s and is rich in fine trees and rare and exotic plants and also features a maze. Spring time brings outstanding displays of magnolias and camelias. Admission is £5.76 or free for NT members.

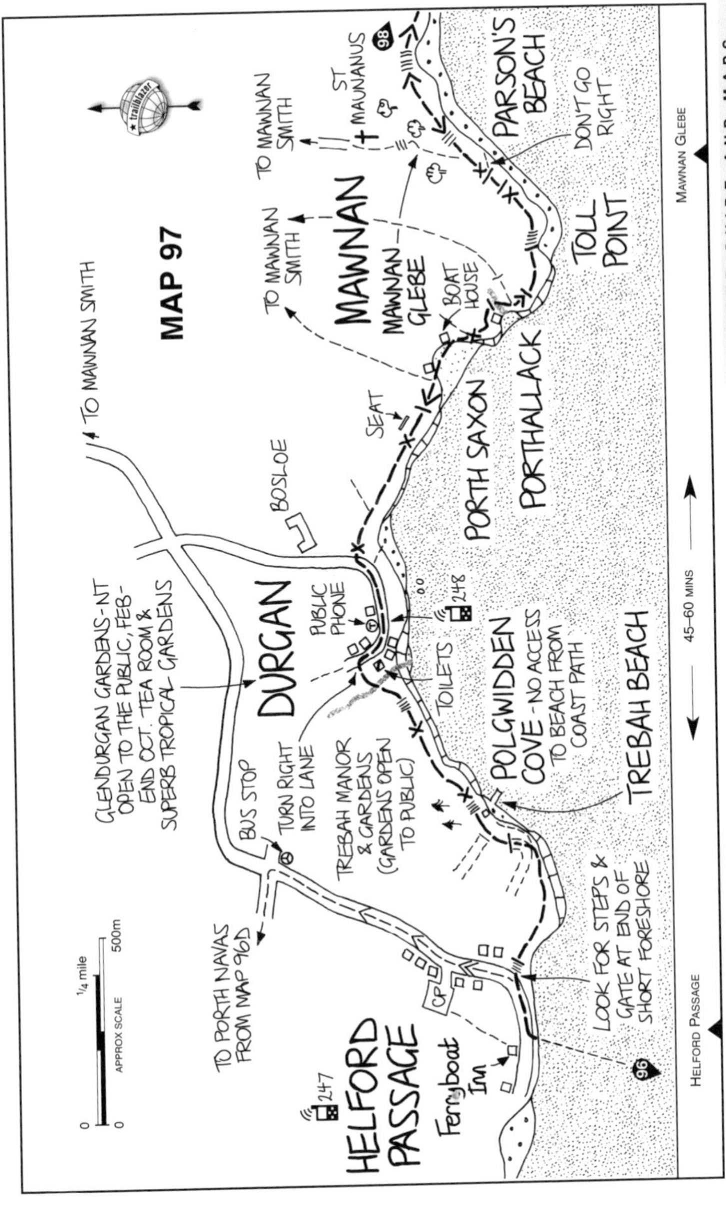

MAP 97

TO MAWNAN SMITH

TO MAWNAN SMITH

TO MAWNAN SMITH

ST MAWNANUS

98

PARSON'S BEACH

DON'T GO RIGHT

MAWNAN

MAWNAN GLEBE

BOAT HOUSE

TOLL POINT

SEAT

BOSLOE

PORTH SAXON

PORTHALLACK

45–60 MINS

PUBLIC PHONE

TOILETS

247

246

DURGAN

GLENDURGAN GARDENS–NT OPEN TO THE PUBLIC, FEB–END OCT. TEA ROOM & SUPERB TROPICAL GARDENS

TURN RIGHT INTO LANE

TREBAH MANOR & GARDENS (GARDENS OPEN TO PUBLIC)

POLGWIDDEN COVE – NO ACCESS TO BEACH FROM COAST PATH

TREBAH BEACH

BUS STOP

TO PORTH NAVAS FROM MAP 96D

HELFORD PASSAGE

247

Ferryboat Inn

CP

LOOK FOR STEPS & GATE AT END OF SHORT FORESHORE

96

HELFORD PASSAGE

¼ mile

500m

0

0

APPROX SCALE

MAWNAN GLEBE

including **Gatamala Cove** and **Bream Cove** before the lovely expanse of **Maenporth Beach** where there's a café and restaurant.

From Maenporth the path is well travelled. After Gyllyngvase Beach suburban pavements take you all the way around **Pendennis Point** and past Falmouth Docks, a popular spot to lean on the fence for a while and watch the boats being repaired below. About 20 fishing boats work from this port of which half either trawl for whitefish or dredge for scallops. There is a native oyster fishery situated in the River Fal.

The final stretch of the coast path is through the streets of Falmouth jostling for space with the shoppers. Although this is an unspectacular finish to your adventures there are plenty of pubs and restaurants where you can celebrate your achievement.

MAWNAN SMITH

The village used to have four blacksmiths so acquired the name to distinguish it from nearby Mawnan. Mawnan Smith isn't actually on the coast path but it can easily be reached by walking from Helford Passage (25-30 mins), Durgan (15-20 mins), or Mawnan (15-20 mins). The **post office** is in the **Spar** (Mon-Sat 8.15am-1pm & 2-5.30pm, Sun 9am-11pm) and has all the usual groceries including filled sandwiches, fruit and crisps.

The *Red Lion* (☎ 01326-250026; Mon-Fri noon-2pm & 6.30-9pm, Sat & Sun noon-2.30pm & 6.30-9pm) is a pub to spend time in, a real beauty with real ales such as Old Speckled Hen, Doom Bar as well as some guest beers. The food is excellent and if you try no other crab bisque (soup) in Cornwall, try it here. It'll cost £6.95.

For B&B try *Carwinion Vean* (☎ 01326-250513, ☐ www.carwinionvean.co .uk; 1T/1D/1F, all with private facilities) hidden away in a large house off Grove Hill. Mrs Spike makes walkers welcome and cooks up a memorable breakfast. B&B costs £30 per person or £35 for single occupancy. *Chynoweth* (☎ 01326-250534, ☐ www.chynoweth.helfordriver.net; 1D/1T, both en suite) is quite small and charges £30 per person, £35-40 for single occupancy. They are about 800m from the coast path but can arrange to pick you up from the trail and will transfer your luggage, though there may be a small charge for journeys other than local ones. Also offering a pick-up service (to/from the Ferryboat Inn free, to/from Falmouth £5, to/from the

Lizard £25) is *Gold Martin* (☎ 01326-250666, ☐ www.goldmartin.co.uk; 1T or D/1D, both en suite), Carlidnak Rd, a beautiful late 18th-century house with a lounge, conservatory and garden. They have a single room but it is only let out in conjunction with one of the doubles. Two sharing a room pay £66 for B&B and if the single room is booked it is £34.

Transport

Mawnan Smith is on First's 35 route between Falmouth and Helston. See public transport map and table, pp46-50.

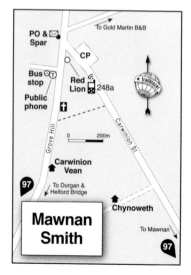

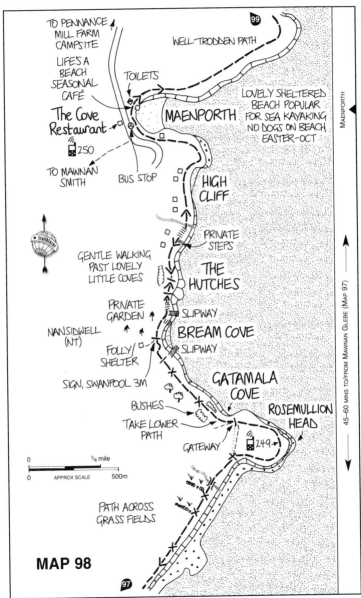

TO PENNANCE MILL FARM CAMPSITE

LIFE'S A BEACH SEASONAL CAFÉ

TOILETS

WELL-TRODDEN PATH

99

The Cove Restaurant

📱250

TO MAWNAN SMITH

BUS STOP

MAENPORTH

LOVELY SHELTERED BEACH POPULAR FOR SEA KAYAKING. NO DOGS ON BEACH, EASTER-OCT

MAENPORTH

HIGH CLIFF

PRIVATE STEPS

GENTLE WALKING PAST LOVELY LITTLE COVES

THE HUTCHES

PRIVATE GARDEN

SLIPWAY

NANSIDWELL (NT)

BREAM COVE

FOLLY / SHELTER

SLIPWAY

SIGN, SWANPOOL 3M

GATAMALA COVE

BUSHES

ROSEMULLION HEAD

TAKE LOWER PATH

GATEWAY

📱249

0   ¼ mile

0   APPROX SCALE   500m

45-60 MINS TO/FROM MAWNAN GLEBE (MAP 97)

PATH ACROSS GRASS FIELDS

MAP 98

97

MAENPORTH [MAP 98, p241]

Apart from its **seasonal café** (*Life's a Beach*), Maenporth has a smart bar and restaurant *The Cove* (☎ 01326-251136, 🖳 www.thecovemaenporth.co.uk; summer daily 11am-11pm, winter Tue-Sat noon-3pm & 6-9.30pm, Sun noon-9.30pm) where you can sit out on the deck and have coffee or sample the tapas (£3.50-6.25) for lunch. The menu changes every six weeks but often features wild sea bass fillet (£19.99); meat and vegetarian dishes are also available.

FALMOUTH [MAP 100, p245]

Falmouth is a working port and holiday resort rolled into one. A small fishing village in the 17th century, it was developed by the Killigrew family who made their money from privateering and piracy, a lucrative trade in those days. Falmouth is still defined by the sea and ships, especially sailing thanks to its large expanse of sheltered water. It is said that an entire navy can anchor safely in Carrick Roads, the body of water between Falmouth and St Mawes. One of Britain's major yachting centres, it is often the first port of call for many a trans-Atlantic sailor and the Tall Ships make it a regular place to visit, bringing out the crowds in their tens of thousands. Two festivals worth attending are **Falmouth Regatta Week** and the **Oyster Festival** (see pp30-1).

The entrance to Carrick Roads is guarded by two castles built by Henry VIII, Pendennis Castle on the western promontory and the other across the water at St Mawes. **Pendennis Castle** (☎ 01326-316594, 🖳 www.english-heritage.org.uk; daily mid Mar to June & Sep 10am-5pm, July & Aug 10am-6pm, to 4pm on Saturdays, Nov-Mar 10am-4pm; £5.50), built by Henry VIII, is well worth a visit. The **National Maritime Museum** (☎ 01326-313388, 🖳 www.nmmc.co.uk; daily 10am-5pm; £8.75), Discovery Quay, has plenty of interesting displays telling the stories of Cornwall's past.

Falmouth Art Gallery (☎ 01326-313863, 🖳 www.falmouthartgallery.com; Mon-Sat 10am-5pm, admission free), The Moor, has a permanent collection of work

You may be too near the end of the walk to stop here but the beach is a real gem. **Campers** should head to *Pennance Mill Farm* (Map 99; ☎ 01326-317431, 🖳 www.pennancemill.co.uk; Easter to end Oct), which charges £6.50-7.75/£13-15.50 for one/two people in a tent. It's best accessed from here or from Swanpool beach: phone for directions.

The Falmouth Explorer (First 400) **bus** calls here; see public transport map and table, pp46-50.

by mainly Cornish artists with several visiting exhibitions throughout the year; the gallery is in the Municipal Buildings and is above the library. The independent **Poly Cinema** (☎ 01326-212300, 🖳 www.the poly.org), on Church St, shows art-house films. The box office is open Mon-Sat 10am-5pm.

Services

The staff at the **tourist information centre** (☎ 01326-312300, 🖳 www.acornishriver .co.uk; July & Aug Mon-Sat 9.30am-5.15pm, Sun 10.15am-1.45pm, Mar-July & Sep-Oct Mon-Sat 9.30am-5.15pm, Nov-Mar Mon-Fri 9.30am-5.15pm), Prince of Wales Pier, couldn't be more helpful.

The **post office** (Mon-Sat 9am-6pm) is next door to the **library** (Mon-Fri 9.30am -6pm, closed Wed, Sat 9.30am-4pm); the latter provides **internet access** (£1.80 per 30 mins). The other place for internet access is **Q-bar** (☎ 01326-210294; Mon-Sat 10am-midnight, Sun noon-midnight) on Killigrew St. They charge £3.50 for the first hour and also provide Wifi access for laptops.

The main High Street **banks** are along Market St, all with cash machines with no charge for withdrawing money and there's a Tesco Xpress (Mon-Sat 7am-8pm, Sun 10am-4pm) on The Moor. In case you need to wash some clothes the nearest **launderette** is further up Killigrew St. The **medical centre** (☎ 01326-212120; Mon-Fri 8.30am-6pm closed 1-2pm), Westover Surgery is on Western Terrace. There is a Boots **pharmacy** on Market St.

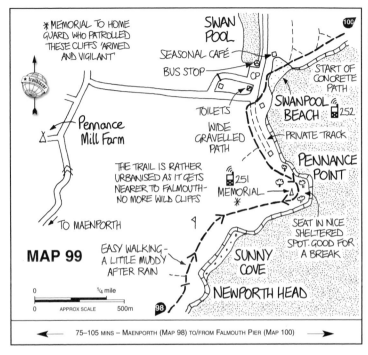

* MEMORIAL TO HOME GUARD WHO PATROLLED THESE CLIFFS 'ARMED AND VIGILANT'

SWAN POOL

SEASONAL CAFÉ

BUS STOP

100

START OF CONCRETE PATH

SWANPOOL BEACH 📱 252

TOILETS

PRIVATE TRACK

WIDE GRAVELLED PATH

PENNANCE POINT

Pennance Mill Farm

THE TRAIL IS RATHER URBANISED AS IT GETS NEARER TO FALMOUTH - NO MORE WILD CLIFFS

📱 251

MEMORIAL *

SEAT IN NICE SHELTERED SPOT. GOOD FOR A BREAK

TO MAENPORTH

EASY WALKING - A LITTLE MUDDY AFTER RAIN

SUNNY COVE

MAP 99

NEWPORTH HEAD

0   ¼ mile
0   APPROX SCALE   500m

98

75–105 MINS – MAENPORTH (MAP 98) TO/FROM FALMOUTH PIER (MAP 100)

Where to stay

Those wanting to **camp** will have to go to *Pennance Mill Farm* (see Maenporth, Map 99). The only **hostel** in town is *Falmouth Backpackers* (☎ 01326-319996, 🖳 www .falmouthback packers.co.uk; 14 dorm beds, 1S/1D or T/1D/2Tr), 9 Gyllyngvase Terrace, charging £24 per person in a single room, £21 in a twin and £25 in an en suite double although the price in a 4-bed dorm is £19.

The following are just a selection from Falmouth's huge choice of accommodation; in terms of quality there is not a lot to choose between them. In summer, and for events such as the Tall Ships gathering, the town can get booked up so make sure you keep this in mind when planning your trip.

Guesthouses are thick on the ground in the Melvill Rd/Avenue Rd area. *Lugo Rock* (☎ 01326-311344, 🖳 www.lugorock hotel.co.uk; 12D, T or F, all en suite with

shower), 59 Melvill Rd, is a good place to start. It's a large comfortable establishment where two people sharing a room pay £65-79, single occupancy is £45; dogs (£5-7 per stay) are accepted if arranged in advance. Just opposite, the half-timbered *Rosemullion* (☎ 01326-314690, 🖳 gail @rosemullionhotel.demon.co.uk; 1S/3T/ 9D, 11 en suite, two with private bathroom) has king-size beds in four rooms and charges £32 to £38 per person for two sharing, £30-35 for the single and £35-45 for single occupancy of a twin/double.

Turn right and on the left are two guest-houses side by side: *Melvill House* (☎ 01326-316645, 🖳 www.melvill-house-fal mouth.co.uk; 2T/3D/2F, all en suite), at 52 Melvill Rd, where the rate is £28-33 per person, £35 for single occupancy, and *Dolvean* (☎ 01326-313658, 🖳 www.dolvean.co.uk; 2S/2T/6D all en suite), at No 50, a welcoming place run by a young couple. The wife is German and, by arrangement, takes visiting groups round the area. The tariff is £35-46 per person, £35-41 for a single room. The extra details include free mineral water in the bedrooms, a nice touch.

Trevu House (☎ 01326-312852, 🖳 trevu-house@falmouth45.fsnet.co.uk; 3S/ 3T/2D, all en suite), at 45 Melvill Rd, charges £25-33 per person; and *Telford* (☎ 01326-314581, 🖳 www.thetelford-falmouth .co.uk; 2S/2D/2T/1F, all with private facilities), costs from £28-35 per person. At No 49 is *Cotswold House* (☎ 01326-312077, 🖳 www.cotswoldhousehotel.com; 1S/2T/8D, all en suite) which has a residents' bar and restaurant (Easter to October only); rooms cost £30-40 per person.

The attractive *Gyllyngvase House Hotel* (☎ 01326-312956, 🖳 www.gyllyng vase.co.uk; 3S/6T/6D/1F) charges £28-33 for a single room with shared facilities and £60-80 for an en suite room. They have a restaurant and bar and you can get free use of the internet. *Camelot* (☎ 01326-312480, 🖳 www.camelot-guest-house.co.uk; 2S/ 4T/2D/1F, all en suite), at No 5 Avenue Rd,

is in a striking black and white property and charges £30 for a single and £56-70 per room with a £2 per person supplement for stays of one night only. Some of their twin rooms can also be doubles or triples. *Trevelyan* (☎ 01326-311545, 🖳 www.bed andbreakfastfalmouth.co.uk; 2S/4D/2F, all en suite), at No 6, is open all year, has Wifi access and takes debit and credit cards; they charge £25-27 per person. *Braemar* (☎ 01326-311285, 🖳 www.braemar-falmouth .co.uk; 1S/4T/4D, most with en suite), at No 9, charges £28 per person and *Trevoil* (☎ 01326-314145, 🖳 www.trevoil-falmo uth.co.uk; 3S/2T/3D, most en suite), at No 25, charges £25 per person.

On Gyllyngvase Terrace, a quiet side road, *The Rosemary* (☎ 01326-314669, 🖳 www.therosemary.co.uk; 1S/2T, D or F/ 3D/2F, all en suite), at No 22, is a highly rated guesthouse charging £34-38 per person with a £2 supplement for stays of one night only. They are open February to October and take some credit cards.

A little further to walk but worth the trouble is *Trevaylor* (☎ 01326-313041, 🖳 www.trevaylorhotel.com; 1S/5D/3F, all en

---

FALMOUTH MAP KEY

Where to stay
12 Castleton
13 Engleton
16 Green Lawns Hotel
17 Trevaylor
36 Trevoil
37 Braemar
38 Trevelyan
39 Camelot
40 Dolvean House
41 Melvill House
42 Lugo Rock
43 Rosemullion
44 Falmouth Beach Resort Hotel
45 The Rosemary
46 Gyllyngvase House
47 Falmouth Backpackers
48 Cotswold House
49 Trevu House
50 Telford

Where to eat
3 Grapes Inn
4 Finn M'Coul's
8 Xen Noodle Bar
9 Nepalese Gurkha
10 Q Bar
11 Wodehouse Arms

Where to eat (cont)
19 Ming's Garden
20 Kings Head
21 Bistro de la Mer
22 Two Ten Bistro
23 Mali Thai
24 Balti Curries
25 Oggy Oggy Pasty Co
26 The Chain Locker
27 The Hut
28 Clark's Restaurant
29 Shelton's Café
30 3 Amigos
32 The Shed
33 Harvey's Wharf
34 Pizza Express
35 5 Degrees West

Other
1 Tourist Information
2 Pharmacy
5 Tesco
6 Library & Gallery
7 Post Office
10 Q Bar (internet)
14 Launderette
15 Medical Centre
18 Poly Cinema
31 National Maritime Museum

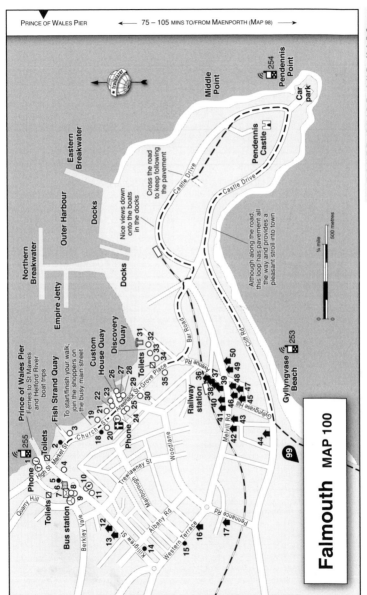

PRINCE OF WALES PIER ← 75 – 105 MINS TO/FROM MAENPORTH (MAP 98) →

Middle Point

Pendennis Point

Car park

254

Pendennis Castle

Castle Drive

Cross the road to keep following the pavement

Castle Drive

Although along the road, this loop has pavement all the way and provides a pleasant stroll into town

Nice views down onto the boats in the docks

Eastern Breakwater

Docks

Outer Harbour

Northern Breakwater

Docks

Empire Jetty

Prince of Wales Pier
Ferries to St Mawes
and Helford River
boat trips

Fish Strand Quay

To start/finish your walk, join the shoppers on the busy main street

Custom House Quay

Discovery Quay

31

32

33

34

Toilets

26 27 28

29 25

Maenock St

Grove Place

35 36

30

24

Phone

18 19 21 22 23
20

Church St

3

255

Phone

Toilets

High St Market St

1

2

4

Quarry Hill

Toilets

Bus station

5 6
7 8
9 10
11

Berkley Vale

12

13

Killigrew St

14

Albany Rd

Western Terrace

15

16

17

Pennance Rd

Marlborough Rd

Trewlawney St

Woodlane

Melvill Rd

Avenue Rd

Bar Road

Railway station

37 38 39 40 41 42 43 44 45 46 47 48 49 50

Cliff Rd

253

Gyllyngvase Beach

Gyllyngvase Hill

99

¼ mile

500 metres

Falmouth MAP 100

suite), 8 Pennance Rd, a large double-fronted house with an open aspect where B&B costs £32 per person with a £2 supplement for one-nighters. They remain open all year.

Close to the bus station are two B&Bs next to each other both under the same ownership: *Castleton Guest House* (☎ 01326-372644, 🖳 www.falmouth-bandb.co .uk; 1S/3D/3F, most en suite), 68 Killigrew St, and *Engleton* (same phone no and website); 1D/2T/2D, T or F, most en suite), at No 67, both charging £25-27.50 per person for B&B; single occupancy rates depend on the season but expect to pay £35-38. They remain open all year.

Finally, two hotels for those who want a bit of luxury after their exertions on the trail are: *Falmouth Beach Resort Hotel* (☎ 01326-312999, 🖳 www.bw-falmouthbeach hotel.co.uk; 16S/104D or T, all en suite), Gyllyngvase Beach, part of the Best Western chain, with rates from £65 to £73 per person for B&B. There's a fitness suite and pool and every luxury known to man. Also quite exclusive is *Green Lawns Hotel* (☎ 01326-312734, 🖳 www.greenlawns hotel.com; 6S/27D or T/6F, all en suite), Western Terrace, charging £65-75 for a standard single en suite and £60-75 per person for two sharing a room. The hotel has a lovely creeper-clad front, an indoor pool and a swanky **restaurant**, open daily year-round.

Where to eat and drink

Falmouth is packed with places to eat ranging from fish and chips through a variety of ethnic restaurants to intimate bistros, swanky restaurants and fine dining. Naturally enough seafood predominates and it is no exaggeration to say you could eat out at a different venue every day for a fortnight.

The two most eclectic dining experiences are probably *Xen Noodle Bar* (☎ 01326-218346; daily noon-3pm & 5-10.30pm), The Moor, where your meal comes and goes with speed and you're out of the door within half an hour having spent about £10 a head. They don't take cheques. The other is *Nepalese Gurkha* (☎ 01326-311483, daily noon-2.30pm & 5.45-11.30pm; above Xen Noodle Bar) serving

Nepalese food. For the familiar Chinese meal look no further than *Ming's Garden Restaurant* (☎ 01326-314413; Tue-Sat noon-1.30pm & daily 5-10.30pm Church St) where the early bird menu for those eating before 7pm costs £8.95. They close on Mondays. *Balti Curries* (☎ 01326-317905, 47 Arwenack St) is open noon-2.30pm and 6pm-midnight every day and *Mali Thai* (☎ 01326-210333, Quay Hill) with the usual Thai menu is open noon-2pm and 5-11pm every day.

On Discovery Quay, there are numerous places to sit and enjoy a coffee or eat a meal. For a trendy bar and restaurant, *Harvey's Wharf* (☎ 01326-314351, 🖳 www .harveyswharf.com; food served daily 9am-10pm, bar open till 11.30pm) or sit on the decking with a cocktail at *The Shed* (☎ 01326-318502; Mon-Sat 9.30am-midnight, Sun 9.30am-11pm). *Pizza Express* (☎ 01326-318841; daily 11.30am-11pm) also has a restaurant there with tables on a balcony. Their cheapest pizza is the Margherita at £5.75 and their dearest the Gamberettini (£10.95).

Heading along Arwenack St, *5 Degrees West* (☎ 01326-311288; daily noon-10pm) catches the eye, with their range of beers and food described as 'light nibbles', 'large nibbles' and 'a bit on the side'. Next comes *3 Amigos* (☎ 01326-317477; daily 6-9.30pm) advertising itself as a Mexican Steakhouse, a challenge to any red-blooded meat eater. If you really want to prove you have cojones go for mole poblano (roast pork tenderloin cooked with three types of chilli) at £12.95. In total contrast but only a few doors away is the *Oggy Oggy Pasty Company*, the obvious choice if your appetite for pasties is still unfulfilled.

Turning down the narrow Quay Hill to the water front, *Shelton's Café* is a good spot for a coffee and maybe a bite to eat – their roasted vegetable lasagne only costs £5.95 – but for an intimate dinner try the secretive little restaurant *The Hut* (☎ 01326-318229; Easter-Oct daily 5-11pm, rest of year 6-11pm) with a wonderful menu including sea bream with sun-dried tomatoes olives and herbs (£13.95), or 1kg of Cornish mussels (£11.95).

Back on Arwenack St, *Two Ten Bistro* (☎ 01326-210200; daily summer noon-9pm, winter Tue-Fri) is a contemporary seafood restaurant with dishes such as roasted monkfish with honey, ginger and soy for £14.50. Next door, *Bistro de la Mer* (☎ 01326-316509; June-Sep Tue-Sat noon-1.30pm and daily 7-10pm, Oct-May Tue-Sat noon-1.30pm & 7-10pm) offers similar fare: you might like to try their seared Falmouth Bay scallops (£17.95).

Clarks Restaurant (☎ 01326-312678; daily 7am-2.30pm & 6-9.30pm), at No 38, serves seafood mainly such as paella (£13.95) but they also have steaks and chicken dishes. Booking is advisable.

If the choice is just too much to cope with, perhaps you feel like falling back on a traditional pub in which case the *King's Head*, close to the church, the *Chain Locker* on Quay Hill, *Grapes Inn* on Church St, *Finn M'Coul's* on Killigrew St, and the *Wodehouse Arms* (food served Mon-Sat noon-3pm & 6-8pm, Sun noon-3pm) opposite the bus station should be choice enough.

Transport

First has **bus** services to: Truro (88/88B, 400); Mawnan Smith, Gweek, Helford Passage & Helston (35) and Penzance (2). The Falmouth Explorer calls in at various beaches in the Falmouth area. The **train** goes to Truro hourly, operated by First Great Western. See public transport map and table, pp46-50.

Map key

Walking track	Cornish hedge	Forest / wood
Minor track	Bridge	Boggy ground
4WD track	Fence	Building
Road	Stone wall	Accommodation
Steps	Hedge	Campsite
Slope	Water	Church
Steep slope	Sand	Public Toilet
Stile	Stones	Public telephone
Gate	Stream	Bus stop
Dunes	Golf course	Car park
Cliff	Lifeguard cover	GPS waypoint
Memorial	Rescue equipment	Map continuation
	Lighthouse	

APPENDIX A: GPS WAYPOINTS

MAP	REF	GPS WAYPOINTS		DESCRIPTION
Map p75	001	50 49 601	04 32 803	Falcon Hotel, Bude
Map 1	002	50 49 685	04 33 330	Compass tower
Map 1	003	50 49 427	04 33 380	trig point
Map 1	004	50 48 861	04 33 242	Upton
Map 2	005	50 48 006	04 33 514	stone seat
Map 2	006	50 47 224	04 33 342	Black Rock Café
Map 3	007	50 46 769	04 33 519	junction with road
Map 3	008	50 46 257	04 34 494	Millook
Map 4	009	50 45 632	04 35 924	trig point
Map 4	010	50 45 425	04 36 795	footbridge, Lower Tresmorn
Map 5	011	50 44 809	04 37 815	footbridge
Map 5	012	50 44 446	04 37 911	Crackington Haven
Map 5	013	50 44 287	04 38 742	boardwalk, Cambeak
Map 6	014	50 43 562	04 38 723	turning to car park
Map 6	015	50 43 039	04 38 957	bench at highest point
Map 6	016	50 42 661	04 39 303	bench
Map 7	017	50 42 458	04 39 721	boardwalk
Map 7	018	50 42 215	04 40 615	gap in hedge
Map 8	019	50 41 826	04 40 942	boardwalk
Map 8	020	50 41 717	04 40 688	stile
Map 8	021	50 41 530	04 41 669	Flagstaff, Penally
Map 8	022	50 41 403	04 41 645	Boscastle bridge
Map 9	023	50 41 030	04 42 489	steps by ruin
Map 9	024	50 41 000	04 43 286	rock arch
Map 10	025	50 40 372	04 43 693	Rocky Valley
Map 10	026	50 40 201	04 44 213	path to beach
Map 10	027	50 40 315	04 44 440	bench
Map 11	028	50 40 058	04 45 399	café at castle
Map 11	029	50 39 854	04 45 277	footbridge
Map 11	030	50 39 553	04 45 777	Tintagel Youth Hostel
Map 11	031	50 39 280	04 45 707	gate
Map 11	032	50 39 038	04 45 396	bench
Map 12	033	50 38 651	04 45 574	Trebarwith Strand
Map 12	034	50 38 365	04 45 818	stream crossing
Map 12	035	50 38 053	04 45 987	gate
Map 12	036	50 37 450	04 45 974	path to Tregardock Beach
Map 13	037	50 37 794	04 46 517	path to Tregragon Farm
Map 13	038	50 36 430	04 46 939	stream crossing
Map 13	039	50 36 209	04 47 190	stepping stones
Map 14	040	50 35 974	04 47 456	stile
Map 14	041	50 35 736	04 48 404	boardwalk
Map 14	042	50 35 609	04 49 200	road at Headlands Hotel, Port Gaverne
Map 15	043	50 35 778	04 50 880	stile at Varley Sand
Map 15	044	50 35 617	04 51 254	bench at Scarnor Point
Map 15	045	50 35 655	04 52 062	bench, Kellan Head
Map 16	046	50 35 437	04 52 187	bench in memory of Sgt Roberts
Map 16	047	50 35 308	04 51 998	stile, Doyden Point
Map 16	048	50 35 097	04 52 795	Trevan Point
Map 16	049	50 34 996	04 53 930	path to Pentireglaze
Map 17	050	50 35 249	04 55 011	path to Pentire Farm

MAP	REF	GPS WAYPOINTS		DESCRIPTION
Map 17	051	50 35 477	04 55 477	stone seat, The Rumps
Map 17	052	50 35 188	04 55 988	Pentire Point
Map 18	053	50 34 770	04 54 940	Pentireglaze Haven
Map 18	054	50 34 414	04 54 989	junction with road, Polzeath
Map 18	055	50 33 838	04 55 769	Trebetherick Point
Map 18	056	50 33 679	04 55 491	steps to Daymer Beach
Map 19	057	50 32 722	04 55 496	Rock car park
Map 19	058	50 32 646	04 55 384	Blue Tomato Café, Rock
Map 21	059	50 32 808	04 56 040	War Memorial, Padstow
Map 21	060	50 33 204	04 56 957	junction with track
Map 22	061	50 33 570	04 56 892	Hawker's Cove
Map 22	062	50 34 052	04 57 090	tower
Map 22	063	50 33 415	04 57 988	path to road
Map 23	064	50 32 681	04 58 601	Trevone Beach steps
Map 23	065	50 32 344	04 59 632	Harlyn Bridge
Map 23	066	50 32 728	05 00 213	bench at viewpoint
Map 24	067	50 32 581	05 00 889	junction with path
Map 24	068	50 32 892	05 02 018	Trevose Head
Map 24	069	50 32 422	05 01 489	first house in Booby's Bay
Map 24	070	50 31 851	05 01 318	beach exit south
Map 25	071	50 31 491	05 01 307	steps up from beach, Constantine Bay
Map 25	072	50 31 015	05 01 571	steps
Map 25	073	50 30 521	05 01 208	bridge at Porthcothan
Map 25	074	50 30 168	05 01 998	footbridge
Map 26	075	50 29 870	05 02 409	cairn
Map 26	076	50 28 830	05 01 861	National Trust shop, Carnewas
Map 27	077	50 27 866	05 01 834	Mawgan Porth
Map 27	078	50 27 586	05 02 163	path to Bre Pen Farm
Map 28	079	50 26 622	05 02 472	Watergate Bay
Map 29	080	50 25 522	05 03 134	bridge at Porth Beach
Map 29	081	50 25 033	05 04 236	path junction with road
Map 30	082	50 25 141	05 05 408	war memorial, Headland
Map 31	083	50 25 104	05 05 779	Fistral Blu
Map 31	084	50 24 720	05 06 060	Esplanade toilets, Fistral Beach
Map 31	085	50 24 420	05 05 883	Penpol footbridge
Map 31	086	50 24 341	05 06 699	Beach Café
Map 31a	087	50 24 319	05 04 641	Laurie Bridge
Map 32	088	50 24 253	05 07 616	Crantock Beach Steps
Map 32	089	50 24 041	05 08 972	footbridge, Porth Joke
Map 33	090	50 23 333	05 08 560	exit from beach, Holywell Bay
Map 33	091	50 23 172	05 08 358	bus stop by Treguth Inn
Map 33	092	50 22 788	05 08 979	stile by isolated farm
Map 33	093	50 22 459	05 08 653	top of path to beach
Map 34	094	50 20 694	05 09 209	Beach Road, Perranporth
Map 35	095	50 20 336	05 10 704	quarry, Cligga Head
Map 36	096	50 19 577	05 11 383	airstrip
Map 36	097	50 19 253	05 11 505	Blue Hills Tin Mine
Map 36	098	50 19 108	05 12 062	WC, Trevaunance Cove
Map 37	099	50 19 057	05 13 888	St Agnes Head
Map 37	100	50 18 027	05 13 926	chimney, Wheal Coates
Map 37	101	50 17 976	05 14 011	Chapel Porth
Map 38	102	50 17 231	05 14 417	Porthtowan Beach

MAP	REF	GPS WAYPOINTS		DESCRIPTION
Map 38	103	50 16 755	05 15 319	chimney
Map 39	104	50 16 578	05 15 513	stream crossing, Nancekuke
Map 39	105	50 16 353	05 16 526	concrete shelter
Map 40	106	50 15 821	05 17 019	car park, Portreath
Map 40	107	50 15 645	05 17 517	Portreath beach
Map 41	108	50 15 528	05 18 117	gate opposite The Horse
Map 41	109	50 15 312	05 18 466	stream, Porthcadjack Cove
Map 41	110	50 14 915	05 18 765	car park exit
Map 42	111	50 14 408	05 19 807	car park, Deadman's Cove
Map 43	112	50 14 196	05 21 639	Hell's Mouth
Map 43	113	50 14 471	05 22 687	trig point, The Knavocks
Map 44	114	50 13 803	05 23 226	Godrevy Café
Map 44	115	50 13 233	05 23 084	Gwithian
Map 45	116	50 12 287	05 24 715	Phillack Towans
Map 46	117	50 11 278	05 25 276	Hayle tidal gate
Map 46	118	50 11 033	05 25 211	Hayle Viaduct
Map 47	119	50 10 651	05 26 484	Lelant Saltings
Map 47	120	50 11 271	05 26 129	St Uny Church
Map 48	121	50 11 804	05 27 714	road at Carbis Bay
Map 48	122	50 12 312	05 28 239	shelter, Porthminster Point
Map 48	123	50 12 538	05 28 612	Porthminster Station
Map 49	124	50 12 856	05 28 707	St Ives post office
Map 50	125	50 12 949	05 29 300	shelter
Map 50	126	50 12 862	05 30 674	stream crossing
Map 51	127	50 12 775	05 31 345	stone circle
Map 51	128	50 12 779	05 32 168	trig point, Carn Naun Point
Map 51	129	50 12 613	05 32 534	stream, River Cove
Map 51	130	50 12 143	05 33 246	stream crossing
Map 52	131	50 11 742	05 34 421	turn for Zennor
Map 52	132	50 11 839	05 34 553	Zennor Head
Map 52	133	50 11 697	05 34 375	gap in hedge
Map 52	134	50 11 473	05 34 002	Tinner's Arms, Zennor
Map 52	135	50 11 669	05 34 485	stream, Pendour Cove
Map 52	136	50 11 385	05 35 028	stream, Porthglaze Cove
Map 53	137	50 11 300	05 35 864	path junction to Gurnard's Head
Map 53	138	50 10 817	05 36 269	stream, Porthmeor Cove
Map 54	139	50 10 503	05 37 096	Bosigran Castle
Map 54	140	50 10 397	05 37 009	stone bridge, Porthmoina Cove
Map 54	141	50 09 924	05 37 839	stream crossing, Trevowhan Cliff
Map 55	142	50 09 935	05 38 345	stile, Morvah Cliff
Map 55	143	50 09 799	05 39 328	buoyancy aid, Portheras Cove
Map 56	144	50 09 823	05 40 178	car park, Pendeen Watch
Map 56	145	50 09 567	05 40 280	stream, Enys Zawn
Map 56	146	50 09 304	05 40 699	footbridge, Geevor
Map 57	147	50 08 654	05 41 465	trig point, Botallack Head
Map 57	148	50 08 071	05 41 667	gate and stone stile
Map 57	149	50 07 926	05 41 953	change of direction to right
Map 58	150	50 07 591	05 42 224	Cape Cornwall car park
Map 58	151	50 07 325	05 42 106	trig point Ballowal Barrow
Map 58	152	50 07 049	05 41 590	junction in path
Map p177	152a	50 07 431	05 40 721	St Just Square
Map 59	153	50 06 892	05 41 843	turn in path

MAP	REF	GPS WAYPOINTS		DESCRIPTION
Map 59	154	50 06 289	05 41 742	stream crossing, Maen Dower
Map 60	155	50 05 874	05 41 699	rocky outcrop
Map 60	156	50 05 273	05 41 237	lifeguard station
Map 60	157	50 04 796	05 41 401	junction with path inland
Map 61	158	50 04 635	05 42 091	car park Sennen Cove
Map 61	159	50 04 634	05 42 263	toilets, Sennen Cove
Map 61	160	50 04 059	05 42 859	Land's End
Map 61	161	50 03 320	05 42 207	Trevilley Cliff
Map 62	162	50 03 197	05 41 470	Nanjizal
Map 62	163	50 02 211	05 40 545	black and white tower
Map 62	164	50 02 235	05 40 283	Porthgwarra
Map 63	165	50 02 333	05 39 575	Carn Scathe
Map 63	166	50 02 599	05 39 059	Porthcurno
Map 63	167	50 02 654	05 38 011	stream crossing, Gamper
Map 64	168	50 02 831	05 37 704	Penberth Cove
Map 64	169	50 03 048	05 37 107	stream, Porth Guarnon
Map 64	170	50 03 024	05 36 363	sign on rock
Map 65	171	50 03 118	05 36 066	Cove Cottage, St Loy
Map 66	172	50 03 201	05 34 887	metal gate
Map 66	173	50 03 319	05 34 096	path junction, Carn Barges
Map 66	174	50 03 657	05 33 788	Lamorna Cove
Map 67	175	50 03 639	05 33 216	steps, Carn-Du
Map 67	176	50 04 207	05 32 616	bench
Map 68	177	50 04 596	05 32 453	road junction
Map 68	178	50 04 977	05 32 283	war memorial, Mousehole
Map 69	179	50 06 366	05 32 907	Newlyn Bridge
Map 70	180	50 06 881	05 31 901	Jubilee Pool, Penzance
Map 70	181	50 07 266	05 31 888	bus station, Penzance
Map 72	182	50 07 388	05 28 424	Godolphin Arms, Marazion
Map 73	183	50 07 398	05 27 485	path leaves road, Marazion
Map 73	184	50 06 756	05 26 496	Perran Sands
Map 74	185	50 05 950	05 25 525	Cudden Point
Map 75	186	50 06 050	05 25 063	steps to beach, Bessy's Cove
Map 75	187	50 06 194	05 24 179	stream crossing, Pestreath Cove
Map 76	188	50 06 217	05 23 484	Chris Old's restaurant
Map 76	189	50 06 053	05 22 860	beach exit, Praa Sands
Map 77	190	50 05 703	05 22 061	car park, Porthcew
Map 77	191	50 05 428	05 21 269	Grey Stone Mine
Map 78	192	50 05 477	05 20 209	stream crossing, Tremearne Cliff
Map 79	193	50 05 053	05 19 370	Grylls Act Memorial
Map 79	194	50 05 085	05 18 911	Porthleven Harbour
Map 80	195	50 04 034	05 17 433	HMS Anson Memorial
Map 81	196	50 03 270	05 16 601	Gunwalloe Beach Café
Map 81	197	50 02 402	05 16 130	Gunwalloe Church
Map 82	198	50 02 005	05 15 507	Poldhu Cove
Map 82	199	50 01 704	05 15 707	Marconi Monument
Map 82	200	50 01 418	05 15 279	steps, Polurrian Cove
Map 82	201	50 00 893	05 15 385	Mullion Cove
Map 82a	202	50 01 613	05 14 488	Mullion Church
Map 83	203	50 00 515	05 15 594	stream, Mullion Cliff
Map 83	204	50 00 045	05 15 816	stile, Predannack Head
Map 83	205	49 59 860	05 15 273	stream, Parc Bean Cove

MAP	REF	GPS WAYPOINTS		DESCRIPTION
Map 84	206	49 59 008	05 14 471	gorge, Gew-Graze
Map 85	207	49 58 487	05 13 818	Kynance Cove
Map 86	208	49 57 583	05 12 541	footpath to Lizard Village
Map 86	209	49 58 092	05 12 165	Lizard Green
Map 86	210	49 57 506	05 12 308	most southerly point
Map 86	211	49 57 803	05 11 800	Housel Cove
Map 86	212	49 57 769	05 11 139	National Coast Watch, Nare Point
Map 86	213	49 58 227	05 11 267	Church Cove
Map 87	214	49 58 372	05 11 332	beacon
Map 87	215	49 58 476	05 11 209	stream crossing, Parn Voose Cove
Map 87	216	49 59 218	05 10 714	Cadgwith Cove
Map 87	217	49 59 832	05 10 337	bridge, Little Cove
Map 88	218	50 00 300	05 09 750	Kennack Sands West
Map 89	219	50 00 535	05 07 610	gate and stile, Zawn Vinoc
Map 90	220	50 00 530	05 07 306	stream, Downas Cove
Map 90	221	50 00 405	05 06 872	stream, Meludjack
Map 91	222	50 00 285	05 06 088	concrete hut
Map 91	223	50 00 751	05 05 906	Bench, Chynhall's Cliff
Map 91	224	50 01 436	05 05 791	Coverack Harbour
Map 93	225	50 02 094	05 04 073	Lowland Point
Map 93	226	50 02 849	05 04 018	stream, Godrevy Cove
Map 93	227	50 03 100	05 04 092	path leaves lane
Map 93	228	50 03 333	05 03 926	Porthoustock
Map 93	229	50 03 766	05 04 609	junction with road
Map 94	230	50 04 023	05 04 703	Porthallow
Map 94	231	50 05 087	05 04 551	Nare Point
Map 95	232	50 05 188	05 06 020	steps, Gillan Creek
Map 95	233	50 04 771	05 07 509	path to Manaccan
Map 95	234	50 05 335	05 06 018	St Anthony's in Meneage
Map 95	235	50 05 558	05 06 496	Ponsense Cove
Map 96	236	50 05 454	05 08 083	ford, Helford
Map 96	237	50 05 512	05 08 000	bus stop, car park, Helford
Map 96	238	50 05 701	05 07 978	ferry landing, Helford
Map 96	239	50 05 184	05 08 475	Kestle
Map 96a	240	50 04 755	05 09 806	crossroads, Mudgeon Farm
Map 96b	241	50 04 851	05 12 114	Mawgan Church
Map 96b	242	50 05 791	05 12 422	Gweek Inn
Map 96c	243	50 06 634	05 10 356	Trengilly Wartha pub
Map 96d	244	50 06 405	05 08 645	Porth Navas
Map 96d	245	50 06 671	05 08 196	Trenarth Bridge
Map 96d	246	50 06 331	05 07 421	crossroads
Map 96d	247	50 05 986	05 07 660	Helford Passage
Map 97	248	50 06 202	05 06 884	Durgan
Map p240	248a	50 06 966	05 06 497	Red Lion, Mawnan Smith
Map 98	249	50 06 587	05 04 958	Rosemullion Head
Map 99	250	50 07 477	05 05 615	Maenporth Beach
Map 99	251	50 08 039	05 04 417	Home Guard Memorial
Map 100	252	50 08 423	05 04 512	beach exit, Swanpool Beach
Map 100	253	50 08 646	05 04 035	Gyllyngvase Beach
Map 100	254	50 08 780	05 02 862	Pendennis Point
Map 100	255	50 09 351	05 04 180	Tourist Information, Falmouth

INDEX

TRAILBLAZER GUIDES – TITLE LIST

Adventure Cycle-Touring Handbook	1st edn out now
Adventure Motorcycling Handbook	5th edn out now
Australia by Rail	5th edn out now
Azerbaijan	3rd edn out now
China Rail Handbook	1st edn early 2010
Coast to Coast (British Walking Guide)	3rd edn out now
Cornwall Coast Path (British Walking Guide)	3rd edn out now
Corsica Trekking – GR20	1st edn out now
Cotswold Way (British Walking Guide)	1st edn out now
Dolomites Trekking – AV1 & AV2	2nd edn out now
Inca Trail, Cusco & Machu Picchu	3rd edn out now
Indian Rail Handbook	1st edn late 2009
Hadrian's Wall Path (British Walking Guide)	2nd edn out now
Himalaya by Bike – a route and planning guide	1st edn out now
Japan by Rail	2nd edn out now
Kilimanjaro – the trekking guide (includes Mt Meru)	2nd edn out now
Mediterranean Handbook	1st edn out now
Morocco Overland (4WD/motorcycling/cycling)	1st edn mid 2009
Moroccan Atlas – The Trekking Guide	1st edn mid 2009
Nepal Mountaineering Guide	1st edn late 2009
New Zealand – The Great Walks	2nd edn mid 2009
North Downs Way (British Walking Guide)	1st edn out now
Norway's Arctic Highway	1st edn out now
Offa's Dyke Path (British Walking Guide)	2nd edn out now
Overlanders' Handbook – worldwide driving guide	1st edn Jan 2010
Pembrokeshire Coast Path (British Walking Guide)	2nd edn out now
Pennine Way (British Walking Guide)	2nd edn out now
The Ridgeway (British Walking Guide)	2nd edn out now
Siberian BAM Guide – rail, rivers & road	2nd edn out now
The Silk Roads – a route and planning guide	2nd edn out now
Sahara Overland – a route and planning guide	2nd edn out now
Scottish Highlands – The Hillwalking Guide	2nd edn mid 2009
South Downs Way (British Walking Guide)	3rd edn out now
Tibet Overland – mountain biking & jeep touring	1st edn out now
Tour du Mont Blanc	1st edn out now
Trans-Canada Rail Guide	4th edn out now
Trans-Siberian Handbook	7th edn out now
Trekking in the Annapurna Region	4th edn out now
Trekking in the Everest Region	5th edn out now
Trekking in Ladakh	3rd edn out now
Trekking in the Pyrenees	3rd edn out now
The Walker's Haute Route – Mont Blanc to Matterhorn	1st edn out now
West Highland Way (British Walking Guide)	3rd edn out now

www.trailblazer-guides.com

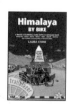

Cornwall Coast Path
BUDE – FALMOUTH

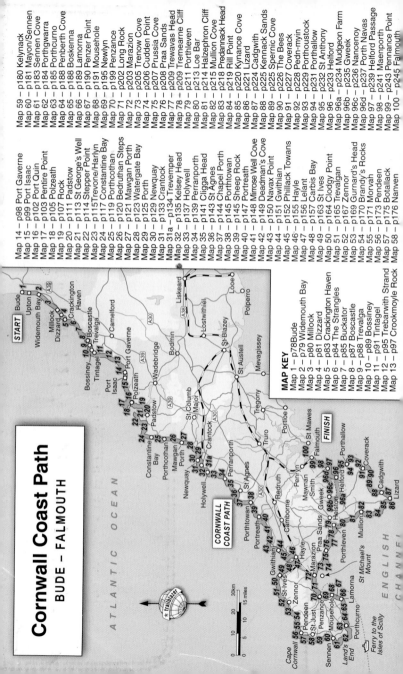